Northern Association

Sermons

On Various Important Doctrines and Duties of the Christian Religion

Northern Association

Sermons
On Various Important Doctrines and Duties of the Christian Religion

ISBN/EAN: 9783337087425

Printed in Europe, USA, Canada, Australia, Japan

Cover: Foto ©Lupo / pixelio.de

More available books at **www.hansebooks.com**

SERMONS

ON VARIOUS

IMPORTANT DOCTRINES AND DUTIES

OF THE

CHRISTIAN RELIGION;

SELECTED FROM THE *MANUSCRIPTS* OF SEVERAL *MINISTERS*,

MEMBERS OF THE

NORTHERN ASSOCIATION,

IN THE *COUNTY* OF *HAMPSHIRE*.

NORTHAMPTON: (MASSACHUSETTS)
PRINTED BY WILLIAM BUTLER.
1799.

A TABLE OF CONTENTS.

I. & II. *THE Christian Religion of Divine Authority.*

By Mr. STRONG, of Williamsburgh.

III. *The true GOD known only from Divine Revelation.*

By Mr. FORWARD, of Belcherstown.

IV. *A View of the Divine Perfections.*

By Mr. EMERSON, of Conway.

V. *A View of GOD, as Creator and Governor of the World.*

By Mr. NEWTON, of Greenfield.

VI. *The Essential Divinity of JESSUS CHRIST.*

By Mr. HALE, of Westampton.

CONTENTS.

VII. *The Personality and Divinity of the* SPIRIT.

By the same.

VIII. *The glory of* CHRIST, *as Mediator.*

By the same.

IX. *On Regeneration.*

By Mr. EMERSON.

X. *A Belief of the peculiar Doctrines of Christianity essential to our Acceptance with* GOD.

By Mr. LYMAN, of Hatfield.

XI. *The true Christian Character delineated.*

By Mr. WILLISTON, of Eastampton.

CONTENTS.

XII. On *living under the eye of* GOD.

   By Mr. EMERSON.

XIII. *The Advantages of Pious Society.*

   By Mr. WILLIAMS, of Northampton.

XIV. *Family Government and Filial Duty.*

   By Mr. LYMAN.

XV. *Symptoms of the Decline, and Importance of the Revival of Family Religion.*

   By Mr. HAYES, of South-Hadley.

XVI. *The Use and Importance of Christian Institutions.*

   By Mr. STRONG, of Williamsburgh.

CONTENTS.

XVII. *Persuasives to an Attendance on the LORD's Supper.*

By Mr. TAYLOR, of Deerfield.

XVIII. & XIX. *Infants of Believers Members of the Church of CHRIST.*

By Mr. HOPKINS, of Hadley.

XX. *Upon the Discipline of CHRIST's Church.*

By Mr. LYMAN.

XXI. *Dissuasives from Excessive and Sinful Diversions.*

By Mr. TAYLOR.

XXII. *Habitual Growth in Grace essential to the Christian Character.*

By Mr. FORWARD.

CONTENTS.

XXIII. *On what constitutes a Criminal Conformity to the World.*

By Mr. JUDD, of Southampton.

XXIV. *Religion frequently corrupted by Human Speculations.*

By Mr. FORWARD.

XXV. *Reasons offered for frequent Meditations on Death and Judgment.*

By Mr. WELLS, of Whateley.

XXVI. *The final and total Disappointment of the Wicked.*

By Mr. WILLIAMS, of Northampton.

XXVII. *The happy and glorious state of the Righteous.*

By the same.

SERMON I.

The CHRISTIAN RELIGION of DIVINE AUTHORITY.

Ephesians, ii. 20, *And are built on the foundation of the Apostles and Prophets, Jesus Christ himself being the chief corner-stone.*

THE subject assigned me, in these discourses, is to shew, that the Christian Religion is of Divine Authority: that is, it hath God for its Author and Original. The text selected for the purpose, it is supposed, clearly comprehends the subject: in which the Apostle asserts, that not the persons but the doctrinal inspired writings of the Prophets and Apostles, with Christ their head, the author, source and subject of their writings, constitute the foundation on which the Christian Ephesians and church are built. Under the terms Apostles and Prophets, no doubt, is comprised all the doctrinal writings; that is, scriptures of the Old and New Testament: having Jesus Christ, the chief corner stone, their original author and founder. Such is the foundation on which christians are built: their religion is the religion of the bible: there, and there only, it is taught and instituted, in its purity and perfection.

A CAPITAL object of this sacred book, is to display to the view of the intelligent system, particularly to man, who is more especially interested; the glories of the divine character, as **God the Redeemer**. To this end, it is replete with excellent and ample direct instruction, in its doctrinal parts, by which the glorious perfections of God, as the God of salvation, are asserted and defined with as great clearness and precision as our necessities require: nay more, to illustrate and enforce these, it gives a grand exhibition of the glorious character of Jehovah, in an extensive historical series of his marvellous works, from the creation to the end of the world, especially in the course of the divine administration relative to his chosen people, the seed of Abraham; under the Jewish dispensation, in which the majesty, wisdom, power, holiness, goodness and truth of the one true God, are notably exemplified: and this, with a benevolent design to impress the minds of men, Jews and Gentiles, with a solemn abiding sense of their obligations to him, and induce them to seek for happiness only in him, as the God of salvation; and by these means to prepare the world, Jews and Heathen, for the greatest and most astonishing event that ever took place in it, viz. the coming of the Son of God incarnate to publish, institute and establish the christian religion; seal his testimony with his blood, and die, on the cross, as an expiatory sacrifice for the sins of men. Of him, the prophets of the Old Testament, those holy men of God, spake as they were moved by the Holy Ghost, and foretold his coming, and minutely described him as the Messiah, the Saviour who was to come: and the inspired writers of the New Testament give us the history of his birth, life, death and resurrection, which with great exactness agrees with the predictions of the Old: thus the New Testament history invincibly establisheth the truth and divine original of the Old, by the accurate fulfilment of its prophesies: particularly those which relate to and with precision characterize the

promised

promised Messiah: on the other hand, the truth and divine authority of the New receives great confirmation from the exact agreement of its principal facts with the predictions of the Old Testament; especially if it be considered that the penmen universally claim the authority of divine inspiration. Both **Testaments** harmonize and conspire in promoting the same great design, and in establishing the same religion, although with different degrees of clearness and in diverse modes of dispensation. The Old Testament clearly revealed and promised a Savior to come, and thus afforded a solid foundation for faith and hope: it was given to the church of Israel as a rule of faith and practice;—well adapted to the then age and state of the church, equally as the New Testament to christians in a more advanced age and state.

THE doctrines of the New **Testament** are comprised in the Old, witness St. Paul, saying, that in preaching the gospel he had said " none other things than those which the Prophets and Moses did say should come."

ALL the prophets are said to have born witness concerning Jesus. Indeed some articles of our faith are more clearly and fully exhibited in the Old Testament than in the New; for instance, the creation of the world,—the fall of man, &c. The Old Testament, in its connection with the New, is said to be the foundation on which the christian church and christian religion are built, as in the text. Saint **Paul** confesseth his faith to be, a " belief of all things written in the law and the Prophets."* Timothy from a child knew no other scriptures than those of the Old Testament; but these were able, sufficient, to make him wise unto salvation, through faith which is in Christ Jesus.

SAINT **Peter** asserts that " no prophesy of the scriptures are of private interpretation," not to be considered as the private sentiment of a fallible man, as is the

case

Acts xxiv. 14.

case with all other writings, "for the prophefy came not at any time by the will of man, but holy men of God fpake as they were moved by the Holy Ghoft." The writers of the New Teftament bare ample teftimony to the infpiration of thofe of the Old Teftament, and exhibit their own writings as equally infpired.

In profecuting the fubject thefe three things naturally and neceffarily are to be illuftrated and evinced, viz. The neceffity—the truth—and divine authority of the fcriptures.

THE neceffity of a divine revelation, I think, will clearly appear from the following confiderations:

1. THE light of nature teacheth that there is a God: a firft *Being*: the efficient caufe and laft end of all other beings; to whom they all have their tendency; who therefore muft be Supreme.

2. THIS Supreme Being ought to be worfhiped, that is, acknowledged, reverenced and honoured, in every refpect as Supreme. If we derive all we are and have from him, and for the very purpofe, that we render or afcribe all to him, in promoting his honour and worfhip; if *He* is infinitely above and more perfect than all other beings, as is moft evident, certainly he is to be refpected, revered and honoured accordingly. Thus, is it completely demonftrated that God ought to be worfhiped.

3. THE worfhip of God is not a bufinefs of nature, fuch as feeing, hearing, walking, &c. which therefore needs no rule to direct it; but is a bufinefs which depends upon art, a divine art, and muft be regulated by certain rules.

4. IN the prefent ftate of mankind, natural reafon is not fufficient to furnifh us with thofe rules, becaufe it is depraved and corrupt as all muft acknowledge who are dictated by reafon. Upon actual experiment made for this purpofe and continued through fucceffive ages, the refult was, *the world by wifdom knew not God*. And *when they knew him*, that is, had the means of

knowing

knowing him, *they glorified him not as God.* Whence compleat demonstration is obtained, that human reason, unassisted by revelation, by its highest improvements, under its present depravity, is not sufficient to regulate our conduct in the worship of God. For the same reason, the sayings and sentiments of wise men cannot afford a sufficient rule, **because they depend** solely on reason for their support; from it, depraved as it is, they borrow all their force. Nor are the dictates of the Fathers to be relied on, for they, as well as we, were men, and as such were not only restricted by determinate rules equally as we, but also were always **fallible and sometimes false**; therefore could frame no other than uncertain rules, a mere nose of wax, equal to none; but **a rule, especially in this case, ought to be certain and infallible**: hence it follows that a revelation from heaven, is of absolute necessity to direct men in the worship of God: **such are** the sacred scriptures.

This may receive farther confirmation if we consider that the nature and requisites of such rule very exactly agree with the scripture, and with that only. They are such as these:

A **rule** to direct our faith and practice towards **God, ought to** be prescribed by God only. *What thing soever I command you, observe to do it: thou shalt not add thereto nor diminish from it. In vain do they worship me teaching for doctrines the commandments of men.* A law or rule of conduct cannot be given by any other but by him whose right it is to rule. The scripture alone is **prescribed by God to be our** rule. *All scripture is given by inspiration of God.* Another requisite to such rule is that it be known, clear and perspicuous; otherwise how could it lead **us** to the knowledge of our duty: such is the scripture, at least in things which more immediately respect our faith and practice, it being **plain and easy to be understood.**

A FURTHER

A FURTHER requisite of such a rule is that it be fixed and determinate, constant and unchangeable, every where consistent with itself : otherwise how could it be a sure guide to our conduct : such is the rule prescribed by God in his written word : it is *a sure word of prophesy*. Again, such rule ought to be compleat and adequate to its design in regulating our faith and practice ; which may neither be increased or diminished : otherwise it were incompetent to measure its object : such is the scripture ; for nothing is incumbent on us which it does not prescribe, either with respect to faith or manners ; nor, on the other hand, does it require any thing which it is not our indispensable duty to receive, or which does not pertain to our duty to God. *All scripture is profitable for doctrine, for reproof,* &c. All things contained in it *are written for our learning,* &c. Finally, such rule ought to be received and made public : otherwise how could it determine and put an end to controversies that may arise between parties ? but the scripture rule was publicly given by divine authority : thus to the Jews *were committed the oracles of God ;* and by them were received with common consent.

IN this manner, the necessity of divine revelation may, in my opinion, be fully demonstrated : That it be committed to writing is also necessary, will appear from the following considerations ; so urgent is this necessity, that the church could not be, or exist without the written word : not indeed in an absolute sense ; for God, had he seen fit, might have made other provision for her being and preservation ; but on supposition that God hath appointed his written word a mean to salvation, she is under a necessity of possessing it : this necessity seems to be expressed by the Apostle Jude, ver. iii. We find many instances in which God commanded the writing of his word, viz. by Moses frequently, by Moses and Joshua conjointly, Isaiah, Jeremiah, Habbakuk, and St. John in the Revelation :

and

and it is more than probable, that all the sacred writers wrote as well as spake by express authority from God and under the constraining influence of his spirit: what adds force to the argument is, that God himself with his own finger first began the sacred writing, on tables of stone: had it not been necessary he would neither have done nor commanded it. The manifold and absolutely necessary use of scripture affords a cogent argument in proof of the point in hand: *all, the whole, scripture was given by inspiration of God and is profitable for doctrine, for reproof, for correction: for instruction in righteousness. These things were written for our learning. These are written that ye might believe that Jesus is the Christ, the Son of God; and that believing ye might have life through his name.*

THE reasons for which infinite wisdom saw it necessary that the revealed word should be committed to writing were probably such as these, first, The shortness of human life. By the time in which Moses lived and the scripture began to be written, the life of man was reduced to seventy, or eighty years, as Moses himself gives the account in the 90th Psal;—For some of the first ages of the world, when the life of man was extended nearly to a thousand years, God was pleased to preserve and propagate the heavenly doctrine by oral tradition, assisted by frequent immediate revelations made to the Patriarchs.—Second, the number of men and members of the church were increased. Third, The danger and insecurity of its safeguard, to be expected from tradition alone: for during the preceding times of tradition, many corruptions had crept in already and more were to be feared; pious Jacob found occasion to purge his family of strange gods, which had gained admittance into it. Gen. xxxv. 2.—Fourth, The uncertainty of things which depend, wholly on human memory, especially things of religion.—Fifth, Because of the permanent stability of revealed truth. Sixth, Because of the perverse cunning and zeal of Heretics and

and Seducers : who might more easily pervert unwritten tradition to favour their own errors.

HENCE the divine revelation recorded in the Old and New Testament is emphatically stiled, *the scripture, the writing*, by way of eminence ; because of all writings it is infinitely the most excellent and interesting : it contains the words of eternal life. It is called not simply, the scripture, but the holy or sacred scripture ; for it is the genuine offspring of the Holy Spirit. Treats of the most holy subjects, our duty to God through Christ :—it tends to answer the most holy purposes, the glory of God, the edification and eternal salvation of men, and produceth the most holy fruits, love and obedience to God, and benevolence to men.

LET us next attend to the evidence of the truth and genuineness of the sacred scriptures. By the truth of scripture, we mean, that what it contains is true ; so that it cannot deceive or err ; it is *a sure word of prophesy*. ' *The testimony of the Lord is sure. It is noted in the scripture of truth. Thy word is truth.*'

IN particular, its doctrinal and historical parts exactly agree ; the former with right reason and truth, the latter with matters of fact : its practical parts with the will of God : its prophesies, promises and threatnings with the event, not otherwise nor less than if both were present face to face. Can it be otherwise ? It hath the God of truth its Author—Christ the truth itself, the faithful and true witness, its Voucher—the holy infallible Spirit of truth, its Inspirer, and *holy men of God as moved* by him, its Writers. It is far more sure and certain than any other revelation, even though it should come from one arising from the dead, or even from the angels themselves. But this may more fully appear when we come to consider the evidence of its divine authority.—At present let us pursue the arguments which demonstrate it true and genuine.

1. WE have, to say the least, as good evidence of the truth and genuineness of the sacred writings as

we

we have of any other ancient writings. What proof have we that the books of Cicero, Homer, or any others, were the productions of the men whose names they bear, more than this, tradition has handed it down for truth, with universal consent, it has been received for truth, it never has been proved untrue. Additional proof is that these books have been mentioned, referred to or cited by various writers in every age since; what better evidence can we have that any ancient book is genuine? It is true, that this is all human testimony, not divine, yet judged sufficient to satisfy us in every other case; but this is as good evidence of the genuineness of the sacred writings, as of any other writings: and if this be not sufficient to give credit to the sacred scripture, it is equally insufficient for any other books; they must all be rejected as spurious.

THAT the Bible, at least the Old Testament, is a genuine authentic book, we have not only all this evidence in its full extent, but we have more, we have over and above, the testimony of the authentic public records of the Jewish nation; but public records in all cases are admitted as good evidence:

IT is found on their records, that the whole of the Old Testament, containing the very same books which we now have, was delivered to their nation by God himself or his special order, and received and venerated by them as a revelation of his will. The five first books, called the book of the law, were received and deposited in the side of the ark of the covenant, by special order. Deut. xxxi. 24, 25, 26. *When Moses had made an end of writing the words of this law in a book until they were finished, that Moses commanded the Levites, saying, take this book of the law and put it in the side of the ark of the covenant of the Lord your God: that it may be there for a witness against thee.* The other books or parts of the Old Testament, written by different *holy men of God as they were moved by the Holy Ghost*, in succeeding times and ages, were received and used by that people as authentic canonical scripture immediately upon their being compiled and given them for that purpose: until the canon of their scripture, the Old Testament, was completed by Malachi: of the truth of this we may be assured from the testimony of authentic church history, particularly that of the Jewish Church.

2. THE sacred scripture exhibits in itself, distinguishing marks and figures of a true and genuine writing; such as these,

THE writers appear to be men of probity and truth, honestly disposed, and also men of abilities and qualifications competent to the undertaking. There is no appearance of their being influenced by interested views of honor or emolument; but quite the reverse. They, the writers of the New Testament in particular, were zealous advocates in a cause, the cause of christianity, from which they well knew nothing but dangers, losses, and even death itself could be the result. That so many different writers, in times and places so diverse, should every where so exactly agree and harmonize on the same subject, affords evidence that their guide was truth and their writings are genuine. The testimony of their most deadly enemies, in not denying but conceding the facts which they relate, and only imputing them to false causes, is invincible evidence that these facts were truly related and could not be denied. They write of things done in their own time, of which they were eye and ear witnesses, and must certainly know and could not mistake. Further, the contents of the Scripture serve to prove its truth. These, so far as they come within its ken, exactly agree with right reason: to instance in moral duties; the scripture teaches nothing which is contrary to reason rightly improved, even moral Philosophers and Sophists being Judges; these teach or require nothing, under the direction of right reason, which is not taught and required in a manner much more excellent and perfect, in the sacred writings.

ings. As to its histories, it every where agrees with facts: as might by an induction of particulars, would time and room permit, easily be made to appear. Should we next turn our view to natural religion, both to its speculative and doctrinal points, we might readily perceive, that even in those in which it comes nearest to truth and right reason, we have much more excellent and perfect instruction from the scripture. To prove the truth of scripture in things supernatural and otherwise unknown is now less difficult; for we have no reason to suspect *that* of falsehood, in things supernatural or miraculous, which we always and every where find to be truth in things natural and known: beside, scripture history and its supernatural miraculous facts are so blended and interwoven that a confirmation of the truth of its history, is an equal confirmation of its supernatural and miraculous events.

Having thus far demonstrated the truth of the scripture in general, it may not be impertinent nor useless to consider the reasons which serve to establish the truth and genuineness of the New Testament, in particular.

1. The same arguments which have been used to prove the truth of the scriptures in general, that taken from the Jewish records only excepted, are all applicable, in all their force, to the writings of the New Testament, and equally prove them true. We have credible evidence from authentic approved history, that the same sacred books, which we now have in the New Testament, were all written by the Disciples, and contemporaries of Jesus of Nazareth, and that they were very early and universally received and used by the christian church, as true and genuine writings.

2. The credibility of the writers: The persons who wrote the wonderful things concerning Jesus appear to have been men worthy of credit. That this may appear in a convincing light, we are to remember, they were eye and ear witnesses of the things which they write;

write: they who saw the facts bare record and knew with certainty that their record was true: they declare what they saw with their own eyes, and heard with their own ears. They were not single witnesses, nor barely two or three, which amounts to legal evidence, but more, they were twelve; nay, the principal fact, without which the truth of all others must fail, the resurrection of Christ, is attested on the authority of five hundred brethren, who at once were eye witnesses of the surprizing all important event. 1 Cor. xv. 6. &c. Of Elijah's ascension to heaven, Elisha alone was the solitary witness; yet his single testimony was always received by the Jews as worthy of credit.

They could have no temptation to narrate a falsehood, either from ambitious or avaricious views, or any other selfish motive: they full well foreknew, for they were forewarned by their Lord, of the sacrifices they must make in his cause, that the things they were to testify, and the doctrines they were to preach would bring upon them, like a deluge, the odium of the world; and thence expose them to every kind of dangers, losses, persecutions, infamy, poverty and even death in its most frightful forms. In their narrations they conceal not their own faults and failings, as an impostor would certainly have done.

They wrote and published their writings while as yet very many were living who were present and eye-witnesses of the facts which they relate: who had seen and heard Jesus, and were knowing as to many of his mighty works: and among these many of their bitterest enemies, who were sufficiently inclined and might easily have detected the fraud, and would certainly have done it, had not a consciousness of the truth of the facts restrained them. These writers are circumstantial in their history, they take particular notice of times, places and persons present when and where his miracles were wrought; nor do they disagree, in any thing material, one with another; although, at the time of

writing

writing they were very diftant one from another, both in time and place.

They relate things done, not here or there fecretly in fome by-corner; but things of public notoriety, acted publicly in the open view of the world, their moft rancourous enemies being prefent. We may add finally, they fealed the truth of their writings with their blood: they, with true chriftian heroifm endured the moft intolerable torments and cruel death. They died as martyrs to the truths of the New Teftament.

3. The truth of the New Teftament may be clearly demonftrated from its univerfal and moft exact agreement with what is written in the Old. The very nature and complexion of its contents prove it genuine: particularly, That all its parts, on fo great a variety of fubjects, and written by fo many different men, diftant one from another both in time and place, without the leaft fhadow of previous caballing or collufion, fhould fo accurately agree and harmonize among themfelves— With the nature of things—with every true hiftory, Jewifh and Heathen, as by adverting to particulars would clearly appear,—We may add its agreement with the Jews themfelves, its greateft enemies; for moft of the paffages of the Old Teftament cited in the New, were explained in the fame fenfe by the ancient Jews, as hath been illuftrated by ancient writers who were well informed in Jewifh literature.—Permit me to add finally, that the enemies of chriftianity, neither ancient nor modern have ever been able, by folid proof, to fupport the charge of falfehood, though often brought, againft the New or Old Teftament, or any part of them; but every writing is to be held true until it is fairly and folidly proved to be falfe.

SERMON

SERMON II.

THE CHRISTIAN RELIGION OF DIVINE AUTHORITY.

Ephesians ii. 20. *And are built on the foundation of the Apostles and Prophets, JESUS CHRIST himself being the chief corner stone.*

HAVING in the preceding discourse illustrated and proved the necessity of Divine Revelation, also of its being committed to writing; and that the Sacred Scripture, containing such revelation, is a genuine writing and universally true; we now proceed in the

3d PLACE to examine the evidence of its divine authority and original: and this may be done with greater facility because its truth and genuineness being now sufficiently established, whatever proof it exhibits of its own divine original, may with propriety be improved and must be admitted as good and decisive evidence in the case; but the scripture every where abounds with testimonies to this purpose: it universally claims, as its unquestionable right, to be received and submitted to, with sacred reverence, as the very *word of God and not of man*; to refer to particular instances would be an implication of such ignorance of the scripture

ture as is reproachful to those who have the Bible within their reach.

A SECOND argument is the necessity of a written revelation from God: which has been already proved: whence we conclude, that either the sacred scripture, which we possess, contains that revelation, or that there is no such revelation given to men, nor ever was; but the last supposition is absurd, we must therefore assert and believe the former, and affirm that our Bible is that word of God: this argument depends on a twofold hypothesis which must be confirmed; the first that of necessity there must be a written revelation from God: in addition to the proof already adduced for this purpose, permit me to say this necessity may be undeniably proved both from the nature of God, and of man; for to God is due worship and obedience, which cannot be rendered unless the manner of his worship, and his will which is to be obeyed, be revealed by God himself: also from the nature of man, which consists of an immortal soul capable of eternal happiness or misery, in another state: he is therefore in absolute need of being directed, by certain prescribed means, how he may avoid the one and obtain the other; but since he is in himself utterly destitute of such direction, and has no other way to obtain it, he is in absolute necessity that it be revealed to him by God. There is and can be no other word of God, as a standing rule of faith and practice but the scripture: this appears both from the induction of particulars made in the preceding discourse, viz, neither natural reason, nor philosophy, nor the documents of the wise, nor the sayings of the Fathers, nor any enthusiastic suggestions, can be that infallible word of God. This is also evident from the very nature of the case: for there are things in the christian religion and essential to it, necessary to be known which are involved in mystery, and not knowable but only by divine revelation:—Such as for instance, the Trinity of persons in the Deity—

ity—the incarnation of the Son of God—the union of two natures in the Mediator—regeneration, &c.—These and other important doctrines, which lie at the foundation of the christian religion, are and can be known no where else but from the scripture.

THIRD, The nature and tenour of the things contained in the Bible invincibly prove it to be of divine original.

THESE are such as could not possibly be dictated by any creature; not by any evil spirit or wicked man, both because the multiplicity of rules and injunctions found in it, requiring, on the severest penalties, the utmost purity, even sinless holiness could not possibly proceed from an unholy being; for they are utterly abhorrent from his nature; and also because, it cannot be admitted that he should have denounced such dire anathemas and curses against himself, as sanction his own eternal punishment, which are frequent in the scriptures: nor could they originate from holy angels or good men; for to be guilty of fraud or imposture is inconsistent with their character, much more to arrogate divine authority to their own inventions; but the scripture universally claims such authority to itself; which clearly demonstrates, that it could not be the production of good angels or good men: it must therefore, of necessity, have had its origin from God, invested with his authority.

FOURTH, The low rank and mean accomplishments of many of the writers of the sacred scriptures, compared with the sublime and mysterious truths which they unveil, afford an incontestable proof that their doctrines are of divine original. For the deep and hidden things there opened to view are such as far surpass the capacity of all created reason, even the most exalted and improved; this is manifest, for instance, in the mysterious doctrine of the Trinity, the origin of sin—the hypostatical union of the two natures in the person of Christ—the redemption of men by the blood of the

Son

Son of God, &c. The most enlightened and penetrating philosophers, aided by all their voluminous authors, should they unite to a man, combine all their sagacity, and exert every nerve of genius, would find themselves utterly unequal to the task of unfolding these mysterious truths which are revealed and written in the sacred volume ; written not merely by men, but men of the lower class of mean condition, shepherds, plowmen, fishermen, mere ignorant laymen, furnished with no kind of literature, without skill either in logic or oratory ; with infallible certainty we may conclude, they had the knowledge of those mysteries, not otherwise than by immediate inspiration from God.

FIFTH. The many signal interpositions of Divine Providence in approbation and support, both of the inspired penmen, and the religion founded on their writings clearly demonstrate it to be the cause of God.—If we consider either the miracles which were wrought in favour of the scripture, which we shall soon more particularly attend to, or the manner in which the doctrines contained in the Bible were propagated, maintained and vindicated, by the instrumentality of the Apostles, we shall every where discover an extraordinary care and watchfulness of Divine Providence : particularly, if we consider the mission of the Apostles to preach and publish the Gospel ; is there not a clear display of the extraordinary interposition of the Most High, that Christ should select, in preference to all others, men of the lower rank, furnished with no advantages of birth, fortune, fame or literature, and send them forth, as his heralds through the world, to proclaim one *Jesus,* crucified in Judea, as the only and *Almighty Saviour* of the world, together with a promise of the reward of eternal life, to them who should receive him, on their testimony ; at the same time denouncing the punishment of eternal death to all who should refuse him ? and that this institution, in itself so unpromising, should, in such hands, in so short a time, make so great a progress through the world; and that in the face of the utmost opposition from earth and hell in combination? Also the effectual support and preservation given to the Apostles on this extraordinary embassy: how remarkably was the arm of the Lord made bare, in that, timid unarmed men, sent among ravenous wolves, equally so that the churches formed by them, which were truly heartless and feeble, should be so powerfully succoured and defended against the assaulting force of nearly all the world, and that even down to this day? In this the approving hand of God will appear yet more conspicuous, when we consider the arduous task imposed on the Apostles, and the insuperable difficulties which attended it; their business was to persuade men, of every nation and religion, to renounce the religion and mode of worship embraced, revered and even idolized, with universal consent, by their forefathers, their contemporaries, their families, neighbours and dearest connections, to which they were almost invincibly attached and bigoted by the prejudices of education, and long established hereditary custom and habit: But to persuade men to alter their religious sentiments, rights and customs, whether true or false, is one of the hardest things in the world, especially when confirmed and deep rooted by the aid of bigotry and superstition: such was the business assigned to the propagators of Christianity: not only this but a still more arduous difficulty was to be encountered, they were sent to disciple all nations, Jews and Heathen, to Christ and his religion: to persuade them not only to renounce and abandon their native religion, but cordially embrace, in its stead, a religion, of all others, the most thwarting and disgusting to the pride of the human heart; the embracing of which, at the same time, they well knew, would expose them to the reproach, angry resentment and cruel persecution of the world around them, and even to the most tormenting death. Can it be thought that any power short of

Divine

Divine and Omnipotent could give success to such an undertaking? We may add, the horrible judgments of God executed on the opposers and persecutors of the Christian cause, for instance Herod, Pilate, Julian, &c. clearly shew it to be under his divine patronage, and that his watchful Providence takes its part and avengeth its wrongs.

If we look to the severe and signal punishments inflicted on the violators of the doctrines, precepts and institutions of the scriptures, both Old Testament and New; to instance only in Nadab, and Abihu, and Uzzah, in the Old, and Annanias and Sapphira his wife in the New; we may see convincing evidence that scripture doctrines and institutions are held under the patronizing care of a watchful and avenging Providence: they who presumptuously disregard them do it at their peril. From all these particulars, considered in connection, it appears, with irresistable evidence, that God hath openly attested his high approbation of the scripture and its religion, and holds them under his fostering care as his own offspring; but he would not nor could he, approve and give such countenance to an imposture: we may therefore on sure ground conclude, without all peradventure, it is of Divine original and authority.

SIXTH. The visible marks and characteristics, inherent in the scripture itself, evince its Divinity. Such as its antiquity; the five books of Moses taken together, make up the oldest book in the world; it has been extant now more than three thousand years; and the whole of the Old Testament more than two thousand, and the New about seventeen hundred. Also its perpetuity in duration while all other antient books have been devoured, either by time, devastations, wars or conflagrations, this by a kind and watchful Providence has been preserved entire, and handed down even to our times. Likewise the harmony and perfect consistency of all its parts. We may add the humble majesty of its ſtile connected with its ſo great power and energy.

SEVENTH. This foundation truth is invincibly ſupported by the miracles which have been wrought in its confirmation.

A PROPER miracle is an act above created power, and beſide or contrary to the eſtabliſhed laws of nature, and can be performed by none but God the author of nature and its laws ; nor is it in the power of God to work miracles in favour and ſupport of that which is not true ; but certain it *is*, he hath done many and great miracles in favour of ſcripture truths :— this is certain both from the teſtimony of other writings concerning the ſcripture, and alſo from the teſtimony of ſcripture concerning itſelf. Which teſtimonies of ſcripture however are not to be here urged as divine, leſt we ſhould argue in a circle, but as human teſtimonies, which we have ſhewn to be true, and fully to be relied on ; having demonſtrated the ſcripture to be a true and genuine writing, we may with propriety improve its teſtimony, though as human, yet of equal, nay of greater validity than any other hiſtory, becauſe its truth is ſupported and eſtabliſhed on better evidence.

THE miracles wrought by a power clearly divine in confirmation of the ſcripture, both under the Old Teſtament and New, eſpecially the latter, were many and mighty ; as is abundantly evident from ſacred hiſtory. By the miraculous hand of the Redeemer, the God of Iſrael, his people were reſcued, with mighty ſigns and wonders, from cruel ſlavery in Egypt, conducted on dry ground through the midſt of the ſea, and through the wilderneſs, and for the ſpace of forty years, by a conſtant miracle, were ſupplied with food, and raiment, and water from the rock. By a notable miracle, Elijah confounded the prieſts and worſhippers of Baal, and conſtrained the ſpectators to acknowledge the Lord the only God.

THESE

THESE and many other miracles were wrought in confirmation of the fcriptures of the Old Teftament.— The prophet Ifaiah foretold and particularly deciphered fome of the wonderful things which fhould diftinguifh the times of the Meffiah, viz. that *the eyes of the blind fhould be opened, and the ears of the deaf unftoped ; the lame man leap as an hart, and the tongue of the dumb fing.* This was literally fulfilled in the miniftry of Jefus of Nazareth, as every one knows who has any acquaintance with his hiftory : we there read, that *the deaf hear, the blind fee, the lame walk, the tongue of the dumb is loofened, and the dead are raifed.* To refer to particular inftances is needlefs. Modern infidels have had the effrontery to deny that Jefus wrought any miracles, and that any were ever wrought by Prophets or Apoftles in favour of the fcripture ; but it is worthy of obfervation, that they, who lived at the time, were eye and ear witneffes of thefe fupernatural works, had not the impudence to deny the facts ; no they were acknowledged not only by the friends, but even by the enemies and warmeft oppofers of the chriftian caufe ; they confeffed they were fupernatural works, wrought by a fupernatural power, they only denied it to be divine. Hear the confeffion of the chief priefts and Pharifees, convened in council for the purpofe of obftructing the fuccefs of the miracles and doctrines of Chrift, thefe were his bittereft enemies and finally his accufers and murderers ; the voice of this council is, *this man doth many miracles, if we let him thus alone all men will believe on him.* The miracles wrought by Chrift and thofe to whom he gave power, properly attended to would force from every difcerning unbiaffed mind the confeffion of Nicodemus, *Rabbi, we know that thou art a teacher come from God : for no man can do thefe miracles which thou doeft except God be with him.*— Whenever a proper miracle is wrought, the hand of God is to be feen and confeffed, as owning and approving both the teacher and his doctrine ; but we have all the evidence that can reasonably be wished for or needed to convince us that many notable miracles have been actually done, both under the Old Testament and the New, in confirmation of scripture truths: of this we have not only the testimony of the scripture itself, as has been shewn, but the concurrent testimony of profane history; some of the miracles of the Old Testament are mentioned in the works of heathen writers; many of the miracles wrought by Christ and his Apostles are taken notice of in the writings both of Jews and Heathen. Thus, I think, the miracles wrought for that purpose, afford full demonstration that the scripture, and consequently the christian religion which is built upon it, are of Divine authority.

EIGHTH. The prophesies contained in the Bible, in connection with their fulfilment, afford another infallible proof that God is its author. It is self evident that none but the omniscient could foretell and minutely describe things hundreds and thousands of years before they exist: such predictions are numerous in the writings of Moses and the Prophets, of Christ and his Apostles; that these are true and genuine writings, and to be received as such, you have seen fully confirmed, in a former discourse; there is therefore no reason to question that the prophesies contained in them were given out and written, from Moses downward to the perfecting and sealing the whole canon of the scripture by St. John the Divine, at the time and by the very persons as there represented.

FROM the death of Moses to this time is more than three thousand years, from the compleating of the Old Testament canon by the prophet Malachi, is near twenty three hundred years, and from the perfecting of the whole scripture by St. John in the Revelation is about seventeen hundred years.

THE enemies of Christianity, to discredit the sacred volume and persuade us to reject it as spurious, tell us " that the pretended prophesies found in it are

" of

" of much later date, and were written after the e-
" vents which they would seem to predict," the events
so exactly correspond with their predictions that they
would consider them rather as histories than prophesies;
having no other way to evade the force of this argument in favour of Divine Revelation; but that this is
a mere evasion and utterly void of truth, you may be
assured from the evidence which has been adduced to
the contrary; for if the scripture is no imposture but
a true genuine writing as has been demonstrated, we
may thence obtain certainty that the prophesies contained in it, were given out at the time and by the same
persons as there related. Had infidels any colourable
pretence for this evasion, with respect to those prophesies which were long since fulfilled, yet certainly they
can have none as to those which are now, at this very time, clearly fulfilling, before our eyes, and in the
open view of all the world: and such there are. I
shall particularly consider but one, of many which are
to the present purpose, it respects the present state and
situation of the Jews; which more than three thousand years since was foretold with great accuracy, by
Moses, as you may see in the 28th Chapter of Deuter-
onomy; a part of his prophesy is expressed in these
words, *And the Lord shall scatter thee among all people,
from one end of the earth even unto the other. And a-
mong these nations shall thou find no ease, neither shall the
sole of thy foot have rest; but the Lord shall give thee
there* " *a trembling heart and sorrow of mind. Then the*
" *Lord will make thy plagues wonderful, and the plagues*
" *of thy seed, even great plagues and of long continu-*
" *ance; and they shall be upon thee for a sign and a won-*
" *der, and upon thy seed forever.* And our blessed
Lord, in his day, clearly forewarned that people, that
these awful calamities were soon to be inflicted by the
hand of the Romans, where he says, *These be the days
of vengeance, that all things which are written may be
fulfilled. For there shall be great distress in the land,*

and wrath upon this people. And they shall fall by the edge of the sword, and shall be led away captive into all nations; and Jerusalem shall be trodden down of the Gentiles, until the times of the Gentiles be fulfilled. We need only to turn our eyes to the present state and condition of this rejected, despised people, to see the exact fulfillment of these prophesies; we shall see them, according to prophesy, in fact *led away captive and scattered among all nations.* There is no civilized nation where they are not found; except where they have been banished in disgrace; yet no where intermixt or united with any other people; but are, in all places kept distinct and known to be Jews: wherever they are, *they have no rest,* in general have no settled habitations or landed property of their own; they enjoy not the rights of citizenship, of electing or being elected to office, civil or military. In no part of the world have they any thing like either a civil or ecclesiastical polity of their own; but are in subjection to the government where they happen to reside, be it despotic or free; they are viewed with an eye of reproach as a people in disgrace. Such have been their situation now for about seventeen hundred years; agreeable to prophesy, it hath been *of long continuance;* and agreeably to our Saviour's prediction will continue *until the times of the Gentiles be fulfilled:* or in the language of St. Paul, *until the fulness of the Gentiles be come in.* No other people of equal or nearly equal antiquity can be found or any remains of them among men; for instance, the Egyptians, Philistines, Chaldeans &c. their name is utterly extinguished and they intermingled and swallowed up in the mass of nations.

The Arabians, who are the posterity of Ishmael, are an exception to the preceding remark; for they, ever since the days of Abraham their father, have been held up in the hand of Divine Providence, as another remarkable instance of the fulfillment of prophesy, in the open view of mankind. This prophesy was announced

nounced by a special messenger from God, called an angel, who appeared to Hagar, and foretold her that the child with which she was then pregnant, by Abram, should be called *Ishmael, and he will be a wild man; his hand will be against every man, and every man's hand against him: and he shall dwell in the presence of all his brethren.* The prophesy respects his posterity in their future generations; his twelve sons called princes settled and dwelt in Arabia, near the borders of Egypt, where they continue to this time, a wild and savage race, who, having *their hand against every man,* they live by rapine and plunder, which causeth the hatred and hostilities of their neighbours; yet none have been able to extirpate them; they have continued in this situation, now for the space of three thousand and seven hundred years nearly, and still *dwell in the presence of all their brethren.* But to return to the Jews, who, although they are scattered among all nations, are yet kept distinct and known from all other people: the great and destructive overturnings and revolutions which have taken place among the nations of the earth for seventeen hundred years, have not been able to blot out their name or make any material alteration in their state; surely the finger of God is here.— We have in this instance twofold invincible proof of the truth and divine authority of the Christian Revelation and religion, the one an exact and undeniable fulfilment of prophesy, in open view before our eyes, and the other a standing continued miracle, of which we and all the world are witnesses, by which that fulfilment is effected; for nothing short of the miraculous hand of God could effect it. As the seed of Abraham were once separated unto God, and set up by him, as a beacon, to diffuse light and instruction from the revelation of his word,* so now they are and have been for ages, by his unfathomed wisdom and miraculous power held up, in the open view of the world, as

D   a standing

---

* To the world around them.

a standing monument, an irrisistable demonstration, of the infallible truth and divine original of his written word. Was this evidence alone properly attended to, there would not, there could not, be an infidel, or a deist in the world, at least where scripture prophesies and the past and present state of the Jews are known.

NINTH. I shall add but one argument more in proof of the great foundation truth we are attempting to vindicate, it is this, The general scheme opened and prosecuted throughout the sacred volume, clearly demonstrates its divine original.

THE author certainly had a mind sufficiently capacious and discerning thoroughly to look through things from the beginning to the end: and minutely view all the intermediate objects, which might, as means, tend either to aid or impede the great design, and the fittest means and methods to obstruct the one and effectuate the other. The scheme is that of man's redemption by the mediation of the Son of God incarnate: to reveal him in his mediatorial character and work, to lead men to know and embrace him as the only Saviour of sinners, is the great design progressively opened and harmoniously prosecuted through the whole scripture, Old Testament and New; in the former with a far less, though increasing, degree of light and clearness, than in the latter. A careful unbiassed attention to this amazing plan as unfolded and carried into effect by the word and spirit of God, will produce full conviction that *known unto the author of it, were all his works from the beginning. That he is God, and there is none like him: declaring the end from the beginning, and from ancient times the things that are not yet done, saying my council shall stand, and I will do all my pleasure.*

THE limits assigned me forbid a more particular discussion of this argument, nor is it necessary; the candid attentive reader will be sensible that cogent and conclusive arguments are not wanting fully to confirm

this

this foundation principle of christianity, the truth and divine authority of the scriptures, which, at the same time, as solidly evince the Christian Religion of divine authority ; the latter is built wholly on the former.

OF the manner in which the word of God was communicated to the Prophets and Apostles, take the explanation from St. Peter, he says, *The prophecy came not at any time by the will of man, but holy men of God spake as they were moved by the Holy Ghost.* These holy men, were the Prophets and Apostles, whence we are said to be built on them as a foundation: the sacred word written by them is the sure foundation of the faith and religion of christians.

IT ought to be observed that the Holy Spirit moved and inspired them in a different manner in different parts of this business, things which were before unknown to them, such as the history of the creation, the fall of man, &c. which were past, yet unknown, and predictions of things future, the knowledge of these they received by the immediate inspiration of the Holy Ghost ; for there was no other way in which they could obtain such knowledge. As to things already known or which might be known by ordinary means, such as the history of Christ written by the Evangelists, the Acts of the Apostles written by Luke, and such like, they had, by a divine influence, such presence of mind, such religious care and caution, that they could not err : at the same time, in both, they had the gentle accommodating influence of the Holy Spirit, in such manner, that the several writers should use such stile and language, as was distinctive and characteristic of the writer, as is observable in their writings. .

THE books of both Testaments are to be accounted authentic and canonical only in their original languages : as all public instruments and writings are valid only in their originals ; because these holy men only, who were furnished with the infallible guidance of the Holy Spirit could utter an inspired and authentic
scripture.

scripture. The original authentic languages are the Hebrew and Greek: the Old Testament was originally given to the church of Israel in Hebrew, with this exception, that some small parts of it, in Ezra, Esther, Jeremiah and Daniel were written in the Chaldean language. That the New Testament was written only in Greek, is acknowledged in the christian church: therefore we receive the scripture as authentic only in those languages. As the church of Israel held no other but the Hebrew of the Old Testament, so the christian church holds none but the New Testament in Greek as canonical. The books called Apocrypha, not having been originally written in Hebrew, and for other good reasons, were never received, either in the Jewish or christian church, as canonical scripture. However the sacred scriptures, for the common use of the church, may and ought to be translated into other languages; and translations in any language are to be received as authentic, so far as they truly copy the original, by which they are always to be cautiously examined. Illustrious and forever to be adored was the kind providence of God, in preserving these fountains of divine wisdom; not only that they have not been wholly and altogether lost, but that they have not been mutilated by the loss of any one book, nor even corrupted with any very material error. While these fountains have been thus secure, not so much as one of the more ancient translations has come down to us entire.

From human translations may be learnt every thing necessary to salvation, provided they only agree with the original in essential parts, as they all have been wont to do which have been received by the churches; although at the same time they may disagree and be deficient in many things of less importance. We may rest assured and satisfied, that the sacred books are come down to us pure and genuine, although seeming inconsistancies, real difficulties or deficiences in things which do not at all affect the essentials of religion, are

to

to be met with in our translations; such things may well be expected, and are to be imputed either to our ignorance of ancient customs, usages, idioms of speech, &c. or to the misapprehension, carelessness or ignorance of transcribers; it could not be otherwise unless they all had been divinely inspired.

TEN thousand such flaws and faults, avidiously hunted up and set in their full strength and most formidable array, by the zealous advocates of infidelity, with a view to bring the Bible into discredit and contempt, have as little force in the ballance of wisdom and a sound mind, against the weighty cogent arguments which give firm support to the belief of its truth and divine original, as a straw in the scale against bulky mountains; while in the mean time, the several* perfectly harmonize in things essential, such as, articles of faith, precepts, promises, threatenings, &c.

THE following reasons may give us assurance that the scriptures, in their originals, have not been materially corrupted. 1. Because to permit it is contrary to the kind and watchful providence of God; will not he who numbers and guards the hairs of our heads, watch over and preserve the foundation of our religion, our eternal salvation? 2. Christ himself has given us his word, *that 'till heaven and earth pass, one iota or one tittle shall not pass from the law, 'till all be fulfilled.* 3. The authority of scripture cannot be supported without the purity of its originals; but sinks at once upon the supposition of any material corruption in them.— 4. Neither the Hebrew of the Old nor Greek of the New Testament hath been corrupted, therefore none: not the former, because it could not have been done by the Jews, for they were assiduous even to superstition, in their zeal to preserve its purity: as appears from their own Masora, a Jewish book so called, and also from the testimonies of Philo and of Josephus, &c.— Christ and his Apostles never upbraided them with this

* Approved Translations.

this fault, nor any where gave the least intimation that the Jewish scriptures were corrupted, as doubtless they would have done, had they been chargeable with it.— Nor was it ever in the power of christians of any denomination, had they been ever so much disposed to corrupt it, the multiplicity of copies widely diffused through the world rendered it utterly impossible:— Likewise by reason of a variety of sects, with a vigilant and jealous eye watching one another; the Jews, at the same time, in great numbers, standing round narrowly eying, and sufficiently prompt to detect every misstep; having been corrupted by none, either Jews or Christians, it remains uncorrupt.

No more has the Greek of the New Testament been corrupted; for the supposition militates against the wisdom and goodness of its divine Author: he, who has engaged that one iota shall not pass from the law, the Old Testament, we may be assured, will take as effectual care for the preservation and purity of the Gospel or New Testament.

We have this farther consideration. The pious zeal of the wise and faithful watchmen, the eminent doctors and teachers in the christian church, and such there have been in every age, hath always moved them with a vigilant eye to guard its purity, and with prudent care and diligence remove and amend any little corruptions that might have been introduced by its adversaries.

The subject opens an extensive field for the cultivation of many interesting practical uses of improvement: but having already surpassed the limits prescribed, am not permitted to enter upon it, farther than barely to suggest, that it is highly incumbent on the teachers, the ministers of the christian religion, seriously and often to urge and inculcate on their hearers, the divine authority of the scriptures: this appears to me of so great use and even necessity to the success of our ministry, in the promotion of the well being of the church,

church, and the falvation of fouls, that I cannot perfuade myfelf to pafs it without fome brief remarks.—This is of great importance, as a mean and the only effectual mean to perfuade men to hear and receive the word, *not as the word of men, but as it is in truth the word of God.* It is of moment that they are led to confider this as the firft element of the chriftian religion, the very firft thing to be learnt and known in it. Knowing this firft, fays St. Peter, to all chriftians, that no prophefy, no part of the fcripture is of human, but of divine authority : it is very obfervable, this conftantly holds the firft place, in moft of the prophetic writings, as may be feen by any one who will look to the beginning of the books of the Prophets : *Thus faith the Lord,* or *the word of the Lord which came* to the prophet by name, is the common introduction to their writings. The divine authority of the fcripture is not only the firft element, it is even the only fupporter and foundation of the chriftian religion : thus much is clearly afferted in the text : this therefore, before all things elfe, as a foundation, is to be rightly and firmly laid, by the fpiritual builder ; fays St. Paul, *as a wife mafter builder I have laid the foundation, &c.*

This is at the bottom, as the foundation ftone of all other chriftian principles, doctrines and practice ; if this be not ftrongly laid, but fails, they will unavoidably all fail and fink with it. It is that foundation without which neither faith nor obedience will have place in our hearers : what is faith but to affent, becaufe God hath fpoken ? Unlefs we have a firm perfuafion that God hath fpoken whatever is written in the Bible, on what can faith reft ? Again, what is obedience, but to do what God commands ? Unlefs therefore we are certain that God hath fpoken thefe things, which are commanded in the fcripture, how fhall we obey him, or be certain that we do fo ? Hence, fays St. Paul to the Theffalonians, *Ye received it not as the word of men, but as it is in truth the word of God, which effectually worketh*

worketh also in you who believe. The more the belief of this first foundation principle is rooted and flourisheth in our hearers, so much the more will they abound in every good word and work, and the whole of their religion flourish, their pious ardour to maintain good works, watch against and avoid sin, &c. will be prevalent and increasing, and so much the more ample will be the harvest of all our ministerial labours. How great is their number who are either ignorant of this divine authority of the scripture, or even deny it, not only without the pale of the christian church, but in its very bowels! How many who carp and cavil at it! How many, finally, who are wavering and in doubt about it. Perhaps the christian can scarcely be found who does not, at times, find in himself some small degree of doubt and hesitancy concerning this first great principle, the foundation of the whole christian religion. How urgent is the necessity such hearers are under of the friendly seasonable aid of their spiritual instructors: Is it not therefore highly incumbent on the latter, seriously and frequently to give them their best assistance, by stating to their hearers, in as plain and forcible a manner as they are able, the reasons which demand their firm belief and cordial reception of this foundation principle: arguments for this purpose, amounting to compleat demonstration, are not wanting, but ready at hand: by these means, the ignorant may be instructed, the carping caviller silenced, if not shamed, the wavering relieved and established, the humble christian strengthened, and the unbeliever, in now and then an instance, perhaps reclaimed, and the whole audience benefitted.

SERMON

SERMON III.

THE TRUE GOD KNOWN ONLY FROM DIVINE REVELATION.

1 Corinthians i. 21. *The world by wisdom knew not God.*

THE knowledge and belief of the being, perfections and government of God are the foundation of all religion.

THE inquiry is, *How do mankind attain that knowledge?* I answer, *by divine revelation.* Whether reason, in the state in which man was created, was sufficient to inform him of all that was necessary to be known respecting God and religion, belongs not to the present inquiry: But what it is capable of now? We have no better way of determining this, than by considering what reason, unassisted by revelation, has done in past ages. The Apostle Paul, a man of great learning, and well informed of the state of mankind, assures us, that "the world by wisdom knew not God." To prevent misapprehensions, and pursue the subject with perspicuity, I shall,

FIRST, Explain and state the meaning of the Apostle in this assertion.

SECONDLY, Endeavour to show the truth of it.

THIRDLY, Answer the principal objections against this assertion, in the sense it is explained and stated.

FIRST,

FIRST, I am to explain and state the meaning of the Apostle in this assertion, "the world by wisdom knew not God."

THE most general sense in which men may be said to know God, is, *to know that there is a God*. The Apostle cannot be supposed to mean that the world, the generality of mankind, had no idea that there was any God. For it is abundantly evident that the Heathen, who were the largest part of mankind, worshipped many Gods. This they could not have done, if they had no notion that there was any.

To know God, properly, is *to know that there is a God, and but one God*, and to have some proper conceptions of his being, character and government—to *know that God is a self existent, eternal, all perfect Being*: that he possesses knowledge, power, wisdom, justice, goodness, truth, faithfulness, &c. in complete fulness—that there can be no addition to, nor diminution of his perfection—that he is, ever was, and ever will be, the same unchangeably great, glorious, holy, wise, powerful and good Being. It implies also that we know him as the Creator, Upholder and Governor of all things; and also the relations God stands in to us, and we to him—what conduct and worship God requires of us, or is becoming from us to him—the worth of his favour, and the way to obtain it.

IT is, however, of less importance to know how much the Apostle included in a just knowledge of God, than it is to know in what sense he denied the world of mankind to have it, or what knowledge of God he denies them to have. I imagine that he denies that they had any just knowledge of God, his character, government or worship.

THE world of mankind, the Jews only excepted, knew not that there was *one only living and true God*. Consequently, they had no proper idea of the divine Being or character, of their relation or duty to him—of the worth of his favour, or the way in which it was to be sought and obtained.

But we must observe, the Apostle's assertion is, "The world *by wisdom* knew not God." That is, the world of mankind, by all their wisdom, learning and sagacity, knew not God. He does not assert, nor intimate, that they had no knowledge of God by revelation or tradition. The heathen undoubtedly had some knowledge of God, originally from revelation, handed down to them by tradition. The true religion was taught by Noah, a preacher of righteousness to his posterity, and handed down, for *a length of ages*, by the Patriarchs to theirs. But such was the depravity of mankind, and the power and policy of Satan, that a great part of mankind "did not like to retain God in their knowledge." They were not contented with the religion revealed and taught by God, nor with the worship he had prescribed. They vainly fancied they could make some amendments in both. They speculated on these things, endeavoured to form a religion and worship more agreeable to men's taste. They made various additions and alterations, according to their own humours and inclinations, till, by degrees, they had totally corrupted religion, and lost the knowledge of the only true God. "They worshipped them which were no Gods, changed the truth of God into a lie." That is, they worshipped images, which are lying vanities, instead of the true God.

And when they had thus lost the knowledge of the true God and religion, they never recovered it, until the gospel was brought to them. All their priests, philosophers and statesmen, by all their wisdom, learning and sagacity, never regained the knowledge of the true God. The wisest and most learned among them entertained false and absurd notions concerning God.— They owned many Gods, worshipped idols, beasts and reptiles.

This was not only the case with the bulk of mankind, but with the wisest of them. Nor was this the case merely in the most rude and dark ages of the world, as among those who were involved in the grossest ignorance, but in those ages, and in those places where learning flourished most. In Egypt and Babylon where learning was first cultivated, in Greece, and in Rome, when it was mistress of the world, the most learned men in all those places, by all their studies and wisdom, knew not the only living and true God—had no just conceptions of his being, character, government, or the way in which his favour is to be obtained. I proceed,

SECONDLY. To show the truth of this observation, *the world by wisdom knew not God.*

THIS is made evident from hence, viz. That the world of mankind, that one nation only excepted which were favoured with divine revelation, fell into and continued in the errors of polytheism and idolatry.— This can be fully shewn both from sacred and profane history. Idolatry was of ancient date. It is generally supposed to have begun in Chaldea or Assyria, where learning flourished sooner than in other parts of the world. Next the Egyptians worshipped several Gods, particularly Osiris, Isis and Apis. It spread into other nations. Many were the idols of the ancient nations. When Greece became famous for arts and arms, they introduced the Gods of other nations. Athens, which had been the seat of learning for ages, in the Apostles days, was full of them; yet even there, the true God was the unknown God.

As the Romans conquered other nations, they brought their Gods to Rome, and worshipped them. The very names of their Gods would make a large catalogue. They had some thousands of them. It is not easy to suppose they would have worshipped such a number of Gods, if they had known the only true God. Would their wisest and most knowing men so easily

easily have fallen in with the errors, superstition and idolatries of the times, if they had known the only living and true God? It cannot be supposed. Therefore, since they embraced polytheism and idolatry, and neither taught nor practised any better, we must conclude they knew no better.

There were in Greece and Rome, for ages before Christ, many sages and philosophers renowned for wisdom and probity. Their writings are yet extant; yet we do not find in them any proper account of God. Their notions of God, or rather of the Gods, were very absurd. Their philosophy consisted principally in morality, logick and ethicks. They were very inquisitive to find out wherein man's chief good or happiness consists. But they were greatly divided in their opinions about it. Those who have been at the pains to collect their opinions, have reckoned up some hundreds of them. This would not have been the case, had they known the true God, *whose favour is life.*— But they laboured in the dark. They wearied themselves in vain to find the door to happiness—what was the true wisdom for the children of men.

In Job's day, the inquiry was, " where shall wisdom be found." The philosophers searched through nature to find it, but in vain. Revelation alone discovered " that the fear of the Lord was the true wisdom for man."

A fair experiment was made, for ages together, when learning and philosophy were at the greatest height in the heathen world ; what it was the utmost human wisdom and learning could do towards finding out the true God, the true way of worship, wherein man's true happiness consists, and the way to it. But all their wisdom and learning failed them. Pertinent, therefore is the inquiry of the Apostle, " Where is the wise ? Where is the scribe ? Where is the disputer of this world ? Hath not God made foolish the wisdom of this world ?" God permitted the experiment to be made,

that

that men in that and in all future ages of the world might be convinced that the boasted wisdom and learning of this world is foolishness—is utterly insufficient to teach men the knowledge of the true God, and the way to happiness—that they need a divine revelation, and that they might be prepared to receive one.

When the world was in this woeful state of ignorance, polytheism and idolatry, from which they could not, by all their wisdom and learning extricate themselves, God was pleased to send his Son from Heaven into the world, to make reconciliation for iniquity and bring in an everlasting righteousness, and to teach men the only true God, and the way to happiness in his favour. He chose, instructed and sent forth a number of Apostles to preach the gospel, open the way to life and salvation, and instruct them in the great and important things which concern their present and future peace and happiness. Thus *when the world by their wisdom knew not God, it pleased God in his wisdom, by the foolishness of preaching to save them that believe.*—Though the doctrine of salvation by Christ crucified was to the Jews a stumbling block, and appeared to the learned Greeks, foolishness; yet it pleased God, by the preaching of the gospel, to bring to nought the boasted wisdom of men, humble their pride, convert and save those who believed on this crucified, risen and exalted Saviour, and obeyed his gospel. I proceed as it was proposed,

Thirdly, To answer some objections which may be made against this proposition, in the sense it has been stated and explained. As,

First, It may be said, that men of reading know that the being and perfections of God can be demonstrated by principles of reason, and have been thus demonstrated as clearly as any principle in mathematicks.

I reply, if this be so easily done, whence is it that there are so many in the world, even of those who pride themselves that they possess a superiority of reason, argument and learning, yet are nevertheless of a libertine and atheistical cast? That this is fact cannot be denied. Most of the grandees in the European courts are of this stamp. However,

GRANTING the objection to be true, it militates nothing against this assertion, that the world by wisdom knew not God. For,

THE question is not whether there is a God, or not: Nor, whether it be agreeable to reason to conclude that there is a God, who possesses all perfection: nor yet, whether the being and perfections of God can be demonstrated or have been demonstrated by principles of reason. The strength or weakness of human reason, in the point before us, is not to be determined by what men favoured with revelation, divine and human erudition can do, or have done; but by what men without the knowledge of divine revelation can discover and prove. The boasters of reason and despisers of revelation can claim no more. And of this the world has had a fair and long trial. There cannot, therefore, be a fairer way, (these men themselves being judges) of determining what mankind can do in this case, than by considering what they have done under these circumstances.

WHAT if men favoured with divine revelation and human learning, have demonstrated the being and perfections of God! Does it thence follow that they would or could have done it if they had not been favoured with divine revelation? By no means.

DIVINE Revelation greatly enlarges our knowledge, especially our knowledge of God and his works. The great improvements which have been made, in latter ages, in philosophy and astronomy, are not owing to superior powers of mind in the moderns above those of the antients; but to superior advantages of culture: And these advantages are derived principally from the clearer knowledge of the gospel and divine revelation.

revelation. From that source we derive many *ideas* which our reason approves, upon which we reflect and reason, and by which we enlarge our knowledge of God and his works; *Ideas*, however, which would never have entered our minds had we been destitute of divine revelation.

LEARNING was cultivated of old in Babylon.— In Egypt, thence brought to Greece, and from thence to Rome, where it was cultivated with great assiduity, for a long time before the days of the Apostles. The Apostle Paul was not only an adept in the learning of the Jews, but in that of the Gentiles; he had travelled into other countries, visited Athens and Rome, and was able to dispute their most learned and subtle philosophers. From him we have this sad and lamentable observation, that the world by all their wisdom and learning knew not God.

SECONDLY, It may be said, that the heathen philosophers and sages taught many excellent things concerning God and moral duties, therefore we cannot suppose them ignorant of God and religion.

I REPLY, that they generally held a plurality of Gods, though sometimes, they might mention the name of God in the singular number—that the characters they gave of the Gods, and the conduct they ascribed to them, are very absurd and such as are utterly inconsistent with the ideas we have of the true God.— Though we find now and then a good moral sentence in their works; yet it is rare to find in them a sentence concerning God which we can fully approve. They appear to labour under great ignorance and darkness, and to have very confused ideas, concerning God and his works. What few things they said concerning God, that had any appearance of truth, are taken special notice of, and highly extolled, by some, who would exalt reason in matters of religion, higher than is just. But if they had any just ideas of God and religion,

where

where did they get them? I answer, from Revelation.

Though mankind did not like to retain God in their knowledge, yet there were some few things handed down to them, by tradition from antient revelation.

And further, **the scriptures of the Old Testa**ment were early translated into Greek, which **was the** language most generally spoken from the days of Alexander to the Apostles. The Jews, being scattered into all parts **of the** world, carried those scriptures, with them. Learned men of all nations had access to them. And though they did not regard them as a divine revelation; nor examine the evidences of their being so; yet they read them out of curiosity, to **know what they** contained. Some things in their writings show **this.** Virgil's Pollio, a Pastoral describing a person **to be** born, who should be a great blessing to the world, from some leading expressions in it, **appears to** be a sort of imitation of some things in the prophecy of Isaiah concerning Christ **to come.** They gained some knowledge by reading those scriptures. They were, however, fond of having what they **wrote** thought to be their own, and dressed their ideas in their **own language;** yet what few things **they** wrote well, they collected either from the scriptures, or from tradition originally handed down from divine revelation.

Thirdly, It may be objected, that though Philosophers and men of learning among the Gentiles, knew God, yet as the religion of their country was Polytheism and Idolatry, and as it was patronized by the ruling powers, they dare not speak against it, or teach any other. Therefore it may be said, the Apostles could only mean that the bulk of mankind were kept in such ignorance that they knew not God. To this I reply,

That this objection has more plausibility than truth in it. For the Apostle asserts, that *the world by*
G *wisdom*

wisdom knew not God. That is, all the wisdom and learning in the world did not bring men to the knowledge of the true God. The common people indeed, were amazingly ignorant, they could neither write nor read. Men of good common learning among us, have far greater advantages to attain knowledge, if they have equal leisure, than the most learned had in those ages. What learning there then was, was either in manuscript or in the philosophers and instructors.—Now printing is brought to perfection. All the valuable writings of antiquity are translated into our language. We have the records of former, and the discoveries of later ages. We have the sacred records.—Bibles are plenty and cheap. We have the labours and researches of the greatest divines, the most famous philosophers, the ablest statesmen and generals; we have a much easier and shorter way to knowledge than they had, and a greater fund of it to repair to: yet under all these advantages, how little do we know of God? Pertinent therefore was the inquiry of Zophar; " canst thou by searching find out God?" It is in vain, therefore, for any to pretend that the light of nature has discovered, or can discover the true God, unless they can bring some instances to prove it. Some have indeed, introduced Socrates for this purpose; but very impertinently, for he owned that he got his opinions in religion from the barbarians, meaning the Jews.—There cannot be a single instance produced of any of the sages of antiquity who by all his wisdom knew God. They acknowledged many Gods. They said that Jupiter was the greatest and best. But could we find an antient hoary sage who gave a proper account of God, it would be reasonable to conclude that his knowledge was derived from revelation, either by reading or tradition.

It is worthy to be remarked here, that the knowledge of the true God and of religion could be handed
down

down by tradition formerly, when men lived to a great age with more certainty than in after ages.

NOAH lived three hundred and fifty years after the flood, and doubtless was a preacher of Righteousness then as well as before. Shem lived under his father's instructions four hundred and fifty years, and survived him an hundred and fifty years. Abraham was under his instructions seventy-five years, travelled to Egypt and other places and conversed with the sages there. Men lived long in the days of Job and Moses. Those who travelled in quest of knowledge had great advantage from habitation, and much knowledge was handed down that way to the Heathen. Though they chose not to retain God in their knowledge.

FOURTHLY, Some may perhaps say, that the Heathen offered sacrifices nearly the same as the Jews.

BUT what does this prove? It is an argument that sacrifices were originally of divine appointment. That the Heathen preserved, in some measure the form of worship, though by multiplying the objects of it, they lost the knowledge of the true one, and offered their sacrifices to devils, and not to God.

FIFTHLY, What the Apostle saith, Rom. i. 20. is objected, " for the invisible things of him (God) from the creation of the world are clearly seen, being understood by the things that are made, even his eternal power and godhead ; so that they are without excuse."

To this I reply. That, however this passage of the Apostle has been understood or applied, the Apostle evidently introduces it to show that the Gentiles were inexcusable in loosing the knowledge of the true God, which they had originally from Revelation, when they had the book of nature before them. The works of creation witnessed the being and perfections of God, and they were inexcusable that they did not attend to them. Had they duly considered the works of creation evidencing the perfections of the Creator, they would not have worshipped them as Gods which are no Gods,
" But

"But they did not like to retain God in their knowledge." They speculated in matters of religion, "they became vain in their imaginations," in the Greek diallogis mois, which may well be rendered reasonings.— When learning began to flourish, those who possessed it became proud. "Knowledge puffeth up." They were not content to continue in that religion which God had revealed, and which had been taught them. They attempted to correct and amend it by their reason and philosophy. But they corrupted and ruined it.— "In pride, in reasoning pride man's error lies." They worshipped the sun, moon and planets, because they found they had influence on the seasons and in producing faults. Then they worshipped great men who had been benefactors. And at length they were so stupid as to worship birds, beasts and creeping things.— Their "reasoning pride," led them astray. They never recovered the knowledge of the true God until the great teacher came from Heaven to enlighten those who sat in darkness and in the region and shadow of death.

These are the principal objections which occur. I hope the answers though brief, will be satisfactory.— Let us attend to some observations by way of improvement.

First, From what has been said, we learn the deplorable state of the gentile world before the gospel was preached to them. They were sunk into the most woful ignorance in matters of religion. Aliens from the commonwealth of Israel, strangers to the covenant God had made with men, and the promises God had made of a Saviour—they had no knowledge of God nor hope of salvation by a Redeemer. They were carried away to dumb idols by the customs of the times.— Their understanding was darkened and they walked in the vanity of their minds. Being past feeling, they gave themselves over to work all uncleanness with greediness. From such progenitors we sprung, and such

such would have been our case, had not the sun of righteousness risen up on the dark parts of the earth with healing in his wings.

Second, Hence we may see the need of a teacher from Heaven to reveal the true God and the way of salvation to men. Both Jews and Gentiles needed such a teacher. The Jews were privileged above the Gentiles, as they had the oracles of God, in which were contained the promises of salvation, and the way of access to God. But the way of worship appointed to them was calculated for that nation only while they lived in the land of Canaan, and until the Messiah came. When they were scattered into different parts of the world they could not worship God according to the law of Moses.

The Gentiles needed to be shewn the promises God had made of a Saviour. Jew and Gentile needed to be shewn how God had fulfilled them, and taught the way of access to God through a Mediator.

Jesus Christ is this teacher from Heaven. He has taught us the nature, perfections and government of God, the way to worship him, and to obtain his favour and eternal life. He selected a number of Apostles, whom he sent into all the world to preach the gospel. They faithfully executed their commission, and, though greatly opposed by men and devils, had great success, in putting down satan's kingdom, and setting up the kingdom of Christ in the world.

Third, Hence we learn the unspeakable privileges which accrue to us from divine revelation. Few are sensible how great these are. We are taught the being, perfection and providence of God. We can see clearly that there is one, and can be but one living and true God. We are apt to wonder at the blindness and stupidity of the Heathen, that they should worship many Gods and the true God be to them unknown.

This

This should lead us to reflect upon and be duly thankful for the advantages we derive from divine revelation. Their capacities were as great as ours; but our advantages are vastly greater than theirs. We know that God created the heavens and the earth; and we see his perfections displayed in the works of creation and providence. We have the account of man's original state, of his apostacy, and of the sad state into which we are brought by the fall, of the promises of a Saviour and the fulfilment of them.—— The way of life and salvation by Christ is pointed out to us. We are told what we must do to be saved.—— We have the wisest counsels, the most weighty motives, the most earnest expectations, and the most solemn warnings set before us.

How could we know God, the acceptable way of worship, and on what terms he will receive sinners into his favour, but from divine revelation?

Many important truths and duties are now plain, which, without divine revelation, would never have been known.

We should seriously consider ourselves accountable for every talent we receive——that if we do not improve our privileges we shall be utterly inexcusable—— that if we continue in unbelief and disobedience, our condemnation and punishment will be greater than that of the Heathen, who never had such light and advantages. "The servant who knows his master's will and prepares not himself to do it, will be beaten with many stripes."

Fourth, Hence also we learn the necessity and advantages of a preached gospel.

Put the case, that the scriptures were in our hands, but we had no gospel preachers, should we be in better circumstances than the Ethiopean eunuch, when he was reading the prophesy of Isaiah, concerning Christ? Philip asked him, "understandest thou what thou readest?" He replied, "how can I, except some man

man should guide me?" we should need a preacher to interpret them—one who made it his study to unfold them. We need to have the evidences of there being a divine revelation set before us, and the truths they contain properly arranged and explained, and the consistency of the whole shewn: lest otherwise cunning and crafty men, who lie in wait to deceive, shake our faith. There are many errors in the world. Preachers are necessary, not only to instruct the ignorant, but for the perfecting of the saints—for the edifying of the body of Christ, and to prevent their being carried about by every wind of doctrine.

So long as these ends are to be answered, a stated ministry and the preaching of the gospel will be necessary and advantageous.

Our duty therefore is to attend upon the gospel preached by Christ's ambassadors, not forsaking the assembling ourselves together for divine worship; but giving diligent heed to the things which are spoken, lest at any time we let them slip. Let us walk in faith and love, grow in grace, and in the knowledge of our Lord and Saviour Jesus Christ. To him be glory and dominion, world without end, *Amen.*

SERMON IV.

A VIEW OF THE DIVINE PERFECTIONS.

Psalm viii. last verse. *O Lord our Lord, how excellent is thy Name in all the earth!*

THE Psalmist, in this psalm, devoutly celebrates the transcendent greatness and glory of God's name, as displayed in his works. The psalm begins and ends with the same pious admiration and acknowledgment of the divine excellency. "How excellent is thy name in all the earth!" The glory of God's name is indeed above the heavens; it is in the clearest manner displayed in the upper world: but it is not confined there; it breaks forth and shines with beams of lustre through all the earth.

By the name of God, we are sometimes in scripture, and particularly in our text, to understand, his being and attributes; or that by which he makes himself known; his wisdom, power, holiness, mercy, &c. as revealed in his word, or discovered by his works. It is in these that he exhibits himself to his intelligent creatures; from these only can we form right conceptions of the nature and perfections of the glorious Creator. But then we must remember, that it is but very little comparatively, that can be known of God, especially in the present imperfect state. Our capacities and

views

views are confined within very narrow limits. God is infinite, and therefore incomprehensible to finite beings. Who by searching can find out the Almighty to perfection? The most enlarged conceptions of the most exalted finite understanding, fall far short of a complete knowledge of the supreme nature and excellence.

WHEN therefore we enter on a subject like this, which respects the being and attributes of God; it should be under a due sense of our weakness; and with an ingenuous confession of our inability, to give a description, that shall fully correspond with the infinite dignity and glory of him whose name is wonderful. Yet the great God has been pleased in a measure to reveal himself to his rational creatures: so that something truly, though not fully, may be known of him. From the discoveries and notices he has made, we may obtain some suitable, though inadequate ideas, of his glorious character and perfections.

AN attempt to give some proper view of these, is the present design.

THE divine perfections have been usually distinguished, by natural and moral; or incommunicable and communicable. The former are such as can only be ascribed to God—Eternity, immutability, omnipotence, &c. the latter are those attributes, which some creatures do in a measure possess;—wisdom, justice, holiness, &c. These last however as belonging to God, are infinite perfections; they are in him essentially, radically and in a supereminent degree; in creatures, imperfectly and according to a certain measure; but as a ray, an emanation from the infinite original source of perfection. In a strict sense there is none wise, holy and good, but one; that is God. Yet renewed men are represented as possessing the image, and partaking of the nature of God; as being his children in an eminent sense, and bearing a resemblance to him.— They are required to be holy because God is holy; and to be perfect as their father who is in heaven, is perfect.

perfect. Those who dwell in love are said to dwell in God, and God in them; from whence it appears that there is, and must be some real likeness in saints, according to their measure, some imperfect resemblance in holy dispositions and affections, to the moral perfections of Deity. But I return to the proposed design, which is to take a distinct survey of the divine attributes, or in the language of the text, to consider the various excellencies of God's name.

I SHALL in the first place mention those divine attributes that are denominated incommunicable, and then speak of those moral perfections, a resemblance of which is to be found in some creatures. I begin with the former, and of those excellencies which are essential to the nature of God, and which cannot be derived, or communicated, the following are the principal, and comprehensive of the rest, viz. Selfexistence, infinity, eternity and immutability.

FIRST, Self-existence is a prime attribute of deity. It is peculiar to the living and true God, to exist in and of himself, independent of all others. His name alone is Jehovah; this title imports independent being and essence. It is the nature of God to *be*, and always to be the same; *I am that I am.* This is my name and this is my memorial to all generations.

THIS necessity of being is the sole privilege of deity; the existence of other beings is dependent and derived. The first cause must necessarily have being and life of himself; and he must be the original source, cause and spring of life and existence, to every living thing. In him they live and move and have their being. There are innumerable living creatures of various ranks and orders; and some beings will forever exist; but these are all absolutely and constantly dependent on God. His almighty power upholds and continues their existence. He alone has life and immortality in himself.

SECOND,

SECOND, The *Infinity* of God is another essential property of the divine nature. By this he is distinguished from all others, and from every thing else.—For all creatures and things in the universe are finite, these have all certain measures and bounds set to them. But the supreme majesty is absolutely without measure or limits. This is the proper idea of infinity. That is infinite that has no beginning, and no end—which cannot be circumscribed by place, nor terminated by time. Such is God.

THIS divine infinity includes, among other things, *ubiquity* or omnipresence which it may be proper in this place particularly to consider.

THE glorious God by his infinite greatness and immensity fills all places. He is every where. His essential presence pervades the universe. "The eyes of the Lord are in every place beholding the evil and the good. He revealeth the deep and secret things, he knoweth what is in the darkness; and the light dwelleth with him, neither is there any creature that is not manifest in his sight; but all things are naked and open to his all comprehending view."

THE essential universal presence of the Deity is every where declared and asserted in the sacred scriptures. But how are we to conceive of the divine ubiquity? I answer this as well as other incommunicable attributes of God cannot be fully comprehended by finite creatures; but for our instruction in respect to this wonderful attribute, we may observe.

THE great God is every where present by his wisdom; directing, ordering and overruling all causes and events in the best and fittest manner.

HE is every where present by his knowledge and understanding which are infinite; he is therefore intuitively and perfectly acquainted with all the various parts of creation; has a full, distinct and perfect knowledge of the nature, properties, situations, relations,
connections

connections and tendencies of all creatures and things in the universe.

God is every where present by his power, exercising a constant and uncontrouled dominion and authority over all his works. I add once more. The supreme being is omnipresent in respect of his goodness, this extends to all places, and is exercised continually. The heavens and the earth and the sea, do not only manifest the divine wisdom and power ; but these are likewise replete with wonderful exhibitions of God's grace and beneficence. The Lord is good to all and his tender mercies are over all his works. We are next to take a view,

THIRDLY, Of the *eternity* of God. This is also included in the divine infinity ; but may be considered as a distinct attribute. He is stiled, "the King *eternal*, and the high and lofty one that inhabiteth eternity." This is a perfection essential to God and by which he is distinguished from all other beings. Eternity in a strict sense can be ascribed to God only. It signifies one perpetual uninterrupted duration of existence, which has neither beginning, end or succession of days, months and years. This cannot be predicated of any created being. All finite beings have a beginning ; though some will never have an end.

THE happiness of the righteous and the misery of the wicked are both said to be eternal, because neither of them will have an end : yet they are not eternal beings, because they had a beginning ; and that which had a beginning is not properly eternal. Eternity therefore in a strict sense belongs only to God ; who has ever existed and will forever exist. " From everlasting to everlasting thou art God."

THE eternity of God denotes the following things. (1) That He ever *was*, and therefore that he never began to be. Reflect back as far as imagination can trace, to millions of millions of centuries, and you come no nearer to the beginning of God's existence,

because

becaufe it had no beginning. He was as ancient, fo to fpeak, millions of ages paffed as he is now, or will be millions of ages to come ; becaufe eternity is not computed by years or ages ; the *Divinity* has no date. (2) That he will have no end. As he never began to exift ; fo he will never ceafe to be. Look forward through the revolution of as many ages as figures can exprefs, and you will come no nearer to the end of God's exiftence : becaufe to his eternal being there can be no end ; having no limits, it is fubject to no meafure or computation.

HENCE, (3) In the eternal duration of God there is no fucceffion. With refpect to him there is nothing paft, nothing to come, but every thing prefent. The everlafting Jehovah poffeffes one eternal *now*. All times and fpaces of duration ; all viciffitudes, events and tranfactions, both paffed and future, which have or will take place in the univerfe, are all gathered and united into one inftant—are all collected to one point. Thefe all, are now and ever were prefent to the all-comprehending view of the eternal mind. This is fome imperfect account of God's eternity.

4th. THE other general incommunicable attribute, to be confidered is the divine *Immutability*, or unchangeablenefs. It is the appropriate character and privilege of the Moft High not to be fubject to any poffible change. " I am the Lord, I change not," it is peculiar to my nature, and to mine only ever to be the fame. This is implied in that wonderful name by which God revealed himfelf to Mofes, "*I AM THAT I AM.*" I am what I was and what I fhall be ; the unchangeable God yefterday, to day and for ever.

BY this perfection he is diftinguifhed from, and exalted far above, all creatures and things.

EVERY created being and thing, we fee is fubject to alteration.

MEN on earth are fickle inconftant creatures. The various and multiplied parts of creation are all liable

ble to as many vicissitudes. Every thing we behold is uncertain—in a perpetual fluctuation—putting on a different face, wearing a different aspect, and all tending to dissolution. This world with all its inhabitants are in constant agitation. What shifting scenes; what various changes and alterations, are constantly taking place on this mortal stage!

And if we raise our views to the visible heavens; if we contemplate the sun, the moon and the stars, we find them changing their positions and aspects. And these all, shall ere long perish; they will wax old as doth a garment, and like a vesture be folded and changed. But the Creator shall endure and remain the same forever. On his own immovable basis he continues immutably fixed; undisturbed by all the revolutions and changes of time.

The sun in the firmament, is the most constant, unvarying and glorious object, of any other in creation; and is therefore the brightest emblem of the unchangeable Jehovah. In allusion to that bright and immense luminary, he is by the Apostle James stiled, "the Father of lights;" but he adds, "with whom there is no variableness or shadow of turning." Here it is observable that while the Apostle compares the Deity to the sun, as the most striking image of the divine immutability; he is careful at the same time by his choice and manner of expression, to signify the vast superiority of the Father of lights. The sun, though more constant, fixed and unvarying as well as more bright and splendid, than any other object, is not without change. It has its parallaxes and tropicks; a diversity of aspects and appearances; but with God there is no variableness or shadow of turning. He is in the most absolute sense an unchangeable being. He is of one mind.

Having thus briefly considered the natural, or incommunicable perfections of God; it remains, according to the proposed method, that we attend in the

next

next place to some of those, which for sake of distinction are denominated his moral or communicable attributes; a shadow or resemblance of which are found in some of his intelligent creatures. Among these are the following; which I will endeavour a little to explain and illustrate, viz: divine wisdom, power, holiness, justice and truth. I include the attribute power; because though not strictly a moral, is yet a communicable property. Though the highest degree of power, of which creatures are possessed, is weakness compared with almighty strength; yet all power being derived from God; in those who possess it in any degree there may be said to be a kind of resemblance, in that respect to the Almighty. And there is spiritual strength derived to the children of God, by which they may be said, in a moral view to resemble their heavenly Father.

I now return to the consideration of those moral attributes above named, as they exist in God. At the head of this class of perfections we place wisdom.

1st. THE great God is possessed of infinite wisdom. This perfection is ascribed to him in the highest and most absolute sense. He is stiled, " the only wise God." He is said to be " wise in heart as well as mighty in strength." " A God of knowledge by whom actions are weighed;" and whose " understanding is infinite;" " the Lord of Hosts, wonderful in counsel, excellent in working." The Apostle breaks out in expressions of admiration of this glorious perfection. " O! the depths of the riches both of the wisdom and knowledge of God."

It might be proper to consider divine wisdom as essentially existing in the divine nature; and as it is displayed and manifested by its operations.

DIVINE wisdom abstractedly considered is a power and disposition to form, direct and dispose all things in the best and fittest manner possible. It is the part of wisdom to concert the best plans, and to devise and

make

make use of the best means for their execution. Such wisdom dwells in God, in the most perfect and consummate manner.

The wisest of men are liable to mistakes in their schemes; or if these are ever so wisely formed; yet for want of a thorough knowledge or sufficient power they fail of success. It is far otherwise with the most High. His judgment is perfect; it cannot err; his plans are all therefore, without the least defect: and infinite wisdom joined with uncontroulable strength must ensure success to every purpose his heart can devise. His understanding is infinite; and his will is perfect; and he worketh all things according to the dictates of that infinite knowledge; and the counsel of that perfect and holy will. In a word the Almighty not only works, so as none can *let* him; but all his operations carry in them the marks of the most consummate wisdom and prudence.

This perfect and manifold wisdom of God is wonderfully displayed, in his works of creation and providence; but in an especial manner, it shines forth in the stupendous plan of man's redemption. Here the subject opens to a field, wide and extensive, in which it would be pleasing and profitable to expatiate; but the short limits prescribed me will not permit my entering upon it.

I must pass on therefore to a distinct consideration of another of the divine attributes, viz.

2dly. That of power. God is excellent and infinite in power. This perfection in the most absolute sense, and in the highest possible degree belongeth to him.

The idea which we naturally form of God, is, that of an infinitely strong, powerful and almighty being. The sacred passages which assert and declare the supreme uncontroulable power and dominion of Jehovah are too numerous to be cited here. You will recollect that he is frequently in scripture called " the mighty

mighty God;" "the strong Lord;" "the Lord almighty;" "the Lord God omnipotent, &c. For the illustration of this divine attribute we will only enquire very briefly into the nature and extent of God's power, and the manifestations and effects of it.

THE divine omnipotence imports an ability to do all things, which are not repugnant to the perfection of his nature. When it is said, God cannot deny himself; he cannot lie; or if it should be said that the almighty cannot cause a thing to be, and not to be; to make that present which is past, or an event not to have been, which has actually taken place, and the like: all this is no impeachment of divine omnipotence, for such things as abovementioned, evidently imply, either weakness and imperfection, in the agent, or absolute contradiction and absurdity in the supposition. The divine power may, notwithstanding, be truly said to be unlimited and without controul. There is nothing becoming an holy, perfect and almighty being that he cannot effect; and it is certain that he doth whatever pleases him in heaven and in the earth, in the sea and all deep places; and there is none can stay his hand. His power is coexistent with his being, and as boundless as his infinity. It extends through the universe; and like his other attributes is unchangeably the same.

THE omnipotence of deity, as well as the divine wisdom, is sufficiently evidenced by the effects that we behold. The formation of the heavens and earth; the production of all those things with which they are replenished; the vast number and greatness; the wonderful beauty and harmony; the exact proportion and uniformity, the connection, order and regularity of the works of creation, do all most conspicuously manifest and show forth the glory of the creator's power, as well as that of his wisdom and goodness.

AND if we attend to the marvellous operations of nature and second causes; the amazing occurrences in providence; the astonishing revolutions and events which take place in the natural and moral world; in these various phenomena we clearly trace an omnipotent agency; and shall be constrained to acknowledge one supreme almighty, though invisible hand, who worketh all things according to the counsel of his own will. How manifold and marvellous are thy works O Lord, both of creation and providence; by thine almighty power as well as in thy perfect wisdom hast though made them all.

3dly. THE holiness or goodness of God comes next to be considered. This is essential to the divine nature, and intimately connected with divine power. Sovereign uncontrouled power, separate from goodness and holiness, would be infinitely dangerous. Such power in the hand of an unjust, unholy and evil being, would be terrible indeed: the very thought excites terror. This must therefore be an entirely wrong idea of God. It is matter of unspeakable comfort that the almighty creator and ruler of the universe is a being as *good* as he is *great*. His sovereignty and dominion are indeed absolute and uncontroulable, but they are perfectly just and holy. All the acts of God's power; all the administrations of his government are under the constant and immediate direction of unerring wisdom and infinite goodness. This renders the attribute of omnipotence equally amiable with all the other perfections. How desirable is it that he, who is wise in heart, should be also mighty in strength; that the God of power, should be no less the God of love. Universal authority and dominion in such a being are perfectly safe for the subjects. None can be injured by the exercise of it; all must be happy who cheerfully submit to it. Well may the truly benevolent and obedient, every where join in that joyful acclamation; " Alleluia for the Lord God omnipotent reigneth."

BUT I am here to speak particularly of the divine holiness.

GOD's

GOD's name and his nature is holy. He is called by way of eminence, "*the holy one*," and said to be "*glorious in holiness.*" This is a part of the divine character, which shines with distinguished lustre. The heavenly host are represented as falling at the footstool of God's throne, and with deep reverence crying "holy, holy, holy is the Lord God, Almighty."

THE divine nature is perfectly free from any the least stain, and infinitely opposed to all impurity. He is of purer eyes than to behold iniquity without abhorrence. Holiness is the intrinsic rectitude and perfection of his nature. It includes in it perfect goodness, benevolence and mercy, justice and truth.

THE benevolence or love of God, which is only another word for holiness, is that attribute by which the divine being necessarily delights in his own holiness and happiness; and desires the holiness and happiness of his creatures, so far as is consistent with his own glory and the general good. Perfect consummate goodness being essential to the divine nature, it must follow, that every thing proceeding from him must be good. All the exercises of his eternal mind; and all the acts and administrations of his universal government, must be so many acts and exercises of pure benevolence.

FROM a fountain perfectly pure, holy and good; nothing corrupt can proceed. To impute to the infinitely holy and good God, any act that implies the least defect of absolute goodness; or the want of the purest benevolence, or the least deviation from the most perfect rectitude and holiness; would be highly derogatory to his honour, and a criminal impeachment of his sacred character.*

4thly. THE Justice of God is by no means opposed to his goodness; but is inseparably connected
with

---

* As an objection to what is here asserted, it will be asked; How are the many evils and miseries which take place in the world
under

with it, and really a branch of it. An idea of goodness and mercy distinct from justice and righteousness, is not a true idea of God; for in his character, these are inseparably conjoined, and in some respect the same: so far at least that every act of God's justice, however individuals may be affected, is really an act of divine goodness and general benevolence. The infinite goodness and mercy of God, therefore, affords no ground of encouragement to impenitent sinners to hope they shall pass with impunity: for he is no less just and righteous than good and gracious.

God has indeed " proclaimed his name, the Lord God merciful and gracious, long-suffering, abundant in goodness; keeping mercy for thousands, forgiving iniquity, transgression and sin:" yet lest impenitent sinners, from these multiplied expressions of compassion, should be emboldened in wickedness, presuming on the divine lenity; it is added in express and emphatical terms; " And who will by no means clear the

under the divine government, consistent with the perfect universal benevolence of deity? Answer. If it is an undoubted truth, (as we believe) that there are no evils of any kind which have or will take place in creation, but were originally designed, and will finally terminate in the greatest possible good: then these evils and miseries are consistent with the perfect goodness of God. But could not God have prevented sin and all its evil consequences from taking place? If it had been best that sin and its attendant evils should not have been in the world; he, who is infinite in wisdom and goodness as well as power, doubtless would not have permitted them: his actually permitting these evils to take place is a sufficient proof and evidence to us that it was best on the whole they should: and this ought to silence every cavil and objection which rises in our minds. Is it not enough for us to know that the plan of providence was the result of infinite wisdom and perfect goodness? Because such short sighted creatures as we are unable fully to comprehend or account for it; shall we therefore presume to arraign the divine wisdom and impeach the divine goodness? Who are we that we should reply against the Almighty? It certainly would better become us; in things intricate and mysterious, to say with the humble Apostle, " O the depth of the riches both of the wisdom and knowledge of God, how unsearchable are his judgments and his ways past finding out."

the guilty." While the goodness and mercy of God incline him to pardon sin, and receive penitent sinners to favour; divine justice, truth and holiness require, that incorrigible offenders be punished and destroyed.

5th. We will just touch upon the truth of God, and with this, finish our brief survey of the divine perfections.

This is likewise an essential part of God's excellent name and character. He is the living and true God in opposition to false deities; and he is the God of truth; the faithful God who keepeth covenant and mercy, with them that love him and keep his commandments.

The veracity and faithfulness of God, are manifested in the exact fulfilment of his word. "God is not a man that he should lie, nor the son of man that he should repent; hath he said, and shall he not do it; hath he spoken, and shall he not make it good?" Numb. xxiii. 19. He most certainly will. Heaven and earth shall pass away, but not one tittle of his word will ever fail.

There is God's word of promise, and his word of threatening; both of which he will invariably fulfil. "Know therefore that the Lord thy God, he is God, the faithful God, who keepeth covenant and mercy with them that love him and keep his commandments to a thousand generations; and repayeth them that hate him, to their face, to destroy them." Deut. v. 9, 10.

Has the merciful God promised to help and save all those who trust in him? On the contrary has the just and holy God declared that he will punish and destroy, all who continue in impenitence and wickedness? It may be relied upon, that to each of these solemn engagements he will be true and faithful.

Thus I have attempted, in some measure, to exhibit the various excellencies of God's name. The subject is immense and sublime; but very little justice

therefore

therefore could be done to it, in a single discourse, and especially, by so feeble a pen: yet what has been offered, will serve, it is hoped, to give the reader some just and raised conceptions of the glorious God. How excellent and wonderful doth he appear in each of those views we have taken! From the consideration of which we may well say in the language of inspiration; "There is none like unto thee O Lord. "Thou art great and thy name is great; who shall not fear thee O thou King of nations," and supreme Lord of all: "for to thee doth it appertain."

MANY important and useful remarks might be made from the subject, considered particularly in its several parts: The following more general ones, can only be mentioned as an improvement of the whole collectively.

FIRST, This view of the divine character and perfections, will serve to confirm our belief, of the *unity* of the Godhead. A being of such attributes, as we have seen, belong to God must necessarily be but only *one*. It is impossible there should be two or more, infinite eternal beings. The supposition is manifestly absurd and contradictory. The scriptures indeed teach us, that this one God subsists in three distinct persons; but they at the same time declare the essential unity of these persons. "There are three," says the apostle John, "that bear record in heaven, the Father, the Word, and the Holy Ghost, and these three are one."*
1 John v. 7.

SECONDLY, The subject of the divine perfections, opens to us a field of most delightful and profitable contemplation. Nothing to intelligent creatures, can afford such rational and sublime entertainment—such real

and

---

* The doctrine of the trinity, it is confessed, is mysterious and incomprehensible to finite beings; but is it more so than the manner of the divine existence, his infinity, eternity and other essential attributes? of these we believe God to be possessed, though we are unable to comprehend them.

and substantial enjoyment. This is a subject, in its nature grand and inexhaustible; the more it is studied, and the longer it is contemplated, the more excellent, glorious and divine, it will appear. It cannot fail to furnish abundant matter of constant, increasing pleasure, admiration and joy, to the enlarged minds of angels and saints; through the vast ages of eternity. At present we can see and know but little of the character and glory of the great Jehovah, because but little comparatively has as yet been revealed and manifested to us; though enough to excite our astonishment—sufficient to draw forth lively sentiments of devout homage and elevated praise. But hereafter, in the future state, the minds of glorified beings, will be vastly expanded; and the divine perfections will be far more fully and clearly displayed.

UNLIMITED space, and eternal duration will then afford ample scope for the continued exhibitions and discoveries of the exhaustless treasures of marvellous wisdom, power, benevolence and love of God, to the enlarged view of all holy intelligences. But then,

THIRDLY, Since the nature and attributes of God are infinite; though it is our highest wisdom to contemplate and admire them; yet it argues arrogance and folly to pretend fully to understand and comprehend them. The height, depth, length and breadth of a single part of the divine character surpasses all finite understanding; who then by searching can find out the Almighty to perfection? This is an expanse unmeasurable! an abyss unfathomable! an ocean without bottom or shore!

FOURTHLY, For any therefore to entertain low and dishonourable thoughts of the glorious eternal God;—for any to withhold those religious acknowledgments and adorations of his sacred being and perfections, which are his due;—for any to refuse that supreme love, honor and obedience, which his exalted character and infinite excellencies demand; shows ex-

supreme

treme ignorance and fottifhnefs; it difcovers vile ingratitude and rebellion.

Again, This fubject may ferve to teach us, that thofe views of God that are partial : which do not refpect his whole character, are wrong and dangerous. Thus if we confine our ideas of the goodnefs and benevolence of Deity; to the exclufion of the divine perfections of juftice, righteoufnefs and holinefs; it will lead to miftakes and conclufions, that may prove injurious and fatal.

Once more. It is of the higheft importance that we get poffeffed of right conceptions of the one only living and true God. His divine character and glory dwell effentially and fully in his eternal Son; the whole is manifefted and fhines forth in the perfon of Jefus Chrift our Lord. " No man hath feen God at any time ; the only begotten Son who is in the bofom of the Father, he hath declared him." John i. 18. To the faving knowledge and love of this Son of God it infinitely concerns us moft ardently to afpire; the obtaining of this is all our falvation. " This is life eternal to know thee, the only living and true God and Jefus Chrift whom thou haft fent." John xvii. 3.

In fine let us love and admire God's true character; praife and extol him for what he is in himfelf and for all the wonderful difplays he has made of himfelf in his word and works. Let us humbly fubmit to his authority, and exalt his great name ; adopting the noble afcription of the royal prophet. " Thine, O Lord, is the greatnefs and the power and the glory and the victory and the majefty : for all that is in the heaven and in the earth is thine : thine is the kingdom, O Lord ; and thou art exalted head over all, both riches and honour come of thee. In thine hand is power and might ; and in thine hand, it is to make, create and give ftrength unto all. Now therefore we thank thee and praife thy glorious name.

SERMON

SERMON V.

A VIEW OF GOD, AS CREATOR AND GOVERNOR
OF THE WORLD.

Pſalm lxxxix. 11. *The Heavens are thine, the earth alſo is thine: As for the world and the fulneſs thereof, thou haſt founded them.*

WHEN we attend to the great and numerous objects which we behold, and contemplate on others which are out of ſight, it is both natural and reaſonable to enquire, how all theſe things came into exiſtence? To whom they belong? And under whoſe government they fall? In the words before us we have what may be conſidered, as an anſwer to theſe inquiries. They teach us, that all theſe things are the workmanſhip of God, are his property and under his diſpoſal.— In the 95th Pſalm it is ſaid the Lord is a great God and a great King. In his hand are the deep places of the earth. The ſtrength of the hills is his alſo; the ſea is his, and he made it, and his hand formed the dry land; but in our text the language of this kind is more univerſal. Here the heavens and earth and the world in general, are repreſented as being made and governed by God. The heavens are thine, the earth alſo is thine; and as for the world and the fulneſs thereof, thou haſt founded, or exalted and eſtabliſhed them.

K THE

The exalted character of God, as creator and governor of the world, I shall particularly attend to and endeavour to illustrate in this discourse.

The acts of the Deity in creating and governing the world, though connected, yet being distinct operations, I shall consider them separately, beginning,

First, With a view of God as creator.

Eternal self-existence belongs to God alone.— The existence of every other must have had a beginning, and be the effect of some cause and this cause we can find only in God. The production of a creature whether angel or man, cannot proceed from himself because thus he must operate before he has a being; and after the creature is made, he is incapable of creating others. This is the case, as experience teaches, with man. He can alter the form of some things already made, but it is utterly beyond his power to create the smallest insect or vegetable, or atom of matter. And we have reason to believe that there is the same inability in angels; therefore the world and the things therein were created by God: they must be created by him, because they are not selfexistent, and the power of God alone appears equal to such an effect.— What reason thus teaches, is abundantly asserted and confirmed by the book of revelation. *Through faith, in this, we understand that the worlds were formed by the word of God, so that all things which are seen were not made of things which do appear.** The scriptures teach us that the world is not from everlasting as is God himself.

Before the mountains were brought forth or ever thou hadst formed the earth and the world, even from everlasting to everlasting thou art God.† These expressions lead us to conceive of the world not as being co-equal with God in point of duration. Moses also gives a particular account of the creation as a work performed by Almighty God, when time first began. *In the beginning*

---

* Hebrews, 11. 2.   † Psalm, 90. 2.

beginning God created the heaven and the earth. The act of creating is not essential to the divine nature and what is to be considered as being eternal like God himself. Some parts of the creation probably took place before others, particularly those of the celestial world. The heaven spoken of by Moses as created with the earth we may conceive of as the material and visible heavens. To this apprehension we are led from his concluding words upon the subject.—*Thus the heavens and the earth were finished and all the host of them.* The empyrean heaven, where is the throne of God, the habitation of his holy angels, might have been brought into existence at an earlier period; and we have reason to believe that it was, from the representation which God made to Job, of the Angels as being the admiring and joyful spectators of his work in creating this world. *Where wast thou when I laid the foundations of the earth—when the morning stars sang together and the sons of God shouted for joy!*† But whatever distinction there may be, among the creatures and things that *exist*, in respect to their original in point of time, and the powers and qualities of which they partake; they are all the workmanship of God. *The heavens are thine, the earth also is thine, for thou hast made them.* As for the world, the wide universal world, and all things which are in it, thou hast created them.

In this work of creation the power, goodness and wisdom of God are conspicuously displayed.

1. His power—the eternal power of God is clearly to be seen by the things which are made, and to be admired from the instantaneous manner in which all these things come into being through the energy of his voice—*God said, let there be light and there was light.* He was pleased, as is related by Moses not to create all the things of this world in the same moment, in their final form and order, but to do it in six successive days,

† Job xxxviii. 4, 7.

days, probably for the benefit of angels who might be spectators upon that great occasion, and also that men in future time might contemplate upon the works of God with the more ease and satisfaction; but whenever any part of the creation was produced, the word of God effected it in a manner most expressive of his power and majesty. *He spake and it was done. He commanded and it stood fast.**

2. VIEWING God as Creator of the world, we behold his goodness. *The earth is full of his goodness, also the great and wide sea.* When God first surveyed the works of his hand, he pronounced them, as Moses observes, to be very good.† Since that time they have suffered an unhappy change in their nature and effects, in consequence of sin; but they still remain good and appear in general to have an existence given them upon a benevolent design. Some of them are a partial evil; but even these may be productive of good. Thorns and thistles, and vegetables of a poisonous nature, barren deserts and mountains of rocks, and venomous beasts may answer some useful purpose. *God hath made nothing in vain;* and from the apparent use of the greater part of his works we may conclude that those things, whose beneficial effects we cannot perceive, are capable in some way, of being improved to the advancement of happiness.

THE most of the evils that arise from the things which God hath made, appear to come by the perversion of them. As the instruments which men form for their benefit, do sometimes accidentally or by being misapplied become a mischief to them: So the fruits of the earth, whether of the vegetable or animal kind, by an improper use of them, may prove hurtful and injurious; but this is no evidence that the design of the Creator in making them, was not benevolent. Every creature of God is good in itself, and when rightly improved, in its effects, and in this the benignity of God appears.

* Ps. xxxiii. 9.   † Gen. i. 31.

appears. Further, his goodness appears in that enjoyment of which all his living creatures are made susceptible, and in the provision that he has made for them universally according to their peculiar nature and situation. Their capacity for enjoyment is very various. The sensitive powers of some creatures are much less than those of others, and consequently they have less happiness; but all may be said to be happy, in that they have an opportunity to enjoy what their nature demands. The divine goodness is not to be impeached merely because all creatures are not put upon an equality. As the human body is the more compleat by reason of the variety of its parts, though some of them are inferior to others: So the visible world may be the more perfect, and contain in it the more happiness, in consequence of that diversity which there is in the nature and gifts of those creatures with which it is filled: and therefore it is no objection against the goodness of God, that some are distinguished by it above others; and to make such an objection is not only groundless but an impious reflection upon the sovereignty of God, especially when any particular man makes it in respect to himself, and complains of his Maker because he is not made equal to some other man or to an angel. *O man, who art thou that repliest against God! Shall the thing formed say to him that formed it, why hast thou made me thus? Hath not the potter power over the clay to make one vessel unto honour and another unto dishonour?** We have not the less happiness because some others have more than we, and being treated with no injustice, *our eye should not be evil because God is good.*

3. GOD as Creator, appears infinitely wise.

THE marks of wisdom are manifest in his works. The nature and form which are given to creatures and things; their great similitude and yet infinite variety and distinction; their relation and mutual dependence and fitness in their particular stations, and subserviency,

---

* Rom. ix. 20, 21.

in all their several parts to some valuable end, make them appear to be the effect of infinite wisdom, as well as of almighty power.

The wisdom of many things relating to creation we, indeed, cannot comprehend. We do not perceive the wisdom of God, in performing the work of creation, just at that time in which it was done. We do not see his wisdom in making, out of an infinite number of possible worlds, such a world as now exists; or in making so many creatures and things as he has done, and no more or less, and with such natures and capacities rather than with others, which were equally possible with him. And judging of some creatures that are made, according to the limited view of our minds, we may suppose that they are defects in the creation which might wisely have been left out of it: but the *thoughts of God are not as our thoughts;* and from his wisdom, which we perceive, displayed in his works in general, and especially in those parts of them with which we are most acquainted, we have reason to believe that there is perfect wisdom exercised through the whole. *How manifold are thy works, O Lord, in wisdom hast thou made them all!**

The perfections of God, when we contemplate upon them, lead us to suppose, that his work must be perfect and incapable of amendment, not only by his creatures but even by his own hand. Time and experience make no addition to the wisdom of God, in the review of his works. He never beholds a mistake made by himself. He is indeed represented, as repenting, that he had made man upon the earth; but he repented of this no otherwise, than as he was offended with the wickedness of man, in consequence of which, his measures and dealings with him, were to be changed. The Most High is possessed of infinite knowledge: by him actions are seen and weighed as perfectly before as after they have taken place; and

therefore,

* Pf. 104. 24.

therefore, he was not disappointed, in the conduct of man, and by the event made to see a mistake, which he had committed in calling him into being. And in every creature and thing belonging to the creation of God, his infinite perfection leads us to suppose, that, when taken together, and viewed in their whole connection, duration and purpose, there is a complete and perfect display of wisdom. He hath made the earth by his power ; He hath established the world by his wisdom and hath stretched out the heavens by his discretion.* Having thus taken a view of God as Creator of the world, I shall now

2dly. CONSIDER him, as the Governor of it.

WHEN he had made the world, he did not neglect and leave it to return back to nothing, or to run on in confusion and disorder as mere nature or chance should direct, but took it under his own care, guidance and management.

As he made all things for certain designs, so from the beginning, he has, and always will exercise a controul over the whole, that the purposes of his wisdom in creation may be punctually and fully accomplished. The marks of the divine hand in the government of the world are equally apparent as in its creation ; and when we attend to them as they appear in the course of events, we cannot but acknowledge his universal kingdom and dominion, and say, *the Lord reigneth forever and ever—thy kingdom is an everlasting kingdom and endureth through all generations*. We are to conceive of God as Governor of the world in the following respects.

FIRST, As he has it under his care and preservation. *In his hand is the soul of every living thing and the breath of all mankind*. Of all creatures and things in existence God is the preserver, either immediately, by himself, or by him who is the *image of the invisible God*. By him all things consist or remain in being under

* Jer. x. 12.

der the situation and circumstances which attend them. Many creatures God makes instrumental of their own preservation and that of others. Vegetables and various parts of the inanimate creation are the means of support to such as have a sensitive and rational life, and some animals afford food and nourishment unto others; but their efficacy in this way is ever owing to the watchful providence and agency of God, and he is the great preserver of the whole. *Even thou art Lord alone, thou hast made heaven, the heaven of heavens with all their host, the earth and all things that are therein, and thou preservest them all.*

2. GOD is the Governor of the world, in that he gives law to the whole. *The Lord is our lawgiver and King.* He is a lawgiver unto all creatures and things, in that he gives to them some principle, or law by which under him they are to be directed. The laws of nature, as they are called, which are uniform in their operations, producing under like circumstances like effects, receive their energy from his power and agency; hence the movements and effects of material and inanimate bodies are represented as taking place under him. *The lightning goeth forth at his word—He commandeth and raiseth the stormy wind. Fire and hail, snow and vapour fulfill his word.*

THE law also which is given to the brutal creation and which is sometimes called *instinct*, by which they are led to act agreeable to their nature, and to seek sustenance and safety in a way which to us appears most proper, and in some instances artful, is given to them by God, hence he speaks of it as the effect of that wisdom, which surpasses the wisdom of man, in his address to Job. *Doth the hawk fly by thy wisdom and stretch forth her wings towards the south? Doth the eagle mount up by thy command and make her nest on high?* Among intelligent creatures God rules by a still higher law, which is of a moral kind, suited to their rational nature,

Neh. ix. 6.

nature, and inforced by such motives as are proper to excite an obedience to it. Under a law of this kind, we have reason to believe all the holy angels of heaven are, and those fallen ones in hell, though with different requisitions; for the dominion of God as lawgiver is represented as including in it *things in heaven and things in the earth and things under the earth*, or evil spirits in the bottomless pit. As to mankind we are more particularly informed, that their maker is their lawgiver, and what the law is by which they are to be governed, and what will be the consequence of their obedience or disobedience. This law is in a measure taught by those principles of reason and conscience which are common to men, and therefore where the light of revelation is not enjoyed, men are under moral obligation, and are excusable or blamable, and may feel so, in their own minds according as they conform to or deviate from the rule of their duty. They who have not the (revealed) law, *are a law unto themselves, their consciences the mean while excusing or accusing them*: But by the book of revelation we are more especially taught that the law of God extends to man; here also the particular precepts of his law, are expressly named and clearly explained; to some of which the knowledge of man could never extend by the mere light of nature; of this kind are various precepts connected with that dispensation of grace which takes place by Jesus Christ; which dispensation itself is a mere matter of revelation, a mystery, hidden from the wisdom of the world, but made manifest by the gospel—and by the commandment of the everlasting God made known to all nations for the obedience of faith.*

3d. God is the governor of the world; in that the affairs and events of it are all under his disposal. Under his own ruling and governing hand are those events which may be called *outward* and *natural*. He maketh the grass and the herbs to grow and to wither in his hand,

* Romans xvi. 26.

hand, are the times and the seasons; he it is that appointeth summer and winter, seed time and harvest.—The condition and circumstances of the brutal creation are all ordered by him; a sparrow falls not to the ground without his notice, he feedeth the young ravens when they cry, and provideth for the cattle upon a thousand hills. He gives to all material bodies, their stations, their effects and various motions. *He hangeth the earth upon nothing; he bindeth up the waters in his thick clouds until the day and night come to an end—the pillars of the earth tremble and are astonished at his reproof—he divideth the sea, by his spirit he garnisheth the heavens; he maketh the sun and moon and all the luminaries of heaven to run their race—he bends the sweet influences of Pleiades, and looses the bands of Orion. He bringeth forth Mazeroth in his season, and guides Arcturus with his Sons.* In respect to mankind he determines the times before appointed and the bounds of their habitation—their prosperity and adversity, joy and sorrow are what he in his sovereignty sees fit to order. *The Lord killeth and maketh alive, he bringeth down to the grave, and bringeth up, the Lord maketh poor and maketh rich, he bringeth low and lifteth up.**

Events in the *moral world* are also under the superintendency of God. Divine light, truth and grace take place under him and all the means, which rational beings enjoy for moral improvement. From him all moral dispositions and actions in his intelligent creatures proceed, which are good and virtuous. He maketh his angels swift to obey him, and worketh in righteous *men to will and to do of his own good pleasure, and though God cannot be tempted with evil, neither tempteth he any man, but every man is tempted, when he is drawn away of his own lust and enticed,* yet the sinner is not self-sufficient and independent in any of the wickedness which he commits, and the most atrocious moral crimes are sometimes made subservient to the particular and special

---

* 1 Samuel. ii, 6.

cial purposes, of infinite wisdom; as we are taught in the example of Pharaoh who hardened his heart against God, whereby the divine arm was eventually made the more conspicuous; also in the enmity and cruelty of the Jews towards Jesus Christ; while they, in accusing and putting this person to death, acted a most wicked part; they fulfilled the determinate counsel of God, and were instrumental in accomplishing the design of Christ in assuming our nature, which was that he might give his life a ransom for the sins of the world.

The disposing hand of God over moral agents while they remain free and accountable, is a process in the divine government attended with obscurity and incapable of explanation by the limited powers of men; but as we are addressed in the word of God, as intelligent beings, capable of judging, choosing and acting, and as we are conscious in our minds of moral agency and volition; it becomes us to consider ourselves as free moral agents, accountable for the exercise of our powers, and that we shall be approved or justly condemned according as our actions are good or bad. *If thou doest well, shalt thou not be accepted? And if thou doest not well, sin lieth at the door!** It becomes us also to acknowledge the supremacy of God, and his superintendency over all the volitions of men, for so far as we are capable of looking into the nature of things, it appears impossible that man should exist or act, in and of himself free of all dependence upon divine power, and the scriptures declare that God has the hearts and ways of all in his hands, *that his council stands through all generations, and that of him and to him and through him are all things to whom be glory forever.*

God in thus governing the world makes not only a display of that power, wisdom, and goodness which we noticed in the works of creation, but also of equity and justice, truth and righteousness: There is no oppression

* Genesis iv. 7.

oppression or wrong done by him to any subject of his extensive kingdom. Nothing is required by his law but what is reasonable and right; and no reward conferred or punishment inflicted but what is righteous and just. *The Lord is holy in all his ways, and righteous in all his works. His law is perfect and righteous altogether.*

From the view which we have been taking of the character of God, I may remark,

1st. That he appears a glorious sovereign, possessed of infinite power, greatness and majesty.

He hath created when, and after what manner it seemed him good; and all the vast multitude of creatures and things which he hath made, he governs according to the council of his own will. *Who hath directed the spirit of the Lord or being his counsellor, hath taught him! Thine, then, must we say, O Lord, is the greatness and the power and the glory and the majesty—for all that is in the heaven and in the earth is thine :—Thine is the kingdom, O Lord, and thou art exalted as head above all.* God is so far exalted above others, that the greatest things in nature are as nothing in his sight, and the highest characters among his intelligent creatures, admit of no comparison with him. Behold the nations are as a drop of a bucket, and are counted as the small dust of the ballance : Behold, he taketh up the isles as a very little thing. All nations before him are as nothing : and they are counted to him less than nothing and vanity. To whom then will ye liken God ? Or what likeness will ye compare unto him ? It is he that sitteth upon the circle of the earth ; and the inhabitants thereof are as grashoppers ; that stretcheth out the heavens as a curtain, and spreadeth them out as a tent to dwell in ; that bringeth the princes to nothing : he maketh the judges of the earth as vanity.

2nd. The character of God as creator and governor of the world, appears most worthy of our love. His works are the works of wisdom and goodness : his own glory is the design of them. *God hath made all things for himself*, or for the display of his perfections; he also herein evidently regards the happiness of his creatures; for God is good to all, and his tender mercies are over all his works; even the judgments administered by him are for a salutary purpose, particularly that the children of men might learn righteousness and become possessed of the peaceable fruits of it.

3rd. We are taught by our subject, the omnipresence of God. He being universal in his agency he must be so in his presence. *He is not far from every one of us: for in him we live and move and have our being.*

4th. The propriety and duty of offering prayer, with thanksgiving unto God, appears from our subject. As we are dependent on God and the subjects of his government, it is no more than a proper acknowledgment of our situation to address ourselves to him, and supplicate his favor. *Be careful for nothing; but in every thing by prayer and supplication with thanksgiving let your requests be made known unto God. Thus casting your care upon him for he careth for you.*

5th. A proper view of God, as creator and governor of the world, may be quieting and consoling to the minds of men under the trials and sufferings of this probationary state: Here we are perplexed and troubled in many ways. Our inquiries are attended with darkness and uneasy doubts—the world about us appears defaced and in disorder; the seasons are many times inclement and pestilential—the elements are seemingly at war and threaten us with ruin. Mankind also, through pride, avarice and madness, oppose and devour one another, and spread desolation through kingdoms and nations, and wantonly destroy in one period, the labours of another. Our most interesting hopes from the objects with which we are immediately connected are destroyed, and we spend our days meeting with successive disappointments and bereavements, and perhaps in pain, and always with the prospect of death before us, without finding any enjoyment in the world that is fully satisfying or certain. In this situation it is quieting and consoling, to consider, that we are created and placed here upon the earth by God, who always has us, our circumstances and the world about us under his care and management, and will ever do that which is right, and overrule all things according to his own wisdom and purpose and in that manner, which may best serve to advance his own glory and the general happiness of his creatures. *The Lord reigneth, let the earth rejoice, let the multitude of the Isles be glad thereof.*

6th. THE subject reminds us that God is the great object of our first obedience. His authority is indisputable, and against the manner in which it is exercised by him, no just objection can be made. His law and providence are holy, just and good. Under the just and powerful government of such a being, the impenitent and disobedient cannot expect finally to go unpunished; but verily there is a reward, (through Christ) for the righteous. *Thinkest thou this, O man, that thou shalt escape the judgment of God!—Who will render to every man according to his deeds—unto them who do not obey the truth, indignation and wrath, tribulation and anguish—but glory, honour and peace to every man that worketh good—for there is no respect of persons with God.*

SERMON

SERMON VI.

THE ESSENTIAL DIVINITY OF JESUS CHRIST.

John i. 1. *" And the Word was God."*

THE sacred scriptures give very different names to Jesus Christ. He is man, God, the son of man, the Son of God, the angel, the Lord, the angel of the Lord, and the word. Correspondent with this diversity of names, all parts of the Bible ascribe to him a very extraordinary character.

THE evangelist Matthew writes, *" The book of the generation of Jesus Christ, the son of David, the son of Abraham." John states,† " In the beginning was the word, and the word was with God, and the word was God." He goes farther,‡ " all things were made by him; and without him was not any thing made that was made." At the commencement of time, when the first creature was made, the word existed, was with God and was God. He is distinguished from God, yet is God.

*" THE word was made flesh, and dwelt among us."§ The man Christ was conceived by the Holy Ghost. God had said by a prophet, " behold, a virgin

shall

* Mat. i. 1.   † John i. 1.   ‡ V. 3.
§ John i. 14.

shall be with child, and shall bring forth a son, and they shall call his name Emmanuel, which being interpreted, is, God with us."* Emmanuel is the word made flesh.

This account, given of Christ by the two Apostolic Evangelists, at the beginning of their gospels, strongly intimates, that to understand his character and works, he must be viewed as possessing two natures, and being both God and man.

A PERSONAL union of deity with manhood, is indeed not easily comprehended. But since we are not able to comprehend the union of body and spirit in ourselves, though more acquainted with the properties of matter than with the divine essence, which is most wise, to reject a doctrine of the Bible, because it is not dictated by our own understandings, or to receive it, because it is taught of God?

CHRIST is to be considered not only personally as Emmanuel, but officially as mediator. In this official capacity he is the angel of the Lord, and messenger of his will to men. The distinction between personal and official dignity is easily understood. In regard to one of them a person may be a superior or equal, while in respect of the other he is an inferior. The mother of king Solomon, in that relation was his superior, but as king he was above her, and did her honor in causing a seat to be placed for her on his right hand, while he sat on the throne and heard her request. And Christ, who in the form of God thought it not robbery to be equal with God, in the form of man, and as mediator, became obedient to death.

In the view which has been taken of Christ, there is no contradiction, in ascribing to him the infirmities of manhood without sin, together with all the perfections of deity. Neither are any of the things spoken of him in regard to his human nature, and official capacity, any objection against his possessing essential divinity, and being God equally as the Father.—
God

* Mat. i. 23.

God himself speaks of him as both a man and his own equal: "The man *that is* my fellow faith the Lord of hosts."

These remarks are designed as introductory to an exhibition of evidence of the essential divinity of Jesus Christ; which, it is believed, is asserted in the text: "The word was God." Notice will be taken of the names of Christ, his perfections, the works attributed to him, the religious homage paid him, and his being equalled with God the Father.

1. The names of Christ in the scriptures are a proof of his essential divinity.

A divine person appeared repeatedly to the patriarchs, to Moses and the children of Israel. In which person of deity did God appear? As the Father, or as the Son, who is Christ?

The distinct official characters given in the gospel to the Father and the Son, are a strong presumption, that all intercourse between God and man, is through the Son as mediator. In Christ God is reconcileable to the world, and through him we have access to the Father. It is moreover expressly asserted,* No man hath seen God at any time, meaning God the Father; but, the only begotten Son, which is in the bosom of the Father, he hath declared him. Again,† "Not that any man hath seen the Father, save he which is of God," that is except Christ, "he hath seen the Father." When therefore we read,‡ Then went up Moses and Aaron, Nadab and Abihu, and seventy of the elders of Israel: And they saw the God of Israel:—Also they saw God, and did eat and drink." The God of Israel, God whom Moses and the elders of Israel saw, was not the Father, but the Son, who is Christ.

When Christ was on earth God owned him, and bore testimony to him, by a voice from heaven. But it is thought that there is no other instance, in which there

---

* John i, 18. † John vi, 46. ‡ Exod. xxiv. 9, 10, 11.

there is evidence or probability, of God's having intercourse immediately with men, otherwise than in the person of the Son. In a number of instances of his appearing, he is called not only the Lord or God, but also the angel of the Lord, or man; as if purposely to designate him as acting in the office of mediator. A prophecy of Christ's coming to his temple is,* "And the Lord whom ye seek shall suddenly come to his temple; even the messenger of his covenant whom ye delight in." The name angel signifies messenger; which cannot be applied to the Father, but belongs to the Son, as descriptive of his official character. Thus the names, the angel of the Lord, and the Lord, show that Christ appeared to Gideon.† "The angel of the Lord appeared unto him—and the Lord looked upon him—and the Lord said unto him."—In relating the events of one interview, both names are repeatedly used.

THE same names evidence an appearance of Christ to Hagar.‡ "And the angel of the Lord found her, and the angel of the Lord said unto her, I will multiply thy seed exceedingly. And she called the name of the Lord, that spake unto her, thou God seest me." The historian gives him the two names, the angel of the Lord, and the Lord. Hagar uses a stronger term, implying that he was God omniscient; thou God seest me." And when speaking by the name of the angel of the Lord, he assumes the character of God, in saying, "I will multiply thy seed." These circumstances are additional evidence, that the angel, who spoke to her, was both Christ and truly God.

AT another time Christ appeared as man.§ "A man" wrestled with Jacob, blessed him and changed his name to Israel:" For he said, "as a prince hast thou power with God, and with man, and hast prevailed. And Jacob called the name of the place Peniel;

for

---

* Mal. iii. 1.
† Judges vi. 11, 24.
‡ Gen. xvi. 7. 13.
§ Gen. xxxii. 24. 30.

for I have seen God face to face, and my life is preserved." In wreſtling with a man he ſaw God face to face; which was God in the form of man.

When Abraham dwelt at Mamre,‖ the Lord appeared unto him; and he ſat in the tent door, in the heat of the day; "and he lifted up his eyes and looked and lo, three men ſtood by him. And when he ſaw them he ran to meet them—and bowed himſelf toward the ground, and ſaid, my Lord." The Lord appeared and Abraham looking ſaw three men. He bowed himſelf to them and ſaid my Lord. The Lord muſt therefore have been one of the three men. "They ſaid, ſo do as thou haſt ſaid. And they ſaid unto him, where is Sarah thy wife. And he," (the Lord) "ſaid, I will certainly return unto thee according to the time of life, and lo, Sarah thy wife ſhall have a ſon." In this manner they talked with Abraham, as the Lord and as the three men, evidencing that the Lord was one of the men. "The Lord ſaid ſhall I hide from Abraham the thing which I do?" "Becauſe the cry of Sodom and Gomorrah is great—I will go down now and ſee—and the men turned their faces from thence and went toward Sodom: but Abraham ſtood yet before the Lord," and interceded for that city, "And there came two angels to Sodom at even."* The character in which the Lord appeared to Abraham, as a man and yet God hearing prayer, agrees to Chriſt and to no other.

After this,† "God did tempt Abraham, and he ſaid, take now thy ſon, and offer him there for a burnt offering." But,‡ "the angel of the Lord called unto him and ſaid, Abraham, Abraham, for now I know that thou feareſt God, ſeeing thou haſt not withheld thy ſon, thine only ſon from me." God commanded to ſacrifice his ſon, the angel of the Lord ſaid,— "thou haſt not withheld thy ſon from me." The angel therefore and God were the ſame perſon.§ And
the

‖ Gen. xviii. 1. † Gen. xxii. 1, 2. § V. 15, 16, 17.
* Gen. xix. 1. ‡ V. 11, 12.

the angel of the Lord called unto Abraham out of heaven the second time, and said, by myself have I sworn, faith the Lord, that in bleſſing I will bleſs the." Here he ſpeaks again in a character which belongs only to Chriſt.

JACOB laying his hands on the ſons of Joſeph, prayed* God, before whom my fathers Abraham and Iſaac did walk, the God, which fed me all my life long unto this day, the angel which redeemed me from all evil, bleſs the lads." This angel God is Chriſt. No other, is both the God of Abraham and Iſaac, and the angel who redeemed Jacob.

GOD, in the perſon who ſpake to Abraham and Jacob, appeared alſo to Moſes, on Horeb the mount of God.† " The angel of the Lord appeared unto him in a flame of fire out of the midſt of a buſh : And when the Lord ſaw that he turned aſide to ſee, God called unto him out of the midſt of the buſh. " And the Lord ſaid, I have ſurely ſeen the affliction of my people—and I am come down to deliver them. Come now therefore, and I will ſend thee unto Pharaoh, that thou mayeſt bring forth my people the children of Iſrael out of Egypt." Theſe names, it has been repeatedly noticed, deſignate Chriſt.

THIS inſtance is the more important, becauſe the perſon who appeared in the buſh, is the ſame Lord that enabled Moſes to bring the children of Iſrael out of Egypt ; was with him in the wilderneſs ; and gave them his law at Mount Sinai. He is firſt called the angel of the Lord ; then the Lord, and God. The angel appeared to Moſes, the Lord ſaw that he turned to ſee, and God called unto him. The angel appeared out of the midſt of the buſh, God called out of the midſt of the buſh, the Lord ſaid I am come down, implying that he was there, and was the perſon whom Moſes ſaw. For it will not be pretended that the angel appeared, but did not ſpeak ; and that the Lord and God

talked

* Gen. lxviii. 15, 16.   † Exod. iii. 2, 4, 7, 8. 10.

talked with Moses, but were not seen. Indeed Moses was charged to say to the children of Israel, the Lord God of your fathers, the God of Abraham, of Isaac and of Jacob, appeared unto me." V. 16.

* " God said unto Moses, I AM THAT I AM. And he said, thus shalt thou say unto the children of Israel, I AM hath sent me unto you." The same person still speaks, though he again assumes a new name, or new names. The Lord had before said to Moses, " I will send thee." That he was the angel who appeared in the bush, is confirmed by the testimony of the martyr Stephen. Speaking of Moses he saith,† the " same did God send by the hands of the angel which appeared to him in the bush." Christ in the character of mediator is the angel of God, and by him God communicates messages to men. As God's messenger he came down to deliver the children of Israel, he appeared in the bush as the angel of the Lord, and as the Lord and God he sent Moses, and afterwards was with him in bringing the children of Israel out of Egypt.

" Moses," having made one attempt without success," returned unto the Lord and said, " Lord, why is it that thou hast sent me. Then the Lord said unto Moses, now thou shalt see what I will do to Pharaoh."‡ Thus plain is it that the person who sent Moses continued to be with him. At the first interview, God said, " certainly I will be with thee." By the same name, at the second time of speaking to Moses, he tells him,§ wherefore say unto the children of Israel, I am the Lord, and I will bring you out from under the burdens of the Egyptians." Thus was it God in the second person, who is the angel of the Lord, that gave Moses his commission to deliver the children of Israel, and favoured him with his presence to enable him to accomplish it. The testimony of Stephen

* V. 14.
† Acts vii. 35.
‡ Exod. v. 22. vi. 1.
§ Chap. iii. 12. vi. 6.

phen is again express:* "This is he," is the Moses, "that was in the church in the wilderness with the angel which spake to him in Mount Sinai, and with our fathers."

In pointing out Christ as designated by his names, which are so different from each other as to belong only to him, several instances have been noticed which are proofs of his divinity. He is the Lord to whom Abraham prayed for Sodom; God to whom that Patriarch was about to offer Isaac for a burnt offering, and to whom he sacrificed a ram instead of his son: the angel to whom Jacob prayed, as the God before whom his fathers Abraham and Isaac walked, who also instructed Moses to call him to the children of Israel the Lord God of their fathers, the God of Abraham, Isaac and Jacob. When he appeared to Moses,† the ground, because of his presence, was holy. "Moreover he said, I am the God of thy father, the God of Abraham, the God of Isaac, and the God of Jacob." He repeated his declaration charging Moses, "Thus shalt thou say unto the children of Israel, the Lord God of your fathers, the God of Abraham, the God of Isaac, and the God of Jacob, hath sent me unto you; this is my name forever, and this is my memorial unto all generations." And when Moses returned to him he said further,‡ " and I appeared unto Abraham, unto Isaac, and unto Jacob, *by the name* of God Almighty, but by my name JEHOVAH was I not known to them." To mention one declaration more; at Mount Sinai he spake these words,§ " I am the Lord thy God which have brought thee out of the land of Egypt, and out of the house of bondage. Thou shalt have no other Gods before me." It is not possible that he should assume names more determinately expressive of essential divinity.

THE

---

* Acts vii. 38.
† Exod. iii. 5, 6. 15.
‡ Exod. v. 3.
§ Exod. xx. 2, 3.

The name Jehovah is peculiar to God and always implies divinity. "That men may know," the Psalmist prayed, Psalm lxxxiii. 18, " that thou whose name alone is Jehovah, art the most high over all the earth." This name is repeatedly given to Christ in the original language of the Old Testament. One instance is, Jer. xxiii. 5, 6. " I will raise unto David a righteous branch—and this is his name by which he shall be called THE LORD." In the original as may be seen in the margin of the large Bible, " JEHOVAH, OUR RIGHTEOUSNESS."

OTHER names given to Christ are, *" Wonderful, Counsellor, the mighty God, the everlasting Father, the Prince of Peace." †" Lord of all :" ‡" The Lord of glory :" §" The true God and eternal life :" ‖" Christ, who is over all, God blessed forever." If it is possible for names, and the manner of using them, to evidence a being to be truly God, the names of Christ, it is believed, are a demonstrable proof of his essential divinity.

THE importance of the doctrine makes it suitable to notice other arguments which establish it.

2. THE perfections of Christ are a proof of his essential divinity.

GOD is known by his perfections, which distinguish him from all his creatures. And these perfections, being possessed by Christ, evidence that he is God, of the same divine essence as the Father.

ONE of the names of Christ, descriptive of his character, is, " The everlasting Father." And a declaration which he made of himself is, *" I am Alpha and Omega, the beginning and the end, the first and the last." In another place, he saith, "† I am Alpha and Omega, the beginning and the ending, saith the Lord, which is, and which was, and which is to come, the

---

* Isaiah ix. 6.
† Acts x. 36.
‡ 2 Cor. ii. 8.
§ 1 John v. 20.
‖ Rom ix. 5.
* Rev. xxii. 13.
† Rev. i. 8.

the Almighty." The Father ascribes to him like perfections, in saying, ‡" thy throne O God is forever." And an apostle calls him, §" Jesus Christ the same yesterday to day and forever." These declarations are strongly descriptive of perfections peculiar to deity. Moreover,

CHRIST said to his disciples, ‖" where two or there are gathered together in my name, there am I in the midst of them :" And when he gave them commission to preach him to all nations he added, *" And lo, I am with you alway, even unto the end of the world." He surely must be God omnipresent, to be in the midst of every society of two or three gathered together in his name, and with his ministers preaching him among all nations. Essential divinity is in like manner necessary, to his being officially given to be " the head over all things to the church ; which is his body, the fulness of him that filleth all in all."† And these declarations well agree with the express assertions, ‡" In him dwelleth all the fulness of the godhead bodily." All the fulness of the godhead, not figuratively, but bodily and substantially, dwells in him. That he is almighty is further evident, in that to him as mediator, " all power is given in heaven and in earth ;"§ he " being the brightness of the Father's glory, and the express image of his person, and upholding all things by the word of his power."‖

WHEN he was on earth, he was omniscient. * He knew all men, and needed not that any should testify of man : for he knew what was in man." Peter appealed to him †" Lord thou knowest all things, thou knowest that I love thee." He and the Father are alike distinguished from all creatures in knowing each other.

‡ Heb. i. 8. † Col. ii. 9.
§ Heb. xiii. 8. ‡ Mat. xxviii. 18.
‖ Mat. xviii. 20. ¶ Heb. i. 3.
* Mat. xxviii. 20. " John ii. 24, 25.
† Eph. i. 22, 23. † John xxi. 17.

other. ‡ "And no man knoweth the Son, but the Father; neither knoweth any man the Father, save the Son, and he to whomsoever the Son will reveal him." To know mankind, as king Solomon professed, is peculiar to God: "For thou only knowest the hearts of the children of men:"§ But Christ knows all men, and what is in them; and he knows God even the Father. His omniscience is also further evidenced, in the revelation of the apostle John, in his opening the seals of the book of the decrees of God, and disclosing in prophecy events, which were to take place in a long series to the end of the world.‖ Thus as eternal, unchangeable, almighty, and omniscient, Christ is truly God.

3. THE works of Christ are a proof of his essential divinity.

THE reason of mankind agrees with the scriptures, in teaching that God is to be known by his works.*— "The invisible things of him from the creation of the world are clearly seen, being understood by the things that are made, even his eternal power and Godhead." He faith,† "I *am* the Lord and *there* is none else, *there is* no God besides me." "Thus faith the Lord, the holy one of Israel, and his maker, I have made the earth, and created man upon it: I, *even* my hands have stretched out the heavens, and all their hosts have I commanded. For thus faith the Lord that created the heavens, God himself that formed the earth, I *am* the Lord, and *there is* none else." Who is God the creator? Is he the Father? So is he the Son, the word who was made flesh.‡ "All things were made by him, and without him was not any thing made that was made.§ For by him were all things created, that are in heaven, and that are in earth, visible and invisible, whether *they be* thrones or dominions, or principalities

N or

‡ Mat. xi. 27.   † Isaiah xlv. 5, 11, 12, 18.
* 2 Chron. vi. 30.   ‡ John i. 3.
‖ Rev. v. 9. 1, 1, &c.   § Col. i. 15, 16.
* Rom. i. 20.

or powers; all things were made by him, and for him. And he is before all things, and by him all things consist. God himself," and not by the instrumentality of another, formed the earth. He saith, "I, even my hands have stretched out the heavens." Yet all these were created by Christ. He is therefore the God besides whom there is none else. Further,

CHRIST, as the word made flesh, possesses all the capacity requisite for his office as mediator. And the works of God, which he performs in obedience to the Father, are as sure proofs of his godhead as if he were to do the same works wholly of himself. He laid down his life, and took it again: is the resurrection and the life; and will be the judge of mankind at the last day. These things, as well as his being the creator and the Lord of providence, show that he is God, in the essential attributes of divinity, as well as in office.

4. THE religious homage paid to Christ is a proof of his essential divinity.

THAT God only is to be worshipped, is a fundamental principle, of both natural and revealed religion.* "Thou shalt worship no other God; for the Lord whose name is jealous, is a jealous God." If religious homage be offered to a good man or angel, he repels it with zeal :† "See thou do it not :—Worship God." But Jesus Christ, even when in the form of man, never declined the divine honors, which in many instances were paid to him. And to worship him is warranted by examples the authority of which cannot be denied. The martyr Stephen, full of the Holy Ghost, closed his life,‡ calling upon God and saying "Lord Jesus, receive my spirit." The Apostle Paul prayed, "God himself and our Father and our Lord Jesus Christ direct our way unto you." And when buffeted by the messenger of Satan, he besought the Lord

---

* Exod. xxxiv. 14.   † Acts vii. 59.
† Rev. xix. 10. xxii. 9. Acts xiv. 15.

Lord thrice that it might depart and received this answer; "my grace is sufficient for thee. Most gladly therefore," saith the apostle, "will I rather glory in my infirmities, that the power of Christ may rest upon me." The Lord to whom he prayed, and whose grace was sufficient for him, was Christ; in the confidence of whose power resting on him he gloried in his own infirmities.

His benedictions to the churches to which he wrote epistles are also so many prayers, most or all of which are made to Christ, and one of them to each person of the Trinity by name. "The grace of the Lord Jesus Christ, and the love of God, and the communion of the Holy Ghost, *be* with you all. The grace of our Lord Jesus Christ be with you."

To call on the Lord or on the name of the Lord is another expression of religious worship. Elijah said to the prophets of Baal, "call ye on the name of your Gods, and I will call on the name of the Lord." In the Psalms it is written, the Lord is nigh unto all them that call upon him, that call upon him in truth. "An apostle also makes the observation. *"Whosoever shall call upon the name of the Lord shall be saved." The Lord therefore on whom Christians call is their God, and this Lord is Christ. He sent Ananias to baptize Saul; who objected,† "Lord he hath authority to bind all that call on thy name." The Lord said go," and Ananias went, and said "brother Saul, the Lord, *even* Jesus that appeared unto thee in the way as thou camest forth sent me." Christ is therefore the Lord to whom Ananias described Christians in calling them, "All that call on thy name." The Apostle Paul describes them by the same term. ‡"All that in every place, call upon the name of Jesus Christ our Lord." In both these instances to call on the name of the Lord
Jesus,

* Rom. x. 13.   ‡ 1 Cor. i. 2.
† Acts ix. 10. 17.

Jesus, is mentioned as the known practice and distinguishing character of Christians.

One example more, of religious worship paid to Christ, will be produced. §" And when he had taken the book, the four beasts, and four and twenty elders, fell down before the Lamb, having every one of them harps and golden vials full of odours which are the prayers of the saints. And they sung a new song saying thou art worthy: for thou wast slain and hast redeemed us to God. And every creature which is in heaven, and on the earth, and under the earth, and such as are in the sea, and all that is in them, heard I, saying, blessing and honor, and glory, and power, *be* unto him that sitteth upon the throne, and unto the Lamb forever and ever."

To the authority of examples precepts are added to show the right and the duty of worshipping Christ as God. In the forty-fifth psalm, after saying to Christ.* " Thy throne O God is forever—God, thy God, hath anointed thee." The address turns to the church, " he is thy Lord, and worship thou him." Another psalm† contains the command, " worship him all ye Gods:" which seems to be quoted by an Apostle in application to Christ, in his declaration.‡ " When he (God) bringeth in the first begotten into the world, he saith, and let all the angels of God worship him."— From whatever passage of the Old Testament the apostle makes this quotation, it is an express command, at least of apostolic authority, to the angels to worship Christ, who is the first begotten of God. The conclusion is certain, Christ being worshipped as God, possesses essential divinity. It is to be considered further:

5. Christ's being equalled with the Father is a proof of his essential divinity.

His equality with the Father in his names, perfections,

§ Rev. v. 8, 9. 13. † Pf. xcvii. 7.
V. 6, 7, 11. ‡ Heb. i. 6.

fections, works, and the worship commanded to be paid him, has been already shown. A few particulars will be noticed, in which the comparison is made and the equality stated.

Christ is the Son of God, in distinction from all others, intimating that the term applies to him in a more proper sense than to any creature. He is God's only begotten Son—the brightness of *his* glory, and the express image of his person. The ideas most proper to the term Son are sameness of nature existing in a state of relative inferiority and dependence on the Father. In these Christ answers to the character of the Son of God: being the word made flesh, in his divinity possessing the same essence as the Father, but receiving human nature of him, and acting in the office of mediator as his Son yielding obedience to him. It is in reference to his two natures, that God applies to him the extraordinary terms. "The man that is my fellow saith the Lord of hosts."

Christ, moreover, is one with the Father, his declaration is, "I and my Father are one." In proof of the truth of this Christ appealed to the works of God which he wrought. "If I do not the works of my Father believe me not. But if I do, though ye believe not me, believe the works; that ye may know and believe that the Father is in me and I in him."— Christ's argument must be allowed to be conclusive. And if his doing the works of his Father evidenced that he and the Father are one, they in like manner evidenced that he is God as the Father is God.

Christ's oneness with the Father, and also with the Holy Spirit is declared in the assertion of the apostle John, *"there are three that bear record in heaven, the Father, the Word, and the Holy Ghost; and these three are one." And this doctrine is so important, that to be a christian every person in all ages of the church under the gospel, is obliged to have his covenant

* 1 John v. 7.

enant with God sealed in memorial and confirmation of it, in being baptized "in the name of the Father, and of the Son, and of the Holy Ghost." It is in their thus making disciples, that Christ promises to be with his ministers alway, even to the end of the world.

These things, it is believed, fully and abundantly prove that the scriptural character of Christ implies his true and essential divinity. His names, perfections and works, his being religiously worshipped and equalled with God the Father confirm and illustrate the declaration, the word was God.

In concluding the subject let it be remarked,

1. Jesus Christ is a worthy and fit mediator between God and mankind.

As he is man, so he is God. The word, which was made flesh, was in the beginning with God, and was God. However he condescended to humble himself in our nature, yielding obedience even to death, he and the Father are one. He knows the Father, is acquainted with all the perfections of deity, and understands what obedience and sufferings in the character of man and as our surety, were necessary to satisfy the law of God and honor his justice, in granting pardon to sinners. His personal dignity gives his mediation all the merit and efficacy, which our guilt and unworthiness render needful, to procure acceptance for us with God. And he is able to save to the uttermost all that come to God by him; for he ever liveth to make intercession for them.

2. If Christ is truly God, men, in not believing his divinity, hazard their salvation.

The Christ of the gospel is precisely the Saviour needed by mankind. One infinitely inferior to him would not be able to save a single sinner. If then Christ is God, in the same sense that the Father is God, which it is supposed has been proved, to deny his divinity is to rob him of that which is essential to the infinite glory of his character: and whatever creature merit you

may

may allow him, you infinitely depreciate his atonement, and power to save. Is a sacrifice for sin, debased infinitely below its real character, a safe foundation to hope for the pardon of sin committed against God?

THE infinitude of God is the measure of the guilt of sin, considered as committed against him. Who will say it is not hazardous, to trust a propitiation of infinitely less value, than the one he has provided?

WHATEVER are your thoughts of Christ, the image or character which you form of him in your mind, is the Saviour to which you trust; whether he be the Son of God who is revealed in the gospel, or another that exists only in a mistaken imagination. But if you have only a creature Saviour, and the Christ who gives life to men is God, what will not be your danger of perishing, in believing in a fancied redeemer, that is insufficient to expiate sin, and deliver from eternal death?

THE gospel declares, *" He that believeth and is baptized shall be saved; but he that believeth not shall be damned." If Christ is God and you deny his divinity, can you say that you have gospel faith? and that you are not exposed to the doom of him that believeth not?

3. IT concerns all who hear of Christ, to learn his character and believe in him.

HIS personal dignity, and the importance of his official character invite, and demand your attention. Do you not need one to mediate between you and God? Who is so worthy to be trusted in that capacity as Christ? He has died for men to be their Saviour, and he will be their final judge. God has committed all judgment to him, that all men should honour the Son even as they honour the Father. Blessed are they who know Christ and believe in him.

SERMON VII.

THE PERSONALITY AND DIVINITY OF THE SPIRIT.

1 Corinthians, ii. 10. *"The Spirit searcheth all things, yea, the deep things of God."*

OF all beings God only is infinite. He fills immensity and eternity, and his counsels extend to all creatures and events. One plan comprehends all his works, from the beginning of creation to the completion of all things in the everlasting ages. "O the depth of the riches both of the wisdom and knowledge of God! how unsearchable are his judgments, and his ways past finding out."

THE greatest of all God's works, as far as the scriptures treat of them, is the redemption of mankind by Jesus Christ. All things belonging to our world, and those of heaven and hell, are subservient to it. "God so loved the world that he gave his only begotten Son." The eternal Word became the seed of the woman, to bruise the serpent's head. These are things far beyond the reach of human wisdom and power: "which none of the princes of this world knew." "But as it is written, eye hath not seen, nor ear heard, neither have entered into the heart of man, the things which God hath prepared for them that love him." But God hath revealed them unto us by his
Spirit :

Spirit: for the Spirit searcheth all things, yea, the deep things of God."

The Spirit is a proper agent to be employed in making God known, even in the extraordinary designs of his divine counsels. The Spirit is able to make a true and perfect discovery; he beholds infinity, he searches all things, even the deep things, the most astonishing purposes, of deity. He sees intuitively whatever belongs to God. "For what man knoweth the things of a man save the spirit of man which is in him? even so the things of God knoweth no man," more properly knoweth no one, "but the Spirit of God."

Two things are taught concerning the Spirit.

I. He is a person.

II. He is a divine person, and truly God.

The doctrine of the Trinity comes necessarily into view in exhibiting the character of the Spirit. The bible represents God as acting in three relations, distinguished by the names the Father, the Son, and the Spirit, or the Holy Ghost, and in each relation sustaining a personal character. The Father is a person, the Son is a person, and the Spirit or Holy Ghost is a person. For this reason it is common to say, God exists in three persons; or, there are three persons in the Godhead. At the same time it is allowed, that the word persons applied to God as three in one, is not used with exact propriety as when applied to men. For in whatever manner God is three persons, he is one being. There is only one God, though the Father is God, the Son is God, and the Spirit is God.

This is the gospel mystery: but the mysteries of nature in the existence of vegetable, animal and rational life, in bodies of matter, which we notice every day, but the consistency of which we cannot comprehend, should teach us so much modesty in judging what is consistent and possible and what is not, especially in regard to God, as not to disbelieve plain and express declarations of his word. It is to be considered,

I. The Spirit is a person.

"The Spirit searches," which implies that he is a person, and not an attribute, or merely a power of God. Understanding or power may be employed in performing actions, but there must be an agent, a person, to whom they belong, to direct operations. God, in wisdom, and by power, created the heavens and earth; but these attributes of deity have no choice or will for acting of themselves, neither do they exist otherwise than as perfections of God. And in their producing effects God is the person who exerts them, and by whose volition they are directed. It is otherwise of the Spirit: His character is not that of an attribute of God, but of a person possessing volition, and one acting of himself. It is true he sometimes is called the Spirit of God, and Spirit of the Lord. He is in like manner the Spirit of Christ. But as Christ is a person distinct from the Father, so the Spirit is a person distinct from both, from the Father and the Son.

The Father and the Son are one, in the same manner as the Father and the Spirit are one. But the distinct personality of the Son is manifest in his appearing in flesh, and being the son of man, as well as the Son of God. And as the personality ascribed to the Son is real, and not figurative, so the same is true of the Spirit, the Holy Ghost. Indeed each person of the Trinity has equal claim to personality. This is instanced in the form of administring baptism; "in the name of the Father, and of the Son, and of the Holy Ghost." (Mat. xxviii. 19.)

The importance of the character of the Spirit to christians, will justify the calling of your attention to some further evidence of his personal agency. Christ speaks of him to his disciples, by both an official, and a personal, name: (John xiv. 26.) "The Comforter, the Holy Ghost, whom the Father will send in my name, he shall teach you all things." As a person, he is the Holy Ghost, the Spirit, and the Spirit of God;

in his official capacity, he is the Comforter. In sustaining this office, and acting in it as a person, he appears in his real character. Christ saith of him again, (John xv. 26.) "When the Comforter is come, whom I will send unto you from the Father, *even* the Spirit of truth, which proceedeth from the Father, he shall testify of me." He is sent by the Father in the name of Christ, and by Christ from the Father, and testifies of Christ. In all these views, he plainly appears as a person, and not as only an attribute of God. Christ gives this further account of him: (John xvi. 7, 8. 13. 14.) "If I go not away, the Comforter will not come unto you; but if I depart, I will send him unto you. And when he is come he will reprove the world." " When he, the Spirit of truth, is come, he will guide you into all truth; for he shall not speak of himself; but whatsoever he shall hear, *that* shall he speak; and he will show you things to come. He shall glorify me: for he shall receive of mine, and shall shew it unto you." We here continue to see the Spirit in the same personal character.

WE will now notice several particular actions, which are ascribed to him. Mary, the mother of Jesus, "was found with child of the Holy Ghost;" and an angel said to Joseph, "That, which is conceived in her, is of the Holy Ghost." (Mat. i. 18. 20.) "The Holy Ghost said, separate me Barnabas and Saul, for the work whereunto I have called them." "So they, being sent forth by the Holy Ghost, departed." (Acts xiii. 2. 4.) "The Spirit itself," or himself, "beareth witness with our spirit." (Rom. viii. 16.) Whatever miraculous gifts were given to christians in the days of the apostles, "All these worketh that one and the self same Spirit, dividing to every man severally as he will." (1 Cor. xii. 11.) And to add only one instance more, an apostle, addressing the elders of Ephesus, uses these expressions, " Over the which the Holy Ghost hath made you overseers." (Acts xx. 28.)

WHAT

WHAT you have heard, is only a specimen of the manner in which the scriptures represent the Spirit. It is thought, that, the evidence of his being a personal agent, is plain, full and undeniable. The multitude and variety of expressions which are used, forbid any figurative interpretations, to do away their literal and plain meaning, and require us to conceive of the Spirit as a person: consistently with the express declaration, "There are three that bear record in heaven, the Father, the Word, and the Holy Ghost; and these three are one." (1 John v. 7.)

II. THE Spirit is a divine person, and truly God.

IN the representation given of God in his word, he, in some sense, is more than one person; in particular, he is the Father, the Word or the Son, and the Spirit or the Holy Ghost; the Spirit has the perfections and dignity of God ascribed to him; and he performs the works of God.

1. GOD, in the representation of his word, is in some sense more than one person: and in particular he is the Father, the Son and the Holy Spirit.

IN beginning to read the bible God is soon presented to view as being in some sense more than one. He uses such expressions as these; "Let us make man in our image, after our likeness:" (Gen. i. 26.) "The man is become as one of us;" (iii. 22.) "Let us go down." (xi. 7.) In the Hebrew, the original of the Old Testament, as men acquainted with it have observed, there are other instances in which the singular and plural numbers are unusually connected together in describing acts of God. The name given him in the first verse of the bible, "In the beginning God created," in the original is "Gods;" though "created" is used as if spoken of one only: Gods he created the heavens and the earth.

THIS manner of speaking of God is to be the more noticed, for its being continued through the bible; and in its progress more and more plainly exhibiting the

doctrine

doctrine of the Trinity. The prophet Isaiah heard the voice of the Lord saying, "Whom shall I send and who will go for us." (Isaiah vi. 8.) At the time the prophet heard this voice, he saw the Lord sitting on a throne, above which stood the Seraphim and one cried to another, "Holy, holy, holy is the Lord of hosts." The acclamation holy spoken three times, agrees with the Lord's saying, "Whom shall I send, and who will go for us?" All will allow that God in the person of the Father is described in the character which is here given to the Lord of hosts: And it is to be remarked, that the New Testament proves this God to be both Christ and the Holy Ghost. Isaiah, when he heard the voice of the Lord, answered, "Here *am* I, send me." Accordingly he was commanded, "Go and tell this people, Hear ye indeed, but understand not; and see ye indeed, but perceive not," which the apostle John repeats as a message of Christ, (John xii. 39, 40, 41.) and the apostle Paul quotes as the words of the Holy Ghost: "Well spake the Holy Ghost by Esaias the prophet, saying, Go unto this people, and say, Hearing ye shall hear, and not understand; and seeing ye shall see, and not perceive." (Acts xxviii. 25, 26.)

ANOTHER declaration of the same prophet, which gives intimation of the Trinity is "My mouth it hath commanded, and his Spirit, it hath gathered them." (Isa. xxxiv. 16.) The words, *my*, *his* and *Spirit*, in this passage, belong to three persons. Again, one who appears in the character of Jehovah, saith, "And now the Lord God and his Spirit hath sent me." (Isa. xlviii. 16.) The person sent is Christ, and he who sent him is the *Lord God* and *his Spirit*; who doubtless are God the Father and the Holy Ghost.

To mention another instance from the prophets; Nebuchadnezzar in his dream saw, "And behold a watcher, and an holy one, came down from heaven," who said, "This matter is by the decree of the watchers, and the demand by the word of the holy Ones." On which Daniel obferves, "Whereas they commanded." (Dan. iv. 15. 17. 26.) One watcher, a holy One came down from heaven, bringing the decree of the watchers and holy Ones; which, interpreted according to the general language of the fcriptures, is Chrift bearing a meffage of the Trinity. But,

In the New Teftament the doctrine is taught more plainly. Two paffages are fufficient to be produced. "There are three that bear record in Heaven, the Father, the Word, and the Holy Ghoft; and thefe three are one. (1 John, v. 7.) Teach all nations, baptizing them in the name of the Father, and of the Son, and of the Holy Ghoft." (Mat. xxviii. 19.) The Spirit being one with the Father, and the Word, poffeffes the fame divinity. And that men fhould believe in him in this character is fo highly important that God, who does not allow his people to have any other Gods before, or with him, requires the feal of our covenant relation to him to be applied with an acknowledgment of his Trinity, by our being baptized in each name of the facred three in one.

2. The perfections and dignity afcribed in the fcriptures to the fpirit prove him to be a divine perfon and truly God.

He is ftyled "The Eternal Spirit." (Heb. ix. 14.) In dwelling in believers, he is in all parts of the earth, in a manner which is true of God only. And the Pfalmift in ftrong terms expreffes his filling immenfity: "Whither fhall I go from the fpirit? or whither fhall I flee from thy prefence?" (Pfalm, cxxxix. 7.) To go from the Spirit, or the prefence of God is alike impoffible. The omnifcience of the fpirit is implied in that he "fearches all things, yea, even the deep things of God." And in this character he is diftinguifhed from every creature: for "the things of God knoweth no one fave the Spirit of God." Accordingly the Spirit reveals God to men. He fpake in prophecy by

thofe

those whom of old he inspired to declare future things; and the scriptures were written by his suggestion: "Holy men of God spake as *they were* moved by the Holy Ghost." (2 Pet. i. 21.)

It should be particularly noticed that the inspiration of the scriptures, and the inditing of prophecy, are ascribed equally, and in like manner, to the Spirit and to God; so that either there are two authors of inspiration, which cannot be allowed, or as is plainly the truth, the Spirit is God. Thus holy men spake as they were moved by the Holy Ghost, "All scripture is given by inspiration of God. (2 Tim. iii. 16.) Well spake the Holy Ghost by Esaias the prophet." And, "Blessed be the Lord God of Israel. As he spake by the mouth of his prophets, which have been since the world began." (Acts xxviii. 25. Luke i. 68. 70.) "Lord thou art God. Who by the mouth of thy servant David hast said," "This scripture which the Holy Ghost by the mouth of David spoke." (Acts iv. 24, 25. and i. 16.) It may be remarked further, that not only is the same agency, which implies divine perfection, attributed to both the Spirit and to God; as in the instances now produced; but both names are so united as to imply that they are one being.

Of this we have an important instance in the last words of David. "The Spirit of the Lord spake by me, and his word was in my tongue. The God of Israel said, the rock of Israel spake to me, he that ruleth over men must be just." (2 Sam. xxiii. 2, 3.) The three names used by David seem to designate the three persons of the Trinity. The Spirit at least is expressly named, and the character given to him is that of God.

In an important manner is divine dignity given to the Spirit, in his being prayed to, and religiously worshipped as God. By him was Sampson enabled to perform his miraculous exploits: "The Spirit of the Lord came mightily

upon

upon him," and he flew a thousand men of the Philistines; after which he was sore athirst, and called on the Lord and said, " thou hast given me this great deliverance." (Judges xv. 14, 18.) The deliverance, which was effected by the Spirit of the Lord, he expresly ascribes to the Lord, on whom he called by prayer.—Simeon in like manner, " blessed God, and said, Lord, now lettest thou thy servant depart in peace, according to thy word," which word it is previously stated was revealed unto him by the Holy Ghost." (Luke ii. 28, 29. with 26.)

The Apostle Paul unites the Spirit with God the Father and the Son, and worships God the Trinity, in blessing the church of Corinth : " The grace of the Lord Jesus Christ, the love of God, and the communion of the Holy Ghost, be with you all." (2 Cor. xiii. 14.) The same may be remarked of the homage of the Seraphim crying, holy, holy, holy, is the Lord of hosts in the hearing of Isaiah, in the instance which has been already noticed. Further,

The dignity, which belongs only to God, is given to the Spirit, in that blasphemy against the Holy Ghost is the unpardonable sin. The Apostle Peter also attributes the same dignity to him, in the manner in which he expresses the aggravation of the falsehood of Ananias. " Why hath Satan filled thine heart to lie to the Holy Ghost ? Thou hast not lied unto men, but unto God." (Acts v. 3, 4.)

To finish this argument, the Apostle Paul exclaims, " O the depth of the riches both of the wisdom and the knowledge of God! How unsearchable are his judgments, and his ways past finding out !" This is certainly spoken of the true God, and it seems to be borrowed from the prophet Isaiah, who speaks essentially the same of the Spirit. " Who hath directed the Spirit of the Lord, or *being* his counsellor hath taught him ? With whom took he counsel, and *who* instructed him, and taught him in the path of judgment, and taught him

him knowledge, and shewed him the way of understanding?" (Isaiah xl. 13, 14.) Thus has the Spirit the same superiority of character as the Apostle in admiration of divine excellence gives to God. And to express more fully the greatness of the character of the Spirit, the prophet adds, " Behold the nations *are* as a drop of the bucket, and are counted as the small dust of the balance : Behold he taketh up the Isles as a very little thing. Lebanon is not sufficient to burn, and all the beasts thereof for a burnt offering. (V. 15, 16.) In such language is divinity ascribed to the Holy Ghost.

3. THE works attributed to the Spirit, in the Scriptures, prove him to be a divine person.

No one will doubt whether there are any works, which exceed the capacity of the highest creatures, and prove their author to be God. Prophecy is expressly challenged as peculiar to deity : " I *am* God," saith he, " and *there* is none else : I *am* God, and *there* is none like me ; declaring the end from the beginning, and from ancient times *the things* that are not yet done, saying, my counsel shall stand, and I will do all my pleasure." (Isaiah xlvi. 9, 10.)

IT is thus God makes himself known, and thus the Spirit is proved to be God, in being as we have seen, the author of prophecy ; " declaring the end from the beginning, and saying *that his* counsel shall stand."

A WORK of God was wrought in the miraculous conception of Christ. At coming into the world the Saviour is represented as saying to God, " a body hast thou prepared me." (Heb. x. 5.) How it was done, we are told in the account of his mother's conceiving him : An angel said to her " the Holy Ghost shall come upon thee, and the power of the highest shall overshadow thee." The highest is God Almighty, and he overshadowed the virgin mother when the Holy Ghost came upon her. Therefore the highest who is God, and the Holy Ghost are one ; and of consequence, as the angel said to Mary, the holy thing born of her was called the Son of God. (Luke i. 35.)

ANOTHER work of God is wrought in the regeneration of those who savingly believe in Christ. "God, even when we were dead in sins, hath quickened us together with Christ." (Eph. ii. 4, 5.) It is this quickening, or new birth, which makes men the children of God. It notwithstanding is wrought by the Spirit. "Except a man be born of water and of the Spirit he cannot enter into the kingdom of God." (John iii. 5.) To be born of the Spirit is to be quickened by God; it is to be begotten by the God and Father of our Lord Jesus Christ; (1 Pet. i. 3.) And in experiencing it men are drawn of the Father to Christ: For no man cometh to Christ except the Father draw him. At the same time all who are the sons of God are led by the Spirit of God. (John vi. 44. with Rom. viii. 14.) The word comes to them in power and in the Holy Ghost; 'God saves them "by the washing of regeneration and renewing of the Holy Ghost;" and they "through the Spirit wait for the hope of righteousness by faith; because God has chosen them to salvation, through sanctification of the Spirit, and belief of the truth." (1 Thes. i. 5. Titus iii. 5. Gal. v. 5, and 2 Thes. ii. 13.) Thus, what God works in them, the Spirit works: through the Spirit they wait for the hope of righteousness; which is, they are "kept by the power of God through faith to salvation."— (1 Pet. i. 5.) The work is God's, and in performing it, God the Father, and God the Holy Ghost, are one. Moreover,

GOD is called "The God of all comfort," and yet the Spirit is officially the comforter. (1 Cor. i. 3. with John xiv. 26, and xv. 26.) Also believers are the temple of God, because the Spirit dwells in them; so that the Spirit is God abiding in believers. "Know ye not that ye are the temple of God; and *that* the Spirit of God dwelleth in you. "What know ye not that

that your body is the temple of the Holy Ghost?"— "If we love one another God dwelleth in us." "He that dwelleth in love dwelleth in God and God in him." (1 Cor. iii. 16. and vi. 19. also 1 John iv. 12. 15.)

AGAIN, The Holy Ghost appears to be God in being the divine person by whom miracles have been wrought. Ezekiel writes, (Ezek. viii. 1, 3.) "The hand of the Lord fell there upon me.—And he put forth the form of a hand, and took me by a lock of mine head, and the Spirit lift me up between the earth and the heaven, and brought me in the visions of God to Jerusalem. The hand of the Lord is his power and this is the Spirit who lifted up and carried the prophet. The finger of God is another expression signifying his power, and it means the same as the Holy Ghost, by whom Christ wrought miracles. For, "God anointed Jesus with the Holy Ghost, and with power." (Acts x. 38.) Christ's casting out devils by the Spirit of God, was his casting them out by the finger of God. It is evident both expressions mean the same ; for his words are in Matthew (xii. 28.)— "If I cast out devils by the Spirit of God, then the kingdom of God is come unto you :" and in Luke (xi. 20.) "If I with the finger of God cast out devils, no doubt the kingdom of God is come unto you." The finger of God by which Christ dispossessed the powers of darkness is God himself manifested in his power, which is in the person of the Holy Ghost. In the same manner Christ laid down his life and took it again : "Who through the eternal Spirit offered himself without spot to God ;" (Heb. ix. 14.) "Being put to death in the flesh ; but quickened by the Spirit."— (1 Pet. iii. 18.) The resurrection of Christ was certainly a work of God, and a display of divine power. "The God of our Lord Jesus Christ, the Father of glory,—According to the working of his mighty power, which he wrought in Christ, when he raised him from the dead, and set him at his own right hand."—

(Eph.

(Eph. i. 17. 19, 20.) "Whom God raised up, having loosed the pains of death." (Acts ii. 24.) But the person of God by whom Christ was raised is the Holy Ghost as well as the Son and the Father: "Being quickened by the Spirit."

ONE other work of God remains to be noticed, which is the creation of the world.

"THUS saith the Lord, the Holy One of Israel and his Maker,—I have made the earth and created man upon it : I, *even* my hands have stretched out the heavens, and all their hosts have I commanded." (Isa. xlv. 11, 12.) "In the beginning God created the heaven and the earth. Thus is the Creator truly God: yet it is said, "and the Spirit of God moved upon the face of the waters." (Gen. i. 1, 2.) So early is the Spirit mentioned in performing the work which is most eminently peculiar to God. Other declarations ascribe creation to the Spirit : "By the word of the Lord were the heavens made, and all the hosts of them by the breath of his mouth. (Ps. xxxiii. 6.) Breath and Spirit are words of so near an affinity, that it is natural to understand the breath of God's mouth to mean his Spirit. In the same manner Elihu in Job seems to use the word : "The Spirit of God hath made me, and the breath of the Almighty hath given me life." (Job. xxxiii. 4.) But whether the breath of the Almighty be or not the same as the Spirit of God, Elihu expressly makes the Spirit his Creator.

THE divinity and real godhead being thus, as it is thought, fully established, though much more, would the time permit, might be added to strengthen the proof of it, one observation will conclude the subject. All to whom the Holy Ghost is revealed in the scriptures, should regard him with pious reverence, placing confidence in him as the renewer and sanctifier of the redeemed of Jesus Christ.

Being God he is able to change the temper of the heart, to beget the new man, and give the disposition to believe in Christ. His grace is almighty, his indwelling and keeping preserve men safely to eternal life. How important it is to be a temple of the Spirit of God! But Oh! how awful to blaspheme the Holy Ghost.

EXCEPT you be born of Water and of the Spirit you cannot enter into the kingdom of God. Your privileges are favourable to your being born of Water externally members of God's kingdom; but trust not to what is only outward and visible. See that you be born of the Spirit. How happy you are, if the Spirit himself bear witness with your spirit, that you are children of God. Pray God to give you the Spirit; yield yourselves to his teaching; be led by him: and grieve not the Holy Spirit of God by whom you are sealed unto the day of redemption. AMEN.

SERMON VIII.

THE GLORY OF *CHRIST* AS MEDIATOR.

John i. 14. "*And the* WORD *was made flesh and dwelt among us,* (and we beheld his glory, the glory as of the only begotten of the Father,) *full of grace and truth.*"

THE Word is a name given to the second person of the Trinity, as existing in the ages of eternity. In the beginning was the Word, and the Word was with God, and the Word was God."

"THE Word was made flesh," in assuming human nature. Conceived by the Holy Ghost and born of a virgin, he was by a divine command called Emmanuel; which signifies God with us, God united with man.

IN this state he dwelt among us, in our world, and among the people of God. His tabernacling in flesh was more than thirty years; from infancy to manhood, and to his finishing the work assigned him of the Father, to do on earth.

EARLY after he commenced his public ministry, he chose twelve apostles, to be the first ministers of his kingdom. That they might enjoy every opportunity to know him, and be qualified to preach him to the world, he made them his family and attendants. John the writer of his gospel was one of them, and he seems to

speak

speak in his own name and that of his brother apostles, perhaps also including other disciples of Christ; "We beheld his glory." They were witnesses of his daily life, heard his conversation and preaching, saw his miracles; three of them were present at his transfiguration. All of them were with him after his resurrection, and looked on when he ascended to heaven. They were taught his exaltation at the right hand of God, his being given to be head over all things to the church, his coming again to raise the dead, and his appointment to judge the world. In his whole character, appearing in his humiliation on earth, his exaltation in heaven, and his finishing his work in the day of judgment, which was in the view of their faith. They saw his glory: it was the glory as of the only begotten of the Father. It emanated from Christ as the Word made flesh, possessing the perfections of deity, the same nature as the Father; but united with manhood, and acting in obedience to God as his Son. The disciples saw Christ in this glory; "full of grace and truth:" The messenger of the infinite love of God, the reality and substance of all the shadows of the Old Testament.

The Word was made flesh that he might be the mediator between God and men. Possessing the natures of both he is able to stand between them. And in discharging the duties of his mediatorship he displays his glory. It will be shown as we proceed, that, his glory is seen,

I. In his person and official character;
II. In his humiliation;
III. In his exaltation.

1. The glory of Christ is seen in his person and official character.

In any office, to appear truly dignified requires a capacity, and disposition, suited to the services which are to be performed. With these qualifications, the more elevated the station, and the more difficult the duties of it, the greater honor is acquired.

To

To be the mediator between God and sinful men, is to fill the most exalted office ever bestowed on any being; an office, for which the Word made flesh, and only he, is qualified. In the union of his two natures he possesses all the dignity of character, and capacity to obey and suffer, which are needful in the surety for mankind to recover them to the favor of God. And his regard to holiness and the laws of Jehovah, together with his love to men, made him willing to obey and die for them; that his Father should be honored in their salvation.

His being God agrees with his being invested with divine prerogatives, to display the harmony of truth, righteousness and grace, in God's showing mercy to men. His being man prepared him to yield the obedience required of mankind, and to atone for their sins by dying for them. And it is honorable to him, that he became man without sin, and innocently sustained the infirmities of human nature.

The disposition of his heart was perfectly suited to his work. Love to God, and delight in his law, united with a love to mankind, that was stronger than death.

In this union and harmony of perfections, with his holiness and benevolence of heart, he is fitted to be the mediator between God and apostate creatures, to use the expression of a prophet, he is the fellow, the equal, of the Lord of hosts: and, he is the elder brother of mankind. Thus is he a daysman betwixt them, that as Job speaks, might lay his hand on them both.

His name Christ intimates that he is appointed of God to his office; is anointed to be the prophet, priest, and king of men: all which offices he sustains as mediator. God gave him commission to reveal him in the world; to declare the way of life, to make atonement for sin, for the justification of mankind by faith;

and

and to rule the nations, as Lord of Providence, and head over all things to the church. He had power to lay down his life, and power to take it again; and this commandment he received of his Father. On rising from the dead, all power in heaven and in earth was given to him, and all judgment, to determine the everlasting condition of men; that all should honour the Son, as they honour the Father. Such is Christ's glorious office as mediator, and such his perfect fitness to sustain it, and be honoured in mediating between God and men.

II. The glory of Christ is to be seen in his humiliation.

The Word in becoming flesh veiled the glory of his deity under the infirmities of manhood. This was necessary to his performing the works of his mediation. But his astonishing condescension did not incapacitate him to make continual manifestations of excellence. It was worthy the dignified character of Christ, an amiable expression of his benevolence, to present to the church, an example of the perfection of obedience and good conduct, for the imitation of his disciples; and to accompany this practice of human virtue and religion with frequent emanations of divine power.

The two great commands, which express the sum of duty, taught in the law and the prophets, are love to God with all the heart, and love to your neighbour as to yourself. Both these commands Christ fully obeyed. He uniformly acknowledged, and honoured, his Father. Obedience was his delight: the law requiring it was in his heart; and his meat, and drink, were to do the will of him that sent him, and to finish his work.

The same heart, that loves God, loves also mankind. It was so in Christ. "God so loved the world that he gave his only begotten Son, that whosoever believeth on him should not perish but have everlasting life." And Christ so loved it, that he willingly laid down his life in obedience to his Father, that men might live in believing on him. His affections, and duty, so harmonized, as to make him acquiesce in his Father's will, though it was to drink the bitter cup of death.

THE actions of his life were also full of kindness. He went about doing good. While he taught the way of salvation, he performed many works of benevolence on the bodies of men. Zeal for the honor of God, and love to mankind, animated him through all his life.

HE was exact to fulfil all the precepts of the divine law, of both morality and religion, that he might honor God, and by his example as well as preaching, teach mankind to be holy. When John objected, that he was not worthy to baptize Christ, Christ replied—" Suffer it to be so now, for thus it becometh us to fulfil all righteousness." Alike perfect was his whole life, in keeping the commands of God.

THE devil, with all his infernal cunning, aided by the opposition, and frauds, of wicked men, could not betray him into any commission of sin, or neglect of duty. Through all difficulties he went so zealously, and uprightly, forward in his work, that when arraigned, that he should be condemned, the devil had nothing in him which was sin; for in all his life he had done no iniquity, and no guile had been found in his mouth.— Even Pilate, who condemned him to be crucified, bore testimony to his innocence; and Herod, to whom also Christ was sent, found no fault in him. But,

HE was not merely innocent; he was an example of whatever is good. Such were his humility, condescension and patience, that with evident propriety he invited his disciples, and mankind, to learn of him; for he was meek and lowly in heart. In the severest trial which he endured, he preserved his mildness and composure. " He was oppressed and he was afflicted, yet he opened not his mouth." " When he was reviled he reviled not again, when he suffered he threatened

ened not, but committed himself to him that judgeth righteously." And in his love to his enemies, and readiness to forgive, he prayed on the cross, " Father forgive them for they know not what they do."

By such holy, benevolent and amiable conduct, Christ honored himself in the character of man. His miracles, at the same time, proved that he was sent from heaven, and was the Son of God. On his changing water into wine, it is remarked, " This beginning of miracles did Jesus, and manifested forth his glory." His miracles were more than that they should be all recorded in the history of his life, and they all uttered the same language, and all ascribed to him like praise. They justified him, in calling God his Father ; for they were a foundation for his appealing to the works of his Father, which he did, as evidence, that the Father was in him, and he in the Father.

God also owned him by a voice from heaven.— One instance of it was on his coming up from the water, after his baptism. The heavens opened, and he saw the Spirit of God, descending like a dove, and lighting on him. And, lo, a voice from heaven, saying, This is my beloved Son, in whom I am well pleased." A like voice was again heard on the mount of his transfiguration, and was attended with other circumstances glorious to Christ. Moses, by whom God gave his law to Israel, and Elias a chief person of the prophets, appeared to him ; he was himself transfigured ;" " his face did shine as the sun, and his raiment was white as the light." On another occasion he prayed, " Father glorify thy name." " Then there came a voice from heaven :" the people said it thundered, but the words uttered were, " I have both glorified it, and will glorify it again."

The lowest abasement which Christ endured was his death : but even then, circumstances of glory attended him. Not only did the wicked judge, who gave the order for his crucifixion, acknowledge his innocence ;

nocence; but God himself interposed, and the frame of nature owned the importance of the event. The vail of the temple, which from the time it was built had covered the place of God's presence, was rent from top to bottom; the sun, at noon day, ceased to shine, and for three hours darkness was over all the land. The earth quaked, when he expired, the rocks rent, the graves were opened; and many bodies of the saints who slept arose, and came out of their graves after Christ's resurrection. At these things the Centurion, and they that were with him watching Jesus, were filled with fear and said, truly this was the Son of God. "Certainly this was a righteous man." And all the people that came together to that sight, beholding the things which were done, smote their breasts and returned." It follows to be observed,

III. The glory of Christ is to be seen in his exaltation.

In his resurrection, which was the third day after his death, and in his ascension to heaven which soon followed, his glory began to shine with lustre. And it will more and more brighten, till the works of his mediation shall be finished.

1. Christ appears glorious in rising from the dead, ascending to heaven, and sitting on the right hand of God.

After suffering an ignominious, as well as cruel death, under a false imputation of sin, it was honorable to Christ to rise from the dead. His resurrection proved the truth of what he had said, that he laid down his life for the sheep; and laid it down of himself, that he had power to lay it down, and power to take it again. (John x. 16, 18.) As in himself he had no sin, and his death atoned for the sins of mankind, the law no longer required his blood. "God raised him up, having loosed the pains of death, because it was not possible that he should be holden of it. (Acts ii. 24.)

Whatever

Whatever imputation of guilt, he was under in his death, was removed in his resurrection. The false accusations of his enemies were contradicted, by the demonstration of his innocence and holiness. And all the sufferings, to which he had made himself liable as the surety for men, were finished. His rising from the grave was a triumph over sin and death. The justification, resurrection and salvation of all that believe in him, were declared by it. He is the resurrection and the life, the first fruits of them that slept; who was delivered for our offences and was raised again for our justification.

The declaration, which was made in his rising from the dead, was confirmed by his ascending to heaven. The Father owned him for his Son, and fulfilled to him the covenant of redemption, in virtue of which Christ had come into the world. As he was declared to be the Son of God with power, according to the Spirit of holiness, by the resurrection from the dead; so God highly exalted him, when he set him at his own right hand in the heavenly places. "He overcame and sat down with his Father on his throne; being made so much better than the angels as he hath by inheritance obtained a more excellent name than they." His dignity, and glory, are "far above all principality and power, might and dominion, and every name that is named, not only in this world, but also in that which is to come. God hath put all things under his feet, and given him to be head over all to the church." His name is above every name, that at the name of Jesus every knee should bow, of things in heaven, in earth and under the earth; and that every tongue should confess, that Jesus Christ is Lord, to the glory of God the Father." Thus he, who was made for a little time, lower than the angels, is crowned with glory and honor, and set over the works of God.

2. Christ appears glorious as reigning on the throne

throne of Zion and judging the world at the last day.

His kingly authority is absolute and almighty.— Angels are his ministers; devils are prisoners held in chains. His government particularly respects mankind and his church. He effectually defends his cause, and will preserve the church to the end of the world. His reign will continue till all his enemies shall become his foot-stool, in being totally subdued under him, and made instruments of exalting his kingdom.

ALL nations, and all events in the natural world, are under his controul. He regulates seasons and ages according to his pleasure, and makes all things subservient to the glory of his reign. After giving mankind opportunity fully to show their depravity, the power of sin, and the folly of human wisdom, he will manifest clearly the wisdom of God and the efficacy of his own grace, in recovering them from their ignorance and wickedness, to virtue and happiness. And in the character of the prince of peace, he will reign a thousand years on the earth. His saints will reign with him, and his church be glorious as the bride, the Lamb's wife, the day of whose marriage shall be come.

AFTER the end of the thousand years, the devil will be again loosed for a little time, and mankind again be left to exhibit their character of depravity and wretchedness. Wickedness with all its evils will quickly prevail, and greatly abound in the earth. But suddenly Christ will put an end to both the glorying of sin, and the probation of mankind, by coming to judgment.

ATTENDED with his hosts of angels, he will descend to our world with pomp and great glory. The dead will be raised, and the living be changed; those, interested in his redemption, will put on the likeness of his glorified body; and separated by the ministry of angels, from the wicked, will be placed on his right hand;

hand; while the wicked shall be made to stand on his left. The books will then be opened; which will show the righteousness of his proceeding, in giving to every man according to his works, and inviting to eternal life all that shall have believed on him while in the present world. Every child of God will be found to have been sanctified by the Spirit, as well as justified by faith; and to have wrought the good works, which are the necessary witnesses of a title to glory. On the other hand,

The works of the wicked will prove their opposition to God and holiness; their wilful refusal of Christ, if he shall have been offered to them; and their worthiness to be punished with everlasting death. Thus, in judging the different characters of mankind, Christ will be glorious in his exhibition of the perfections of God, declaring his truth, honouring his justice and holy law, and displaying his grace. He will be glorious in the total disappointment, and confusion, of the devil and all his adherents; and the salvation of such a number of mankind, as will most strongly declare the love of God, and ascribe the highest honor to their redeemer.

3. Christ will appear glorious in his delivering up the kingdom to God the Father.

To receive an office of dignity is honorable; but to resign it, after all the purposes for which it was conferred are answered, is a greater honor. Christ received his mediatorial kingdom in trust; and when he shall have finished God's design in giving it to him, he will deliver it up to the Father. His judging the world at the last day will be the last exercise of his mediatorial authority. His enemies will then be all put under his feet; and the more numerous, subtil, and powerful, they are, the more will he be exalted in triumph over them.

His redeemed, being adjudged to eternal life, will enjoy it as their everlasting inheritance, with no further

further need of his interceding for them, or acting as mediator between them and God. His public declaration to them, from his throne of judgment, " Come ye blessed of my Father, inherit the kingdom prepared for you from the foundation of the world," will eternally secure them in the happiness and glory of heaven. There, like the holy angels, they will have free access to God their heavenly Father, and behold him face to face. After raising his redeemed to this exalted and permanent felicity, it will be honorable to Christ to resign his mediatorial kingdom.

A CIRCUMSTANCE of high importance will be, that all, whom God has given to Christ, and predestinated to eternal life, will be saved. And they will be exactly the number necessary to give the brightest view of the love of God, and most forcibly represent the efficacy of the blood of Christ, and the truth of his bruising the serpent's head.

THE more God is glorified in the manifestation of all his perfections, the more is the devil disappointed, confounded and destroyed. God eternally knew how to manifest his own glory. In covenanting with Christ to save mankind, and giving to him as his redeemed, as many as his wisdom and love determined to save, he had in view all his perfections, and the most honorable display of his own name. He is always of one mind, and the counsels of the Son are the same as of the Father. These in the issue will be perfectly accomplished. The love of God will be satisfied ; the death of Christ will produce the most illustrious effects : and the foundation will be laid for the most complete felicity of all good beings ; in beholding God in the brightest lustre of his glory. No enemy shall remain unsubdued, or without being placed under the feet of Christ, to add to his exaltation ; no circumstance shall be found to diminish the glory of God or Christ ; but all things in heaven and in hell shall unite to ascribe wisdom, and power, and glory, to the Father and the Son, forever and

and ever. "Then cometh the end when he shall have delivered up the kingdom to God, even the Father, when he shall have put down, all rule, and authority, and power. For he must reign till he hath put all things under his feet. And when all things shall be subdued unto him, then shall the Son also himself be subject unto him, that put all things under him, that God may be all in all."

In the imperfect review which has now been taken of Christ in the office of mediator, he appears in amiable and majestic glory. How astonishing is the condescension of the word in being made flesh? how desireable the example of virtue and holiness exhibited in the life of Christ? Love to God, love to men, humility, and obedience to his Father, invite our imitation; and powerfully persuade us to walk after him in the way of life. His love, and obedience were even to the voluntary laying down of his life. When, in the near prospect of the awful sufferings of the terrifying conflict, he prayed, that if it were possible the cup might pass from him, he resigned himself to the sovereign disposal of God and said, "Father, not my will, but thine, be done." In heaven he appears in more majestic glory. Though equally mindful of his redeemed, interceding for them in the presence of God. And in the completion of the work of his mediatorial kingdom, at the day of judgment, and delivering the kingdom to the Father, of whom he received it, the manifestation of his glory will be finished; and in all respects it will be perfect.

The glory of Christ teaches several instructive truths.

1. To own him in the world is a tribute of respect due to his glory.

A condition, on which he promises to own mankind in the presence of the holy angels and of his Father, is, that they own him before men. What condition can be more reasonable? The glory of Christ makes

makes him worthy to be acknowledged before all descriptions of creatures. They, who know him, and have right views of his glory, will not be ashamed to confess him and place confidence in him, though wicked men and devils should hear. Even should the owning of Christ expose to the most malignant rage of his enemies, they can do no more than kill the body; but he can kill, and destroy, both body and soul in hell; and he can save from destruction. The goodness of his disposition, the eminence of his character, the greatness of his power, and his final triumph over his enemies in the salvation of all who trust in him, invite to own him in the world, in the hope of being owned of him in the kingdom of his glory. To be ashamed of him, in a sinful and adulterous generation, is to manifest such depravity and baseness of Spirit, as to be unworthy of a place among his disciples. And justly will he in heaven be ashamed of all those who are ashamed of him on earth.

2. To be truly honorable in any station, it must be filled with capacity and fidelity. There is no higher station, in which even the Son of God could be placed, than that of mediator between God and mankind; and his glory in it, is reflected from his ability as God man, and his disposition, manifested in the performance of all the duties of his arduous undertaking. To be a christian, a disciple of Christ, is honorable; but to be worthy of the respect which is due to the name, you must have the mind of Jesus, and imitate his example. His ministers act in a higher station than ordinary disciples, and to be truly respectable must possess proportional knowledge, prudence and zeal, in performing their Lords work.

WHATEVER be your condition or official dignity, you must reflect honor on your station to have it do honor to you. Let your undertakings suit your capacity, and after the example of our blessed Lord, perform duty with fidelity, and you will be honored.

3. THE

3. The amiable virtues of Christ's humiliation strongly invite to imitate him in love, meekness, condescension, obedience to God and the performance of good works. After beholding the life of Jesus who will be afraid of being dishonored by the practice of true humility, love, and consciencious obedience? To glory in the haughtiness of pride, and to be ashamed to practise meekness and condescension, and to forgive affronts, is to be unworthy to be called christians.

4. You should study and contemplate the glory of Christ, that you may believe in him, and increase your faith.

After viewing his life on earth, look to him in heaven; see him sitting on the right hand of God; behold him coming to judgment, and after the completion of his work of mediation, delivering up the kingdom to the Father. Look at him again, view, and review his glory; and be not faithless, but believing.— In fine,

5. You should keep your eye fixed on Christ, that you may imitate him in a cheerful enduring of trials, and be uniform and zealous in obedience unto the end of life. "Looking to Jesus the author and finisher of your faith; who, for the joy that was set before him, endured the cross, despising the shame, and is set down at the right hand of the throne of God." (Heb. xii. 2.) O the blessedness of being with him, where he is, to behold his glory, which the Father hath given him. (John xvii. 24.) Amen.

SERMON IX.

ON REGENERATION.

John iii. 5. Jesus answered, verily, verily, I say unto thee, except a man be born of water and of the Spirit, he cannot enter into the kingdom of God.

THE doctrine of regeneration is of the highest importance: Of that religion which Christ has taught, it lies at the very foundation; insomuch that all our pretensions to this religion, or expectations of the saving blessings of it, are vain, without an experimental acquaintance with this fundamental doctrine. That all unregenerate persons will be excluded from those spiritual and everlasting enjoyments which are the fruits of the Redeemer's purchase, is evident from the whole tenor of scripture; but this is no where expressed in more full and decided terms, than by our Lord himself, in his discourse with Nicodemus, of which our text is a part.

This eminent Jew, if we may judge from the circumstances of his application and the manner of his address to our Saviour, was not only convinced of the divine authority with which he was cloathed; but was desirous of being informed of the nature of that religion which he came to reveal.

"There was a man of the Pharisees named Nicodemus, a ruler of the Jews: the same came to

Jesus

Jesus by night, and said unto him, Rabbi, we know that thou art a teacher come from God; for no man can do these miracles which thou doest except God be with him."

WHETHER this respectful address, flowed from a real conviction of Christ's divine character and mission; or whether he only meant thus gracefully to introduce himself, is not certain. Be that as it may, our blessed Lord takes the opportunity to instruct this man in a matter of the highest concern, not to him only, but to all others. He begins with the following most solemn and emphatical declaration, " Jesus said unto him, verily, verily, I say unto thee, except a man be born again he cannot see the kingdom of God." q. d. You profess to own me as a teacher come from God: and that the miraculous works done by me, afford demonstrable evidence of this: you say right; your conclusion is just. I am indeed that great prophet whom the Father hath sent into the world to instruct mankind in things of infinite moment: As such a divine infallible teacher, I do now in the most solemn manner declare to you, that except a man, that is, *any one*, be he who he may, male or female, Jew or Gentile, except he experience a new birth, he never can see the kingdom of God. Nicodemus, taking the words merely according to their literal sense, expresses his surprize at our Lord's declaration: " How, he asks, can a man be born when he is old? can he enter the second time into his mother's womb and be born?" Christ, to let him know that he spake not of a natural, but of a supernatural, spiritual, and heavenly birth, explains himself as in the text. " Verily, verily, I say unto thee, except a man be born of water and of the Spirit, he cannot enter into the kingdom of God." This is plainly but a repetition of the former assertion, only in different words: They both have precisely the same meaning; the latter being only explanatory of the former: what our Saviour had expressed by the terms, " born again." He here calls,

the

the being born of water and of the Spirit. The regeneration therefore of which Christ speaks, in his conference with Nicodemus; and which he declares to be so necessary a qualification for the kingdom of God, consists in being "born of water and of the Spirit."

"Jesus answered, verily, verily, I say unto thee, except a man be born of water and of the Spirit, he cannot enter into the kingdom of God."

A declaration like this, made in so solemn a manner, expressed in terms so emphatical and peremptory; and by one of such incontestible authority, must certainly claim our most serious regard.

The importance of the words before us appears not only from these circumstances; but will be farther manifest by attending more particularly to their sacred and interesting meaning. This I shall attempt with divine help to explain and illustrate, by shewing,

I. What we are here to understand by the kingdom of God, and entering into that kingdom.

II. What is the import of the phrase, "born of water and of the Spirit," and describe the change it imports.

III. The absolute necessity of such a change, in order to an admission into the kingdom of God.

1. What we are here to understand by the kingdom of God, and entering into that kingdom.

The phrase kingdom of God, and kingdom of heaven, which are synonomous terms, very frequently occurs in the new testament. It means in general the church of God, including the constitution, laws and privileges of it; as well as the members who compose it. But this kingdom subsists under two distinct forms; the one imperfect and preparatory here on earth; the other complete and consummate in heaven. These have both the same appellation, kingdom of God and kingdom of heaven, on account of the divine nature, origin and end of this kingdom. These two different forms or states of Christ's church are distinguished by

the

the kingdom of grace and the kingdom of glory; or the present gospel state of the church in this world, and its future glorious and triumphant state in heaven.

In the numerous places where we meet with this phrase, kingdom of God and kingdom of heaven, it sometimes refers to the one and sometimes to the other of the above mentioned states of the church.

Thus when John Baptist exhorted the people to repent, saying the kingdom of heaven is at hand; he plainly means that the gospel state of the church was about to be set up in the world. And where our Lord compares the kingdom of heaven to a grain of mustard seed; to a net cast into the sea, which gathered of all kinds good and bad; to a field of wheat intermixt with tares; to ten virgins, wise and foolish, &c. it is manifest he has reference to the present visible and imperfect state of his church, which consists of various and opposite characters. But where he declares; " Not every one that saith unto me Lord, Lord, shall enter into the kingdom of heaven; where he assures his disciples, " Except their righteousness exceed the righteousness of the Scribes and Pharisees, they shall in no case enter that kingdom; and where the apostle declares that all unholy and wicked persons shall be inevitably excluded the blessings of it; in these and other similar places by the kingdom of God is meant the future glorious and happy state of that kingdom or heaven itself.

Now a little attention to the declaration of Christ in our text will convince us that it is in this last sense the phrase, " kingdom of God," is here to be understood. In a verse preceding, he had declared to Nicodemus that " except a man be born again he cannot *see* the kingdom of God. Our text is the same declaration repeated, only here some of the expressions are varied; what our Lord had termed, " born again" he here expresses by being " born of water and the Spirit" which are terms of the same import.

This

This then is the qualification which in this place is made an indispensable term of admission to the kingdom of God. But persons may be admitted to this kingdom as it respects the present form of it, who are destitute of this qualification. Baptism with water will constitute persons regular members of Christ's visible kingdom; but something more is certainly implied in regeneration or being born of water and the Spirit: this latter is required as necessary to enter into God's kingdom, as this kingdom is here to be understood; therefore by this phrase we must here understand, the future perfect state of the church.

This will be farther manifest if we attend to the import of the expression "entering into God's kingdom;" this was expressed before by "*seeing*" that kingdom. To see spiritual objects in the sense of scripture is to enjoy them; therefore to *see* the kingdom of God here undoubtedly means an admission to the complete enjoyment of the spiritual and everlasting blessings of it in the future world.

According to our Lord's positive and repeated assertion no one can be admitted to this, except he is born of water and the Spirit.

What this means will be seen under the next head of discourse; where we are to shew,

2. What is the true signification of the expressions "born of water and the spirit, and describe the change which they import.

Some suppose that here is an allusion to the application of water in baptism, and hence have contended that baptism is the regeneration required.

But that more is intended than the mere washing or sprinkling with water in that ordinance, is clearly evident: for the expressions are "born of water *and* of the Spirit." Now if it should be admitted that the former expression denotes baptism: yet by the latter something more is required as a qualification for the kingdom of God, in the sense in which this kingdom is here to be taken,

taken, viz. the being "born of the Spirit." But to be born of water understanding by this baptism, and to be born of the Spirit, are things distinct in their nature, and may be separated in the subjects.

MANY, who have been baptized, were yet never born of the Spirit : and on the other hand there doubtless have been those who have experienced the regenerating influences of the divine Spirit who were yet never the subjects of water baptism. It is obvious therefore that more is here implied.

PERHAPS our Saviour doth not allude at all to that rite, but by the two clauses intends to express, as *Dr. Doddridge* thinks, one idea, viz. the " purifying influences of the Spirit, cleansing the mind, as water doth the body : as elsewhere to be baptized with the Holy Ghost and fire, signifies to be baptized by the Spirit operating like fire." But if water baptism is here intended or alluded to, in the first clause, then the following paraphrase on the passage by the above named author appears just and natural. " Whosoever would become a regular member of the kingdom of God must not only be baptized, but as ever he desires to share in its spiritual and eternal blessings, must experience the renewing and sanctifying influences of the Holy Spirit on his soul, to cleanse it from the power of corruption and to animate and quicken it to a spiritual and divine life."*

WITHOUT such a work of the divine Spirit on the heart no one can be said, in the sense of the text, to be " born of the Spirit." This phrase in short denotes that moral change of the temper and character of persons by which they are freed from the defilements of their natural condition ; delivered from a state of condemnation ; have God's image and nature restored and of consequence become the objects of his special love. Such a change is every where in scripture represented as indispensibly necessary to constitute a truly religious

* Fam. Expos. Vol. I. pag. 148.

religious character, and entitle to the divine favour: But it is variously expressed, as, by a *new heart and Spirit* ; a *pure heart* and *clean hands* ; *love* to God, and other holy affections ; *repentance* and turning to the Lord ; by *faith* which works by love ; sometimes more directly by *believing* **in the Lord Jesus Christ** ; loving him and keeping his commandments ; likewise by the *New Creature* ; coming out of *darkness* into *light* —passing from Death to life, &c.

THESE various expressions all denote the same thing : they only serve to give different views of the *change* called *regeneration*, and which our Saviour explains in the text by the terms, " born of water and of the Spirit."

To give a full and complete description of this work of the Holy Spirit upon the hearts of men, in its origin, nature, and cause ; the means by which it is produced, with the blessed effects produced by it ; and the happy and glorious end to which it ultimately leads, and which will be the final issue and result of it ; would require more time than is allotted to the present discussion.

I SHALL only mention some of the more important qualities of this change ; which will, however, open, in some measure, its divine nature and effects. And I observe,

1st. THAT the change effected in regeneration is real, great, and remarkable.

IT dont consist merely in assuming the Christian name, or a speculative belief of the peculiar doctrines and principles of the Christian religion ; nor yet in an external conformity to its excellent rules, institutions and duties. All this is indeed important and even necessary. Without such a profession, faith and practice as this, tis true, you cannot deserve the name of christians. But then with all this you may be christians, only in *name* and still be strangers to regeneration and not know what it is to be " born of water and of the Spirit,"

Spirit," without which you must be excluded the kingdom of God.

FROM the representations given of this change in the word of God, and the strong figures and phrases there made use of in describing it, we must conclude it is no slight, superficial or circumstantial alteration, which affects only the head and outward conduct, of such as are the subjects of it; but that it influences the heart as well as life.

To be " born again ;" to become " new creatures ;" to be " transformed by the renewing of the mind ;" to be " turned from darkness to light ;" yea to be " raised from death to life ;" are expressions, though chiefly metaphorical, yet must signify some great and signal revolution to have taken place in the condition of the persons to whom they are applied.

A CHANGE like that, an infant experiences when brought from the darkness and confinement of its mother's womb, into the light of this world; opens its eyes to new objects; hears new sounds, receives till now an untasted food; and lives and acts in a quite new and different manner from before: or like a person born blind who is made to see: or, in fine, like one that is raised from a state of perfect insensibility and death, to motion, activity and life.

2dly. IT is an universal change. It respects the whole man. As sin has spread its hateful contagious influence through all the several powers, parts, and members, and infected the whole mass: so we need to be thoroughly cleansed; that the remedy may be equal to the disease, and the plaster as wide as the sore. Regenerating and sanctifying grace is such a remedy. The change it produces extends its salutary, as far as sin had diffused its malignant effects. In short this blessed, renovating work of God's Spirit is so general and universal, as well as great and remarkable, that the person who is the subject of it, becomes " a new creature, old things are passed away, behold," and admire at

the

the wonderful transformation, "all things are become new."

THE body, although itself incapable of any moral exercises, is yet reprefented as fharing in this change and is really affected by it: For, as, while in an unrenewed ftate, the members of the body, through the influence of the carnal mind, were proftituted to a carnal and criminal ufe, or as the apoftle fpeaks, were "inftruments of unrighteoufnefs unto fin." So in confequence of the renewing grace of God on the foul, thefe fame bodily members are *converted* to a fpiritual and holy ufe, and become "inftruments of righteoufnefs unto God." It is to be remembered, however, that the foul is the principal feat and fubject of this change: For I am to obferve in the next place,

3dly. THAT it is an internal fpiritual change. As the heart is that corrupt fountain from whence all kinds of impurity and wickednefs proceed, it is abfolutely neceffary that this fhould be firft cleanfed; otherwife all the ftreams will remain polluted; for "who can bring a clean thing out of an unclean?

ACCORDING as the real ftate of the heart is, fuch will be the quality of the life and conduct, whether good or bad. "A good man out of the good treafure of his heart bringeth forth good things; and an evil man out of the evil treafure of his heart bringeth forth evil things." "By their fruit fhall ye know them." "Do men gather grapes of thorns, or figs of thiftles?" Even fo every good tree bringeth forth good fruit: but a corrupt tree bringeth forth evil fruit."

So then, would you perform truly good and holy actions, your hearts muft be firft renewed and fanctified by divine grace, you muft experience that internal change of which we fpeak.

UNDER this particular it might be proper to defcribe this change as it refpects the inward man; the underftanding, will and affections of the foul. But I fhall here only obferve in general that regenerating grace

grace effects an essential alteration in the temper, disposition, and character of those who are the real subjects of it. The internal state and exercises of their mind, are totally changed, from what they were while in an unrenewed condition. Their views and apprehensions; their hopes and fears; their pleasures and pains, and prospects are quite different. These spring from other and better principles; are excited by higher motives; are directed to and fixed upon more noble objects: which leads me to speak,

4thly. Of the excellent and dignifying nature of this change. Sin and guilt have grievously debased and vilified the once noble nature of man; and deeply sunk and involved it in wretchedness and misery. We were " planted a noble vine, wholly a right seed; but we are become the degenerate plants of a strange vine." " The gold is become dim and the most fine gold is changed."

While in an unrenewed state every thing is disordered *within*, and *without*; the powers of the soul and the members of the body are deplorably weakened, distempered, debased and corrupted.

It is the design of regenerating grace to recover man from these miseries and ruins of his depraved and fallen condition; and restore him to his pristine glory and happiness. It lays a foundation for this, and in a good measure effects it in this life. For the person who is the subject of that divine and heavenly principle, experiences a most glorious transformation. He is thereby turned from darkness to light, and from the power of sin and satan to the living God. He is restored to the divine image, and partakes of the divine nature. He was a slave to sin, and under the dominion of satan, but is now delivered from the bondage of that corruption and " vindicated into the glorious liberty of the children of God." His soul, which was seduced and drawn away by headstrong passions and impetuous lusts, is recovered from that foul dominion, and subjected to

the

the controul of sanctified reason, and to the dictates of pure religion. In the place of those fleshly appetites and carnal propensities which reigned in his heart, are implanted the graces of the Spirit which shine out in those fruits of righteousness which by Jesus Christ are to the praise and glory of God. The affections which clave to the dust and were held and confined down to earthly objects, are raised to the contemplation of those which are spiritual and heavenly. In short, by regeneration the soul is renewed after the image of him that created it. The person is exalted to the dignified relation of a child of God: and is transformed to a likeness of his heavenly Father, and blessed Redeemer. But although this change is thus dignifying and ennobling; yet I observe that it is nevertheless,

5thly, An humbling change. While in one view it exalts, in another, it abases the soul. This is intimated in the very terms by which it is expressed. To be "*born again*" signifies, to become as a little child: and our Saviour elsewhere declares as much, in so many words; "Except ye be converted and become as little children ye shall not enter into the kingdom of heaven." To resemble little children is to possess an humble, docile, pleasant, and pliant disposition; unassuming; not arrogant and lofty. It is of the nature of converting grace to beget and improve such a temper. It subdues that obstinacy of will, and mortifies those carnal affections and lusts which naturally reign in the unrenewed heart, and which, by habitual indulgence, become exorbitant. Sanctifying grace calms those turbulent passions. It divests the mind of that pride, ambition, envy, hatred and revenge by which it was *swoln*; and disposes to peace and quietness, benevolence and love. It consists of that *charity* which suffereth long and is kind; envieth not; vaunteth not itself; is not puffed up; nor easily provoked; thinketh no evil; rejoiceth not in iniquity, but rejoiceth in the truth; beareth all things, believeth all things, endureth

dureth all things. Or it is that, "wisdom from above which is first pure, then peaceable, gentle, easy to be entreated, full of mercy and good fruits, without partiality, and without hypocrisy." I add,

6thly, THE change, of which we speak, is Divine and Supernatural.

THE carnal sinner of himself will never change his own heart. His heart is utterly opposed to such a change. No human mean or effort is sufficient to this purpose. Regeneration is the glorious effect of Almighty Agency. Those, who experience it, are, "born not of blood, nor of the will of the flesh, nor of the will of man, but of God." Of his "Spirit." Yet let it be remembered, we do not say, the divine Spirit in effecting this work, makes use of no means; nor do we mean to assert, that in regeneration, taking the term as we do in this subject, in a large sense, and the same with repentance, conversion, &c. I say, we do not here mean, that in this change the soul is wholly passive. Regeneration, in the sense we consider it, necessarily supposes activity in the subject: it implies moral and spiritual exercises. The agency of the Spirit herein is not contrary, but perfectly agreeable to the rational nature. The persons, who are the subjects of this agency, are not merely acted upon, but do themselves act, and they act in a free and voluntary way. In short, the regeneration of which we speak, or the new creature and new heart essentially consists in the exercises of evangelical repentance, faith, love and new obedience; all of which are exercises of the creature: and exercises which are altogether rational and fit, to which all are under the highest obligations: and which all are therefore called and commanded to possess and put forth; and that on the severest penalties. But so great is the opposition of the will to those acts and exercises that nothing short of almighty, sovereign grace is sufficient to overcome it: and therefore without the special influence and operation of that grace and
Spirit

Spirit of God, this change can never be effected. The holy scriptures every where afcribe it to a divine agency. In the old teftament, where this change is expreffed by a new heart, turning to the Lord, loving God, and the like, we are clearly taught to confider thefe things as gifts beftowed by God, and effects produced by his power. Thus David prays that *God* would *create within him a clean heart.*"

Ephraim, bemoaning himfelf, cries—" Turn thou me and I fhall be turned." It is prophefied that God's people fhould be willing in the day of *his power.* Mofes faid to Ifrael, The Lord thy God fhall circumcife thy heart and the heart of thy feed to love the Lord thy God with all thy heart. And God himfelf promifes to his people, " A new heart alfo will I give you, and a new fpirit will I put within you: and I will take away the ftony heart out of your flefh, and I will give you a heart of flefh, and I will put my Spirit within you, and caufe you to walk in my ftatutes."

In the new teftament, this change is in the fulleft terms afcribed to God, and fpoken of as the work of his power. Not by works of righteoufnefs, faith the apoftle, which we have done, but according to his mercy he faved us by the wafhing of regeneration and renewing of the Holy Ghoft. Chriftians are reprefented as being the fubjects of a fupernatural and divine birth. " Born not of blood nor of the will of the flefh, nor of the will of man, but of God." By regeneration we become in a fpecial fenfe God's children; but this, we are told, is in confequence of a fpecial divine operation. " As many as received him, to them gave he *power* to become the fons of God, even to them that believe on his name." Regeneration, we have obferved, is the fame with evangelical repentance and faith; but thefe we are taught are the gifts of God. Chrift is exalted to be a Prince and a Saviour to give repentance and forgivenefs of fins." " By grace are ye faved though faith, and this not of yourfelves, selves, it is the gift of God." And to mention no more, the apostle prays that the Ephesians might be led to see and admire, "the exceeding greatness of God's power to them-ward who believe, according to the working of his mighty power which he wrought in Christ when he raised him from the dead."

Having thus in some measure described that change which is called regeneration, and which our Saviour in the text expresses by being born of water and the Spirit, I pass on as was proposed,

3dly, To shew the necessity of it in order to an admission into the kingdom of God.

On this head we must not enlarge. By kingdom of God, it has been shewn, we are in this place to understand the kingdom of glory, or the future perfect glorious state of God's kingdom. Now the absolute necessity of such a change in order for an admission into this glorious kingdom, appears from the many express declarations of that God whose kingdom it is: And from the nature of the happiness of which it consists.

1. He, whose kingdom this is, has frequently declared, that none but those, who have experienced such a change, shall ever be received into it—that all unregenerate persons shall be excluded from it. The solemn and most emphatical declaration of Christ in the text is full to this purpose. Here the *amen, the true and faithful witness;* He who was sent and commissioned of the Father to preach the gospel of the kingdom, to determine the qualifications of the members of it, and prescribe the only terms of admission into it. This divine infallible teacher here declares and with a repeated asseveration, that except a man be regenerated or born of the Spirit he cannot enter into this kingdom, that is, all unregenerate persons will be shut out of it. And there are a multitude of passages in the word of God which declare the same thing, though in different words. All unregenerate persons, in the scripture sense, belong to the character of the wicked; but all

of this character and class it is declared shall be cast into hell; and if so, they cannot surely be admitted to heaven. Regeneration, as we have seen, implies true repentance and saving faith; but it is declared that except men repent they shall all perish: and "He that believeth not shall be damned." To be regenerated, in the sense explained, is to be truly sanctified, in part: It implies a principle of holiness in the heart and the practice of holiness in the life; but we are told that, "without holiness no man shall see the Lord;" and consequently, without this, no one can enter into his kingdom.

In short, from the express and peremptory declarations of scripture, we are assured that the unregenerate of every description; all such as are impenitent and unbelieving in heart, or who are disobedient and ungodly in life, will not only be shut out from God's kingdom of light, and glory, and blessedness above: but that all these characters will be sent down to the dreary regions of eternal darkness, misery, and woe: and that even those who by profession had a name and standing in this kingdom, in its present imperfect state, and held a distinguished rank in it; but were destitute of the internal qualifications of Christ's real subjects, will be at last taken out of it and forever banished from its future glories.

From the oracles of truth we are made to know not only that openly unrighteous, profane and ungodly sinners shall not inherit the "kingdom of God;" but that insincere hypocritical professors of Christ, however high and plausible their religious standing, claims and pretensions may be, will, notwithstanding, be excluded at last. "Not every one that saith unto me, Lord, Lord, shall enter into the kingdom of God; but he that doth the will of my Father which is in heaven."

"And many will say unto me in that day, Lord, Lord, have we not prophesied in thy name? And in thy

thy name have cast out devils ? And in thy name done many wonderful works. And then I will profess unto them I never knew you, depart from me ye that work iniquity."

Thus it appears to be the unchangeable determination of God, by the express repeated and solemn declarations of his word, to exclude finally, all unregenerate people from his kingdom above : Hence in order to an admission into this kingdom, we " *must be born again.*"

And the necessity of such a change might be argued not only from those solemn declarations of that God whose kingdom this is, but also

2dly. From the nature of those blessings and that happiness of which it consists, which are of such a kind, that it is impossible that any, while in an unrenewed state, should partake of them. The idea indeed which we are wont to conceive of heaven is, that it is a most glorious and blessed place, and that if we could but once arrive there we must of consequence be completely happy.

It is truly a place of inconceivable felicity ; but it is intirely a mistaken notion that unregenerate sinners would be happy there. Admitting it possible that persons while remaining in their carnal unsanctified condition could be admitted to heaven, yet it is certain they would find no happiness for *them*. Because the happiness of which heaven consists is of such a nature, that in their present state they could have no sort of relish for it. Infinitely lovely and glorious as heaven is, it would nevertheless prove to the wicked an undesirable, nay a disagreeable place. This thought would receive clear and abundant illustration, if we should take a particular survey of the several branches of the heavenly felicity ; I shall only observe in general that it consists of a society, and of exercises and employments which, though the most noble and sublime ; yet being all pure, spiritual and holy ; carnal, unsanctified minds cannot

relish

relish or be delighted with them: They are utterly destitute of those spiritual and holy dispositions and affections, that are absolutely necessary in order to a participation in them. On the whole, it appears that not only the immutable God must recede from his own most solemn declarations, and revoke his unalterable decrees; but heaven itself must be changed and the very nature of its enjoyments become essentially different from what they are, before unregenerate, unsanctified sinners can be received into that heaven or partake of those enjoyments. But we know that the immutable God will not change his word; and heaven cannot alter its nature; and therefore unless sinners are changed and renewed in *their* nature and character they will assuredly be shut out of heaven.

I HAVE now finished what was proposed for the illustration of the general propositions laid down. What has been offered in doctrine, naturally suggests a variety of things to our minds, which might be profitably enlarged upon by way of improvement. To avoid farther prolixity I shall only deduce a few inferences from the subject, and with the brief mention of them, conclude the discourse.

1st. WE infer that the hopes, which sinners entertain of heaven and future happiness, while remaining in an unrenewed and unsanctified condition, are entirely vain and presumptuous.

THE gospel is indeed a dispensation of mercy and free grace, proclaiming peace and pardon; and offering heaven and all its infinite blessings to sinners of every description, even the very chief; and on the most reasonable terms: But *there are* terms and conditions required, and which the gospel makes to be indispensibly necessary in order to the receiving and partaking of the grace and salvation which it reveals and offers. These are true evangelical repentance and faith which imply regenerating and sanctifying grace, or that change of heart and life which has been described. Without
this,

this, we have seen, it is impossible that sinners should enter into the kingdom of glory: or participate in the glories of that kingdom. Their hopes and expectations of heaven while destitute of the necessary qualifications must therefore be altogether vain, groundless and absurd.

2dly. WE infer that merely having a place and standing in Christ's visible church and kingdom on earth, or even a regular attendance upon its outward forms and institutions, will by no means constitute persons the real subjects of Christ, or give them a title to Heaven. We may have received the initiating seal of the covenant, and thereby be brought into the fold of Christ; we may have explicitly recognized our baptismal obligations, and in a solemn manner joined ourselves to the Lords people, and ratified our vows at his table. We may have eaten and drunken in his presence, and become familiarized with the important doctrines and instructions of his word; and yet all this while strangers at heart to sanctifying grace, we may at the same time be in the gall of bitterness and bonds of iniquity; and so utterly disqualified for the society and enjoyments of saints in the heavenly world, may be forever excluded and banished therefrom with a " Verily I say unto you I know you not."

TRUST not then to a form of godliness without experiencing the power of it on your hearts. Again,

3dly. WE learn from this subject that regeneration or conversion does not consist in those religious impressions and affections, however powerful and strong they may appear to be, which are transient and not attended and followed with good and lasting effects. It is of importance that we notice this, because too many, it is feared, deceive themselves by mistaken conceptions of the nature of true conversion; placing it in some uncommon and extraordinary workings of their own minds, or religious operations which are not thorough and saving. The mind may be greatly affected

and

and agitated both with what may be called religious fear, and religious joy; and there may be a remarkable transition from the one to the other, in the view of religious truth: The mind, I say, may be thus exercised when the heart is not really changed nor the life made better. Such sudden impressions and emotions often wear off and no good effects are produced; yet many build too much upon them, and even ground their hopes of salvation on this false foundation.

But the operations of the Divine Spirit in regeneration are productive of the most salutary effects. A real change takes place in the temper and character of the subjects; and this change is substantial and abiding, nay, the divine principle by which it is affected will grow and increase. The truly righteous and sanctified person will hold on his way and be continually acquiring new degrees of spiritual strength. His path will resemble the rising sun which shines more and more until the perfect day.

To conclude. Of how much importance is it that we all experience a real work of God's Spirit on our hearts.

How dangerous and miserable is the state and situation of carnal unsanctified men? Let such be alarmed: You have verily cause to tremble, for you are each moment exposed not only to be shut out of heaven but cast down to hell. O! Labor to see and feel the misery and danger of continuing in an unconverted condition. Rest not while in this state. Remember that however great, supernatural and divine the work of regeneration is; yet the Divine Spirit whose office it is to change and renew the hearts of men is ever ready and willing to effect this work upon all who will attend to his merciful calls, and receive his gracious influences.

The essence of conversion you have seen consists in turning from the love and practice of sin to the love and practice of holiness—in believing on the Lord Jesus fus Chrift, and conforming to the excellent requirements of his word and gofpel. All this is but a reafonable fervice. All this is plainly your duty ; and to the exercife and performance of which you are under the moft indifpenfible obligations.

To neglect this will argue the higheft ingratitude, criminality and guilt. " Repent then and be converted that your fins may be blotted out." " Turn ye, turn ye, from your evil ways, for why will ye *Die !*

SERMON X.

A BELIEF of the PECULIAR DOCTRINES of CHRISTIANITY, ESSENTIAL TO OUR ACCEPTANCE WITH GOD.

ii John 9. first clause. *Whosoever transgresseth and abideth not in the doctrine of Christ, hath not God.*

IN the primitive ages of the christian church a profession of gospel doctrine exposed our Lord's disciples to the severe reproaches and conflicts of the cross. The power and malice of Jews and Gentiles inflicted upon them the most distressing trials and persecutions. To counterbalance the evils of self denial, ignominy and martyrdom, they were furnished with inward, spiritual supports, and the joyful expectation of an heavenly reward. A mind illuminated to see the beauty of divine truth, and supported by conscious rectitude and a sincere devotion to God and the Redeemer, in addition to the hopes of a better life, were the causes which animated multitudes to a profession of the gospel.

But it is hard to account for the conduct of those, who, in that early age of the church joined themselves to the society of christians, without a due conviction of the spiritual beauty and glory of Christ, and a heart sincerely attached to him; and whose hearts and practice were repugnant to our Lord's doctrines and precepts.

cepts. Why should men void of hearts divorced from the world and its advantages, and destitute of a well founded hope of God's favour in the world of retribution, adopt a religion which teaches men to renounce this world and its vanities, and to embrace for their portion in time the vilest indignities and persecutions? Yet we learn that considerations of present ease and advantage, and the menaces of divine wrath against impostors and hypocrites did not prevent the intrusion of false brethren, deceitful workers and heretical seducers into the apostolic church. Some crept in, whose heads and hearts were essentially estranged from christian doctrine; they brought in damnable heresies, doctrines inconsistent with salvation by Christ.

HOWEVER strange these facts, they are verified by scripture testimony. Possibly the ambition of being leaders in a new sect, the splendor of miracles and the expectation of a glorious church, which they were convinced would eventually triumph, were the temptations which prevailed with so many corrupt men to attach themselves to a persecuted church.

BE this at it may, the evangelist John, the last surviving apostle, set himself vigorously to appose and counteract the evils arising from the introduction of false doctrines into the church of Christ. He has levelled the most alarming denunciations against the heretical sects which sprang up under the eyes of the inspired apostles.

AMONG other arguments to prevent the growth of heresy, our apostle has premonished his fellow christians against the numerous and subtle errors which had then arisen and should soon spring up in the christian church. He forewarned them of the ruin which would accompany the adoption of religious error and taught them in our text, that men are not at liberty to adopt false sentiments in the great articles of religion. He is a transgressor who embraces a capital error in religion. However this fault may be more aggravated in some than in others, yet there is a degree of criminality in all who imbibe false sentiments in religion, since all have the means of better information and would not be misled were not some criminal inattention or prejudice at the foundation of their unscriptural faith. This appears to be a clear maxim from our text. In treating of it I shall endeavour to establish this important sentiment: viz.

Doctrine. THAT a belief of the peculiar doctrines of christianity is essential to our acceptance with God.

WE are not to apply this proposition to infants and children incapable of understanding the gospel system. These may be saved by the merits of Christ, through sanctification of the Spirit, although they know not Jesus as the Mediator. So also may persons whose mental powers are deranged or impaired by disease or bodily habit.

OUR present enquiries are designed for the benefit of those who have heard the gospel and have opportunities to come to the knowledge of it.

SHOULD it be thought possible for heathen to be made partakers of God's saving goodness by becoming new creatures, sanctified in their affections, and by believing some doctrines, received by tradition, concerning the divine attributes of justice and mercy through some appointed atonement for sin; yet those who live under the light of the gospel cannot be saved by any such vague and general faith in God and his placability to sinners. These must sincerely adopt the christian doctrine and abide in it would they hope for acceptance with God.

FOR a better understanding of this main point we may consider the propositions following; viz.

I. THAT, there are certain peculiar and leading doctrines in the christian religion which distinguish it from all other schemes of religion and morality.

II. THAT,

II. That, thefe peculiar doctrines of chriftianity are marked with fuch light and evidence, that no man of common ability can miftake or mifapprehend them without incurring guilt upon his foul and betraying an alienation from the true God.

III. Consequently, the belief of thefe peculiar doctrines is effential to our acceptance with God.

IV. An improvement of the fubject.

1. I am to fhow, that there are certain peculiar and leading doctrines in the chriftian religion, which diftinguifh it from all other fchemes of religion and morality.

The chriftian religion is in our text denominated the doctrine of Chrift. This doctrine comprizes thofe great truths which the Father, by his Spirit, has revealed, in the holy fcriptures, concerning his Son Jefus Chrift: and alfo thofe effential truths which Chrift as a divine prophet has in the fame fcriptures revealed concerning God, a Saviour, the human race, the way in which God can be reconciled to men and men be rendered obedient to God and happy in his love. This doctrine of Chrift has a characteriftical diftinction from all other religions ever publifhed to men.

That fable and philofophy have fuggefted opinions and maxims which bear fome refemblance to chriftian doctrine will not be controverted. But fair examination will teach us, that what fabulifts and philofophers have written in conformity to the chriftian fcheme has come to their knowledge, not by the inveftigations of reafon, but through the medium of tradition or by a perufal of the facred books of Chriftians or of other books compiled from the Chriftian oracles and grounded upon them. So far as this is the cafe, they are enlightened by Chriftian doctrine and felect their opinions from it.

Examine thofe productions which have little or no affiftance from Jewifh and Chriftian revelation and you will find no fimilarity between them and our facred

fyftem

syftem of doctrine. Peruse those books which christians view as divinely inspired and you will find copious evidence to support the position, *that Christianity comprizes doctrines peculiar to itself and such as distinguish it from all other moral and religious systems.* While it assumes to be the living and only way you will perceive it to be a *new* way of access to God. Christianity claims the distinction of being different from all other religions; and as far as we admit its authority we must allow its claim to a peculiar preeminence and glory. Christians must believe the claims of scripture to be well founded and real.

But in addition to the testimony of scripture which so often and so plainly asserts the essential difference between christianity and other systems, let us establish the fact by specifying various important doctrines which are clearly taught in the christian religion and no where else.

It is peculiar to christianity to inform us of the first formation of the human race in a state of moral rectitude, possessed of the image of God and placed under a law of works, with a power and disposition to keep the law of his maker and with an assurance of endless happiness as the reward of constant obedience. No other system has justified the ways of God to men by recording his care and goodness to them in their primitive state.

Nor from any other system do we gain a probable account of the introduction of sin or moral evil into our world, and that consequent depravity and misery which are entailed upon the children of men. True it is, that reason and experience have taught men that they are guilty miserable beings; but the way in which those sad events have taken place, would have forever been involved in darkness, had not this perplexing doctrine been unravelled in the scriptures of truth.

Reason and philosophy might in some feeble degree discover the guilt and wretchedness of the human

man race, but all the inveſtigations of moraliſts and the inventions of fable would have forever failed in pointing out the method in which man could ſecurely hope to regain that favour of heaven which he had loſt. No religion but the chriſtian can make the comers to it perfect in reſpect to that light which they need for obtaining a knowledge of that ſervice and worſhip which ſhall recover ſinners to their loſt dignity and the approbation of their God.

HEATHEN idolaters have multiplied their oblations of beaſts and fruits as a ſacrifice for ſin ; yet they knew little or nothing of the origin or uſe of thoſe ſacrifices as the figures of that great atonement which the Father had appointed for the expiation of ſin and the ranſom of the guilty. The appointment of Chriſt the Son of God, to become incarnate, to obey, to ſuffer and to die in order to magnify God's law, appeaſe his juſtice and to open the door for an exerciſe of forgiving and ſaving mercy to ſinners, this is a doctrine wholly unknown to other religions and peculiar to the chriſtian. Chriſtianity alone reveals Jeſus the ſurety for ſinners and the Redeemer of God's elect. It aſſures us of what we ſhould never have learned in another way, that now God through Chriſt is reconciling the world unto himſelf, not imputing unto them their treſpaſſes.

FROM the ſame ſource of divine illumination we learn, that men are all depraved and utterly helpleſs and ruined in themſelves, wholly indiſpoſed to that faith in God and reliance on mercy, and to that holineſs of life which are indiſpenſible conditions of divine favour.

CHRISTIANITY alone informs us, how this ſcheme of redemption could be planned and executed, ſince it reveals to us that wonderful myſtery of a trinity of perſons in the unity of the godhead, ſo that from the works and paſſion of Chriſt, we ſee how our ſins can be expiated and divine attributes harmonize in our ſalvation ;

vation; and by the operations of the divine spirit, those who are dead in sin and are under the absolute dominion of their lusts are renewed and sanctified to the exercise of a pure heart and a willing subjection to the laws of Christ.

CHRISTIANITY alone enjoins the important duties of purity of heart, repentance of sin and faith in the righteousness of Christ in order to our justification before God. It teaches the unfailing faithfulness of God in maintaining the graces of his redeemed to their final salvation. It states clearly the necessity, the use and the saving fruits of regeneration, that work of God which he will never forsake. It teaches the way to grow in grace and in a preperation for heaven by fervent prayer through a redeemer, by an attendance on those ordinances and sacraments which Christ has appointed for the edification of his body the church.

CHRISTIANITY teaches us, that this world is our only school of discipline, our state of probation—that when we shall leave it our souls shall go to God to receive according to our works—that these bodies which shall moulder in the dust for so many ages, shall all revive at the last day and become unperishable and immortal bodies, and after their union to the souls from which they had been separated by death, they shall be sentenced by Christ to an endless state of blessedness or woe. These are maxims clearly revealed in the christian oracles, they are taught in no other system. Whatever other writings have supposed of these truths they are indebted to christianity for their knowledge.

THESE are not only peculiar but they are practical doctrines of essential importance to the illumination and happiness of the human mind.

I ADD only, under this head, that the practical doctrines of a heavenly mind—meekness—resignation—patience—charity and forgiveness of injuries are taught in the christian religion, in a manner and from motives
peculiar

peculiar to that religion and infinitely superior to that of all other religions or systems of morality. I proceed to observe,

II. THAT these peculiar doctrines of christianity are marked with such light and evidence, that no man of common capacity can mistake or misapprehend them without incurring guilt and betraying an alienation of mind from the true God.

THOSE who object to Christianity, its dark and incomprehensible mysteries and use them as arguments for rejecting its sacred doctrines and precepts would do well to consider, how probable it is, that in a manifestation of God and his attributes to creatures there should be many things inscrutable and beyond the reach of their finite understandings. It is enough to silence our doubts if those mysteries be not self contradictory and repugnant to reason and other doctrines of revealed truth.

WERE mystery a sufficient argument against the admission of religious doctrines, it would equally apply to destroy all our reasonings in natural philosophy.— For the laws of motion, the circulation of the blood, the union between an animal body and a rational soul are as incomprehensible as any of the most intricate doctrines of the christian religion. As well may one deny the existence of motion, the circulation of the blood, and the union of soul and body because he cannot comprehend the manner and laws of them, as deny the christian mysteries of the Trinity, the incarnation of the divine Jesus, the union of Christ and believers, and the renewing influences of the Holy Spirit. To reject all mysteries from religion or common practice, is to open the door to universal scepticism and infidelity.

ONLY reflect how infinitely God and his ways are above us and you will readily acknowledge, that you cannot reach the extent of his counsels or comprehend the mode of his existence. Meek humility will forever silence the cavils and objections which pride and infidelity, so promptly, alledge against the high and essential truths of our holy faith.

THIS also may reconcile us to christian mysteries, that we are not required to comprehend them, but, upon plain testimony, firmly, to believe them. These mysteries are not of a speculative and useless nature: They are admirably calculated to give comfort to the desponding hearts of contrite sinners; to lay for them a foundation of hope in God and to unveil to their view a wonderful plan of redemption by a vicarious sacrifice for sin, through the sanctifying operations of the Spirit of holiness. Christian mysteries explain and render consistent and glorious the great scheme of man's redemption. Set aside these mysteries and the wit and wisdom of men may labour through eternal ages and never discover a way in which the dignity of Gods government and the harmony of his attributes can accord with the pardon and salvation of offenders. As I have intimated, these christian mysteries, the trinity and unity of God, the incarnation of Jesus, the mystical union of Christ and believers, the new birth, the indwelling of the Holy Ghost in the sanctified and the resurrection of the body at the last day, are all expresly revealed in our sacred writings; they are not speculative opinions merely; they are important practical doctrines: They enkindle in the heart vigorous exercises of veneration, hope, faith, love and gratitude to God our Saviour. They amend our conduct both towards God and man. So admirable are their effects upon morals, that no ingenuous mind can fail to see an excellency and glory in these doctrines as the truths of God. So fully has God testified in their support, by miracles, by prophecy, and by providence that the untutored arrogance of reason, the vanity of human science and misleading philosophy alone can lead the mind to contest these glorious and saving mysteries of our holy faith.

LET

SER. X.   *Doctrines of Christianity.*   161

LET the candid, docile mind examine the doctrines of faith in Christ's atonement—of repentance of sin—of purity in heart—of christian mortification and self denial—of patience and meekness—of charity and forgiveness of injuries in order to find acceptance with God, and the moral sense will bear such testimony in favour of these divine sentiments as to feel it to be some guilty prejudice, some faulty passion or selfish interest which can excite us to controvert and disbelieve the great and peculiar doctrines of christianity.

Is there any authority in our holy religion? Then are we sure, that its leading sentiments are intelligible to every honest mind; they are plain to him who understandeth, that is, to him who sincerely wishes to understand and regard them. The scriptures speak of it as some essential fault and error in the hearts of men, when they are disposed to reject Christ and his doctrine. They are no less averse from the knowledge and service of God than from the obedience of Christ. For Christ is God; one with the Father; has revealed all his Father's will and nothing more. If any man love the Father, he will also love his Son Jesus Christ, and submit to him as his guide and lawgiver.

OUR text unites in this sentiment, that it is a faulty disposition which leads men into unbelief or a rejection of christian doctrine. For, saith the Apostle, " Whosoever transgresseth and abideth not in the doctrine of Christ, hath not God." The doctrine of Christ is so plain, so useful, so important, that whosoever doth not embrace and abide in it, is a transgressor and betrays a criminal mind; he neither regards nor loves God in his true and essential character. He is as much an enemy and stranger to God, as he is to the Saviour.

THEREFORE as a consequence, I observe,

III. THAT, the belief of the peculiar doctrines of christianity, is essential to our acceptance with God.

W   CHRISTIAN

CHRISTIAN revelation I shall consider as authentic proof upon the point we are now discussing. We have plenary evidence, both internal and external, that the christian oracles are divinely inspired, and are the unerring word of God. What those scriptures affirm concerning the necessity of believing the great doctrines of christianity, in order to acceptance with God and our final salvation is the most conclusive argument which can be alledged upon the subject.

THOSE scriptures make an allowance for men's doubting and even their disbelieving some truths of christianity which are of less importance. They inculcate mutual forbearance and charity in the smaller matters of faith and practice.

BUT while they give scope for the exercise of a rational liberality of sentiment and a favourable opinion of those who may differ from us; they, at the same time, alledge, that a sincere and honest heart will lead men to agree and harmonize in the distinguishing articles of our faith.

THERE is a wise medium to be observed between a narrowness of sentiment in religious matters and a latitudinarian indulgence to persons of all opinions. The former is bigotry, the latter a licencious indifference to religious doctrines, which nearly approaches to downright irreligion and impiety.

THE example and instructions of Jesus and his Apostles teach us to love men of all religions and to seek their welfare; but this we do not by allowing all their sentiments to be just and their salvation to be secure in case they sincerely believe what they profess. This kind of sincerity in error is oft times the effect of a corrupt heart and a mind powerfully opposed to God and his perfections, to Christ and his adorable excellencies. In this case the tenderest expression of love and friendship is to testify of their doctrines and their works that they are evil and tend to ruin.

This the scriptures assume as an indisputable fact,

that

that Christian doctrines are clearly revealed, easily understood by honest minds, that they are useful and necessary to God's glory and human happiness. So that if a man do not understand and approve the peculiar articles of the christian faith, it argues him to have a perverse and proud heart and that from some sinful motive and selfish interest he does not wish to know the truth nor like to retain God in his knowledge. Our Lord lays this down as an evident principle, " If any man will do his will he shall know of the doctrine whether it be of God." So that a pure and ready mind is an infallible security against a man's rejecting the essential tenets of the gospel.

THIS being a settled principle of scripture, *that gross error is a proof of moral turpitude,* let us next enquire, whether such persons can have God or whether they can enjoy his favour and approbation.

CERTAIN it is, that the word of God speaks of all men as by nature criminal and the mere objects of his displeasure and that until they pass under a total change, in regeneration, they cannot see and enjoy God. His word assures us, that we must repent and in humility become as little children, must renounce all for Christ, embrace him, and cast all our interests upon him, or we can never be justified and saved.

OUR text is explicit, " whosoever transgresseth and abideth not in the doctrine of Christ," that is, whosoever transgresseth by not abiding in the doctrine of Christ hath not God." God has good right to prescribe his own terms of restoring sinners to his love.— This way he has prescribed in the scriptures. He has told us, that this is the effectual, the only way. Whoever does not come in God's way and submit to his terms, he will infallibly cast him off.

AND does it betray no guilty pride and arrogant self conceit, for vile man to say, I will take my own way, I will follow my own counsels in order to gain divine favour and future blessedness ? Will not God be

wroth

wroth with him, who thus casts contempt upon the counsels of eternal wisdom and goodness; and refuses that Saviour whom he hath exalted to give repentance and the remission of sins? Certainly Christ Jesus is embraced as the only Saviour by every one of us, except we be reprobate from God.

To come to God without a mediator is a mad presumption. Those who make the experiment shall find, that they have rushed upon that flaming sword which turns every way to keep the way of the tree of life. Faith in Christ's righteousness, in his testimony and doctrine is the high, indispensable condition of God's favour. This faith is not merely historical and a speculative assent of the mind; it is wrought in the heart and so assents to and approves its glorious object as to produce all the blessed fruits of the spiritual and christian life. It is a faith transforming us into the very image of our dear Redeemer, or it will avail nothing to our justification.

Such faith in the merit and testimony of Christ, will be, invariably, accompanied with divine forgiveness; it will be followed by sanctification with eternal glory. But let those who speak lightly of christian doctrines, and make important differences in religious matters of no moment to man's securing the favour of his God, let such seriously reflect upon this fixed maxim of holy writ. "He who abideth not in the doctrine of Christ, hath not God," "and he who believeth not shall be damned."

IV. We come to an improvement of our subject.

Our subject teaches us, that the blessed God, in his sovereign goodness, has pointed out the only way of life to guilty, dying men. This way is through his Son whom he hath given a ransom for many. By him we are to make our approaches with humble confidence, to the throne of grace, with an assurance that we shall find acceptance.

To deter us from every false hope and pursuit of
divine

divine favour, we are assured, that if we come not in this true and living way, we shall never find a reconciled God, but shall, finally, be excluded from the heavenly inheritance.

SINCE the method of finding acceptance with God is by embracing the christian faith and abiding in it, let us reflect upon the hazardous error of those, who would reduce all systems of religion to one common level; and make the doctrines of Christ of no greater value and effect than the maxims of human philosophers and moralists; and encourage mankind in the fatal delusion, *that a sincere persuasion of the truth of any system of religion and a practice correspondent to that persuasion is all that is requisite to render men acceptable to the Supreme Being.* This sentiment originates from a criminal inattention to the instructions of God's word and from gross ignorance of the supereminent excellency of christian doctrine.

MEN are too licencious to submit to the restraints of Christian duty, and too proud to yield their judgment to the wisdom of God. And therefore they will set up their own schemes of doctrine and duty in opposition to the gospel of God our Saviour.

MUST we be holy and happy in God's appointed way? Must we be christians both in name and reality? Let us then seriously reflect upon the practical importance of embracing the truth of Christ in the love of it: Let us prudently consider the folly and danger of contesting and refusing the peculiar and distinguishing doctrines of the Christian religion.

WE may not be able to ascertain the exact degree of error in doctrine which is incompatible with a state of grace and acceptance with God. We know that men may entertain several false sentiments in religion, and yet be the true followers of Christ. And men of different powers of mind, and possessed of different advantages and opportunities of knowing the truth, may adopt different degrees of error without excluding them from acceptance with God. The same errors may be more hazardous to one man than to another. Proper allowances must be made for the weakness of human nature, the pressure of outward temptations, the byass of a corrupt education and the prejudices of preconceived opinions. We must therefore be cautious neither to concede too little, nor too much to the prepossessions of misleading customs and sentiments. But however, men may err and be in doubt as to some points of christian doctrine, yet there are leading sentiments which they must adopt and firmly believe, in order to be saved.

God in his word has revealed a system of doctrine and duties, which he has required us to believe and practise. According to his sovereign right he has prescribed the way of sinners return to himself and the terms upon which he will be at peace with them. He has assured us that we cannot make our own terms; that he will not regard or approve the will worship and services of sinners; that we must feel and confess our vile and helpless condition and be brought to rely upon the scheme of life which he hath ordained through his Son: we must chearfully subscribe to the great doctrines and duties which he hath testified to us by his Son from heaven. Will we then be so presumptuous as to hope and seek for divine favour in a way of our own invention, and upon conditions which have not received the sanction of our offended sovereign.

To rely upon a method of favour which God has not expresly pointed out and approved, would be to make a most fearful plunge in the dark, and to rest our highest interests upon conjecture and uncertainty. But when he has told us, that Christian doctrines must be believed and Christian duties practised, or he will take no pleasure in us, will utterly reject and cast us off forever; what an arrogant and mad defiance of God and his unsearchable wisdom is it in us, the offending children of men, to hope for pardon and lay claim to his

favour,

favour, while we reject many of the principal maxims of the christian faith and disbelieve the testimony of the anointed Jesus?

Shall we rebellious worms presume to come to God in a way which he has not consecrated, and expect an interest in his love upon terms which he has refused to accept? When we despise the constituted way of access to God, do we shew any reverence for his character or conformity to his will? Can he have a kind regard to us? Or we a dutiful submission to his authority? Will God lightly overlook the indignity which, by our inventions, we cast upon the counsels of his eternal wisdom, and the reproach we affix to the character of his beloved Son, our anointed Redeemer?

God hath assured us, that he will not be sought unto nor be reconciled to men, except through a mediator: That as he is one God, so there is but one mediator between God and men, the man Christ Jesus: Him he hath set up from everlasting to be a Prince and a Saviour, to give repentance with the remission of sins, that through faith in his blood we may not perish but have everlasting life. This is the testimony of the Father concerning his Son, and when we disbelieve this testimony, we make God a liar. And will God hold those in his favour, who make him a liar? Who will not submit to his king whom he hath set upon his holy hill? And who blaspheme those deep counsels of his redeeming goodness in which he has manifested himself so infinitely wiser than men?

According to his promise to the Fathers, he hath raised up unto us a prophet like unto Moses unto whom he hath commanded us to hearken. He hath given awful assurances, that the man who will not hear and obey the voice of this prophet, that soul shall be cut off from the congregation of the Lord. To this prophet, Immanuel, God with us, the Father hath given witness by a voice from heaven, by the signs and miracles which he wrought, by the unsullied purity of

his

his life and doctrines by the wonders of his death and by raising him again from the dead and receiving him up into heaven. To this prophet God hath commanded us to give heed as to a light shining in a dark place, as to the light of the world who alone hath revealed the will of his Father and the way of life to guilty men. This prophet has revealed all necessary and useful doctrines to sinners, and has made it an indispensable condition of divine favour that they embrace and continue in those doctrines. If we abide in those doctrines we do well and shall never come into condemnation; but if we deny them and lead a life repugnant to them, God has assured us, that his soul shall have no pleasure in us. He will treat us as the despisers of his grace, such impenitent sinners, such habitual transgressors and enemies to the divine character that we can never see or enjoy God; we have neither his image upon our hearts or an interest in his love. Pretend what veneration we may for God and moral duty, we remain strangers to him and to moral duty, until we adopt the christian scheme. Let us then, not only, believe christianity in general to be a good and true religion, but imbibe into our minds and hearts the great peculiar sentiments of it. Unless we imbibe the doctrine of **Christ** there can be no root of grace in our hearts nor any hope of safety in our condition. No other scheme will ever give us proper views of God or of ourselves: Nor open to us any door of access to his propitious presence.

Unless we cordially believe the peculiar doctrines of Christ, we must remain under the dominion of sin and the curse of the law; under darkness and condemnation with the world; in the gall of bitterness and in the bonds of iniquity; enemies of God and the children of that wicked one. With this guilty character can we have God?

When God has unveiled to us a way to his favour and has told us that it is the living and the only way, shall we debase this way to a level with other

schemes

schemes of religion? Shall we say, why this is a good religion but other systems may be as effectual to our safety as this? Shall we thus set up the image of Christ in the temple of the heathen Gods? Shall we arrange his inspired oracles upon the same shelf with Plato and Seneca, Confucius and Mahomet, with Hume and Shaftsbury, Paine and Volney? No! In all things let Christ have the preeminence.

If we yield not to him the honour of being our only Saviour; if we receive not his religion as the only true and saving religion, and his peculiar doctrines as worthy of our unshaken faith and essential to our salvation: If we yield not this dignity and glory to Christ and his holy doctrines we reject the Father who hath testified of him; we refuse the only door of mercy; we are ignorant of that transcendant excellency which belongs to the adorable and divine Jesus; we practically deny the Father and the Son and there is no light in us.

For this will remain a solemn truth while the Gospel is preached to sinners: It will be awfully verified when this earth and these heavens shall be dissolved. "He that believeth shall be saved and he that believ-
"eth not shall be damned."

"Now unto him that is able to keep you from
"falling, and to present you faultless before the pre-
"sence of his glory with exceeding joy, to the only
"wise God our Saviour be glory and majesty, domin-
"ion and power, both now and ever, AMEN.

SERMON XI.

TRUE CHRISTIAN CHARACTER DELINEATED.

Philippians ii. 5. *Let this mind be in you, which was also in* CHRIST JESUS.

THE apostle, in these words, improves the example of Christ, as an argument with his Philippian brethren, for their cultivating the grace of humility. An example so amiable, he doubted not would have its weight with them. Their minds had been enlightened to behold the glory of Christ—they valued him above every other object—hitherto they had regarded his will, and they were still in a situation to receive further instructions respecting it. The apostle was acquainted with their love to Christ, and had frequently been witness to the effect of his example in leading them more cheerfully to obey his precepts. He had just been exhorting them to love and union—he now exhorts them to an humble spirit and behaviour; and he is happy in availing himself of the example of Christ to inculcate upon them the exercise of a grace of so much importance.

ALL those who have been brought over to the faith of Christ, are disposed to love him. They are formed to approve of those things which he approves, and to love those things which he loves. They feel it their

their duty to cultivate the christian graces; and they find themselves strengthened and animated in their endeavours to excel in every one of them by the consideration of his example. They learn by this that every precept may be reduced to practice, and that they are not called to the exercise of any one grace but what was easy to him, and attended with pleasure.

Jesus Christ was remarkable for his humility, and was distinguished for the exercise of every virtue. Very fitly, therefore, may he be improved for an example by all who hear of him, and especially, by those who have named his name, and call themselves his disciples.

It was the case with the first christians that they exercised a temper like Christ's, and adopted his line of conduct into their practice. And as it was in their day, so it is in ours. Those who are real christians imitate Christ in his humility, and in every thing which pertains to the christian character. They are like him—have the same mind; being renewed in his image they have wrought in their hearts all those graces which appeared in his life to the greatest advantage, and—they are called to encrease in them and to abound more and more.

As the grace of humility belongs to the christian character, the words of the text might pertinently be improved to illustrate and enforce it; but as this is only a part of the character, and the object in the ensuing discourse is to delineate this character in a general view, the words will be improved as a foundation for mentioning a number of particulars in which christians have the mind, or, are like Christ.

I. They are like Christ in their love to God the Father. The bias of their minds is changed from what it has been. While disobedient and serving divers lusts, their carnal mind was enmity against God, and they liked not to retain him in their knowledge. Indeed they saw not any thing in him wherefore they should love him,

him. But love has now taken place of their enmity. Their understandings having become enlightened, and their wills and affections renewed and sanctified, they have obtained some proper conceptions of God, and love him in a measure as they ought. Those objects which before had engrossed their affections they see to have no excellence compared with the being they now love: for in their apprehension he possesses every excellence, and possesses them to an infinite degree. And this apprehension is independent of the consideration of any good he may do to them: for though they rejoice in his goodness, and love him for those displays of it in which they are themselves most immediately concerned, yet, they love him principally on account of his perfections, especially those which are moral. Hence we find, *Thou shalt love the Lord thy God with all thy heart, and with all thy soul, and with all thy mind,* (Matt. xxii. 37.) is a precept which accords with their feelings. Such beauty, such excellence, do they discover in the divine character as eclipses all other objects; and it appears to them infinitely reasonable that they should love him in the manner required. They have the example of Christ before them in this duty. Love to his Father is an affection of the heart which was very manifest in him. He loves with a perfect love. They who are like him see his example, and endeavor to act under the influence of it. Cheerfully would they love with the strength and constancy he does; but owing to their indwelling corruptions, and the strength of their spiritual enemies, they are defective in their love. They however love, and the breathings of their souls are ardent to have this love perfected.

2. They are like Christ in their cheerfulness to do the will of God. His cheerfulness was early manifest: for before his incarnation, he is represented, in view of the obedience he was to perform, as saying, *Lo, I come:—I delight to do thy will, O my God; yea thy law is within my heart.* (Ps. xl. 7, 8.) When he came

in the flesh, and entered upon his ministry, he observed to the Jews, *I came down from heaven, not to do mine own will, but the will of him that sent me.* (John vi. 38.) They had the evidence that doing the will of his Father was a matter which lay very near his heart. He entered upon his work with cheerfulness, pursued it with constancy; and, therefore, when it was accomplished he was enabled to lift up his eyes to heaven, and say, *Father, I have glorified thee on the earth: I have finished the work which thou gavest me to do.* (John xvii. 1. 4.) The disciples of Christ have learned of him; and though they are not alike perfect in their obedience, yet they perform it with cheerfulness. The law of God is his will to them—it is the very image of his heart—a transcript of the perfections of his nature. As they love God, they therefore, love his law—love to do his will. While opposed to God, they were opposed to his will, and, at variance with every thing revealed to them as their duty: but their hearts of stone are now taken away, and a heart of flesh is given them, so that the law appears differently to them from what it did formerly. They now discern its spirituality, purity and extent: and, as a thorough change has been effected upon their wills and affections, they delight themselves in the law of the Lord, and yield a willing and cheerful obedience to all its precepts. Indeed, they can do no other while feeling with the psalmist, and sweetly constrained to adopt his language, *I esteem all thy precepts concerning all things to be right; and I hate every false way.* (Ps. cxix. 128.) It is true, as they are sanctified but in part, that instances frequently occur where the obedience required of them militates against their feelings. The actings of grace at those times are feeble, but when enlivened, and the subjects of them are made more spiritual, they confer not with flesh and blood, in relation to any duty they are called to perform, however hard or difficult. They consider the will of God revealed in his law as a rule to them: and though Christ has perfectly obeyed the law, and they are to be justified by his righteousness, yet, they do not consider the law as set aside, or, their obligations to observe and keep it as in any measure weakened. The idea may sometimes enter their minds that their obligations to observe the law *are weakened* on the account of what Christ has done, but then it is an idea that they immediately reject with horror: for they are loth to view Christ as being the minister of sin, and they have no desire to be excused from a life of the most holy obedience. The authority of God is a powerful motive with them to do his will, and, another of weight, is the pleasure connected with their doing of it. As they love God they will revere his authority and endeavor to please him: and in pleasing him they will derive pleasure to themselves. Hence we find the psalmist saying, *The law of the Lord is perfect—the testimony of the Lord is sure—the statutes of the Lord are right—more to be desired are they than gold, yea, than much fine gold; sweeter also than honey, and the honey comb—moreover, in keeping of them there is great reward.* (Ps. xix. 7, 8. 10, 11.) Very few christians attain to that eminence in grace which David did, and are equally cheerful in their obedience to the divine will; and yet, all of them are cheerful in a degree, and do the will of God from the heart.

3, They are like Christ in their hatred to sin. God the Father is represented as saying to Christ his Son, *Thou hast loved righteousness, and hated iniquity.* (Heb. i. 9.) And one of the evangelists speaks of him as *looking round about on some with anger; being grieved for the hardness of their hearts.* (Mark iii. 5.) The most of mankind think they feel and exercise some hatred to sin; but sin in itself is not hated by them. The *punishment* of sin they hate, but sin is their delight, and will continue to be until they are renewed and sanctified by the spirit of God. Christ has no punishment to fear: for he knows no sin; (2 Cor. vi. 21.) neither

was

was guile ever found in his mouth. (1 Pet. ii. 22.) Neither is the hatred to sin those exercise, who have the mind of Christ, *occasioned* so much by the punishment threatened sin, as by other considerations. They are feelingly sensible to their desert of sin; but they humbly hope in the mercy of God through Christ, that they are delivered from it. Christ hates sin because it is hateful in itself—hates it because it is contrary to the purity of the divine nature, and tends to the destruction of all good. And it is on this account that real christians hate it. There are other things they hate, but they hate sin more than every thing else; especially at those times when they reflect on the great dishonor it has brought upon God; the sea of sufferings the blessed Jesus passed through on account of it; the distress it has occasioned them; and, the stores of eternal wrath it has procured for such as die impenitent. Though justified, and of the number of those who will finally be saved, yet, whenever they review their sins their hatred rises. They feel the greatest detestation against their sins whenever the eye of their minds is enlightened to see the beauty of God's holiness and the purity of his law, or, whenever they are brought suitably to reflect on the obligations they have always been under to be utterly opposed to sin, and so of course to the commission of it. They not only hate sin, but they hate sin of every kind: and though their hatred is excited principally against the sins of their own hearts and lives, which they are better acquainted with than with those of others, yet, they hate sin wherever they see it.

4. They are like Christ in their benevolence, or, good will to mankind. The rays of his benevolence like the rays of the sun shone all around him. His benevolence shone through every stage, through every scene of his life, especially in his agonies in the garden, and in the excruciating pains he endured on the cross. Indeed his benevolence hath ever been in exercise.

There were special manifestations of it while he was in the flesh; but the rays of it were seen before his incarnation, and have been abundantly since his resurrection, and ascension into heaven. This temper, this friendly disposition of heart belongs to those who act agreeably to their christian profession. (Matt. xxii. 39.) *Love thy neighbor as thyself*, is a precept which comes to them with the same authority, as, *Love the Lord thy God with all thine heart.* And they are sensible it would be folly in the extreme for them to pretend, that they exercise love to one, while they withhold it from the other. Neither would this be agreeable to their new nature: for being formed in the image of Christ, who is love, they cannot but love. And, therefore, we find that their love or good will does not rest merely in the expressions of the lips, but is expressed in benevolent acts: As they love all they do good to all, *especially unto them who are of the household of faith.* (Gal. vi. 10.) Mankind, universally, share in their affections; but it is *the excellent of the earth*, in whom they principally delight, and whose comfort and happiness they are most engaged to promote. The graces of Christ's spirit are manifest in them; and though the resemblance of Christ they exhibit is very imperfect, yet they love that resemblance. They love every thing in which Christ is to be seen. Their love is not a party love as some imagine. They love not the members of Christ merely on account of their bearing the same name with them, or, because they are united with them in the leading points of christianity, but they love them because they have the image of Christ, are members of his mystical body, and, of the number of those whom he will eternally delight to acknowledge as his friends. This love of theirs will prompt them to exert themselves in such ways as Christ hath shown are evidential of love to himself. They will feed the hungry and clothe the naked. They will communicate to them of their good things as they may need; and they will strive not only ly to make them comfortable in this world, but to be useful to them in their progress to a better.

It is said of Christ that, *Having loved his own which were in the world, he loved them unto the end.* (John xiii. 1.) The benevolence of his heart hath been wonderfully displayed towards mankind; but there are none who share his love as his followers do. How frequently in the days of his flesh, when retired from the multitude, and seated in the company of his disciples, did his whole soul go forth in love to them! And how strongly does the ardor of his affections appear when he was about to leave them and go to the Father! Indeed since his ascension, they have every evidence that his love to them is indescribably great, strong and vehement. For their sakes, in subserviency to his Father's glory and the reward he has in view, he is governing all things. He is interceding for them in heaven, and purposes speedily to receive them to himself, to be where he is, to behold his glory and be happy forever. And shall Christ love them to the degree he does and they not love one another? It is not to be supposed. Therefore we find that one evidence among others which they have of their loving Christ is the love they have one to another. (John xiii. 35.) There can be no love to God, or Christ where this love is wanting. (1 John iii. 17.)

5. They are like **Christ** in their humility. *Though he was in the form of God, and thought it not robbery to be equal with God, yet he made himself of no reputation, and took upon him the form of a servant and was made in the likeness of men, and humbled himself, and became obedient unto death, even the death of the cross.* (Philip. ii. 6, 7, 8.) The extraordinary action of Christ's in thus abasing himself is above their power to copy, but they may copy the disposition he manifested in this action of his. He was humble under all circumstances; and his humility at all times appeared to advantage, whether he was alone with his disciples, or with a large multitude.

Y

tude. How fully was this disposition acted out when he condescended to wash his disciples' feet. Nor was it less manifest at the time the air was rent with the acclamations of the multitude, crying *Hosanna to the Son of David: Blessed is he that cometh in the name of the Lord.* (Matt. xxi. 9.) Imperfectly indeed do those who are like Christ imitate him in this particular: but yet they put on humbleness of mind. A grace so excellent as this fails not to attract their attention. And though they meet with many obstructions to retard its growth and encrease, yet their constant endeavor is to grow more humble, to possess more and more of the disposition so apparent in him, whom they call their Lord and Master.

6. They are like Christ in their meekness under provocations. *When Christ was reviled, he reviled not again.* (1 Pet. ii. 23.) *As a lamb before his shearers is dumb, so opened he not his mouth.* (Acts viii. 32.) Under all the provocations, insults and abuses he received from sinners, there never was an intimation on his part, that he wished to revenge himself upon them. And, therefore we find that under the grossest provocations and abuses which he received at his trial, and upon the cross he imprecated no curse upon them, but prayed, *Father, forgive them, for they know not what they do.* (Luke xxiii. 34.) An excellent example is this for the friends of Christ to imitate. They act under the influence of it so far as they are sanctified. The occasions are frequent where they are tempted to rise into resentment under the provocations and abuses they receive. So strongly is pride interwoven in their nature (a passion surprisingly operated upon by abuse) that grace will never so thoroughly subdue it while they are in this world, but they will be in danger of returning one abuse for another. This is a weakness which they seek for grace to overcome. Sensible how easily they may be led astray they consider the example of Christ, and seek for grace to preserve them from a vice which so

easily

easily besets them. And they endeavour to keep in mind the direction of the Apostle Paul to *put off anger, wrath, malice and filthy communication; and to put on, as the elect of God, bowels of mercies, kindness, humbleness of mind, meekness, long suffering and a spirit of forgiveness.* (Colossians iii. 8. 12, 13.)

7. THEY are like Christ in their resignation to the will of God under trials and sufferings. Christ was a pattern of perfect resignation. Under circumstances more distressing than any mere human creature was ever put into, he could say, *O my Father, if this cup may not pass away from me, except I drink it, thy will be done.* (Matthew xxvi. 42.) When those, who are real christians view themselves in a just light, and have their faith strengthened to behold the wisdom, power and goodness of God, and are led to trust in his covenant faithfulness, they are willing, however trying it may be, to bear whatever God is pleased to put upon them. They know they are not their own but God's, and that he has an unquestionable right to order all events in regard to them as he pleases. Their duty to submit is past dispute with them. The hand which afflicts they verily believe will lay no more upon them than he will enable them to bear. And as he has promised that his grace shall be sufficient for them in every time of trouble, they trust the promise, and leave it with him to order their trials in those seasons and measures he sees to be best,

8. They are like Christ in their contempt of the world. The world is a good one, and fitted for their reception while passing through it. And as every creature of God is good, and, is to be received with thanksgiving, so they are to be thankful to him for the world; but they are not disposed to portion their hearts in it. There is something preferable in their view, and, therefore they treat the world comparatively with contempt. The pleasures of the world's affording are empty and transient—and not suited to their immortal minds.

minds. They, therefore, cannot but despise them.—A better good engrosses their affections. Their desires are after God as a portion; and, from the experience they have already had, they expect to find him sufficient to satisfy their wishes to the fullest extent. They have Christ for their example. While he was in the world he used the comforts of it as not abusing them; but they were not things on which he set his heart. They were light—were vain and contemptible compared with other things he had in view. He was willing to be in the world while doing the will of his Father; and when it was accomplished he was as willing to leave the world. There was not any thing in it to urge his stay longer.

9. THEY are like Christ in their hearts being in heaven. His heart—his affections, while in the flesh, were placed on things above. He loved to dwell in his thoughts upon those things which are out of the sight of mortals. This is the case with those who respect Christ, and revere his precepts and example. As their treasure is in heaven their hearts of course must be there. (Matthew vi. 21.) God and Christ are there—saints and angels are there, and there are employments that will be suited to their natures when they shall be wholly freed from sin and are made perfect in holiness. And there is the place where they are to praise and rejoice, to wonder and admire forever and ever. Though the heavenly world is invisible to them, yet faith brings down these things to the view of their mental sight. The view serves to excite and raise their affections, and dispose them more and still more to strive for the free, uninterrupted enjoyment of all the good they have in prospect.

THE limits of a single discourse will not admit of bringing into view all the particulars in which those are like Christ who make him their example. It would be easy to adduce and enlarge upon the zeal of Christ for his Father's honor (John ii. 14.) and the good of men.

(See

(See his life as recorded by the Evangelists.) His regard for the sabbath and public worship, (Luke iv. 16.) his abounding in prayer in all its forms, in public, (Luke xi. 1.) with his disciples, (Luke ix. 18.) who were his family, and in private. (Mark i. 35.) But these and other things which Christians are careful to imitate must necessarily be omitted from being particularly considered at present.

WHAT remains of the subject is some improvement.

I. How encouraging to a life of christianity is the example of Christ! The precepts of christianity are neither above, or below our nature. Different from many human theories which appear beautiful till an attempt is made to reduce them to practice, this system of precepts bears the closest examination, and opens new beauties to the mind, in proportion, as men conform themselves to it. The evidence of divine original these precepts carry in them, and their obvious tendency to refine, ennoble and make happy are arguments of great weight in favour of a life of christianity. A considerate mind views them sufficient, independent of any other: and yet, as men proceed with more resolution and cheerfulness in attempting a thing which they know has been done by another, it cannot fail of being desirable to have an example of holy living. Such an one we have to perfection in the life of Jesus Christ. Instead of leaving us in the wide field of conjectures respecting a matter of so much importance, he hath gone before us and proved to a demonstration, that it is a practicable thing to be like God and do his will. How greatly encouraging is the example of Christ, and powerfully strong does it plead with us to rise and follow him!

II. How unlike Christ are many who call themselves christians! There is something in the christian name very significant: It supposes of those who consent to be called by it that they possess the same excellent

lent spirit which was manifest in Christ, and that they walk as he walked. This must be supposed, if it is allowed that there is any significance in the name; and yet there are many called by it who have no likeness to Christ. Of these are those who profess Jesus Christ to have come in the flesh, while yet, they hold not to one half of the essentials of Christianity. And this is also the case with those who profess to believe in all the essentials of christianity, and yet are openly profane, vicious and immoral. There is, truly speaking, no propriety, in considering those to be christians, who deny the principal doctrines of christianity, though they may profess to receive as truth, some things which Christ hath taught. Neither are those to be thus considered who hold to the essentials of christianity by their profession, and yet, contradict their profession by their impious practices. Such are really infidels, or worse than infidels, as Paul intimates to Timothy, *but if any provide not for his own and specially for those of his own house, he hath denied the faith, and is worse than an infidel.* The same may be said of all who live, with allowance, in the neglect of any of the precepts of Christ's holy religion. Allowing this representation to be just, how great a proportion of those who are called christians may therefore be considered as being unlike Christ?

III. We see the gross inconsistence of those who profess to be like Christ, and yet do not follow him. There are probably those of this character in every part of the world called *christian*, and there may be reason to fear that there are some of them in every religious assembly. The inconsistence is so great that no considerate person can think it an honor to him to be guilty of it. And, therefore, it is hoped, no exceptions will be taken while an attempt is made to detect and expose it. Should any such be present, they will be pleased to suffer some plainness of speech.

You who are destitute of the meekness and gentleness

tleness of Christ—who put on anger and rise into passion at every trifling offence, how absurd is your conduct! You profess to be like Jesus Christ; to be his followers, while yet you have none of his meekness and gentleness. There is something very pleasing in a view of his conduct under trials. To see him when he was reviled, not reviling again—to see him enduring the contradiction of sinners against himself, and praying for his murderers even in the agonies of death, what sight can be more pleasing! more delightful! Is it not a shame, a scandal, a reproach to the holy name, by which you are called, to rise into angry resentment at every little offence committed against you?

You who are grasping after the world, and setting your affections on things which are seen and temporal, how widely does your conduct differ from his whom you wish to be thought to resemble! He was dead to the world and its vanities. He despised the world as heartily as you love it. Was he such as you represent him, setting his affections upon these things? Was he thoroughly engaged in laying up treasure on the earth? He was not, but just the reverse.

You who are sabbath breakers—who neglect, or carelesly attend upon the duties of the sanctuary, are you not chargeable with the grossest inconsistence?—Christ did not thus; and yet you profess to be like him. Do you not know that Jesus Christ had a sacred regard to the sabbath—that he loved the places where God has recorded his name. And that he manifested a great regard to the duties of public worship by a constant and careful attendance upon them? And do you not know that he left his example for you, and that he requires you to do as he has done?

Ye who are so swallowed up in self that you care little about the honor of God or the good of your fellow men, so be that your own interest is advanced, how little of the christian do you exercise and manifest! What a lying profession do you make when you profess

to

to be like Chrift—like him who flamed with inextinguifhable ardor for the glory of God and the good of mankind! It is one of the groffeft inconfiftencies conceivable to pretend that you are like Chrift, and have his mind while *you are living to yourfelves.*

YE who are profane—are intemperate—are formalifts in religion—in a word, all of you who are not in heart and life really like Jefus Chrift, are you not guilty of the groffeft inconfiftence? You profefs to believe that one end of Chrift's coming into the world was *to deliver his people from all iniquity,* while yet you run into it with greedinefs. You have chofen him for your example, and yet you are not careful to copy him in a fingle particular. Certainly you are chargeable with great inconfiftence. It becomes you therefore to take fhame to yourfelves, and humbly look to God, through Jefus Chrift, to difpofe and enable you in future to live agreeably to your profeffion and engagements.

IV. WHAT has been faid may be improved for matter of humiliation to all chriftians. However they are like Chrift—and with propriety may be faid to have his mind, yet, they are by no means fo fully like Chrift as they ought to be. Let thofe of you who are chriftians, for a moment, think what you profefs to be, and what you are bound to be by your profeffion. O how meek—how humble—how dead to the world—how alive in his affections towards heaven—how zealous—how indefatigable in God's fervice, and for his honor and the good of mankind was he whom you acknowledge your Lord and mafter! When you confider him, who is the high prieft of your profeffion, can you help reflecting how holily you ought to walk; and can you at the fame time, fail, of being deeply humbled under a fenfe how exceedingly you have fallen fhort of his example? Certainly the very beft of you have abundant caufe for deep humiliation.

V. BE

V. Be exhorted therefore to make it your principal concern to be what you profess yourselves to be. Dread nothing so much as dishonouring Christ by a life of unlikeness to him. Keep ever in your view the amiable pattern Jesus Christ has set before you. In that you may see what you ought to be. While you love God—are zealous for his honor—cheerfully do his will—love all men—are patient under injuries—submissive to the divine allotments—are weaned from the world, and are heavenly in your affections, you will advance the glory of God, the honor of the Redeemer, serve the cause of truth and be eminently useful in your generation. And this will be for your comfort in this world, and for your everlasting advantage in the world to come. Sensible of your need of divine influence to enable you to be more like Christ—be exhorted with frequency and fervency to ply the throne of grace that you may have large measures of the spirit of Christ; and see that you carefully improve every mean appointed for the purpose. In this way you may hope to adorn your profession, and to be to the honor and praise of him, who hath loved you and washed you from your sins in his own blood, and hath made you kings and priests unto God and his Father; to him be glory and dominion forever and ever. *Amen.*

SERMON XII.

OF LIVING UNDER THE EYE OF GOD.

PSALM XVI. 8. *I have set the Lord always before me.*

THESE words with what follow in this psalm have ultimate respect to Christ. Some expressions the psalmist uses can be true of none but him; particularly those in the tenth verse; "Thou wilt not leave my soul in hell," or the grave; "neither wilt thou suffer thine holy One to see corruption." David here speaks in the name of the Messiah, of whom he was an eminent type: and the words contain a plain prediction of the speedy resurrection of the Son of God from the dead. Thus are they explained and applied in the New Testament, where we find our text, and the passage with which it is connected, cited at large. (Acts ii. 25. and xiii. 36.

THE words of our text, therefore, as applied to the Saviour, must speak the special presence of his Father with him in his mediatorial undertaking. But these words may likewise, with propriety, be applied to christians, who are the members of Christ, and animated by the same spirit. "I have set the Lord always before me." The pious sentiment here expressed, may and should be adopted by every christian.

To

To set the Lord always before us, means, in general, the living under the immediate eye and inspection of God. To do this, is both our wisdom and happiness.

WHAT is proposed in this discourse is to shew what is implied in such a life; and what are the advantages that will result from it.

First, LET us enquire what is implied and signified in a person's living constantly as in the presence, and under the inspection of the great God. This implies,

1. A BELIEF of the divine Omnipresence. That the God with whom we have to do is every where; that he filleth immensity, and cannot be circumscribed by place or time; but in respect of his being and essence is equally and always in every part of the universe; that the heaven of heavens cannot contain him, and no place can either include or exclude his presence; therefore there is no creature that is not manifest before him, but all things are naked and open to his all-comprehending view.

2. THE living under the eye of God, or setting the Lord always before us, implies not merely a speculative belief of the divine ubiquity; but a realizing, feeling sense of this important truth, and with a special application to ourselves. The devout christian believeth and is deeply impressed with the belief that the omnipresent God is really present with *him*. He can heartily adopt that pious sentiment expressed by Sarah's maid; "Thou God seest me;" or can join in the more full and explicit language of David in the 139th psalm; "O! Lord thou hast searched me and known me; thou knowest my downsitting and mine uprising; thou compassest my path, and art acquainted with all my ways; thou hast beset me behind and before and laid thy hand upon me. Whither shall I go from thy Spirit? or whither shall I flee from thy presence? If I ascend up into heaven thou art there; If I make my bed in hell, behold thou art there; if I take the wings of the morning

ing and dwell in the uttermost parts of the sea, even there shall thy hand lead me and thy right hand shall hold me."

The views of one who lives under the eye of God, are totally different from those foolish and mistaken people, who conceive of the supreme Being as absent, and at a vast distance from them; having his residence far beyond the height of the visible heavens; and that the clouds are a thick veil through which his piercing eye cannot penetrate. The believer, on the contrary, though he considers, the heaven of heavens as God's throne, where he makes peculiar manifestations of himself; yet is he far from supposing the most High to be confined by local situation, but believes that his essential presence and inspection extends as much to earth as heaven: that though the celestial spirits are blessed with clearer views, and brighter discoveries of his ineffable glory; yet the creatures of this lower world are also within his ken, and the subjects of his providential care and munificence.

If the great God is every where, he must, of consequence, know all things: his knowledge, doubtless, coextends with his presence; and a realizing belief,

3. Of the divine Omniscience is implied in the character we are considering. He who lives under the eye of God, is conscious that his glorious Maker and Judge is privy to his whole conduct; that he perfectly knows and particularly notices not only all his actions, but the secret springs by which they are moved, and the inward motives by which they are excited.

The scriptures every where represent God not only as an all-seeing, but an all-knowing Being. He is revealed and described as a " God of knowledge by whom actions are weighed;" and whose prerogative alone it is to search and know the hearts of the children of men. It is declared, that " the Lord seeth not as man seeth, for man looketh at the outward appearance, but the Lord looketh on the heart." (1 Sam. xvi. 7.)

xvi. 7.) "His eye, faith holy Job, feeth every precious thing; he underftandeth the way thereof, and he knoweth the place thereof: for he looketh to the ends of the earth, and feeth under the whole heaven." (Job. xxviii. 10. xxiii. 24.) And again, "He revealeth the deep and fecret things; he knoweth what is in the darknefs and the light dwelleth with him." (Chap. xii. 22.) "Woe unto them, faith the Prophet, "who feek deep to hide their counfel from the Lord, and fay, who feeth us, who knoweth us?" (Ifai. xxix. 15.) Am I a God at hand faith the Lord, and not a God afar off? Can any hide himfelf in fecret places that I fhall not fee him; do not I fill heaven and earth?" (Jer. xxiv. 23, 24.) Chrift taught his difciples to pray to their Father who feeth in fecret. (Matt. vi. 4.) And to mention no more; the apoftle affirms, that known unto God are all his works from the foundation of the world. (Acts xv. 18.) The important truth declared in thefe and many other fimilar texts is in a good meafure realized by the pious chriftian. He fets God before him as one who is perfectly acquainted with him, and with every thing that concerns him; that there is no action of his life, no word of his tongue, nor even a fingle thought of his heart that can efcape his notice; that God "knows the things which come into his mind every one of them," and therefore he muft obferve, not only the internal pious exercifes of his heart; but his fecret fins are likewife in the light of his countenance. Nor doth he confider God as an unconcerned fpectator of his conduct; but that he takes particular cognizance of it as a Father and a Judge; approves or difapproves, is pleafed or difpleafed, according to the moral quality of it: hence I obferve,

4. ONE who lives under the eye of God is impreffed with a believing fenfe of his accountablenefs to him for all his conduct. He fets the Lord before him, not only as his Creator, heavenly Benefactor and Friend, to whom he is under infinite obligations; but

as

as his divine Lord and Judge to whom he is amenable, and before whose tremendous bar he must shortly stand; acquitted or condemned; therefore he will be deeply concerned, that his conduct and behaviour be such, as, through the merits and grace of the Redeemer, he may finallly meet the divine approbation and acceptance. I add once more,

5. THE character and life we are describing, implies a life of piety and devotion. He who lives under the eye of God and sets the Lord ever before him, is continually seeking and aspiring after a more intimate acquaintance with his glorious Maker and Redeemer, and endeavours to maintain and keep up a spiritual intercourse and communion with him in and by those means and ordinances which he hath appointed.

HE will diligently and daily attend to the holy scriptures to learn from thence more of the character of God; and his own character and duty. His mind will be much employed in serious and devout contemplations on the being, attributes and works of God: He often retires from the world and its concerns, for the purpose of religious meditation and prayer; and converses much with the Deity in these spiritual and holy exercises. In short the christian who possesses the temper, and lives the life expressed in my text, and which we attempt to illustrate and recommend—such an one maintains a close walk with God; lives in his fear every day, is habitually disposed to and takes peculiar satisfaction and delight in the practice of universal piety and Godliness.

AND thus by a natural transition we pass on, as was proposed,

2dly, To point out some of the important advantages resulting from such a life; or shew the salutary influence and effect the living under the eye of God will produce.

I. SUCH a sense of God as is implied in this, will excite in our minds holy fear and reverence. A view of
God

God in his real character as a being of infinite majesty, holiness and glory, and at the same time a realizing apprehension that we are always in the presence and under the immediate inspection of this dread being, will certainly tend to give an habitual seriousness and solemnity to our minds; yea this belief of the omnipresence of Jehovah will convey a sort of solemnity and sacredness to the places and objects around us. With good Jacob at Bethel we should cry out, surely the Lord is here; how dreadful is this place! This is none other than the house of God, and this is the gate of heaven.

Had we a constant realizing sense of the divine presence and glory, every place would become a Bethel, and each spot on which we stand would be consecrated ground.

II. A sense of God as present with us, and the living under his holy eye and inspection, will tend to produce deep humiliation and repentance. For this implies, as we have seen, a realizing belief of the perfect knowledge, that God hath, and the exact cognizance which he takes of all our real character and conduct; that he knows all our foolishness; beholds the deep and dreadful corruption, deceit, and wickedness of our hearts, as well as the sinfulness of our lives.

Now a believing view and consideration of the infinitely pure and holy God as seeing all our vileness by nature and practice; as being present and privy to all our impure and sinful thoughts, words, and actions; will tend to abase us in his presence, and fill us with shame and confusion of face; for hereby we shall be led to draw a comparison between the infinite purity and perfection of God, and our own exceeding vileness, and nothingness. From that clear view which Job had of the divine presence and purity, he was constrained to break out into the following penitential confession; " I have heard of thee by the hearing of the ear; but now mine eye seeth thee, wherefore I abhor myself,

and

and repent in duſt and aſhes." The like divine maniſeſtations produced, ſimilar effects in the mind of the prophet Iſaiah. "Then ſaid I, woe is me, for I am a man of unclean lips: for mine eyes have ſeen the king, the Lord of hoſts."

A REAL ſight of God as *he is*, perfectly ſpotleſs; tranſcendently great and glorious; and a believing ſenſe of this infinitely pure and majeſtic being, as preſent before us, and looking down upon us, will bring us to view ourſelves *as we are*, poor, impotent, vile, and worthleſs creatures; and this, while it excites high and exalted thoughts of God, will, at the ſame time, produce humbling abaſing thoughts of ourſelves.

That generation who are pure in their own eyes, though not waſhed from their filthineſs, have never truly ſeen and known, either their Maker, or themſelves.

III. The living under God's eye, and a realizing view of his preſence and inſpection, will have a powerful influence to reſtrain from ſin.

Those who are poſſeſſed of a conſtant and lively ſenſe of God and religion on their minds, will be careful to avoid and guard againſt every thing which they know to be diſpleaſing in his ſight. It was this principle, deeply impreſſed on his mind, that ſo effectually reſtrained good Joſeph when violently aſſaulted.— "How, ſaid the pious youth, can I do this great wickedneſs and ſin againſt God."

He was alone with his tempter, the foul act would be wholly concealed from the view of men; but he knew and felt himſelf to be in the preſence of an holy God, and that his all-ſeeing eye was upon him.— This conſideration, joined with a ſenſe of the turpitude of the crime, fortified his heart, and enabled him to repel the temptation. But thoſe who have no ſenſe of the evil of ſin and the omnipreſence of an holy God, are not aſhamed or afraid to commit wickedneſs, eſpecially in ſecret.

That

THAT which more than almost any thing else encourages and emboldens people in their impious ways, is a stupid insensibility and disbelief of the being and presence and purity of God. A vain imagination which they secretly foster in their breasts, that either there is no God, or that he does not see and observe them.

"THE fool in his heart hath said there is no God," it follows, "they are corrupt; they have done abominable works.

To such infidel wretches as these, who say, "the Lord shall not see, neither shall the God of Jacob regard it;" may that pungent expostulation, in the 94th Psalm be pertinently addressed; "understand ye brutish among the people, and ye fools when will ye be wise? He that planted the ear shall he not hear? He that formed the eye shall not he see? He that chastiseth the heathen shall not he correct? He that teacheth man knowledge shall not he know? Again,

IV. A CONSTANT believing apprehension of the divine presence and inspection will not only restrain from the commission of sin; but it will be a strong incitement to a religious and holy practice. The due consideration and belief that God's omniscient eye is ever upon us will serve, through the influences of his spirit and grace, to beget and increase that holy, filial fear of him which is the beginning of wisdom: that implies both the principle and practice of true religion. For to have the fear of God in the heart and to live under its influence is a scriptural description of a truly religious, obediential walk and conversation. And to such an holy life will those be influenced who, in the sense we have explained, "set the Lord always before them."

WILL not those who believe and realize that God Almighty, the great and holy God on whom they constantly depend and to whom they are accountable; that this glorious and dread being is present with them as a strict and impartial observer of their whole conduct;

as well the internal exercises of their hearts, as their outward behaviour; will not the view and consideration of all this have a constraining power and efficacy to excite them to endeavour after a rectitude of temper and practice? Will it not influence them to great watchfulness and circumspection; and to see that their thoughts, words and actions, be such as are pleasing in God's sight and which he will approve and accept? But finding, as they must, by comparing their hearts and lives with the absolute perfection of the divine character and requirements, that their best exercises and performances, fall far short of a due correspondence to the perfect purity of God's nature and law, will they not at the same time be induced to repair to the blood of Christ for pardon and cleansing, trusting in him alone for righteousness, strength and salvation? I observe once more,

V. If we live under God's eye and set the Lord always before us in the manner explained; this will conduce to true peace, comfort and security. Surely it must be a most blessed and happy thing to a pious soul to have God before him, and to believe and know that he is present with him as his heavenly Father and Almighty Friend; one who is both able and ready to help and succour, deliver and save, those who trust in him. With what holy confidence and triumph will such lively views of God inspire the believer. "I have set the Lord always before me;" it follows, "because he is at my right hand I shall not be moved; therefore my heart is glad, and my glory rejoiceth! Such an one dwelleth," as the Scriptures speak, "in the secret place of the most high, and resides under the shadow of the Almighty;" "the place of his defence is the munitions of rocks." The Lord of the universe being present with him and on his side, who can be against him to disturb or harm him? God is our refuge and strength, a very present help in trouble; therefore will not we fear?

These

These are some of the advantages and happy consequences of possessing the character and living the life we have described.

And from what has been observed on this subject concerning the nature of such a character and life we are led to see,

I. That carnal unbelieving men are utter strangers to it, and therefore their state is very unhappy and dangerous. Not to live under God's eye—not to possess believing views and apprehensions of his universal presence, inspection and providence, implies a heart void of religion. Those who are destitute of a sense of their Maker on their minds, do live, as the scripture expresses it, "without God in the world," that is, they live and act as if there was no God to see them; no being to whom they are accountable for all their conduct; no Almighty Judge to arraign and punish guilty offenders.

These inconsiderate foolish people, instead of setting the Lord before them, do set him at a distance from them; they say the Lord doth not see, neither doth the God of Jacob observe it. The language of their unbelieving hearts and irreligious practice, is to the Almighty; depart from us for we desire not the knowledge of thy ways.

But though you do not in the sense we have considered, set the Lord always before you; though you are strangers to those pious sentiments and holy affections which are implied in living under God's eye and in his fear; yet you must know that nevertheless the great God is not far from any of you. It is in him that you constantly live and have your being. He is ever present before you and his omniscient eye is always upon you; nor is it possible that you should get one moment from under his holy inspection, or escape from his dreadful presence. He is perfectly acquainted with your whole character; he has been an eye witness of all your behaviour. Your secret sins are in the light of his countenance; and these are recorded in the book of his remembrance.

membrance. You are to know likewise, that this great Almighty, omniscient and holy God is angry with you. By your numerous and heinous sins you have incensed his displeasure, and are continually exposed to the tremendous effects of his wrath. And remember moreover that you are not only under his eye, but in his hand and there is no power that can take you out of his hand.

Now consider this, ye that forget God, left he tear you in pieces and there be none to deliver.

II. From what we have heard of the beneficial and happy effects accruing to the godly from the constant practice of the duty explained and recommended; let us be induced to live in the practice of it. Let us endeavour to maintain and keep up an habitual sense of the great God as every where present, whose eyes are on the ways of men, who searches their hearts and tries their thoughts. Let us believe this truth with special application to ourselves and keep it in the imagination of the thoughts of our hearts continually, that this great and glorious being sees and knows us, and that we must shortly be called to render an account to him of all our conduct. Let us set this omnipresent Lord before us as our God and Judge, as our heavenly Father and Almighty friend.

Such believing views as these will be attended with the most blessed effects; they will inspire a principle of love and reverence for the character of God; we shall be filled with a humble awe of his sacred majesty: we shall be hereby restrained and kept back from acts of iniquity; from what is displeasing in God's sight; on the contrary we shall be constrained to walk in his ways; and to strive to regulate our temper and conduct according to his will, and so as finally through the merits of Christ to obtain the divine approbation, and receive the rewards of good and faithful servants.

SERMON

PSALM xvi. 3. *But to the saints that are in the Earth, and to the excellent, in whom is all my delight.*

THIS pfalm is called *Michtam of David.* From which title fome have inferred the exceeding value of the matter which it contains. Though the remark may be applicable to this particular pfalm, as it treats partly of the temper of Chrift, his protection, his death, his certain and early refurrection, his complete enjoyment of his Father and the tranfcendant happinefs of his condition, (which, with chriftians, are very precious fubjects of meditation,) yet it fails in its general application : as a candid and careful examination of the 56, 57, 58, 59, and 60 pfalms will convince every reader : to which no very peculiar excellency is attached. It may refer to the mufic ; which, with its peculiar ufe in thefe inftances, may ever be unknown to us. Had the knowledge been material it would have been handed entire to the lateft ages of the church. It not being confonant with divine goodnefs that information which is ufeful at leaft needful for their faith and comfort fhould be loft or withheld from his people. Of fuch information God muft be an unerring, and, of courfe, the beft judge. Let not

this

this ignorance then produce much regret. This pfalm hath a twofold reference: To David and to Chrift. Or if we refer it only to David he muft be viewed both as a faint and as a type of Chrift. Some parts of it cannot hold of him as a faint. The latter part is exprefsly applied to Chrift in the fecond and thirteenth chapters of the Acts. The firft part may ftrictly and literally apply to David as a pious man. In the firft verfe he requefts or expects or modeftly requires fecurity from fome overwhelming evils. The requeft or expectation or demand being built upon his confidence in the word of God. *Preferve me, O God: for in thee do I put my truft.* As if he had faid; I know myfelf, my enemies and God. I know my own weaknefs, the fubtilty and malice of my enemies and the character of God. What he has done for me I gratefully recollect. What he can do for me I devoutly acknowledge. Experience recommends what his word enjoins. What neceffity requires wifdom fuggefts. Duty and intereft are intimately joined. His will and my choice harmonize. I muft truft in him; I do truft in him; I will truft in him; I defire to truft in him for he is willing and able to preferve me. This purpofe and choice do not originate in a fuppofition, which feeds pride, that, though pleafing, they will be profitable to God; that, though I fhall effentially benefit and honor myfelf, I fhall bring him under fpecial obligation to me. *O my foul, thou haft faid unto the Lord, thou art my Lord: my goodnefs extendeth not to thee.* Ver. 2. He addreffes his own foul in folemn converfe as he would a neighbor. Such addreffes are not unufual nor improper. This work was familiar to him. *Thou haft faid unto the Lord, thou art my Lord.* What thou haft faid that God is thy creator, owner and difpofer, thou doft now fay, thou wilt never recall and deny what thou haft faid. The declaration muft continue a truth. This truth abides forever. *My goodnefs extendeth not to thee.* God is independent. He hath in himfelf all perfection. He is the inexhauft-
ible

ible fountain of his own infinite happiness. If I have inward goodness it is the work of his spirit. If I have led a life of religion strength has been continually communicated to me from God. From him *cometh every good and every perfect gift*. The exercises of piety may have contributed to the advantages of others, but not to God. It is no gain to him that I trust in him; though it is to myself. It is no profit to him if I distribute what I have freely received. If others bless me, and praise him for my existence, and wealth, liberality or example, yet for the whole I am indebted to him. *No one hath first given to him, and it shall be recompensed to him again. For of him, and through him, and to him are all things.* Rom. xi. While these declarations proclaim his greatness and fulness, they remind us of our place: teach our dependence and remonstrate against pride.

But to the saints that are in the earth, and to the excellent, in whom is all my delight. The former declaration was negative: this is positive. The exclusion is not universal. God is excluded, but fellow creatures are not. Though he could not be profitable to him, he might be and was to them. He exercised and manifested his sincere regard towards those who bore a spiritual resemblance to their heavenly Father; were transformed by the renovation of their minds and hearts: this moral and encreasing and everlasting excellence was the special ground of his esteem and delight. The effect likely answered to the producing cause. According to the perception of this moral resemblance to God, which constituted their chief excellence, were his delight and joy in their society. Though he and all of the same character then and now extend their benevolence to all men; wishing them well, seeking and advancing, as they have opportunity, both their present and future, their temporal and spiritual interest, yet their complacency is obviously and necessarily more restricted than their benevolence: to them who love and

please

pleafe and refemble **God.** Hence the pfalmift **calls** them *the excellent of the earth.* The honorable, the noble, the worthy, the amiable, the ufeful of mankind—diftinguifhingly, confpicuoufly fo. Such heaven born **fouls** he highly efteemed—he ardently loved them, he longed after **frequent,** clofe and lafting communion with them, and cherifhed genuine **gratitude** to God for their holy endowment**s**, for **opportunities of intercourfe** and for the manifold advantages refulting to himfelf from it.

By calling them *excellent* he might intend to diftinguifh **between** them and the mafs of mankind ; that were then idolaters, and now **are** ftrangers and **enemies** to God. He might **oppofe his** veneration **and efteem** to the **ridicule** and contempt of the world. While they **calumniated** and neglected and rejected them from their **fociety ;** he honored them, delighted in them and readily **affociated with** them. As **he** loved God fupremely, he muft love **thofe** who are **born** of God : As he affiduoufly fought and habitually maintained **communion** with **God fo he** would, if practicable, feek **and maintain** communion with his fincere friends : As he defired nearer conformity to God, he **would** unaavoidably ufe the fitteft **means to** promote it ; this mean of the communion of **faints belongs** to that defcription ; would at once be **chofen** and applied for that purpofe. The opinion and practice **of** David **have** been juftified **and followed** by the generation **of the** Lord's people. Though the mutual in**tercourfe of** chriftians is peculiarly pleafing and beneficial to themfelves ; it is ftill advantageous to **others ;** would be **in** the higheft degree if wifely improved by them. There is **nothing** in the nature **of** religious fociety which **narrows** and confines its advantages to a few. Multitudes may partake largely in them : all, if difpofed, may partake in them without **reft**raint and interruption.

WHAT is now further propofed is, To defcribe and illuftrate the nature and advantages, the pleafures and obligations of **pious fociety.**

I. A VIEW

I. A VIEW of its nature.

IT is founded upon the importance and excellence of evangelical sentiments, holy dispositions, growing moral attainments, religious pursuits, and spiritual interests.

IT is founded upon the constitution of **man**: He being evidently intended **and admirably** fitted by his mental powers, his social affections, his needs and circumstances for society.

IT is founded upon his exposedness, unless enlightened by the word, protected by the grace and assisted by the friends of God, to overlook his highest good, to plunge into sin, and live and perish in it.

IN seeking intercourse with those who love God, and who, as the fruit and evidence of it, keep his commandments, it is now supposed that persons admit the truth and importance of the Christian religion: That they desire to be more acquainted with it, and more firmly established in it.

THAT they believe the suitableness of such conduct; its probable tendency to produce those effects: That there is an encouraging prospect of success presented before them.

THAT they discern a difference of character among their fellow creatures; all not being entitled to the same respect: A promiscuous connexion with them and an indiscriminate regard to them, are not judicious and useful: That they have a predilection for the professed and practical friends of Christ.

THAT they esteem them for their christian knowledge, spirit and practice. They appear honorable to them. As they think well, they also speak respectfully of them; are pleased when others bestow a tribute of respect upon them; and are grieved and offended when reproach is cast upon them by the unthinking and licencious and impious.

THIS intercourse naturally implies that we converse

verse plainly and seriously with the Saints—use freedom with them—open our hearts to them—state our views, difficulties, snares, dangers and burdens to them, and desire and expect the assistance of wisdom and love.

It not improperly supposes that to some particular christians we open ourselves without reserve and reluctance, put much confidence in them, and admit them to the largest share of our friendship and intimacy, and entrust them with all our spiritual concerns.

WHEN this intercourse is most unreservedly maintained it implies a similar cast of religious character:— That we ourselves are subjects of the grace of Christ: Are partakers of the divine nature, recipients of like spiritual blessings, and expectants of the same eternal mercies: That we walk by the same rules, mind the same things, confide in the same righteousness, depend upon the same strength, and live upon the same fulness.— This cast is supposable and unavoidable, *For can two walk together except they are agreed?* Amos iii. 3. *What communion hath light with darkness? What fellowship hath righteousness with unrighteousness? What concord hath Christ with Belial? What part hath he that believeth with an infidel?* 2 Corinthians vi. 14, 15. The only solid and effectual basis of union and communion must unquestionably be laid deep in a similarity of temper and life: A temper wrought by the spirit of holiness, and a life correspondent with the Gospel of Christ.

It is very evident that this intercourse primarily if not wholly respects the things of the kingdom of God; the weighty concerns of religion and of our own souls and the everlasting welfare of mankind.

II. WE propose to notice the advantages and pleasures of pious society.

1. THESE result from the nature of religious subjects and concerns. They must, beyond all others, be important and interesting, vast and wonderful, beneficial and delightful to renewed hearts. Renewed or not their

their intrinsic importance and relative interest to every one cannot be diminished. The being and perfections, the providence and government of God, the mediation of Christ, and the special influences of the spirit, the immortality of the soul, and a state of retribution are doctrines which form the most prominent features of our religion. These carry their own importance with them. A sober and steady view must impress it deeply upon the mind. In proportion as they are examined, believed, and realized will their importance collect strength and fall with their ponderous weight upon the heart. Habitual meditation and conversation upon these and other gospel subjects and duties, with those who study them, and love them, will strengthen rational impressions, promote inquiry, encrease mutual acquaintance, and further a life of religion.

What a being is the Most High God? The inexhaustible and infinite fountain of existence, activity, perfection and enjoyment. Who fills with his presence heaven and earth: Who upholds and animates the natural, intellectual and moral creation: Who diffuses his influence through immensity: Who guides, controls and disposes of all classes of his creatures and existences from the smallest mote, which plays in a sun beam, to the highest rank of heavenly principalities: Who governs all by laws suited to all the diversities of powers and situations: Who knoweth the end from the beginning, accomplishes his purposes and obtains his ends with and without the knowledge, and contrary to the designs and expectations of men; furnishing instruments for his work at pleasure, and employing the most unpromising means and events with ease and honor to effect essential good to mankind; taking the wise in their own craftiness, rebuking the proud, weakening the mighty, confounding the wicked—making the wrath of men praise him, preserving and rewarding the upright and establishing his church by the ruin of other kingdoms powerful and ancient

cient. *Great is the Lord, and greatly to be feared, and greatly to be praised. The works of the Lord are great, sought out of all them that have pleasure therein. His work is honourable and glorious: and his righteousness endureth forever. The works of his hands are verity and judgment. He hath made his wonderful works to be remembered: The Lord is gracious and full of compassion. His praise endureth forever. And his truth endureth to all generations.* It must be profitable to converse frequently and seriously upon the character and works of an infinite God with those who worship and love him. Our understandings will expand, our hearts glow with devotion and confidence: Religion and, with it, as an usual and a natural attendant, peace will flourish in our souls: Moral light and moral joy will thrive in that soil which grace cultivates and enriches.

WHAT a glorious and divine person is the Lord Jesus Christ! What a suitable, what an interesting, what an useful and delightful object of contemplation and conversation! He is the brightness of the Father's glory, and the express image of his person. (Heb. i. 2.) The mighty God, the everlasting Father, the wonderful counsellor, the Prince of Peace, the Lord of Glory, the sun of righteousness, the light of the Gentiles, the salvation of the ends of the earth, the desire of all nations, the foundation and head of the Church, the fulness of him who filleth all in all, the disinterested procurer of all good to men, the author and finisher of our faith, the source of our hopes, the medium of acceptable and perpetual intercourse with the Father, and the bestower of a far more exceeding and an eternal weight of glory. How beneficial must it be to converse with his friends upon his dignity, his divinity, his design, his work, and his accomplishment of it, and the immense blessings, the fruit of it? How delightfully in such society may we dwell upon such subjects! Upon love which is unspeakable—upon mercy which passes knowledge—upon riches of grace which raise the

admiration

admiration of angels, which will become the subject of wonder, and contemplation, of praise and joy forever. Pious conversation upon the discoveries and glories of the gospel is adapted to strengthen faith, animate hope, enliven gratitude and constrain to obedience.

What a wonderfully gracious and wise, and holy being is the divine Spirit! Most excellent and desirable is that work of grace, which the sacred Scriptures ascribe to him in its beginning, encrease, preservation and completion. Begun in regeneration, advanced in sanctification and finished in a perfect moral likeness to God in heaven. His operations are illuminating as the light; piercing as a two edged sword; his influences are chearing as the spring, refreshing as the mildest dews, beneficent as the former and latter rain, nourishing as the most healthful food, essential as the principle of natural life: His graces are fragrant as the rose, and delicious as the richest fruit, sweeter than the sweetest **spices,** and more beautiful than Eden itself. *Covet* **earnestly** *the best gifts: Yet shew I unto you a more excellent way,* (1 Corin. xii. 31.) To this Apostolic instruction and declaration succeeds a just and rapturous description of that *charity which never faileth: Which hopeth, believeth, beareth and endureth all things.—* (1 Cor. 13.) How useful and pleasing must it be to converse upon that variety observable in divine operations? To relate the wisdom and grace, the sovereignty and efficacy of the Spirit's influences discovered in arresting, reforming and converting sinners? Religious conversation upon these important subjects will tend directly to enlarge our knowledge, remove doubts, excite our wonder, strengthen brotherly love and aid devotion and promote spiritual peace.

An animating and delightful subject of consideration and conversation is the immortality of the soul. While the modern philosophy of annihilation after this life blasts our hopes and benumbs our exertions and contracts our views and debases our dignity, the contrary scripture doctrine

doctrine of a future and an everlasting existence stamps a singular value upon our rational nature, wakes into vigorous action all the hidden energies of the soul, inspires with hope, and impels to habitual improvement and eminence in knowledge and holiness. Conversing freely with those who believe and exemplify this truth, will serve to heighten our respect for ourselves and for others, to convince us of the transcendent worth of the soul, establish our faith and encourage us in the discharge of our universal duty. In this way pious intercourse will conduce to our advantage and delight.

THE *retributions of the final judgment may profitably employ our conversation when with the saints.*

THOUGH some never mention the day of judgment and the consequences of that solemn season to all living, nor think much and seriously about them; tho' some deny them, and though some still bolder and more impious ridicule them, yet the word of God abides firm: Which declares, *that we shall all stand before the judgment seat of Christ. So then every one of us must give an account of himself to God. For God shall bring every work into judgment, with every secret thing, whether it be good, or whether it be evil.* (Rom. xiv. 10, 12. Ecclesiastes xii. 14.) To converse without reserve upon these subjects with those who venerate the oracles of God tends to solemnize the soul, to check levity, to restrain from secret sins, to strengthen vigilance, to prompt to the closest self inspection and a course of heart examination, to engage us in a steady walk with God and promote habitual preparation for the decisions of that day, and beget a joyful assurance that our *righteousness will then be brought forth as the light.* Thus both profit and pleasure will accrue from these frequent and serious interviews.

I MIGHT *also observe that similar desirable effects will follow from conversing often and much upon the subject of death—upon the different relations which we bear—and the characters which we sustain and the obligations*

which

which adhere to them; and on all the duties which are enjoined upon us; but I wave them. Their importance is obvious. The utility and pleasure of such a course are evident. Experience has proved it to those that pursue it. *And they said one to another, did not our heart burn within us, while he talked with us by the way, and while he opened to us the Scriptures.* (Luke xxiv. 32.)

2. THE advantage and delight of pious society result from the observations, experiences and christian exercises of the saints.

THEY speak freely to one another upon the things of the kingdom of God. There is a mutual interchange of religious sentiments; formed upon the truth. Pious and wise persons *lay up knowledge. In the lips of him that hath understanding wisdom is found.* With them *wisdom is the principal thing.* They desire to benefit one another; being knit together in the strong bonds of brotherly, that is, christian affection; longing after one another in the bowels of Christ, striving together for each other's spiritual profit. *Hence the tongue of the just is as choice silver.* Hence, *the lips of the righteous feed many. The lips of the righteous know what is acceptable: And the mouth of a righteous man is a well of life.* Their communication is that which is good, to the use of edifying, that it may minister grace unto the hearers. *Being fellow citizens* of the *heavenly country—fellow heirs of the grace of God, and of the same body, and partakers of the promises,* they became mutual helpers in the business of their common salvation, and they chiefly study those things by which they may effectually serve one another. They bring into one common stock their religious knowledge, obtained by reading, hearing, observing and reflecting, and their own christian experiences for mutual benefit. They disclose in friendship the counsels which have been imparted and received: The errors which they imbibed and rectified; the doubts which were harboured and removed; the burdens which they experienced and sustained; the conflicts in which they engaged and succeeded;

ceeded; the discouragements and difficulties which they met with and surmounted; the assistances which were afforded and used; the comforts which were granted and gratefully acknowledged; the means of godly proficiency which were bestowed and blessed. There is an unrestrained and general disclosure of these and of all other things which respect their furtherance in knowledge and piety. They advise and admonish, rebuke and encourage, animate and confirm one another in the ways of godliness. Being taught of God they teach one another: Being warned of God they warn one another: Having suffered both from within and from without, the reproaches of conscience and the censures of the world, they administer mutual friendly cautions: Having been tempted and succoured they succour one another: Having fallen and risen they fortify one another: Having been comforted themselves they comfort one another with those consolations which have been their portion: Having persevered and advanced in the christian life they mention and recommend the means which they found the most suitable and effectual for these ends. They encourage one another to be diligent, to resist, to press forward, to hold out and labour to be compleat in the will of God, perfect, lacking nothing. Thus their pious society is exceedingly beneficial to one another; evidential of cordial affection for their religious interest. An interest which engrosses their attention, which claims and shares their vigorous efforts and kindles their secret and social devotions. They *love one another in the truth, they wish above all things that their souls may be in health and prosper. They rejoice greatly when others shew that the truth is in them, while they walk in the truth.* (3rd of John.)

It may also be further noticed, *that the acceptable manner in which the saints perform religious duties, and the amiable spirit which they discover* have their influence and utility, and endear and stamp a value upon pious society.

WHEN

WHEN they convene in small circles to read devotional works, to pray and praise and confer on important subjects, and grace is drawn into proper exercise, the holy fervor, the humble yet near communion with God, the lively hope, the strong faith, the extensive charity, the divine philanthrophy which they breathe forth, and the esteem of sacred truth and the love of souls which they discover operate powerfully and beneficially upon kindred characters. There will be an extensive diffusion of the rich savor of these christian graces. The whole will prove like the precious ointment poured upon the head of the legal High Priest, which ran down upon his beard and went down to the skirts of his garments. (Psalm cxxxiii. 2.) When in their private conversation and general deportment, the saints exhibit and adorn that *wisdom which cometh from above; which is first pure, and then peaceable, gentle, and easy to be entreated, full of mercy and good fruits, without partiality and without hypocrisy.* (James iii. 17.) It operates like the electrical fluid upon christian societies : It instructs, it enlivens, it delights, it compels to imitation : It produces impressions permanent, and sensations joyous—effects advantageous—consequences everlasting. Those accidentally present, who are not the friends of the saints, may worship God and report *that God is in you of a truth.* (1 Cor. xiv. 25.) *May be won to the obedience of faith by your conversation,* and spirit and example. (1 Peter iii. 1. Rom. xvi. 26.) which they observe. When they hear your chaste, sober, discreet, instructive, benevolent and holy conversation, mark your evangelical temper and notice your humble, meek, inoffensive and useful deportment. This is an imperfect view of the advantages and pleasure of pious society.

III. I PROCEED to consider the obligations to seek and prefer such society.

1. IT is the will of God that we should act this part.

THOSE passages of the Scripture which require us *to love one another*—*To do good unto all men, especially unto the houshold of faith*—*To teach and admonish one another*—*To comfort and exhort ourselves together, and edify one another*—*To exhort one another daily, lest we be hardened through the deceitfulness of sin—and lest Satan get an advantage of us*, we being apprized *of his devices*—*To confider one another, to provoke unto love and to good works*—*To please our neighbor for his good to edification*—*Not to feek our own, but every man another's wealth*—*To be of the fame mind one towards another*—*To rejoice with them that do rejoice, and weep with them that weep*—which prohibit us to *go in the way of evil men*, and urge us to walk with wife perfons—To look well to ourfelves. Thefe and many other paffages, containing fimilar inftructions and exhortations, may teach us the will of the Lord our God. His will we fhould ftudy and love. What he enjoins muft be fitteft for us—muft advance our welfare and fpiritual joy. It may always be afked with confidence, what doth or what will or can the Lord our God and Savior require but what is for our good here and much more hereafter? The branches of our duty point, like the right lines drawn from a circle to the centre, to our furtherance and mutual fellowfhip in the gofpel and religion of Chrift.

2. THE obligation arifes from that regard and affiduous care which we fhould inviolably exercife towards our own religious intereft. This intereft is worth more than any other intereft. It vaftly exceeds any other. It incomparably outweighs all others collectively taken. All others fhould be made fubordinate and fubfervient to it. We fhould fteadily purfue it. Employ the beft means to fecure and promote it and eftablifh it to the end. We fhould labor to do ourfelves the moft effential fervice. We fhould alfo choofe and participate freely of the pureft and moft rational and folid enjoyments. We fhould encreafe continually as far as may be our own moral improvement. Hence we fhould devote

vote ourselves to the fear of God and observe all his righteous judgments, continue and abound in our obedience to God: We must honor them that serve God—associate and confer much with them—ask counsel of them—worship with them—cultivate their spirit and exercise their virtues. By such a course we shall gradually fill our minds with knowledge—reflect much honor upon ourselves—regard the end of our being—build up our soul's interest and partake of the richest joy. *Great peace have they that love thy law.* Pf. cxix. 165.

3. THE society of saints should be sought by us because of their acquaintance and converse with God and their love for him and because of the blessing of God which rests upon them.

THEY stand in a near and honorable relation to God. He is their father, their friend, their covenant God, their portion—Jesus Christ is their elder brother, their intercessor, their benefactor, their redeemer—The Holy Spirit is the author, upholder and finisher of a gracious, necessary and glorious inward change. They are hence the children of their heavenly parent, the faithful disciples of Christ, heirs of glory, the blessed of the Lord. *Because they set their love upon him, they shall dwell in the secret place of the most High, and abide under the shadow of the Almighty. When they call, he will answer them: he will be with them in trouble: he will deliver them, and honor them; satisfy them with his favor, and shew them his salvation.* Pf. xci. What a favor, what an honor, what pleasure, to be closely allied to them, to dwell near them, share in their fervent and devout intercessions at the throne, partake in their mercies and witness their good conversation and winning example? If the gracious presence and friendship of God and intercourse with him are blessings of the first magnitude; it must be desirable and beneficial to live in habits of intimacy with the saints. Great good will result from it. We may rationally desire and hope to be blessed with the same blessings ourselves.

We

We may hope that the protection which encompasses, the wisdom which guides, the presence which blesses and the grace which refreshes and sanctifies the saints, will be applied to us. If afflicted with them that we shall also be refined and comforted with them.

4. WE should seek and duly appreciate the society of the saints, because without it we shall be exposed to suffer much from that which is ensnaring and pernicious.

FEW seek comfort in gloomy solitude. Few will exchange the enlivening scenes of social life for the hermit's cell. Those who make the exchange are either disappointed in their hopes, opposed in their pursuits, sink under the weight of trouble, or imbibe false moral opinions; and wholly mistake the design of their creation; deny themselves what they might innocently enjoy and withhold those labors which society may demand. The thirst for intercourse with others is keen. But the objects of its gratification are uncertain. The selection which it occasionally makes or finally resolves on may be wise or foolish, useful or useless, worthy or unworthy of our rational nature and productive of consequences extensively beneficial or detrimental. We may greatly err. Many, daily observation and long experience teach us, have erred. And multitudes, one cannot suppress the fear, will probably yet err, be deceived by their companions, drawn into the vortex of infidelity and perish in the greatness of their folly. *He that walketh with wise men shall be wise; but a companion of fools shall be destroyed.* Prov. xiii. 20. A thirst for company, unless moderated by reason and guided by discretion and sanctified by the Spirit, will retard our moral improvement, prejudice us against religion, lessen our usefulness and expose us to corrupt habits. To company of an unfavorable, a vain and loose turn we shall be too strongly inclined from the depravity of our hearts. Young persons, especially, also from their ignorance and inexperience

rience, rashness and **vanity**. Hence it becomes very requisite that they should early join themselves to pious society and depart wholly from those who are dead in trespasses and sins. They must guard against the sentiments, resist the spirit and shun the example and dread the intimate intercourse of men of corrupt hearts and vicious lives.

5. An obligation to embrace this society arises from the fitness and utility of being prepared for all conditions and events. We pass through many changes; times and seasons roll over us in which we need the assistance of christian friendship. *In prosperity*, for instance, *we may be ensnared*. Danger often lies hid. An enemy lurks undiscovered; ready to surprize and spoil us. The snare which is unseen may be spread near to us. We may be placed upon a dangerous precipice when we feel most secure. This holds of worldly prosperity. Hence we need the seasonable cautions of pious friendship, lest, when riches encrease, we set our heart upon them; abuse them; overlook and deny the author; live to ourselves, and cultivate that friendship for the world which is enmity with God.

In adversity we need the wisdom of the saints. Lest we faint when corrected—indulge that worldly sorrow which worketh death; living upon our losses—or refuse to receive correction—quarrel with God—despise the rod—lest our heart fret against the Lord and pervert its way, and we bring upon ourselves more accumulated evils. We then need the experience and advice of the saints to open the sources of consolation, and declare the end of the Lord; our sanctification and salvation.

While distressed and tormented with the charges and stings of conscience we stand in need of the prudence and compassion and prayers of the friends of God. We surely should not apply to those who had been our partners in and tempters to sin. We should not expect that wise and kind counsel which doth good like a medicine. From them we should expect mirth and contempt: To have

our

our wounds flighted and not probed—our diftreffes fharpened, not affuaged. We fhould naturally and inftantly turn to the faints, who know how an accufing confcience can be fcripturally quieted—how the deepeft diftreffes can be effectually removed—the deadlieft wounds radically healed and the polluted cleanfed from iniquity. From fuch an application we fhould promife ourfelves much benefit : nor fhould we be afhamed.

WHEN *meeting the laft enemy, death, the mighty and univerfal* **deftroyer,** *we require the efforts of chriftian* **benevolence.** Who of us, when lying on the bed of daily languifhment and the fhadows of the long night of death were ftretching themfelves over our eyes and views, the profpect was dark and the anticipations were fearful, would turn our faces and direct our fpeech for guidance and fupport to the children of difobedience, the feducers of virtue and the advocates of infidelity and the fervants of iniquity ? How unnatural, how abfurd, how odious would be fuch an application ? Certainly we fhould enquire after and defire and felect thofe, on this occafion, who would direct us to him who came to feek *and to fave that which was loft*—to deftroy *the works of the devil*—to *bring life and immortality to light*—to deliver us from the bondage of flavifh fear— to give us the victory over death—to convert it into a covenanted mercy—and put into our mouth that triumphant fong, *Oh death! where is thy fting ? Oh grave! where is thy victory ?* **the** *fting of death is fin ; and the ftrength of fin is the law.* But thanks be to God who giveth us the victory through our Lord Jefus Chrift 1. Cor. xv. 55, 56, 57. From them alone we fhould expect light and comfort, counfel and prayers. It is our duty to prepare for what awaits us—To make feafonable and acceptable and ample provifion for ourfelves againft all probable, much more againft certain exigences and troubles and events ; it is then to prefer the fociety of the *faints ; the excellent of the earth : of whom the world is not worthy.* Heb. xi. 38.

IMPROVEMENT.

IMPROVEMENT.

I. This subject corrects the groundless mistake and condemns the guilty conduct of those who avoid and despise the saints.

It has long been fashionable and by some accounted reputable to heap reproach and contempt upon those that fear God and keep his commandments; who hate evil—who abstain from the appearance of it—watch the motions of their own sinful hearts—dread fellowship with the works and friends of darkness—who copy the example of Christ; who did no sin—who daily implore the protection of divine grace—and labor in all things to keep a conscience void of offence both towards God and man. But he, who judges righteous judgment; who cannot be blinded or prejudiced, deceived or warped, speaks of them and treats them with respect in his word, honors them and delights in them and manifests himself to them and dwells in them. *Since thou wast precious in my sight thou hast been honorable, and I have loved thee.* Isa. xliii. 4. *For the Lord delighteth in thee: and as the bridegroom rejoiceth over the bride, so shall thy God rejoice over thee.* Isa. lxii. 4, 5. *The precious sons of Zion, comparable to fine gold, how are they esteemed as earthen pitchers. Her Nazarites were purer than snow, they were whiter than milk, they were more ruddy than rubies, their polishing was of saphire.* Lam. iv. 2. 7. They are called *saints*—the *excellent*—*chosen of God and faithful.* They are comely through Christ's comeliness put upon them—They are the *lights of the world*—the *salt of the earth.* If the word of truth justly describes their dignity, their worth, their usefulness and importance to mankind, while it strengthens the patience and hope and obedience, and the joy of christians, it proclaims the palpable error and aggravated guilt of those who cannot think justly nor speak respectfully of them, nor associate with them, nor bear with them, nor give them rest, nor endure their continuance on the earth, who rejoice in present attempts made

made by a nation of avowed Atheists and others in different countries to scourge them as with the besom of destruction and overthrow the foundations of government and religion and destroy the church of Christ. Let such, and all scoffers and despisers of saints renounce their errors, repent of their contempt and join themselves to the cordial and excellent friends of the truth. God will not always keep silence: he will do terrible things in righteousness. At which you may wonder; but despise the saints no longer lest you perish.

II. UNSPEAKABLY preferable is the holy fellowship of saints to the intercourse of other society—especially of all vicious society.

MULTITUDES are buried in the world. They vigorously pursue no other concern. Other concerns, though important and spiritual, appear as nothing to them: Their hearts and their conversation are full of the world—Some are bent upon the acquisition of wealth—some of honor and some of pleasure. An intimate connexion with them will probably alienate us from heaven, produce neglect of religious duties and confine us to earth. If we associate with those who live in immorality, our dread of it will likely abate, our detestation of it will decline; we shall approach nearer to it, become familiar with it. If we closely connect ourselves with those who explode and banter the fundamental articles of christianity, with those who never introduce them, and do not desire to understand them, we shall suffer manifold evils. Such an intimate union will prove like the fiery and fatal darts of the evil one. We shall neglect those articles, disbelieve them, and, probably, make shipwreck of faith and a good conscience. If we gladly or incautiously yet frequently associate with the known children of disobedience, the slaves of their lusts, the enemies of vital piety and the haters of the truth, shall we not also become the same perverse children, the same miserable slaves, the

same

same bitter enemies, the same undisguized haters of the best things? Preservation we cannot expect—we cannot pray for it. The means of safety will be neglected. While, if the children of the light, the friends of piety, the defenders of the truth, the excellent of the earth are our chosen companions, that which is good and delightful may be expected to flow from such holy intimacy. When these two situations are compared and understood a doubt of the excellency of the holy communion of the saints cannot prevail nor exist.

III. LET real christians be pursuaded to revive the spirit and power of genuine christian communion and render it more exceedingly beneficial and desirable to themselves and to others.

WHEN religion generally declines, this communion may dwindle into formality, the original design of it be too much overlooked, and the primitive spirit with which it was upheld and characterized awfully degenerate. It has been conveyed to us in the history of the earlier times of christianity, that christians, their condition being peculiarly trying, entered into solemn leagues of holy friendship, entrusted all their spiritual concerns with each other, put the care of their own souls into one another's hands as a most sacred deposit, not neglecting of them themselves; but to obtain stronger security for their preservation from sin and their growth in godliness and eternal life: They became pledges to each other of procuring spiritual blessings for all who had brought themselves under the bonds of so solemn a covenant. They most solemnly stipulated in their several distinct and small societies to caution, reprove, keep, comfort, pray for and bless one another and labor continually for their mutual, holy and eternal welfare. A practice somewhat correspondent is worthy of recommendation and our imitation. Let us, my christian brethren, follow in very evil times a practice of so good report, so replete with solid benefit and productive of satisfaction. At least let christians, in their different circles, use freedom about their religious concerns, impart their whole souls to one another, counsel, admonish, rebuke, watch over, pray with and for one another, quicken, edify, settle and establish one another in the faith and religion of the gospel. While your zeal is according to knowledge, and your love without dissimulation, and your love of one another groweth, you cannot serve one another too effectually in love. The more abundantly you thus strive together for mutual profit, and a plentiful bestowment of divine mercies the more useful and fruitful and joyful will you be. Besides, a steady and more impartial conformity to the will of Christ and a brighter imitation of his life, the model of perfection, will silence slander, confound opposition, recommend your communion to others and tend to encrease the number of disciples. When they believe that God is in you of a truth: When, they say, as formerly, *behold! how these christians love one another;* when they testify for you how soberly, uprightly, inoffensively, charitably, exemplarily and usefully you live, many may glorify God on your account and yield themselves to be the Lord's in an everlasting covenant: and say to you, We will join your christian and brotherly assemblies, for surely you have the spirit of God: surely God is with you. Thus you will diffuse the rich favor of your good ointments far and wide, further and wider, augment your present joy and brighten your future crown of unfading glory.

IV. WE infer the superior excellency of the communion of saints in heaven. Christians are now sanctified but in part. The best have mixtures of imperfection and weakness, of passion and corruption which depreciate their fellowship and mar their excellence, and detract from their usefulness and diminish the advantage and joy of union to them. In heaven imperfection will wholly cease. There will not be the least discoveries nor the feeblest exercises of envy, jealousy, selfishness

selfishness and ill will. The light will be strong, the love vehement, the communion uninterrupted, the union indissoluble, the joy full, the benefit immense and everlasting. Let all then prize and thirst ardently for the perfection of heavenly blessedness.

V. Let the importance of divine friendship and spiritual union to Christ deeply impress all our hearts.

If we should cultivate such an esteem for the fellowship of saints—such a desire for it, and express such delight and joy in it and acknowledge such gratitude for it and pray for its advancement; how much more should we prize the favor and seek the presence of God—desire friendship with him and communion with him—likeness to Christ and a participation of the grace of the Spirit. God is a Friend that will never leave us—a Father who will never reject his children—a Portion that will always satisfy us. Jesus Christ is a Prophet who will always guide us—an High Priest who will always intercede for his disciples—a King who will always rule in us and subdue all enemies for us. The Holy Spirit can always work within us, comfort us, keep us from evil; furnish us for all services, sustain us in all conflicts, sanctify all events to us and perfect that which concerneth us. These divine persons will be our faithful, merciful, sufficient and unfailing friends—in trouble and joy, living and dying, in time, at the day of judgment, in heaven and through eternity.

SERMON XIV.

FAMILY GOVERNMENT AND FILIAL DUTY.

Hebrews xii. 9. first clause. *Furthermore, we had Fathers of our flesh, which corrected us, and we gave them reverence.*

FROM the discipline and corrective restraints, which earthly parents lay upon their children, the Apostle argues the necessity and utility of those rebukes and chastisements, which the people of God sustain, from his fatherly rod. From that filial respect and reverence, which dutiful children render to their earthly parents, under those wholesome rebukes and constraints, which they lay upon their passions and conduct, the Apostle infers, that humble and cheerful submission, which the children of God should yield to him, when he inflicts upon them his faithful rebukes and corrective visitations.

Our text affords a reason, not only, for our entire submission to God and humble veneration of his power and wisdom; but, also, clearly establishes the authority of parents over their offspring and the obligations of filial piety towards earthly parents. I shall, therefore, take occasion from our text to discourse to you upon those two great and important subjects, *Family Government and Filial Piety.* These are duties, intimately

timately connected and mutually dependent; and bear a place of first consideration, in the scheme of christian morality.

Our subject, then, divides itself into two main branches:

I. To treat of that authority and government which parents and heads of houses should exercise in their families. "We had fathers of our flesh which corrected us."

II. To define, that submissive reverence and piety which children and other domestics should render to parents and the heads of families.

"And we gave them reverence."

I need not labour to prove a point, so obvious, from our text, that the correction, which parents had given to their children, was a discharge of duty and merited approbation. And the return of reverence, from their children; was an indispensible obligation and a natural expression of gratitude. This construction of the Apostle's words being admitted, we deduce from them a conclusive argument, in support, both, of parental government and filial piety. We proceed

I. To treat of that authority and government which parents and heads of houses should exercise in their families.

"We had fathers of our flesh which corrected us."

Under the denomination of Fathers of our flesh we include those, who are, actually the parents of children, and, also, those who, in the providence of God, are placed at the head of families, with children and domestics committed to their care and inspection.—Every master and mistress of a family should cultivate the tender affections of real parents, towards their offspring; and exercise that watchful solicitude and concern, for all the subordinate branches of the family, which will prompt the most active exertions, for the best improvement and happiness of those committed to their trust.

trust. In this way, the loss of real parents will be in a good degree, compensated to orphan children. These tender dispositions, in the heads of families, would operate as lively incentives to a good and impartial government of their children.

PARENTAL love is the first and most effectual principle of an equal and wise discipline of the children, and domestics of a family. That parental love, which is the spring of an equal and wise discipline in families, is, wholly, diverse from that fond and indulgent weakness, which restrains some parents from checking the lustful desires and pursuits of their offspring. It is not parental love, it is a faulty weakness of mind, which prevents parents from laying vigorous restraints upon the licencious appetites and violent passions of youth, in their age of inexperience and folly.

PARENTAL love ought to be tempered with justice and directed by prudence, or it will be poorly qualified for the wise and happy management of a family. Parents, who love without discretion and exercise an attention to their children, without a supreme regard to moral rectitude, may show, indeed, their fondness and indulgence; but their management of the family will scarcely deserve the name of government: It may command our pity; but never our approbation and esteem.

HAVING stated those moral and social affections which, most essentially, prompt parents to the faithful discharge of family government, I shall now endeavour to show in what this government consists, and how it may be well administered.

FAMILY government is the right ordering and management of the temporal concerns and the moral and religious state of those, who, usually, dwell together under the same roof or in one family. The prerogative of government belongs to the Father of the family, with the assistance of his wife, who is given to him, by God, to aid him in this important work.

WHEN

WHEN a family is deprived of the Father or the Mother, then the whole administration devolves upon the survivor, and however inconvenient, must be managed by the remaining parent. The other members of the family must yield a dutiful submission to the surviving head.

As it is a requisite qualification in a good ruler to provide for the subsistence and safety of his subjects; so it is necessary in the Father of a family, that he take measures to secure the members of his household from wrongs and injuries, and provide for their healthful, comfortable and reputable subsistence in the world;— that he administer such accommodations to all, as will render their lives the least burdensome and most easy and agreeable to them. Parents are to nourish and cherish their children in such a diligent manner as to evince that their growth and prosperity are objects of their attention and solicitude and that they take a pleasure and satisfaction in supplying their wants. They are to provide for their household. For he, who neglects this service, proves, that he knows not the duties and feels not the tenderness of a parent. " But if any provide not for his own, and specially for those of his own house, he hath denied the faith, and is worse than an infidel." To sustain our children is an obligation of nature and an injunction of religion. This implies, that a parent by prudence and industry should exert himself, in those occupations, by which, the property of the family may be so increased, as to afford a sufficient and comfortable subsistence to all the members.— For this end the children and inmates of the family must be, early and carefully, educated in a course of active diligence, in some lucrative calling, for the benefit of the whole.

AN indulgence to sloth and idleness or to useless and unproductive employments is a gross neglect on the part of parents and tends, directly, to impoverish and render miserable their children, and eventually, to make

them

them unprofitable to themselves and a nuisance to society. Heads of families, therefore, must see that their children, when able, earn their own bread and not waste and squander the fruits of other peoples labour. If necessary, they must use, not only, counsels and instructions but, authority, restraint and discipline to produce among their children these salutary effects.

ANOTHER branch of family government is, to excite in the minds of children, a grateful sense of their dependence, and of their obligations to their parents and a dutiful respect for their authority. Parents never can discharge the duties of government until they have established their authority and a prevailing influence over the minds and conduct of their children.—The pleasure of parents must be regarded as a law and the children's attention be bent upon gratifying their wishes and fulfilling their expectations. This ascendency must be employed in directing, aright, the inclinations and pursuits of the whole family.

PARENTS should labour to render their authority easy and their commands acceptable to their children. In this way they will gain such an habitual controul over their offspring as will enable them to pursue their best spiritual and temporal interests with efficacy and success. Having, by wise, benevolent and uniform exertions confirmed their authority with their children, parents should use this singular advantage, to mould their hearts and practice, to a decent and virtuous deportment in the world.

FOR this end, the Parent is to apply himself to the instruction of his children, in those principles and duties, which are of the first magnitude. And first of all labour to eradicate that narrow and selfish disposition of the heart, by which, they are engrossed, solely, with their own interests and concerns. From their infancy children should be taught, that they are related to others, that they are not made for themselves, nor are they to live to their own private advantage. They

should

should be led to regard the rights of others and to pursue their happiness, as a leading branch of conduct through life.

COULD parents, by wholesome instructions, by a speaking example and by frowning upon and punishing all instances of a narrow selfishness and negligent regard of other people's happiness, cultivate in the minds of children an enlarged and disinterested method of thinking and acting, they would lay the foundation of all the great and beneficial affections of social life;— they would set their offspring in the path of true honour and substantial usefulness. By such early cultivation children would be able, in the progress of life, not only to enjoy society but, materially, to subserve the interests of it, by a generous and virtuous course of practice. It is a great object to make children feel the obligations of their social relations and excite them sacredly to fulfil those obligations, however laborious and painful the task.

SHOULD parents find their children inclined to any dishonourable and vicious course or guilty of any little and unworthy action, they must labour for their immediate amendment before the principle be rooted and the vice habitual. An attention, too early, cannot be paid to the opening passions of youth to curb those which are excessive and eradicate the criminal; and to substitute in their place noble and generous sentiments of benevolence and virtue. Every thing useful and liberal in the infant mind is to be encouraged and cultivated by suitable testimonies of approbation and animating rewards. Every thing selfish, base, fraudulent, false and malicious is to be reprobated, restrained and punished with uniform strictness and in many cases with a stern and rigid severity. Children are to be taught, by the loss of parental favour, by wholesome rebukes and faithful corrections, that vice is infamous and destructive to happiness.

The discipline of the rod is not designed for the common and daily correction of childish follies and foibles; but if some base and degrading fault has been committed, which argues a perverse and malicious mind, the evil ought to be cured by applying the correction of stripes. Base offences should be corrected with servile punishments.

But corporal punishment is the last remedy; it is to be applied with much caution, with much accompanying instruction and rebuke; with the utmost coolness and deliberation and for low, sordid and malignant offences. Such is human depravity that very few perhaps can be reared to mature age without requiring at one time or another, the correction of stripes: But, certain it is, that all children do more or less require, not only useful counsel and exhortation, but stern reprehension and rebuke. The timely exercise of such rebuke may, in most cases, prevent all the future labour and difficulty of training children to a decent and virtuous life.

Probably no method is more effectual to excite children to shun vice, than the showing of them the infamy and evil consequences of it, in some person, with whom, they are acquainted or by setting before them the more pleasing example of one made useful and respectable, by the practice of the opposite virtues. The parent's own example has the greatest effect, either, in confirming or weakening the good dispositions of his children. He may let his own good example speak for itself and operate its own happy effects. But, if he be wise, he will studiously propound the virtuous example of others to the notice and imitation of his children. The reputation and advantages, which, one man has gained, by conquering his lusts and extirpating deep rooted habits of wickedness, may animate children to attempt a reformation, where they find themselves most inclined to transgress and guard them from falling into snares laid for their ruin. The dreadful miseries and remorse,

remorse, which habitual offenders incur, when properly, represented, are a useful and striking lesson to children and youth. But in some way or another, either by persuasion or constraint, by example or precept, it should be the unwearied labour of all parents and heads of families to cure the narrowness and selfishness of their children's minds; that narrow selfishness, which renders them so insignificant and useless, if not, so injurious and mischievous to society.

PARENTAL influence and authority must be, vigorously employed to strangle the baneful lusts of the carnal and sensual mind and to nip the first shoots of sin and vice, which show themselves, in the early practice of their tender offspring.

It is a great point gained, when the minds of children are furnished with good moral sentiments and those useful propensities, which will lead them to regard the happiness and secure the approbation of those, with whom, they are connected in life. For this end they must be taught social duties and be dissuaded and restrained from all illiberal feelings and practices; be led to consult the interests of the family and society in which they dwell, and to demean themselves as wholesome members of the civil community, where providence has fixed their lot. They should be taught to become active, virtuous citizens of the state, and to fill, with dignity, all those stations, to which, they may be called in the progress of life; to be obsequious and submissive to their superiors, to be kind and benevolent to their equals, and to be courteous and condescending to their inferiors.

PARENTS should, not only, bend their attention to the production and cultivation of these social virtues, but, learn their children to reverence themselves; to exercise sobriety, temperance, chastity and self-government; to mortify their unruly passions and subdue their sensual appetites. They must be restrained from all those excesses, however pleasing to flesh and sense,

which

which will debase their character, as rational, accountable and immortal beings.

ABOVE all, parents are to direct their principal labours, in the government of their families, by good examples, by virtuous counsels and by salutary corrections to discipline the minds of their offspring to a sense of their dependence upon God, their obligations to worship and obey him; and, especially, to elevate their minds to the high duties of the christian religion; to repent of all sin; to look for mercy and forgiveness through Christ Jesus; devoutly to attend his ordinances; sincerely to keep his laws; and to expect final happiness, solely, through his righteousness and the sanctifying influences of his holy spirit.

To this, as an ultimate object, must all the attention, care and watchfulness of parents be directed; even, to make their children, the children of the Most High God and wise to their eternal salvation in Heaven. This is the first, this is the last duty of parents to govern their children for God and to train them up in the nurture and admonition of the Lord. We now proceed to speak,

II. OF that submissive reverence and piety which children and other domestics should render to parents and the heads of families.

"AND we gave them reverence."

THE obligations of filial piety lie, not only, upon children to their own parents, but also, upon all youth placed under the care of masters and guardians. Masters and guardians are, in the providence of God, placed in the parent's stead: And are bound to the same affectionate care, as though, the children committed to them were the fruit of their own bodies. For this reason, the master or guardian is entitled to a grateful return of filial affection and reverence. My observations, therefore, will apply, with equal force, to children by birth and adoption.

LET

Let us reflect upon the nature of this duty of filial piety—the principles upon which it is founded—and the manner in which it is to be exercised by children towards those who have the inspection and care of them.

What we denominate *filial piety*, in our text, is denominated *reverence*. This is a respectful veneration and esteem for the persons and characters of parents—a cordial affection and dutiful submission to their authority—a ready obedience to their commands——and a watchful attention to every intimation of their will. Those, alone, truly, reverence their parents, who stand in awe of their displeasure and deprecate it, as an essential evil ; who labour to fulfil their just expectations and accomplish their wishes ; who study to render themselves pleasing and acceptable, and to promote their parent's happiness.

Filial piety prompts youth to shun those connections and pursuits which are painful to their parent's hearts ; to watch the indications of their pleasure and to anticipate their desires ; to relieve them of their burdens and anxieties ; to administer to their necessities ; and by every method to alleviate the troubles and cares of declining age. It is the solicitude of pious children, that their parents enjoy, as much satisfaction, as will consist with the vicissitudes and frailties of this transitory life, and die with the tranquillizing hope, that, when they are lodged in the dust, they shall be succeeded by an offspring eminent for a reputable and virtuous deportment.

The highest earthly felicity of parents depend upon the character and conduct of their children : Upon no earthly object are their hearts so, earnestly, intent, as the good conduct and happiness of their descendents. Filial affection and piety will lead children to regard these feelings of their parents ; not to mar their enjoyments nor disappoint their hopes. By an obsequious deportment, they will convince their parents, that their

pleasing

pleasing expectations will, probably, be answered. Dutiful children will multiply the tender offices of love and gratitude to their parents; will discover their deep and feeling sense of obligation and dependence; will practise the duties of gratitude; and upon every occasion will prove, that their humble reverence is equalled, only, by their parent's fond and endearing love.

They prefer the society, the counsels, and instructions of their parents to those of all others. By their meek submission they teach others to respect their parent's character. They conceal their failings, patiently sustain their infirmities and animate and enliven their joys.

This filial piety is explained, in scripture, by obeying our parents; by submitting to their authority with humble reverence; by yielding, quietly, to their corrections and restraints; and by crowning them with every possible honour.

Children, who reverence their parents, will not trespass upon their overweaning indulgence; nor take advantage of their weakness; nor expose their defects; nor conceal their good properties and virtues. A true child will feel his own reputation, comfort and usefulness to be, intimately, connected with those of his parents. He will neither despise the instructions of his Father nor forget the law of his Mother: remembering, That a wise son maketh a glad father, but a foolish son is the heaviness of his mother. This alluring motive will quicken affectionate and dutiful children to virtue and wisdom, *That parents have no greater joy than to see their children walking in the paths of truth and honour.* The pleasure of a dutiful child, in his own honours and advantages, arises, essentially, from a consideration of that joy and satisfaction, which it imparts to an aged father or mother.

Thus, in a numberless variety of ways, do filial piety and reverence display themselves—by grieving at the displeasure and rejoicing in the favour and approbation

tion of parents—by accounting the parents frown a severe punishment and his smiles a rich reward—by setting a uniform example to the family of quiet submission—by an active and chearful difcharge of every duty:—by amending a fault upon the first notice of the parent's difpleafure—and by purfuing, with redoubled diligence, thofe virtuous purfuits which have engaged his approbation.

THE pious youth leans his underftanding to parental wifdom and experience for inftruction, what courfes to purfue, and with what companions to affociate. Thus does he learn to go in the way of the wife and the good; to forfake the paths of finners and the feat of the fcorner. He is obfequious to the orders and regulations of the family, in which, he lives, efpecially, thofe regulations, which relate to the improvement of the mind, the promotion of morals and virtue, and the worfhip and fervice of our God and Redeemer. When children honour and reverence their parents, family order and peace are fecure; all, mutually, enjoy reputation in the world, comfort with each other and favour with God. The fecret of God's love is upon their tabernacle.

Now let us fee, upon what principles and foundations, this excellent and ornamental grace of filial piety is grounded.

DUTIFUL refpect and filial reverence in children is, but, the natural and eafy expreffion of gratitude, to thofe tender and difcreet parents, who bear a prudent and vigilant affection to their offspring. Love begets love. An open and generous mind will, ever, prompt youth to honour and reverence their parents, and to repay their watchful care with humble, obfequious duty.

IT is the wife ordination of heaven, that a faithful government exercifed by parents fhould be followed by humble fubmiffion and filial obedience. Nature and reafon dictate to virtuous children the exercifes of

filial

filial piety. In no other way, can they answer those obligations, which, a sense of right and wrong impose upon them. If there be any virtue, any good moral sense, any commendable disposition in the hearts of youth, they will feel the obligation of esteeming and honouring their parents, as next, in order and importance, to that duty, which they owe to God, the Universal Parent. Does one remember his obligations to the Almighty Father? he cannot be unmindful of his earthly parents; he cannot forget those pains and cares and labours by which he is brought into life, is reared to age and taught to discern between good and evil. The many anxious toils and watchings, which, his parents have exercised for him, he cannot fail to repay, with fervent affection and habitual obedience.

Has he no disposition to esteem and reverence his parents? He has no foundation laid, in his mind, for the faithful discharge of any other relative duty in life: He has no ingenuity, no gratitude, no sense of decency and propriety, which may lead him to respect the laws, either, of God or man.

The principles of justice and benevolence to men and of homage and subjection to God, seem to be laid in the hearts of children, by an exercise of dependence upon and gratitude to their parents, with whom, they are first conversant and from whom, they realize the first benefits and advantages of life.

The Author of being has implanted, in the minds of children, a sense of their dependence on their parents and of their obligations to please and obey them; and not only so, but, he has made these duties the subject of frequent injunctions in his written word. They are inculcated by repeated divine precepts. And multiplied evils are threatened to those, who neglect to fulfil these obligations. God's word and providence combine their testimony, in favour of those, who reverence their parents and in frowning upon all, who dishonour and grieve them.

The

The command to honour our father and mother is the firſt commandment with promiſe; that is, this commandment has temporal rewards and penalties annexed to it. So that thoſe, who honour their parents, do, more commonly, live long and proſperouſly in this world; while thoſe wicked children, who contemn and diſgrace their parents, do not live out half their days. "The eye, that mocketh at his father, and deſpiſeth to obey his mother, the ravens of the valley ſhall pick it out, and the young eagles ſhall eat it." Numerous examples of God's favour, to ſuch as obey their parents and of his anger againſt thoſe, who diſhonour them are recorded in his word and in the hiſtory of his providence. We read God's reſpect to filial piety, in the inſtances of Iſaac, Obadiah and Timothy. His wrath hath been revealed againſt filial diſobedience in the inſtances of Abſalom, Adonijah, the ſons of Eli and the ſcoffing Iſhmael.

As God has inſpired a ſenſe of filial duty into the hearts of children; has teſtified his diſpleaſure againſt ſuch as neglect it and his favour to thoſe who regard it; has made parents inſtruments of the being and happineſs of their children; and as he has made the felicity of parents and children, the well being of ſociety and the glory of the church of Chriſt to depend, eſſentially, upon the exerciſes of filial piety; ſo we muſt conclude, that this duty is, not only, well founded, but, of infinite conſequence to human happineſs, both, in this life and that which is to come.

APPLICATION.

Uſe 1ſt. LET parents and heads of families be excited to a wiſe and uniform government of their children and houſeholds.

IT is a ſervice well pleaſing to God. He has given his gracious approbation of it; and, alſo, ample directions for the faithful performance of it. He has granted ſuch encouragements, ſuch aſſurances of ſuccefs, as may well animate parents, refolutely, to begin, and, diligently, to purfue a duty fo important and falutary. In the good regulation of families a foundation is, early, laid for a life of virtue and religion. The honour of God is promoted; that honour of God which fhould be the great object of our defire and purfuit.

By the wholefome difcipline of youth, parents are the happy inftruments of fowing the feeds of early piety; of producing a veneration for the great God and a cordial fubjection to the laws and ordinances of Jefus Chrift. They are employed in bringing their children and domeftics, into a near and faving relation, to the bleffed Redeemer of finners. They train up their offspring, not only, for a life of confcious rectitude, of inward peace and of important ufefulnefs to their fellow men; but, they prepare them to meet death with fortitude and ferenity, and, after death, to go and dwell with God in the city of his prefence, there to be forever engaged in the rapturous employments and to participate the ineffable joys of a glorious immortality. Parents, are not thefe advantages, to be obtained for ourfelves, in conjunction, with our dear families, argument fufficient and more than fufficient to roufe our attention to a duty fo fruitful of prefent and eternal benefits?

CERTAINLY, a well regulated affection for our children muft excite us to educate them, by an wholefome difcipline, for Chrift; to train them up in the nurture and admonition of the Lord; by a fpeaking example of fobriety, of virtue and religion, by ufeful leffons of wifdom, by neceffary checks and reftraints upon their faulty and vicious propenfities, to lay a foundation for this fond and confoling hope, that when we fhall be called, another day, to account for ourfelves and our families, we may be able to fay, " Here are we, Lord, and the children whom thou haft given us."

AN

SER. XIV.   *and Filial Duty.*

AN additional argument, to enforce my important exhortation, is, that children stand in great need of parental discipline and restraint. At times, to lay the check of restraint and the compulsion of authority upon children is the best earnest and expression of parental love. Youth are ignorant and inexperienced. They want the friendly counsel and experience of years to guard them from the snares which lie, constantly, in their way.

HAPPY would it be for youth, if they had nothing, but ignorance and inexperience, to mislead them. Alas! they have a vitiated body, defiled with impetuous and seducing appetites. They have a depraved soul, given over to the dominion of unhallowed lusts. They see things through a false medium. They perceive objects through the channel of misguiding faculties. Their passions impel them to dishonour; to courses vile and degrading to their rational and immortal nature. Shall not parents, then, watch against the indulgence and growth of these vicious propensities? check the rising desire of forbidden enjoyments? and, early, discipline their children to that mortification and selfdenial which is requisite to an honourable and useful life? When these propensities are urgent, shall not parental authority be fixed and decisive to repress and subdue them? Let parents neglect this correcting care and they and their children shall be the immediate sufferers. By such neglect, parents, the youth shall grow up in our families a seed of evildoers, to provoke the fierce anger of the Lord against them. They shall become crooked serpents to hiss at their parent's authority; to poison their reputation; and to sting their souls with the most subtle and penetrating anguish and remorse.

Alas! fond, indulgent Parents, blind to the follies and vices of your children; What a mass of reproach and agony are you heaping up for yourselves? How shall your negligence spoil the dear offspring of
your

your bodies? How fast will they ripen for infamy and ruin in time and for eternity? Do they make themselves vile and you restrain them not? Do you not, early, bend them to the yoke of obedience; to regard your orders and to fulfil your demands? They shall be the abhorrence of the good; the grief of your own souls: They shall teach the Lord's people to transgress: They shall be the scourge and pest of the community in which they dwell: And the Lord will, soon, do a thing in your houses, at which, both the ears of him, who heareth it, shall tingle.

But will you govern them as you ought, and as God will enable you if you seek to him aright? They shall be your ornament and rejoicing; the comfort of your pilgrimage; the stay of your declining age: They shall enjoy as much of this world as shall conduce to their permanent happiness: Those who dwell around you shall rise up and call you blessed: extensive connections and future generations of men and of christians shall find occasion to extol God for that wise and understanding heart which he hath given to you and which you have so, prudently, employed in ordering your house in a perfect way and in commanding your children, after you, to keep the way of the Lord.

Use 2*d*. Let children reverence their parents.

My young friends, the rising hope of the church of God, be assured you have never more occasion to venerate and love your earthly parents than, at those times, when they maintain a wise and strict restraint over your unruly passions and lusts. They, commonly, correct with reluctance and from an overbearing conviction, that it is useful and necessary for you and will conduce to your present and future happiness. Under all their counsels, instructions and restraints, reverence that fidelity and discreet love, which has taught them, for good and sufficient reasons, to check both their own inclinations and yours. Cultivate, for your parents, an uninterrupted affection. Venerate their authority; do

honour

honour to their character and obey their commands; for this is good and well pleasing in the sight of God. "Honour thy Father and thy Mother; that thy days may be long upon the land which the Lord, thy God giveth thee. *Amen.*

SERMON XV.

SYMPTOMS OF THE DECLINE, AND IMPORTANCE OF THE REVIVAL OF FAMILY RELIGION.

GENESIS xxxv. 2. *Then JACOB said to his houshold, and to all that were with him, put away the strange gods that are among you, and be clean, and change your garments.*

THE Patriarch Jacob, when he was journeying from his Father's houſe to Padan Aram, bound himſelf by a ſolemn vow to almighty God, that provided he would ſpread his pavilion over him, and return him in peace, the Lord ſhould be his God; that the ſtone which he had erected for a pillar ſhould be God's houſe; and that all that God ſhould give him, he would ſurely give the tenth to him. The prayer-hearing God was graciouſly pleaſed to grant him more than he had requeſted: but, it ſeems, Jacob, in the midſt of proſperity and fulneſs, had forgotten his vow; or, at leaſt, deferred the payment. And in the beginning of our context God reminds him of it. In the text we ſee the pious care and attention of Jacob in the matter; like a true ſon of Abraham, he exerciſes his paternal authority, and excites his houſehold to their duty. He was not afraid to ſpeak as becomes the governor and head of a family. He lays an injunction on his family

in

in two things: not on his wives and children only, but on his servants also.

1st. To put away the strange gods that were among them. How surprising that strange gods should be harboured in the family of so good a man as Jacob! And who had so largely shared in the bounties of divine Providence, as well as the riches of grace! But the best of saints are imperfect— His connivance at them must be considered as his infirmity—Certainly this was not a spot of God's children: for, what concord hath Christ with Belial? What agreement hath the temple of God with idols? Jacob, being awakened to a sense of his duty and obligations to his covenant God, requires them immediately to abandon their detestable images.

2d. He commands them to purify themselves and change their garments. Simeon and Levi, in a peculiar manner, had need to change their garments, for they had been defiled with blood. This was but a ceremony symbolical of changing and purifying the heart.

The sum of the matter is, they must be in readiness to attend on a solemn ordinance. Jacob, as the head of the family, and as one invested with parental authority, charges them to prepare themselves to meet the Lord, in solemn acts of religious, instituted worship. In the prosecution of this subject, my object is,

To give some symptoms and evidences of the declension of family religion among a professing people— then show that when family religion is evidently on the decline, it is highly incumbent on heads of families to use strenuous and unremitting endeavours for its revival.

I. To give some symptoms and evidences of the declension of family religion among a professing people.

Is it not an undeniable fact, that in families, where there has been much of the appearance of religion, at times there are but partial fruits of it? The house which has been a Bethel, instead of continuing to be a
house

house of prayer and religious exercises, rather becomes a den of thieves. Family religion which is so excellent and amiable, and the glory of a people, is departed from; or at least, it is exceedingly on the decline. The

1st. SIGN I shall mention of the declension of family religion is, family conversation being engrossed by the things of this world. The state of family religion may be clearly ascertained from family discourse. Inspiration teaches us, that where the treasure is, the heart will be also. And whether the heart and affections be placed most intensely on earthly, or heavenly things, may usually be learned from general conversation. (Though, possibly, some may so play the hypocrite, as to be undiscovered all their days.) When worldly things uninterruptedly occupy the attention, and the daily topic of family discourse is, what shall we eat? What shall we drink? Wherewith shall we be clothed? How shall we execute our worldly projects? How shall we increase riches? Or, as the Psalmist expresses the same thing, "who will shew us any good?" And the conversation of the family is rarely seasoned with a word concerning God, their duty, and the eternal world: I say, when this is the case, it is an indication, that family religion is in a very languishing condition. How can family religion be said to be in a flourishing state, when there is not a syllable uttered respecting divine and eternal things from one week, or month, to another? Solemn and frequent discoursing of the things of God and the soul, has a great tendency to promote religion, and maintain the power of it in a family. And indeed, this is an essential branch of family religion: God gave commandment to Israel, to maintain religion in their families; and to this end directed them, to teach his laws diligently to their children, and to talk of them when they sat in their houses. Were religious conference unimportant, and useless, we cannot suppose, God would have so strictly enjoined it upon the families of his people.

How

How deplorable the condition of that family in which there is no semblance of piety! How surprisingly forgetful must such be of their own immortal souls and eternity! All posting, on the wings of time, towards that world, "from whose bourn no traveller returns," and still perfectly secure and unconcerned! None making the inquiry, "what shall we do to be saved." But not to digress, in a word, will any deny that religion is on the decline in that family, where there is no discourse either of the nature or importance of it?

2dly. WHEN the heads of the family are not careful that the several members of it, both children and servants, who are adult, attend on family worship, it argues not only remissness in duty, but a great want of piety.

Is it not a melancholy truth, that some indulge their household in absenting themselves from morning or evening sacrifice? Are not some negligent as to the choice of the fittest season, unitedly, to offer their supplication to Heaven for family mercies? Have we not reason to think, and say, of such houses, as Abraham did to Abimeleck, Surely the fear of God is not in this place? Has not every member of the family a precious and immortal soul? Does not each one stand in need of the pardoning mercy of God? Why then should not every one have an opportunity, and be directed, in union with the family, to seek it at the throne of divine grace? Reasons and motives, certainly, are not wanting, to enforce this as a duty. When parents are so negligent, what reason is there to expect, that their children will ever entertain a sacred regard for religion? The probability is, that there will be less appearance of it, from time to time, in such a house, till the very form of it become extinct. When Cain left the worship of the altar which his father had erected, he soon cast off fear, restrained prayer, and became a vile profligate, and vagabond in the earth.

G o 3dly.

3dly. A NEGLECT of reading the word of God in a family is an indubitable symptom of the declension of religion. To be very religious, and to neglect conference with the word of God, is an absurdity. All true friends to religion entertain a cordial regard for the word of God, which is its source. The psalmist gives it as the character of truly pious persons, that they take delight in God's word, and make it familiar to them, " Blessed is the man who walketh not in the counsel of the ungodly, nor standeth in the way of sinners, nor sitteth in the seat of the scornful: but his *delight is in the law of the Lord;* and in his law doth he meditate day and night." Such make use of the sacred oracles in application to their own particular circumstances, and for the instruction and direction of their household. They make them daily the man of their counsel, and improve them as a light to their feet and a lamp to their path. And, in common, it may be laid down as a maxim, that in those families where the Bible is frequently resorted to, and intimately conversed with, there is true religion; and where it is treated with neglect, and seldom read, there is no religion. Some portion of the holy scriptures, extraordinaries excepted, should be read in families daily. And in proportion as this duty is omitted, contempt is cast upon them, and their divine author. And such omission is an argument of the great want, if not of the entire destitution of true religion.

4ly. THE neglect of pious instruction is a sad evidence of the declension of family religion. Where family religion is in its glory, godly instructions drop as the honey and the honey comb. The children and domestics are taught the fear of the Lord—the preciousness of their souls—their danger of perishing, while unregenerate—their need of an interest in the Saviour—the excellency and gain of godliness—the wisdom of seeking God without delay, and making sure a title to his favour. They are informed, that it is not the command

command of man merely, but of God himself, to seek the Lord while he may be found, and to call upon him while he is near. In that house where such parental instructions are faithfully administered, we may hope there is something of the power of religion; but how great the reverse, where no suitable care and pains are taken to instruct the family in the way of duty and happiness! And indeed, are not some heads of families so indifferent and unconcerned, whether or not their household be made acquainted with necessary truth and duty, that they grudge a little expense, to teach them to read the holy scriptures? Do not some practically declare, that they think that lost, which is expended in education? And it may be, their children are as ignorant of the very first principles of religion, as of the Koran of Mahomet. Judging from appearances, may we not well conclude, that too many heads of families are far from realizing, that the command given to Israel, is still in full force? Deut. vi. 6, 7. "And these words which I command thee this day, shall be in thine heart, and thou shalt teach them diligently unto thy children, and shalt talk of them when thou sittest in thine house, and when thou walkest by the way, when thou liest down, and when thou risest up."

ABRAHAM, the father of the faithful, has set a good example for heads of families to train up their household in religious knowledge, and wisdom's ways; the happy fruits of his care and fidelity may encourage parents to this duty: if we cast our eye on Gen. xxii. 7. we may see how intelligent his son Isaac was in the law and custom of sacrifices: "And Isaac spake unto Abraham his father; and said, my father; and he said, here am I, my son. And he said, behold, the fire and the wood; but where is the lamb for a burnt offering?" In this instance he discovers the fruit of his good education, and instruction in matters of religion. Abraham felt the importance of supporting family religion, and well instructed his house. This fidelity in him is

assigned

assigned as a reason, why God would not hide from him his design to destroy the cities of Sodom and Gomorrah—" And the Lord said, shall I hide from Abraham that thing which I do: Seeing that Abraham shall surely become a great and mighty nation, and all the nations of the earth shall be blessed in him? For I know him, that he will command his children, and his houshold after him, and they shall keep the way of the Lord, &c. But when heads of families have not, like this pious patriarch, faithfully discharged parental duties, what melancholy instances have there been in all ages of the world, of disregard to piety, and depravity of manners, in their offspring? Hence we may make this observation, that, as the prosperous state of family religion will be discovered in parental, pious ininstructions; the reverse may be inferred, when such instructions are neglected.

5thly. WHEN immoralities are perpetrated by the members of the family, and parents neither administer correction, reproof, or restraint, it is an evidence of the declension of family religion. Their neglect to reprove iniquity in those under their charge, is a tacit connivance at it; or, a silent approbation of it. They virtually bid them God speed in their sinful ways; and hence are partakers with them in their guilt. And have we not reason to fear that more than a few heads of families are thus culpable? This was Eli's fault; his sons made themselves vile, and he restrained them not. For this neglect, God informed him, that he would judge his house forever. And those who would wish to escape Eli's curse, must cautiously avoid his sin. The wise man's advice is, " Chasten thy son while there is hope, and let not thy soul spare for his crying"—He likewise says, " The rod and reproof give wisdom; but a child left to himself, bringeth his mother to shame. Correct thy son, and he shall give thee rest; yea, he shall give delight unto thy soul." Too many are criminally careless in this matter; like Gallio in another

case,

case, mind none of those things. Some may be timorous, and afraid of grieving, or displeasing their children, should they chasten them for offences: but whatever may be the cause, this is a very faulty omission. And when sin is winked at by them, or not reproved, it is a very sure token that family government is not supported, and religion is on the decline.

6thly. IRREVERENCE and disrespect of parents are another argument of the same truth. Parents themselves are usually the blamable cause of such delinquency. Their careless inattention to parental duties naturally breeds contempt in their children. If parents do not keep their places as heads of the family, and support their dignity and authority, it would be a wonder, should their children treat them with due reverence; or, that piety should flourish in the family. But as to the virtuous woman, it is said, "her children rise up, and call her blessed." Solomon has set children an example of a respectful behaviour towards their parents: Though he was the king of Israel, and lived in the greatest splendor of all earthly monarchs, yet, (instead of forgetting his obligations to the mediate authors of his being, as too many do,) he exhibited a reverend respect to his mother; sensible that this would be an honour to him, as well as his duty. See 1 Kings, xii. 19. "Bathsheba therefore went unto king Solomon, to speak unto him for Adonijah; and the king rose up to meet her, and bowed himself to her and sat down on his throne, and caused a seat to be set for the king's mother, and she sat on his right hand." This one instance of respect, was a greater honour to him than his crown. And this proclaimed his good education; that he had been, "trained up in the way he should go." But when children are heady and ungovernable, and walk in the ways of their own heart, and in the sight of their own eyes, and instead of reverencing, trample on their parents; their demeanor exhibits a striking proof of the declension,

sion, yea, the destitution of family religion. For, were this duly supported, it would create a reverence and filial fear in the hearts of children towards their parents; which is their indispensable duty. Agreeably to Levit. xix. 3. "Ye shall fear every man his mother, and his father; I am the Lord your God."

7thly. THE same truth appears very evident, when there are contentions, and discords in the family. Families of piety are families of peace. Is it supposable, that piety is operative in the hearts of those, who live in bitter disagreement and animosity? Piety and discord have no more fellowship, or connexion with each other, than Christ with Belial. Those, who live in christian love and peace, may hope and expect, that the God of peace will dwell with them; but on no other grounds may families look for the favourable presence of Deity; the contrary spirit and practice being totally repugnant to the christian character. A holy and jealous God is so far from winking at the sin of family contention, that he views it with abhorrence. This monster, this demon of discord not only banishes the *power* of religion from the *hearts* of men; but often the very *form* of it from *families*. Is it not a common case, that in that house where there is lasting contention, there is little or no prayer, religious communion or concern how they may promote each others best and eternal interest? On the whole this observation may be made, without exception, viz. in whatever family there is much contention, and lasting division, religion, (if there be any at all) is on the decline. Though possibly there may be the form, yet the power of it has departed.

ARE these things so? Are these things which have been suggested, symptoms and evidences of the declension of family religion? Then have we not abundant cause to fear and conclude, that family religion is greatly on the decay, even in this land of light? And this is a gloomy omen, and bespeaks our fervent supplications

plications to Almighty God, that he would pour out his spirit, revive his work, and excite and quicken heads of families, especially those who have been thus negligent, to their respective family duties. Which leads me to consider the

2d. THING proposed, viz. That, when family religion is evidently on the decline, it is highly incumbent on heads of families, to use strenuous and unremitting endeavours for the revival of it.

THE state of religion in Jacob's family was such, when he was commanded to go up to Bethel, that it was requisite something effectual should be done, to redress its defects, and bring about a thorough reformation. It was necessary that Jacob should exert himself in so good a cause, when they had introduced strange gods among them. So it is highly necessary, when religion in the family, either in its power or form, is manifestly declining, that the heads of it should vigorously exert themselves, in the use of all proper means, that a revival and reformation may take place.

1st. ARGUMENT I shall adduce to enforce this duty is, that unless endeavours be used, religion, where there may be some appearances of it, will continue to decline. It is easier to loose two steps in religion, than gain one.

DECLENSION is agreeable to unrenewed nature. It is to swim down the current. It is consentaneous to the corruptions of the depraved human heart. And the world is suited with it. Were a revival natural and easily obtained, it might be effected without zealous efforts; but it is far otherwise, on account of the strong opposition to it from the world, Satan, and inward moral corruptions. The case before us is very parallel with that of entering into the kingdom of heaven. Men must *strive* and be in *good earnest*, if any thing be done to effect. We may hope that God will bless and succeed suitable exertions; but what grounds have we to expect this revival, when it is not so much as *attempted* by the heads of the family? Jacob had no expectation that the disorders of his family would be remedied, should he himself remain supine and inactive: We find, he not only commanded them to put away the strange gods that were among them, but took effectual care that his orders should be obeyed; and that they should have no further opportunity to pay divine honors to their idol gods, as in the 4th of the context, "And they gave unto Jacob all the strange gods that were in their hands, and all their earrings which were in their ears; and Jacob hid them under the oak which was by Shechem."

2dly. The flourishing of real christianity in communities depends much on the good state of family religion; which should be a powerful inducement with heads of families to exert themselves in this important business.

I am far from insinuating, that it comes within the verge of their power, to change the hearts of the members of their family, or implant a gracious principle in them: This is a work peculiar to deity; but as to external reformation, they may do much, by the common assistance of divine grace. Jacob could not inspire the hearts of his family with reverence and purity, and thus prepare them for the solemn occasion upon which they were going to Bethel; yet he could prevent their carrying strange gods with them. And the prospect of success may be a stimulus with parents to engage in this duty their faithful labours, accompanied with their own good example, and have the most direct tendency, to influence their household, to attend to the one thing needful—to awaken from security—to promote religious thoughtfulness, and induce them to seek and serve the Lord our God. Their constant, pious endeavours will habituate them to religious services, and tend to keep down, and even eradicate that powerful antipathy to holiness and divine services, which naturally possesses the human heart.

WHAT probability is there, that pure religion and undefiled will flourish among a people, if family religion be not supported, and if parents do not strive to purge out the leaven of wickedness? Civil rulers may make good laws, and see them well executed. Ministers of the gospel may be faithful in warning others of the danger and demerit of sin, decrying the vices of the times, and urging a compliance with the terms of gospel grace; yet in vain shall we expect the flourishing and spread of vital piety, if family religion be not supported, or parents be remiss in performing the duties they owe their children. The good seed will soon be choked for want of domestic cultivation. But let family religion revive; and the houses of God's professing people become Bethels, places of religion and godliness, and then we may hope for a glorious revival of religion in our land. To behold religion growing as a vine, and sending forth its roots as Lebanon.

3dly. ANOTHER cogent argument to the duty recommended is, that the family in which religion is declining and dying, lies exposed to the judgments of God. The Most High is angry with such families, and sometimes testifies his displeasures in this world by his judgments: agreeably to Jer. x. 25. " Pour out thy fury upon the heathen who know thee not, and upon the *families who call not upon thy name.*" God, with a jealous eye, observes the families of his people, whether, like David, they walk before him with perfect hearts. Holy Job was apprehensive that his sons, in their feasting, had sinned; which he, doubtless, feared, would incur tokens of the divine displeasure, in judgments upon his house. See his pious care, chap. i. ver. 5. " And it was so, when the days of their feasting were gone about, that Job sent and sanctified them, and rose up early in the morning, and offered burnt offerings according to the number of them all: for Job said, it may be, that my sons have sinned, and cursed

cursed God in their hearts." Thus did Job continually." God threatened to judge Eli's house forever, for the wickedness of his sons, and in that he did not exercise his authority in suppressing it as *became a parent*, as well as an high priest and a judge in Israel. God exercised Jacob with sore afflictions in his family, not merely, because he had not performed his vow, but in that he did not suppress their idolatry. Do family sins and declension expose to the judgments of heaven? Then is not this consideration a loud call to the work of reformation?

4thly. ANOTHER motive for assiduous endeavours to effect a revival is, that declension incurs a forfeiture of God's protection and blessing. The divine favours ought by no means to be considered as unimportant; but more to be valued than gold, yea, than much fine gold. They are safe, whom God keeps, and blessed indeed whom he blesses. But when God withdraws his protection and blessing, the very walls and bulwarks of the family are thrown down, and a gap is made in its hedge of defence, for judgments to enter. And God justly withdraws from those who withdraw from him. With the froward, we are taught, God will shew himself froward; while the righteous he compasses with his favour as with a shield. Do you, who are heads of families, value personal and family blessings? Do you wish for the smiles of a gracious God on your houses? Strive to reform whatever may be amiss; lest you kindle the divine resentments, and provoke the Most High to say of you and your house, as he did of Eli's, that he will judge it forever.

5thly. ANOTHER argument for studious endeavours after a revival may be, that this effected, will give a hopeful prospect of the order, piety, and happiness of the rising generation. Those who are now upon the stage of life, must soon quit it: one generation after another passes away in rapid succession. And what consolation would it administer to serious christians

tians in a dying hour, to realize a good foundation laid for the piety and well-being of the rising generation; especially, if they themselves in their proper stations, have contributed their mite towards the good work—But, on the other hand, if family religion be apparently decaying, and dying, how dark a cloud overspreads the rising generation! What confusions and miseries await them! All will readily concede to this as a truth, that if children and domestics be trained up in irreligion and disorder, there is a very slender foundation laid for their well-being here or hereafter. But should family religion revive; and parents adopt the virtuous resolution of Joshua, the servant of the Lord, that as for them and their house, they will serve the Lord, they might justly hope, that God would be the God of their seed and bless them. Surely love to posterity should excite us, who are heads of families, to do our utmost in the promotion of that which is so desirable and important. And how should we tremble at the thought, of teaching irreligion by our own practice! Children are too prone to pattern the neglects and vices of their parents; yet, for the encouragement of parents it may be said, they often entertain a high esteem of their virtuous and religious counsels and examples, and are happily influenced by them. The consideration of which gave rise to that pertinent direction of the wise man, " Train up a child in the way he should go: and when he is old, he will not depart from it."

IMPROVEMENT.

1st. From what has been observed, have we not too great reason to fear, and conclude, that family religion is languishing, *even in this land* which is *exalted to heaven* in point of religious privileges? How wide the difference between the present and former days! Do not sin and iniquity unabashed rear their brazen front? Will not this observation apply, not to a few individuals

als merely, but to many families? To what an height has immorality arrived! Where shall we discover the ancient spirit of strictly sanctifying the sabbath; or, the fervors of heavenly conversation? Where similar pious counsels, and solemn warnings of parents to their children? In how few instances shall we discern that sacred regard for public worship, and zeal for the honour and glory of God, which appeared in our forefathers? How much has the spirit of prayer and supplication abated? Might we be made acquainted with the state of religion in many of the families of God's professing people, should we not, probably, be filled with astonishment at their negligence in point of religious and instituted duties; and adopt David's exclamation, (were grace in lively exercise in our own hearts) viz. " horror hath taken hold upon me, because of the wicked who forsake God's law!" And might our pious Ancestors rise out of their graves, they could scarcely realize, from present appearances in the moral world, that this was the land which they left at death. Were houses to pass under a thorough examination, should we not have abundant cause to conclude, (and by the same tokens which have been exhibited,) that family religion is on the decline? How much have parents lost their authority? and how few children pay them due fear and reverence?

THESE, with other omissions which might be mentioned, are the fruits of declension and evidences of deep degeneracy in religion. Hence,

2dly. IF we may draw any inference from past dispensations of divine Providence towards a professing, backsliding people, have we not grounds to fear, that this land is ripening for ruin? Is not this intimated to us by the decaying, dying state of family religion? We may expect that all true piety will soon disappear, if family devotion expires: the latter is the prelude to the former—And declension is a step towards rejection. It is true, God exercised long suffering towards the

Jews

Jews under their backslidings : "How, says he, shall I give thee up, Ephraim? How shall I deliver thee, Israel? How shall I make thee as Admah, and set thee as Zeboim?" Yet at length he cut them off for their unbelief and wickedness—"In the place where it was said ye are my people, it was said ye are not my people." And negligence of family duties, we may suppose, was at the bottom of their national wickedness, served to fill up the measure of their sin, and hasten their ruin. Hence,

3dly. We may infer from our subject one reason, why the rich and inestimable means of grace with which we are favoured, are not more effectual, viz. the unfaithfulness of parents to their important trust. There is not a people under heaven, who are more highly favoured and distinguished, in point of religious priviledges, than we are. And we do not jeopard our lives in the profession of Christ, as many, in former ages, have done : But though we are indulged such choice means of grace, how few are there, comparatively, who are savingly benefited by them ? How amazingly does a careless Laodicean spirit prevail ! How many at the present day excuse themselves from the gospel entertainment, for no better reasons, than those assigned by those grave dispisers in Luke xiv. ? What multitudes are so ravished with the love of riches, and worldly enjoyments, that they are chearful, constant votarists at Mammon's shrine. And we may expect that these things will be so, till family religion revives. The want of this often renders the most powerful means ineffectual. When the word makes some impression on the mind, it is soon lost. Though the tender minds of children and youth are solemnly affected, yet, through the delinquency of their parents, how often does their goodness become as a morning cloud and the early dew ? Hence,

4thly. We may infer the present indispensable obligation of all parents, to use their unfainting efforts

for

for the revival of family religion. Among the various things which are needful in our land, this is one, not of small moment. And the great inattention to the things of our eternal peace, which is so visible, is deeply to be deplored.

Let us then, who are heads of families, exert our authority and influence for effecting a reformation in those under our charge; and never think we can take too much pains in the cause of God and religion. Instead of countenancing iniquity, let us boldly appear on the Lord's side, and stem the torrent, lest we be considered and treated, as partakers in the guilt of others. If we are not partakers in the sins of others, neither shall we be in their plagues, especially, in the coming world! Noah had the manly, commendable fortitude, to separate himself, by exemplary piety, from the wicked world around him. And righteous Lot refused to swim down the current of the times; and they were both happily exempted from the common destruction.

Should our endeavours for the revival of religion be succeeded in our own families only, we shall secure the blessing of God to ourselves and our household. And we may place an holy confidence in the God of all grace, that he will bestow his favour on our offspring for a great while to come. For we read, " He hath given meat to them who fear him, *he will ever be mindful of his covenant.*" Should not true religion revive, many will eternally perish; yea, many of God's professing people will fail of grace and glory. The bare form of godliness will never ensure future felicity. Our Saviour has, in few words, decided this point, " except a man be born again he cannot see the kingdom of God."

This matter merits careful examination. Let us examine the state of our families by those symptoms of declension which have been exhibited, and labour speedily

dily to rectify whatever defects we may descry, either in principles or morals.

It might not be unprofitable for us, frequently and seriously to consider, that our time is short at the longest, in which we can sit at the head of our families. And we may, very suddenly and unexpectedly, be removed by death; at which period it will be forever too late to amend our error. Let us, therefore, now shake off sloth, awake to duty, and adopt the pious resolution of that eminent servant of the Most High God, depending on divine grace, that "as for us and our houses, we will serve the Lord." If we faithfully execute such purpose of heart, we shall not only have the solace of an approving conscience; but meet the plaudits of our great Lord and Master before the assembled universe, at the judgment of the great day, and receive from him that blessed sentence, "Well done, good "and faithful servants, enter ye into the joys of your "Lord." AMEN.

SERMON XVI.

THE USE AND IMPORTANCE OF CHRISTIAN INSTITUTIONS.

Acts ii. 41, 42. *Then they who gladly received his word, were baptized : And the same day there were added unto them about three thousand souls. And they continued stedfastly in the Apostles' doctrine and fellowship, and in breaking of bread, and in prayers.*

JESUS, the Head and King of the church, having purchased it by his blood, made the necessary provision for its constitution, and appointed the means requisite to its edification, commissioned his Apostles to teach in his name and disciple all nations to his religion, to gather and organize churches, and administer his ordinances. He ascended into heaven ; and on the day of Pentecost, (this was a festival celebrated by the Jews at the finishing of their harvest, in testimony of their gratitude to God for giving them the blessings of harvest.) Some, have observed that this day of Pentecost, was the very day on which the law was given at Mount Sinai : And on this day, about ten days after his ascension, Christ endowed his Apostles with power from on high, by the extraordinary effusion of the holy Spirit in the miraculous gift of tongues. The text informs us of the signal succefs of the sermon preached by St. Peter on this occasion, the plenteous spiritual harvest reaped by it; about three thousand converts to the christian faith, were added to the church, on that memorable day, and as the fruit of a single sermon.— How many thousand sermons have since been preached without the appearance of the conversion of one soul!

In this instance several favouring incidents concurred to give efficiency to the sermon. Peter's hearers were the very persons who, but a short time before, had been active or accessary in crucifying that same Jesus whom Peter now preached, and testified to their faces, " that God had made him both Lord and Christ." His wounds were yet bleeding in their guilty consciences. Also the miraculous gift of tongues conferred on Peter and other illiterate fishermen, his fellow Apostles, did much to prepare the way for such signal succefs. We may add, his hearers, as the fifth verse informs us, were devout men, studious to know the truth, grossly ignorant, but disposed to receive information and conviction. Above all these the extraordinary cooperation of the holy spirit which attended the word preached and produced that rich harvest.

These three thousand new converts were baptized and added to the church the same day. Their admission to fellowship in the church was not suspended to give opportunity either for themselves or others to gain greater evidence of their gracious sincerity; they were admitted without delay: This Apostolic example may doubtlefs be safely imitated. These added to one hundred and twenty of whom we find previous mention, at that time made up the church in Jerusalem, the first christian church ever formed.

The two verses, which I have now read, informs us of the manner how christian institutions were used and celebrated by these primitive christians, in their public assemblies: Having gladly received the word, at Peter's mouth, they readily submit to and receive baptism, as the institution of Christ; in which they chear-

I i fully

fully give up their names to him, to be his voluntary disciples and followers, and signify their earnest desire and humble expectation of being purified from sin by his atoning blood, regenerated by his spirit, and of choice seal their engagements to be faithful and loyal in his service, and their stedfast hope of inheriting through his mediation, all the blessings of the new covenant.

Being baptized into Christ, they put on Christ, and become incorporated with him as members of his body, the church; and sacredly engage to abide and walk with it, in all the commandments and ordinances of the Lord blameless; how they fulfilled these sacred vows the text informs us,

2. That they adhered stedfastly to the Apostles doctrine, that is the doctrine which the Apostles preached; the doctrine taught in the scriptures. As all christians are built on the foundation of the Apostles and Prophets, i. e. the doctrinal writings of the Old and New Testament, so this was the foundation on which these primitive converts were built; to this they stedfastly adhered: this they relied on as the foundation of their faith, and the rule of their practice: this they received, revered and trembled at, not as the word of men; but as it is in truth the word of God. They continued stedfast and firm in their adherence to this foundation. The original word is of stronger import, it signifies that they adhered, with fortitude, patience and perseverance, to the divine word: with christian heroism they dared every difficulty and danger, with patience they endured the greatest sufferings and with perseverance maintained their profession and practice in the face of all opposition and peril: they continued stedfast though with the jeopardy of their lives, and every thing which men hold dear.

They were stedfast and constant in their attendance on the public institutions of religion, the dispensation of the word and sacraments; although constrained ed from a regard to their own safety to hold their religious assemblies in the dead of night and in places of retirement. As they were constant hearers, so also they were conscientious doers of the word: with cautious precision they formed their hearts and lives by the rules of that heavenly doctrine: this they embraced, not by an implicit faith in their teachers, but upon careful examination; "they searched the scriptures daily to see if these things were so." Assiduous to "prove all things and hold fast that which is good."

3. They continued stedfast, not only in the Apostles doctrine, but also in fellowship. This may include these three things, viz. fellowship with the Apostles— their social communion among themselves—and their reciprocal communication of aid and benefits one to another. This evidently intends fellowship with the Apostles and is what is especially implied; "they continued stedfast in the Apostles' fellowship as well as doctrine, i. e. they adhered closely to their own teachers, their own ministers, and communion with them in their ministrations: and by their example discountenance and reprove the schismatical conduct of professors who without just cause withdraw from their own ministers and the congregations with which they are connected. The first christians, with one accord, were constant in their attendance on the public institutions of religion, dispensed by their own ministers; and in doing so, give an example worthy of imitation, which may administer reproof and correction to those who either, through carelessness and inattention, are negligent or unsteady in their attendance on christian institutions, or for mere curiosity, slight of their own ministers, or an itch for novelty and change, forsake their own assembly and minister, and go otherwhere without necessity or any good reason. This example may be of use to instruct and convince us that it is incumbent on every christian to continue stedfast in fellowship with those teachers who have been regularly set over them in the Lord.

The

The word fellowship signifies company or joint partnership; they, who manage business in company, whether trade or any other, are in **fellowship**, as they severally share the labour, expense, loss and gain of the business. People have fellowship with their ministers when they willingly share with them in the toil, the cost, **the hazard** and incalculable profit of a due attendance on the public use of christian institutions: That is, when they attend with constancy, with a docile temper, truly desirous of religious instruction and animation, ready to submit to and obey them, as their spiritual fathers and guides. They then have fellowship with their ministers when they so improve the word and other christian ordinances as to answer their great design, viz. The promotion of the **common cause** for which both ministers and their people are set apart, jointly with **united** diligence and zeal, **to** labour; it is the cause of **christianity, the cause** of Christ and of all his true disciples.

They also continued stedfast in fellowship among themselves, and communion one with another. As the social intercourse of saints in heaven constitutes no small part of the happiness of heaven, so the christian fellowship of saints on earth, affords a degree of heaven upon earth.

Social feelings and exercises are essential to the happiness of man; but in order to these there must be a suitableness of sentiment and disposition: The primitive christians were of one mind and one heart, and thus adapted to coalesce in one body: For although man loves and is happified in society, yet it is only the society of those whom he loves: He cannot be delighted and in society with those whom he hates. It is the nature of love to attract and unite men one to another, on the contrary, hatred in its nature tends to disunite, make them distant and shy one of another.— Hence it is evident that brotherly love is of essential importance to the delights and advantages of christian
fellowship:

fellowship : the very term imports concord, agreement and friendly intercourse.

THE fellowship of christians is that holy communion and partnership which they have with Christ, in all his benefits, by faith and among themselves by love; and is a joint participation in the common privileges and duties of christianity, and a reciprocal interchange of the offices of love and brotherly kindness : It is held and exercised in great variety ; by no means principally in a mutual communication of temporal benefits, tho' this is necessarily included ; but especially of spiritual, particularly, they have fellowship in doctrine or faith as in the text, they embrace the same doctrines, and as to things essential to salvation, at least, they hold to the same system or confession of faith. They have fellowship in mutual brotherly exhortation ; as required, they exhort one another daily. Also in consolation and joy ; they not only share jointly in the consolations of the spirit ; but have a feeling participation in each others comforts and joys. In love, they are kindly affectioned one to another in brotherly love ; cordial affection, and to love as brethren is common to all the saints ; in which they all have fellowship. In humility and proper submission : always ready to submit themselves to God, and one to another in his fear. In pity and tender compassion one to another. In prayer ; but this being particularly noticed in the text, will of course be considered in its place.

FARTHER, christian fellowship includes a mutual communication of benefits. " The multitude of them who believed were of one heart and one soul ; neither said any of them that ought of the things which he possessed was his own ; but they had all things common." The intire union of these early converts is worthy of remark and of imitation ; they were not merely one in doctrine and sentiment, but one in affection, " *of one heart and of one soul.*"

THEY

They were in reality what the members of the christian church in all ages and places ought to be and profess to be, a band of brothers: An excellent pattern for christians to imitate to the end of the world. They behaved one towards another as members of the same body, animated by the same head. Their ardent love and fellow-feeling was not concealed in the heart, it was operative, and expressed in its visible genuine fruits of liberality: "They called" and considered "nothing as their own, of all which they possessed," when the necessities of their brethren called for a distribution: The possessors of goods sold them and formed a common stock, from which the poor equally as the rich were supplied; for "they had all things common."

This example however is not designed to be a pattern which christians, in ordinary times, are required to imitate; because the state of the church, at that time, was such as it never since has been, nor is it probable ever will be: It was then in its infancy, there had not been opportunity to make provision for the regular supply of the wants of the poor, at least of poor christians; the whole church was then contained in one city, Jerusalem, and harrassed by persecution; liable soon to be dispersed, as they soon were in fact. This important and necessary instruction however may be gained from this extraordinary instance of christian liberality, that they to whom God hath given ability ought, according to their ability, be it more or less, to abound in ordinary, and as occasion may occur, in extraordinary acts of charity. Christians in all times and places ought to exercise the same love and tender affection one towards another as these primitive christians, and to as high a degree, and be as ready to express it in outward act whenever occasion may require.

Another and emminent instance of christian fellowship, in which they continued stedfast, was breaking of bread; not common but sacramental bread, i. e.

SER. XVI.   *of Christian Institutions.*   263

in celebrating the Lord's supper : So ardent was their zeal and devotion that none of their religious assemblies were held in which they did not solemnly commemorate the death of Christ at his table : They seem to have considered their other public exercises of religion as incomplete without this.

The Saviour's blood was yet warm, and they wished to keep it warm in their hearts, by a frequent remembrance of it, at his holy table. Their constancy in celebrating this christian institution, as a mean, gave life to all their other religious services ; and qualified them both for doing and suffering their Lord's will. Their frequent partaking of the cup, that symbol of Christ's blood, seemed to fire them with zeal and fortitude in shedding their own blood in his cause.

Alas ! What account will men give, a day of accounts is approaching, for having, of their own choice, neglected so useful and so necessary an institution, always in their offer !

Are they apprized that it is the institution of a dying Saviour, appointed by infinite wisdom and love, as a mean highly important to the salvation of his redeemed people !

Are men now above these helps to a good life, and preparation for heaven, which christians once so highly esteemed and so carefully improved ! Have we not as great need to use the best means to arm ourselves against sin, the world and temptation ; and to animate our exertions to secure a blessed immortality ?

Is not the true and obvious reason why this institution is neglected by so many, because men are not willing to be so holy, so strictly bound by the rules of duty, as they then were used as christians always ought to be ? Are there not those, in great numbers whose own hearts bear them witness, if not void of all serious reflection, that the holy sacrament would bind them to greater strictness in religion than they can endure the thought of submitting to ? If they join themselves

selves to the Lord and approach to his table, they are conscious, they must leave their sins, depart from all iniquity, deny themselves of every unlawful gratification, live soberly, righteously and godly, to which their hearts are utterly opposed and are ready to revolt at the very thought. They must forgive and love their enemies, on whom they have vowed revenge, and which they cannot be willing to relinquish: They must enter into sacred engagements, which they heartily wish to be free from: Are therefore reluctant and shy of laying themselves under personal obligations to love God, keep his commandments, attend his ordinances or abridge their fancied liberty to the contrary. If God, by his sovereign authority, lays them under the obligations of his law and gospel, to refrain from those ways of sin, which persisted in, would unavoidably issue in destruction, and choose the path of life, they can neither resist nor avoid their force, though little felt; yet utterly thwarting to the governing inclination of their hearts: and, was it in their power, would gladly burst these bonds of divine restraint and rid themselves of every tie to a religious life: Is it not hence clearly manifest that, by whatever self-flattering excuses such persons may seek to quiet their own minds and keep themselves in countenance, their neglect of this and other ordinances is to be resolved into the prevalent wickedness of their own hearts; their unmortified love of sin, and a criminal aversion to a religious life? And they would excuse themselves and feel nearly blameless, and perhaps in the way of duty in not attending christian institutions, from the consideration of their own unfitness, and thence conclude it is not their duty, but would be sin to attend them; but can disobedience to the express commands of God and a neglect of his positive institutions be innocent? Can transgression and duty be the same thing? Then sin and duty are the same: But such neglectors would act more wisely and safely would they set themselves with serious

solicitude

solicitude to examine and explore what it is that makes up that unfitness which they consider and rely on as sufficient to excuse and exculpate them in a neglect of special ordinances: Would they not easily find it to consist wholly in an evil heart of unbelief, which occasions their departure from the living God, a criminal aversion to an holy God, and his holy institutions? That they love sin rather than duty, the perverse wickedness of their own hearts, would be found their only excuse. Was this their unfitness truly the grief and burthen of their souls; what they detest, lament and truly wish to be freed from, it would at once be removed; but instead of this, it is what they love and cherish, and refuse to part with.

The last thing mentioned in the text, in which the primitive christians continued stedfast in fellowship, is prayer, i. e. in solemn social addresses to God in their public assemblies; in which they poured out their souls to him in fervent supplications with thanksgiving.

Public prayers and intercessions are always to be used, and solemnly attended as an important interesting branch of christian worship; to be held in high esteem by all; this high esteem and a sacred regard for them ought to be witnessed, in a diligent and seasonable attendance on them: pious caution is to be used in avoiding an unnecessary late attendance on, and too early a withdraw from the public administrations of God's house. The whole congregation, if it be practicable, ought to be present and composed in their places, when divine worship begins, and continue so until it be ended. The use of this caution would prevent several evils which so far as may be, ought to be avoided, such as these, viz. A slow and tardy approach to the house of God, and a too early departure from it, have the appearance of too little esteem and respect for divine institutions, and shew them to be burthensome and grievous, which tends to the dishonour of God, disesteem of his worship, disserve the cause of religion, and encourage and strengthen the hands of the irreligious and profane, in their neglect and contempt of christian institutions: This is not all the evil; for the neglect of this caution, interrupts the attention and profit of others and impedes the worship of God: The worship of the Deity, in all cases, ought to be celebrated with profound reverence and devout uninterrupted composure.

The public exercises of religion in general, of prayer in particular, properly solemnized, serve to glorify God in the most illustrious manner, are highly acceptable to him, keep alive some sense of God and religion in the minds of men: No sacrifice is more pleasing to God or beneficial to men than the united pious homage of his people in their public assemblies. The Lord loveth the gates of Zion more than all the religious services in the private dwellings of Jacob.

The people of God, when with one accord, they come up to his public worship, do at least externally give him public honour: In open view they give their testimony that he is worthy and ought to be worshiped, and that they regard and reverence his authority and institutions: and by their example openly and loudly invite and encourage others to come and with them partake in the fatness of God's house. On the other hand, when professors of religion shew themselves remiss and negligent by their total or frequent absence from the worship of God, instead of giving him honour, in a public manner they reproach and dishonour him; for by their neglect they bear public testimony that the authority and law of the Supreme Ruler are not binding and may well be trampled on, and his institutions so far from being sacredly important and useful that they are vain and unprofitable, a grievous burthen, worthy to be treated with disregard and neglect. Such unchristian example has great influence upon others, especially the loose and profane, to bring religion in general, and its public institutions in particular,

ular, into disrepute and disuse, and thus serves to encourage and embolden them, not simply to imitate, but if possible, to exceed the pattern.

READING the best books, the Bible not excepted, though joined with prayer or other religious services, in our own houses on the sabbath, may not be substituted in the place of a personal attendance and fellowship in the public exercises of religion; for this at best would be a mere selfish business; but we are required to regard not every one his own benefit only, but the good of others also: Such private devotion, be it ever so devout, does not give that public encouragement and animation to others, nor that visible countenance and honour to divine institutions which God requires and is well pleased with in preference to any or all religious worship in private; for these, as they are timed, are mere humane inventions set up in place of divine institutions, with which God is not well pleased, nor the worshipper really profited: "In vain do they worship me teaching for doctrine the commandments of men." Without the blessing of God success is not to be hoped for; but we are warranted to expect his blessing only in the way of his own institutions; to these only hath he annexed and promised it. It will one day appear that God is acceptably worshipped in no other way but precisely in that which he himself hath prescribed: we are not warranted to substitute any thing else in the place of divine institutions.

BESIDE, we are to consider that the public exercises of religion, serve above all other instrumental means, to maintain and give life to true devotion and the fear of God among men: They, who in a land of light, of choice habitually neglect the former, shew themselves to be without the latter: And that open disregard and neglect with which they treat religion in public, is a proper index to point us to their neglect of it in private. Hence we may justly conclude that a prevailing neglect of christian institutions in public directly tends

and

and iminently threatens to erase from the minds of men a proper regard for the Lord's day, and for religion in general, and in this way to extirpate the church with all its ineftimable privileges from among a people, and fink them down into a state more forlorn and hopeless than that of the heathen.

Surely every true friend to the christian cause, will be vigilant and cautious, at least with respect to his own conduct, to avoid every thing both in word and example which might tend to forward so destructive an evil; and strenuously labour by every mean in his power to obstruct and prevent it.

The example of the primitive christians which we have been contemplating is fruitful, in a variety of instances, in profitable instruction relative to our own duty.

I. A stedfast adherence to the doctrines of christianity: That we embrace them in our understandings, and that in their genuine sense; receive them as divine and infallibly true: Approve and esteem them as excellent above gold, highly interesting and necessary to salvation: That we consult and attend to them with sacred awe as the very word of God: With candour search them daily, with a mind open to instruction, with an honest aim, not to support a favourite opinion and because it is so, but to learn the truth and avoid error. That we constantly and devoutly attend and have fellowship with our spiritual instructors, in their public ministrations: Solicitous to come with minds free of prejudice, open to the truth, eager to embrace and practise it; penetrated with the sentiment that our governing end in hearing should be that we may be doers of the word, forming both our hearts and practices by it.

II. That we are stedfast in fellowship one with another: To that end our hearts must be warm with love to God and man: We must imitate the example before us, in being of one heart and one soul; having a mutual sympathetic feeling as members of the same body, animated by the same spirit, governed by the same head: sharing in common the dignity, privileges, duties, labours, trials and rewards of christianity.

It may be of some use here to obviate a mistake which enthusiasts have fallen into in their notions of christian fellowship, who have made it to consist essentially in certain inward feelings which christians have one towards another, a kind of undescribable communion or rather communication of heart to heart, peculiar to true christians, by which, they imagine, they are able to discern and distinguish, with infallible certainty, the real christian from others, by their own feelings towards him; in their own words they can feel him, and thence know him to be a saint indeed: This they have considered, if not the only, the most exalted kind of christian fellowship: By this they gain, as they imagine, absolute certainty, both of their own sonship, because they love the brethren, and that of others, because they love them as saints, having no respect to the moral character or fruits of the one or the other: Of this kind of fellowship the scripture gives no account; and it is delusive, useless and dangerous. A christian temper is to love all as saints who profess and appear to be so: The good man will exercise the same love to the hypocrite as to the saint, while he considers him as a saint.

From the example in the text it appears that the fellowship of primitive christians consisted not in such inward feelings or emotions as imply an immediate and direct intercourse of heart to heart; but in a common participation of the privileges, ordinances, duties and blessings of christianity: They, it appears, had fellowship in gospel doctrine, in breaking of bread and in prayers; their fellowship consisted in a joint participation of those outward and ordinary means which God hath appointed and given to his church for her edification: Which are always to be used under the influence of supreme love to God, faith in his promises and brotherly affection one to another. Their

Their example invites and even binds us so to love one another as to be ready to every work of goodness: Ready to communicate, according to the ability which God hath given us, to relieve the necessities of others; especially to supply the wants of our fellow christians. Perhaps no duty of our religion is more frequently or with greater ardour inculcated in the New Testament; yet how little attended to? Certain it is, it will be found of capital importance and influence in the decisions of the final judgment: This will then be respected and honoured above every other kind of good works; perhaps, because by the want of this every other will then be proved insincere and hypocritical: It seems to be established as the test of the sincerity and soundness of our personal religion: It will be alledged by the judge himself as the declarative ground of that transporting sentence, "Come ye blessed of my Father, inherit the kingdom prepared for you from the foundation of the world; for I was an hungred and ye gave me meat, &c." And the want of this will be announced as the reason of the awful sentence against the wicked, depart from me, ye cursed, into everlasting fire, &c. For I was an hungred and ye gave me no meat, &c.

III. The practice of the primitive church may be of use to instruct and persuade us as to our duty, with respect to the holy supper.

Their stedfastness, zeal and frequency in celebrating that sacred solemnity, with great force may admonish us to go and do likewise. When we view their ardent love to Christ, their fervour, stedfastness and delight in his worship and institutions what abundant reason have we to take shame to ourselves and in deep humiliation before God, lament our want of love, at least a warmer love to him; our coldness in his service and reluctance to approach to him in his sacred institutions: That we are no more constant, conscientious, fervent, devout nor delighted in attending them.

How

SER. XVI. *of Christian Institutions.*

How much is it to be regreted, and what cause of deep humiliation before God, that the name of Christ is so greatly dishonoured and his institutions, particularly baptism and the Lord's supper, vilified by that neglect with which they are treated by great numbers, even of those who would not be accounted the enemies of the cross of Christ; nor even unfriendly to his religion: Nay, of those who, at least, implicitly profess to be his followers, his disciples and even his friends, and that their only hope of salvation is through the merit of his blood.

ALL, without exception, are to be considered the professors of the christian religion, who have and receive the word of God as his word, acknowledge its divine authority, and that they, equally as others, are holden to observe and obey it: Who commonly attend the public prayers and instructions of his house: All such persons do publicly, though implicitly own themselves under all the obligations of his covenant, his word is this covenant, for that reason is often called the book of the covenant: Such professors, in that they receive the scripture as the word of God, are under all the obligations that the authority of God, in his word can lay them, agreeably as the members of the church: His positive command to the former equally as to the latter is, "Obey my voice," and they are as strictly holden to depart from all iniquity, be holy in all manner of conversation, and neglect no part either of natural or instituted worship; no, not any one divine institution. Nor is it possible that professors of the above description, should be free of such sacred obligations; they cannot free themselves, unless they can successfully resist God and shew themselves stronger than he; nor can God himself free them, for in so doing he must deny himself, lay aside his kind regard for his creatures, forfeit his word, become like to the sinner and connive at transgression: Thus solemnly and invincibly are they bound to believe and do all that

God

God requires in his **word,** which he hath put into their hands, and they receive as his word.

Dear souls, your only wise and safe course, in this serious situation is, not to wish or seek to be freed from these sacred and salutary obligations, or to reduce them to little ; but chearfully and heartily embrace them in all their extent ; because it is your life : Subscribe them with **all your** souls : Make open and public confession of their **reasonableness and** excellency and your full consent **and closure with** them : **thus by y**our own personal vows bind yourselves to the **Lord** as his willing people, to walk in all his commandments and ordinances blameless, this do in a firm reliance on, and with fervent prayers to God for his holy spirit to help you both to vow and **also to pay your** vows in a manner acceptable to him and salutary to yourselves. *Amen.*

SERMON

SERMON XVII.

PERSUASIVES TO AN ATTENDANCE ON THE LORD'S SUPPER.

Luke xxii. 17. *last clause*. *This do in remembrance of me.*

OUR blessed Saviour, on the evening preceding his crucifixion, abolished the passover, and instituted the sacrament of the supper.

The passover was a feast annually celebrated, in commemoration of the miraculous deliverance of the Jewish nation from their bondage in Egypt. A Lamb, or figuratively, *innocence*, was slain and eaten, in a solemn manner.

This Lamb was a type of the innocent Jesus, who, as the Lamb of God, was slain from the foundation of the world; and was now ready to make an actual sacrifice of himself upon the cross, for the liberation of men from the bondage of sin.

This sacrifice, being an event of the first importance, as it would demonstrate the love of God to this lost world, and open the mysteries of redemption, Christ, while eating the passover, instituted the sacrament of the supper—appointed the symbols—gave his disciples an example of the manner he would have it

L L observed—

observed—explained the design of the institution, and by an explicit command, and in a solemn manner enjoined their observance of it. *And he took bread, and gave thanks, and brake it, and gave unto them, saying, This is my body which is given for you:—This do, in remembrance of me. Likewise, also, the cup after supper, saying, This cup is the New Testament in my blood which is shed for you; or, according to St. Matthew, for the remission of sins.*

THE nature and design of this sacrament, together with the time, place, and manner of its institution, unite, to impress the reflecting mind with a deep sense of its importance. The death of Christ is, indeed, the central point of all the doctrines and mysteries of redeeming love.

BUT however important the institution, however explicitly, and solemnly, the observance of it is enjoined, yet many, who hope for acceptance with God, thro' the merit of Christ's atonement, disregard the injunctions of the Saviour, and treat the sacrament with total neglect.

FOR the consideration and benefit of such, this discourse is designed. Read and contemplate with candor, and a feeling concern for your spiritual interest, the motives I here lay before you, to influence you to an attendance on this commemorative sacrifice of the Lord Jesus.

YOU have had your minds perplexed with vain janglings, and intemperate disputes respecting proper subjects for this ordinance, and modes of admission to it. This I lament, as it has weakened your sense of obligation to the duty, and has had a tendency to remove from your minds a consciousness of guilt, while living in the open violation of the authority of the Saviour.

BUT, from whatever cause your neglect may have arisen, since, what hope you entertain of pardon, and of final admission into heaven is founded on the doctrines

rines of the cross, you can have no argument of sufficient force to justify you in this neglect. That you may be sensible of this, and be stimulated to an immediate attention to your duty—I invite you, first, to a serious consideration of the designs of the ordinance.

1. ONE great design of it is, to preserve a lively impression on the mind, of the death and passion of the Lord Jesus.

THAT this end might be answered, our Saviour appointed bread and wine as symbols of his body and blood. That the bread should be broken, or bruised, as a visible representation of the bruising of his body on the cross. And that the wine being poured forth, should lead us to contemplate his streaming blood.— That, by the united influence of these symbols, our minds and hearts might be kept alive as to a sense of his dying agonies.

HAD there been no sacrament instituted for the purpose of calling back our naturally forgetful and wandering minds, to the sufferings of the great object of our holy religion, our sense of them would have been weak, and to them our thoughts would seldom have recurred.

OUR feelings are naturally sympathetic. Objects in distress make deep impressions. And when the Lord Jesus, who ought to be the object of our love and dependance, is visibly represented in all the agonies of the cross, we must do violence to ourselves, to remain unaffected.

THIS sacrament you neglect. Is not this an evidence that you have no desire to retain a suffering, bleeding Saviour in your minds? But, you acknowledge that what hope you entertain of salvation, is founded on the atoning blood of Christ. Does not that hope forbid your forgetfulness of the anguish he suffered when sheding it on the cross? Are you not, indeed, inconsistent with yourselves, when you indulge an hope of pardon, and of acceptance with God, and yet neglect

lect the appointed means of recalling to your minds, those sufferings of the Saviour which he endured, to procure these ineftimable bleffings for you? Can you lift up your eyes, and hearts, to Jefus in heaven, for the benefits of his crofs, and not feel the impropriety of your conduct in neglecting the fymbols of his fufferings?

2. THE facrament of the fupper is defigned, to exhibit Chrift in the higheft act of his fufferings, as an evidence of his unbounded love for us.

GREATER love hath no man than this, that he lay down his life for his friends, but the love of Chrift, manifefted by his dying agonies, exceeds our higheft thoughts; while we were yet enemies he died for us. His facred body was broken, and his foul preffed down under the weight of divine wrath, becaufe the chaftifement of our peace was upon him.

WHAT muft have been his love for us, voluntarily to have borne our ftripes inflicted in fuch a cruel manner?

THIS facrament being defigned to lead us to a contemplation, and to revive in our minds a fenfe, of this love, with what propriety can it be omitted? Does not this omiffion evidence the higheft ingratitude? Is it not expreffive of fuch indifference to the love and compaffion of the redeemer, as on reflection, to excite a confcioufnefs of unworthinefs?

You pretend to believe in Jefus—to exercife an affection for him—to entertain a grateful fenfe of his love, manifefted for you, in his fufferings and death; yet you refufe the fymbols defigned to exhibit this love. What is the language of this neglect? It is, that you are infenfible of the benevolence of your redeemer—are ungrateful to your divine benefactor; and that all your pretenfions to chriftian virtue, and to an affection for the Saviour, may, with propriety, be confidered on as pretenfions. They, who love Chrift, keep his commandments.

3. ANOTHER

3. ANOTHER defign of the facrament is, that all fuch as hope for falvation by the crofs, may, by an attendance upon it, exprefs their humble and public acknowledgment of the fundamental articles of the chriftian faith.—*That the death of* **Chrift** *is the only ground of hope for pardon.*

A FIRM belief of this truth is effential to the chriftian character. For, without the fheding of blood, there is no remiffion.

To the virtue and efficacy of Chrift's blood you look for falvation. What poffible reafon can you give why you fhould not publicly acknowledge it, by your attendance on this commemorative facrifice? Are you afhamed of the foundation of your hope? If fo, will not **Chrift** be afhamed of you in his kingdom?

4. THE facrament of the fupper is defigned as a ftanding witnefs to the world, of their infidelity, and ingratitude. As oft as ye eat this bread and drink this cup, ye do fhew the Lord's death till he come. Chrift is exhibited in this facrament, not only for the benefit of believers, but as a teftimony againft the unbelieving world. *There are three who bear record in heaven, the Father, the Word, and the Holy Ghoft, and thefe three are one. And there are three that bear witnefs in the earth, the Spirit, and the Water, and the blood; and thefe three agree in one.*

WHATEVER may be fignified by the witneffes in heaven, it is probable that by the blood, one of the witneffes in the earth, is meant, the facrament of the fupper. They, who, as the friends of Chrift, attend on the euchariſt, make to the world a public manifeftation of his death, which was the witnefs of his love, and of his placing himfelf in a condition to beftow everlafting bleffings on fuch as believe on him.

If thefe remarks are juft, it follows, that you are fo far from being witneffes for Jefus, or from ufing your influence to preferve the witnefs of him in the world, that you are included with others, againft whofe infidelity,

delity, negligence, and ingratitude this facrament bears teftimony. Whatever the fecret exercifes of your heart may be, and however amiable your private character, yet in a public view you are out of the kingdom of Chrift, are unbelievers, vifibly in the kingdom of darknefs, and feparated from the commonwealth of Ifrael.

5. THE facrament of the fupper is defigned to recal to our remembrance the exceeding finfulnefs of fin, together with the holinefs, and juftice of God.

WHAT can prefent to our view in more lively colours the nature of fin, and the divine difapprobation of it, than a reprefentation of the fufferings of the Son of God? When we confider his true character, as the only begotten of the Father, in whom dwelt the fulnefs of the godhead, and that when he took upon him the form of a fervant, he could not be accepted as a mediator, until he had fuffered the full penalty of the broken law, the nature of fin, and the juftice of God muft be forcibly impreffed upon our minds.

WHY did Chrift agonize in the garden? Why, on the crofs did he cry out in anguifh, and in bitternefs of foul—*My God, my God, why haft thou forfaken me?* It was becaufe he was preffed down under the weight of our iniquities. Though he knew no fin, he was made fin for us. The chaftifement of our peace was upon him. He was involved in the wrath of God. The fupporting influences of heaven were withdrawn from him—and he funk into death.

IN various inftances God has manifefted his indignation againft fin. The rebel angels, or the morning ftars he thruft down from heaven, into darknefs, without hope of recovery. Man he expelled from the earthly paradife—The old world he deftroyed by a flood of waters—and the cities of Sodom and Gomorrah he confumed by fire. In all thefe inftances there was a wonderful difplay of divine wrath. In none of them, however, was there fuch an exhibition of his inflexible juftice, as in his frowns upon the Saviour. When Chrift

Christ was chastised for our peace, and God hid his face from him, and denied him every divine comfort under his greatest distresses, then it was that his indignation against sin was manifested, and his holiness and justice were displayed. It was evident God could not spare even his own Son when our iniquities were upon him; but justice pursued him as a fugitive, and criminal, and required of him full satisfaction to the broken law.

But, the sacrament which exhibits these things, you neglect. Is not this neglect a painful evidence that you have but a faint impression on your minds of the justice of God, and of the nature of sin? Can it be, that you are disposed to obliterate from your souls every impression of the wrath of God, in which the Saviour was involved, when your iniquities were upon him? Surely not; why then neglect the instituted means of recalling these things to your minds?

6. ANOTHER design of the Lord's supper is to remind us of the blessed fruits, and effects of Christ's death.

HEREBY the law, as to believers, was disarmed of its condemning power—Christ having passed to the end of it. Hereby the prince of darkness was vanquished; for by the cross Christ spoiled principalities and powers, making a shew of them openly, triumphing over them in it. Hereby the hand writing of ordinances, which was against us, was blotted out, being taken away, and nailed to his cross. As a blessed fruit of Christ's death the Holy Ghost is sent into the world, by whose powerful operations the believer is born again, and receives earnests of a glorious immortality.

THESE are only a specimen of the benefits of the atonement. And do you neglect that institution which is designed to impress your minds with a just sense of such blessings? If so, does it not follow that you ought *in Justice*, to be deprived of the enjoyment of every

blessing

blessing flowing from the cross of Christ? I leave you to answer the question to your own minds.

7. THE sacrament of the supper is designed for a standing confirmation of the covenant which God, by his Son, has entered into with man. And our attendance upon it, is a practical confession of our grateful acceptance of the conditions of pardon offered in that covenant; of which the blood of Christ was the seal. The Testament was not of force whilst the testator lived, but by his death received its efficacy. That sacrament, therefore, which is appointed as a memorial of the sealing of the covenant, is of the first importance: And our attendance then on it is the strongest external evidence we can give, of our grateful acceptance of the pardon it offers. It follows, that such as refuse this sealing ordinance give the strongest evidence, that they refuse to accept of pardon on the conditions of the covenant.

I WILL not further enlarge on the nature and designs of the institution; but will turn your attention to other considerations, tending to impress your minds with a sense of the importance of an immediate attention to this christian sacrament.

YOU are not insensible that the Lord Jesus, by a positive command, has enjoined your attendance on this institution; and that, as an indispensable requisite in the christian character. And it is impossible, you can be so ignorant, as to suppose, that you can recommend yourselves to him by disobedience. What possible reason can you have to hope, that the Great Head of the church will receive you into favour, and make you the subjects of his grace, when you are the practical despisers of his authority, and of the riches of his table?

POSSIBLY, you may have, in some respects, misunderstood the command, by considering it as binding on none but those who have very satisfactory evidence
of

of their regeneration, and union to Christ ; and therefore, have not felt the criminality of disobedience.

If you consider the command in this light, you labour under an error. All the commands of Christ are binding. And a personal disqualification to keep them, is an aggravation of the sin of disobedience :— For, if a personal disqualification is a sufficient justification of disobedience it follows, that it is in the power of men to render void all the commands of God. Let them love and practise sin, till the habits of iniquity are become rooted, and they are disqualified from keeping the commands.

But you, who endeavour to justify your disobedience to the command of the redeemer respecting the eucharist, would be surprised, to hear a man plead his voluntary incapacity, to keep the divine law, as a matter of self-justification. Yet, where is the difference between his conduct and your own ? Here is a command which you acknowledge to be binding on believers ; but you have not certain evidence that you are believers ; therefore not binding on you : The consequence unavoidably follows, that you justify sin, by sin ; for you will not pretend but that you are bound to believe. Does not this appear like trifling with the authority of God ? And is it not virtually subjecting the laws of the Redeemer to your own will.

You consider the Lord's supper as a solemn sacrament, designed for the benefit of such as hope in the righteousness of Christ. In this you are right. Your error lies in the consequence you draw from this important truth, which is, that you are not sufficiently holy, and are not possessed of that satisfactory evidence of your title to the benefits of Christ's purchase, which gives you a right to the ordinance. At the same time when asked on what foundation you hope for eternal life, you say, on the atonement of Christ. But, how can you hope for life and happiness on this foundation, and yet be disqualified to keep that command which is

designed

designed to preserve on the mind a lively sense of the sufferings of the Saviour. If you have hope in Christ, according to your own construction of the command, you have a right to the sacrament, and all its important blessings.

The evidence, say you, that your hope is well founded, is weak—too weak to justify your attendance on a sacrament of such solemnity and importance. I enquire—Has your Saviour made a weak hope, the want of assurance, or of certain evidence of sanctification a bar against communicating his dying love in the eucharist? There is no such thing in the New Testament. If there were, who could obey? But is disobedience a proper course to be taken, in order to strengthen the evidences of grace? If you reasoned wisely you would conclude, that this is the cause of your doubts, and fears, and that while the means of strengthening are neglected you will always remain feeble.

You seem to fear obedience to this command because of the solemnity of the sacrament. You consider it more solemn and awful, than any other institution of divine appointment. Whether you are right in drawing this comparison, and in affixing different degrees of solemnity to the ordinances of God, I will not decide. Every religious duty ought to be performed with reverence and Godly fear. Is there any thing more solemn in calling the mind back to a contemplation of the sufferings of the Saviour, by external symbols, than there is in addressing the infinite Jehovah by prayer? But you will not, surely, justify the neglect of this duty on the principle of its being solemn. You go to the throne of grace, and speak to God, though sensible you cannot order your speech aright. You do not neglect the duty because of its awfulness. Neither ought you on this account to neglect the sacrament. If you consider it, a solemn ordinance you ought to attend to it for that very reason: You need solemnizing.

And

And this will tend to strengthen your hope, and remove the gloomy apprehensions you entertain of yourselves.

FURTHER, as a motive to influence you to attend on this commemorative sacrafice, you ought to contemplate your baptismal obligations. Baptism is an external seal of the covenant of grace: And an evidence that you are solemnly dedicated to the service of God. "Know ye not that so many of us as were baptized into Jesus Christ, were baptized into his death, therefore we are buried with him by baptism into death, that like as Christ was raised up from the dead, by the glory of the Father, so we also should walk in newness of life." From hence it appears that you are visibly in Christ, and are members of his household; lying under covenant obligations to walk in obedience to all his commands. You, therefore, who, having received baptism into Christ, seperate yourselves from the communion, are covenant breakers. You turn from the holy commandment, in violation of that covenant which is sealed by baptism. You are visibly of the household of God, but refuse to partake in the provisions of the house; or to submit to the authority of the master. Instead of possessing that temper, in the exercise of which, you would receive with thankfulness and joy the crumbs of his table, you have not a disposition to obey the command, to partake of the full provisions of your master's house. This, you must be sensible is walking in the course of the world; and not in that newness of life which your Saviour requires.

CONSIDER also, the benefits to be derived from this holy ordinance, as a motive to influence you, to an immediate attention to your duty. You cannot suppose that the benevolent redeemer, whose object was the joy and salvation of men, would have instituted this solemn sacrament, without intending it as a medium through which to communicate special blessings. Accordingly he has promised his gracious presence with

the

the ministration of it. This has a direct tendency to banish fear, and to promote joy and gladness of heart, to increase the graces of faith, hope, meekness and love—to excite in your souls a **desire to fulfil all righteousness**—to wean you from the vanities of the present world—to lead you to contemplate with unshaken confidence, the power and majesty, of the glorious redeemer—and to familiarize the thoughts of immortality—to **enable** you to look forward to the appearing of the great God, and your Saviour with a composed mind and a glorious hope. What then does your neglect imply? Have you **no wish** that your faith should be strengthened, your hope, **love**, and joy increased; nor, indeed, that any of the graces of the spirit should be **revived in your heart, or** appear in your life?

THE dangers also, **to** which you expose yourselves by **disobedience to** this command, you ought **seriously to contemplate.** Does not your violation of the authority of Christ, in this important **instance, amount to a revolt** from his sovereignty; and to a voluntary enlistment **of** yourselves under the banners of the prince of disobedience? True, you have not had this apprehension of the nature of your conduct: And may be surprised to hear it suggested. But, contemplate the words of the Saviour.—" Whosoever shall confess me before men him will I *confess* also before my Father who is in heaven. **But whosoever** shall deny me before **men,** him will I *deny* before my Father who is in heaven." What does Christ design by this confession? Is it not **the** giving of public testimony that you are his disciples, and that you look to the cross for salvation? But you make **no** public confession. And do you find in any of Christ's discourses, that he considered such as his disciples who, from any cause, did not make a public confession of their belief? This declaration of our Saviour is solemn, and requires the close meditation of neglecters.

You

You pretend that you are chriſtians : What evidence do you give that you are ſo, when a poſitive command of Chriſt is by you, openly diſregarded, a ſolemn inſtitution neglected—a ſpecial mean of preparation for heaven ſlighted, and the preſence of the glorious redeemer avoided ? What greater evidence of an unchriſtian temper than this, can be given ? How can you pretend that your hope is founded on the croſs of Chriſt ? Aſk a Jew, or Mahometan, whether you give evidence that you are Chriſtians : He will anſwer that, " you have no part, or lot in him, on whom you pretend to believe." The argument may, indeed, be brought into a very narrow compaſs. " He that is not with me, is againſt me"—ſaid the Redeemer : Are you with, or againſt him ? There is no middle ſtand : Can you be with him and yet live in the open violation of his authority ? If you can—what is it to be againſt him ? This queſtion, I leave for you to anſwer to your own minds.

Were Chriſt preſent, we may well ſuppoſe he would addreſs you in the following language. " In love and compaſſion for you I have died a cruel death. I command you to remember me, in the exerciſe of a benevolent temper. Senſible, from my perfect knowledge of the human heart, and the temptations of the world, that you are expoſed to looſe a lively ſenſe of my death and paſſion, I have in mercy appointed an important ſacrament calculated to diſtinguiſh you from the unbelieving world, and have adapted it to your particular uſe and advantage. This ſacrament you neglect, tho' as a *friend*, I have ſolicited your attendance, and as your *Sovereign* have commanded it. As your *friend*, and *Saviour* I ſtill continue my ſolicitations. I urge you by the love and compaſſion of my nature—by the ſufferings I endured, and by the bleſſings you may receive from a compliance with my will, to defer no longer. If you have any love for me, who have loved you unto death. If you have any reverence for my memory—

any

any gratitude for the important services I have rendered you, or any fear of punishment hereafter, for disobedience to my laws, immediately come forward and take the vows of the altar. I entreat you, not to suffer an ill-grounded fear to operate as a self justifying argument for disobedience. Fear of obeying my command, lest you offend, you know to be unjust. I delight in your obedience, not in that slavish fear which leads you to a violation of my authority.

"You know that all things are ready—the feast is prepared—Come, then, oh friends! Eat and drink, yea drink abundantly, that your souls may be satisfied with the riches of my house." *Amen*.

SERMON XVIII.

INFANTS OF BELIEVERS MEMBERS OF THE CHURCH OF CHRIST.

GENESIS xvii. 7. *And I will establish my covenant between me and thee, and thy seed after thee in their generations, for an everlasting Covenant, to be a God unto thee, and to thy seed after thee.*

GOD made a Covenant with Abraham, saying, "Unto thy seed have I given this land." (Gen. xv. 18.)

THIS promise respected Abraham in his natural posterity, and these in the line of Isaac; and was God's covenant with him, and with them. The promise, (Gen. xxii. 18.) "In thy seed shall all the nations of the earth be blessed," was God's covenant with Abraham, and all nations of the earth, Jews and Gentiles. Therefore the Jews are said, to be "children of the covenant, which God made with their fathers; saying unto Abraham, in thy seed shall all kindreds of the earth be blessed." (Acts iii. 25.) And the Gentiles are said, to be "fellow heirs of the same body, and partakers of his promise in Christ, by the gospel." (Ephe. iii. 6.) The word of God by Moses, was his covenant with him, and the children of
Israel

Ifrael. "Write thou thefe words; for after the tenor of thefe words, I have made a covenant with thee, and with Ifrael. (Exod. xxxiv. 27.) Of the fhew bread it is faid, (Lev. xxiv. 8.) He fhall fet it in order before the Lord continually, being taken from the children of Ifrael by an everlafting covenant;" that is, *by a perpetual ftatute.* (See ver. 28.) God's promife, to continue the priefthood in the line of Phinehas, was his covenant with him. "Behold I give unto him my covenant of peace; he fhall have it, and his feed after him, even the covenant of an everlafting priefthood. (Numb. xxv. 12, 13.) The ten commandments were God's covenant, fee (Exod. xxxiv. 28. and 1 Kings viii. 9, 21.) Threatnings, and curfes, as well as promifes of the word of God, are his covenant. "All the curfes of the covenant that are written in this book of the law." (Deut. xxix. 21.) *Thefe* then were conftituent parts of the covenant. The whole word of God, is his covenant with fuch as have his word. Hence the *law* by Mofes, and the *gofpel* by Chrift, are God's covenant. "If that firft covenant had been faultlefs, then fhould no place have been fought for the fecond." This, and other paffages of fcripture above, ferve to fhew, that the word of God to men, is his covenant with them, in the fenfe of the fcriptures; in which fenfe we are to fpeak of God's covenant with us; at leaft in divinity. For the things contained in God's covenant with Abraham, we muft confult the book of *Genefis*, the revelation, and promifes made to him by God, and the injunctions given him.

In God's covenant with Abraham, Gen. xvii. the words of my text are important, and claim our particular attention. Such things therein, as appear to me moft material, will be noticed under feveral particular heads of difcourfe.

I. In the text God's covenant is the fame, with his feed after him in their generations, as with Abraham himfelf. "My covenant between me and thee,

and

and *thy seed after thee in their generations.*" Then follow the words of the covenant. *To be a God unto thee, and to thy seed after thee :* This may be considered as a promise to Abraham, *to be a God to him ;* and as the same promise *to his seed after him in their generations, to be a God to them,* or the whole may be considered as a promise to Abraham ; *to be a God to him, and to his seed after him.* And (thus considered) the same promise is implied to his seed ; *to be a God to them, and to their seed after them :* Otherwise God's covenant with Abraham in the text, is not his covenant *with his seed after him in their generations ;* contrary to the text itself, *my covenant between me and thee, and thy seed after thee in their generations.* In either view of the promise—*such* as it was to Abraham, *such* it was to his seed after him ; and *therefore* to the believing Gentiles ; *his seed* in the sense of the promise. I am not disposed to contend for either of the above constructions of the words, in opposition to the other. Suffice it, that God's covenant with Abraham, *is* his covenant *with his seed after him in their generations.*

II. The opinion, that the promise in the text, implied the promise of eternal life, is, *at least,* probable. It is much favoured by our Saviour adducing these words, *I am the God of Abraham, of Isaac, and of Jacob,* in evidence of the resurrection, and a future life. The covenant of grace is also summarily expressed, by *being their God.* "I will set up one shepherd over them, my servant David, he shall feed them, and I the Lord *will be their God.*" And the token of the covenant with Abraham, being *a seal* also *of the righteousness of faith,* is a further evidence, that it was the covenant of grace, summarily expressed, and implied a promise of eternal life : For righteousness is by faith, according to the covenant of grace ; and was by faith according to God's covenant with Abraham *in the text.* If righteousness had not been *by faith,* according to this covenant with Abraham, the token of it would not have been *a seal*, (or token) of the righteousness of faith. And whatever the promise in the text implied with respect to Abraham, it implied with respect to his seed after him. If it was a promise of eternal life to him, it was so to such as are his seed, in the *sense* of the promise, and to one on the same condition, as to the other, for the covenant (whatever it was, and whatever it implied) was *the same* with his seed after him, as with Abraham himself.

III. *Thy seed after thee*, as far as to be understood of the natural posterity of Abraham, respected such in the line of Isaac. "Thou shalt call his name Isaac, and I will establish my covenant with him, and with his seed after him." *In Isaac shall thy seed be called*. Esau was excluded from the covenant, for his impious flight of its blessings.

IV. Not only the posterity of Abraham in the above line, but *the believing Gentiles also*, are the seed of Abraham, in the *sense* of the text. "If they which are of the law be heirs, faith is made void, and the promise of none effect; therefore it is of faith, that it might be by grace; to the end the promise might be sure to all the seed: Not to that only which is of the law, but to that also, which is of the *faith* of Abraham; who is the father of us all, as it is written, I have made thee a father of many nations." In the context, God said to Abraham, "My covenant is with thee, and thou shalt be a father of many nations; a father of many nations have I made thee;" and in the text, "I will establish my covenant between me and thee, and *thy seed after thee*, for an everlasting covenant." The connection of the text with what preceded, (if the Apostle had said nothing) would seem to teach us, that more are intended by *thy seed*, than the posterity of Abraham in the line of Isaac. But, after the Apostles comment, it is beyond doubt, that it respects believers of all nations; of whom, the Apostle faith, Abraham is the father, *before God*. In the view
of

of God, and in the sense of his covenant in the text, Abraham is the father of believers, (Jews or Gentiles) and all such are the seed of Abraham. And this (according to the Apostle) was early prefigured, in Isaac (a *child of promise*) being the heir of the promise. "They are not all Israel that are of Israel: Neither because they are the seed of Abraham, are they all children: But in *Isaac* shall thy seed be called. That is, they which are the children of the flesh, these are not the children of God; but the children of the promise are counted for the seed. We brethren, as Isaac was, are the children of promise." The believing Gentiles are the children of Abraham, according to the promise, or in the sense of it; and are heirs of the promise, as Isaac, (the child of promise) was. The above, and other passages of the New Testament, teach us, that such as are not his natural posterity, are the seed of Abraham, in the sense of God's covenant with him. *The children of promise are counted for the seed.* Alluding to the promise in my text, the Apostle saith, "Is he the God of the Jews only? Is he not also of the Gentiles? Yes of the Gentiles also." They (saith he) which are of faith, the same are the children of Abraham." John teacheth the same, saying, "Think not to say, we have Abraham to our father; for I say unto you, that God is able, of these stones to raise up children unto Abraham. He did not intend an impossibility in the nature of things; that God could change stones into men, who, being so formed, should be the natural posterity of Abraham: But that God was able, of stones, to form men, who should receive the gospel, and be children of Abraham, in the *sense* of God's promise: In the sense of which such as believe the gospel, are the *seed* or children, of Abraham, with whom God's covenant was made in their generations. "My covenant between me, and thee, and thy seed after thee in their generations."

V. How

V. How was God's covenant with Abraham? And how is it with his seed after him in their generations? By the word of God to Abraham, (by him believed to be the word of God) God's covenant was with him; and by his word to them (believed by them to be the word of God) his covenant is with his *seed* after him in their generations. Having the word of God, his covenant was with Abraham; and is in the same manner, with his seed after him. For the word of God *is* his covenant; and such as have his word, with them is his covenant made; and this *without* any promise, or engagements made by them, on their part. Two parties mutually bound to each other, is all that is essential to a covenant between them. This cannot be, but by mutual consent and engagements, when the parties are on equal ground; neither having power over the other, to bind him, but by his own consent, and act. It is otherwise with respect to God and man; mutual obligation exists, between God and man, by the word and will of God only. Thereby man is bound to whatever God requires of him, and is entitled to whatever God promises him, on the condition of the promise; and, in case of failure, is subjected to the penalty, by the will, authority, and power of God only; and God, by his word, binds himself to the performance of it. All that constitutes mutual or covenant obligation, and relation, *is*, with respect to God and man, by the word and will of God only. So by the word of God to Abraham, his covenant was with him, and Abraham in covenant with God; and such as have the word of God, *with them* is his covenant, and they are in covenant with God. The scriptures speak of his word, as God's covenant with men, and we are so to consider it. To imagine that there cannot be a covenant of God with men, without consent, and promise, on the part of man, is in direct contradiction to the scriptures. Revelation was made to Abraham, and continued to his posterity, in the line of Isaac and Jacob.

Jacob. These had his word, and were, thereby, in covenant with God. God often speaks of his covenant with them, and of their breach of it. To them, saith the Apostle, pertained the covenant, and the promises. It was not so with the rest of the natural posterity of Abraham. The word of God, or revelation, was not continued to them *in their generations ;* and his covenant was not with them. To them the oracles of God were not committed, as to the Israelites. *These,* having his word, were God's covenant people, while the rest of the natural posterity of Abraham, were not. In the same manner as the Israelites *were,* the believing Gentiles *are,* in covenant with God; having the word and promises of God, under the present dispensation, as the Israelites had, under the former: *The promise is unto you,* saith the Apostle to the Jews, *and to your children, and to all that are far off, even as many as the Lord our God shall call.* The Gentiles are here respected, as *far off,* and the promise, as being to them, when they should receive the gospel, sent to them, and be, *(as many* as should receive it) called by it the promise, respected by the Apostle, is, probably, the promise made to Abraham in the text: *The word which he commanded to a thousand generations ; the covenant which he made with Abraham.*

The believing Gentiles are respected as Abraham's seed, when called *the children of Israel.* " Call his name *Loammi ;* for ye are not my people, and I will not be your God. Yet the number of the *children of Israel* shall be as the sand of the sea: And it shall come to pass, that in the place where it was said unto them, *ye are not my people,* there it shall be said unto them, *ye are the sons of the living God.* When the Jews were broken off from the stock of Abraham by unbelief, the believing Gentiles were grafted in, and became, as the Jews had been, the visible church of God. Therefore to Zion (the church) it is said, " the children which thou shalt have, after thou hast lost the other,

other, shall say, the place is too strait for me; for more are the children of the desolate, than of the married wife. Thy seed shall inherit the Gentiles." Of the believing Gentiles, as graffed into the stock of Abraham, and succeeding the Jews, (broken off by unbelief) as the visible church or people of God, the Apostle treats particularly in 9th of Rom. and God's reception of the Gentiles to be his people, upon their reception of the gospel, and forsaking idolaters, and their idolatry, is thus expressed. "Come out from among them, and be ye seperate, saith the Lord, and touch not the unclean thing; and I will receive you, and will be a father unto you, and ye shall be my sons and my daughters, saith the Lord Almighty."

VI. THE external token of God's covenant with them, belongs to the *infant posterity* of such as are the seed of Abraham, in the sense of the text. With respect to his natural posterity, this is beyond a doubt by the context, V. 10, 11.

THEREFORE God's covenant was with their infant posterity. For the token of it could not, with any propriety, belong to them, if the covenant was not with them, and there had been no covenant between God and their infant posterity. And if the infants of such of the natural posterity of Abraham, as were his seed in the sense of God's covenant, were in covenant, and the token of the covenant belonged to them; why not to the infants of the believing Gentiles, who are as truely the seed of Abraham, in the sense of God's covenant with him and his seed after him, as the Israelites were?

INFANT Israelites received the token of God's covenant by divine appointment. This teacheth us, in what light the infant posterity of such as are the seed of Abraham, in the sense of God's covenant with him, and his seed after him, are to be considered, and were considered by God himself; viz. as those with whom his covenant is made, and to whom the token of it belongs.

longs. Such infants were in covenant under the former dispensation, and, by divine appointment, had their covenant relation recognized, in the administration of the token of the covenant to them. The believing Gentiles, as hath been shewn, are the seed of Abraham in the sense of God's covenant with him. The infants of such, certainly, had a right to the token of the covenant under the former dispensation. Hath Christ disannulled their covenant relation under the Gospel dispensation, by disowning of it? Hath he not rather avowed it? By saying, " Suffer little children to come unto me, and forbid them not; for of such is the kingdom of Heaven;" and by receiving them into his arms, laying his hands upon, and blessing them. Such was the mode of adopting into the number of the church and people of God. Witness Jacob's adoption of the sons of Joseph, to be of his seed, and of the covenant people of God, with others of his posterity. *He laid his hands upon and blessed the lad!* Christ did the same to the little children brought to him. Of the lads Jacob said, " Let my name be called upon them, and the name of my fathers, *Abraham* and *Isaac*:" The same as saying, let them be of the visible church and covenant people of God. What our Saviour said of little children brought to him, *of such is the kingdom of Heaven,* is of the *same* import, *with respect to such,* as the words of Jacob were, *with respect to the sons of Joseph,* when adopted by him to be his, and the seed of Abraham, and Isaac. And there is the same reason wherefore the token of God's covenant with us, should belong, of right, to us, from infancy, as there was with respect to the Israelites. They were the seed of Abraham in the sense of God's covenant with him and his seed after him in their generations; and with them, by his word, God's covenant was made. The same is true of the believing Gentiles. And as God's covenant was by his word with the Israelites in their generations, therefore the token of

it

it belonged to them from their infancy; and God's covenant is, by his word, with us in our generations, and is equally a reason wherefore the token of the covenant should belong to us from our infancy. And baptism is, by the Apostle, called *the circumcision of Christ*, importing it to be the token of the covenant, as circumcision had been.

WITH respect to God's reception of the believing Gentiles, and the federal holiness of his covenant people, the Apostle saith "That the offering up of the Gentiles might be acceptable, being sanctified by the Holy Ghost."

UPON the Gentiles that received the Gospel, the Holy Ghost was shed down, in his extraordinary gifts. In this, God gave his testimony of his reception of them as his people. As saith the Apostle, " God, which knoweth the hearts, bear them witness, giving them the Holy Ghost, even as he did unto us. Again, " After that ye believed, ye were sealed with the Holy Spirit of promise." (Received this divine token, or seal, of God's reception of them).—And, upon such divine testimony, the Apostles knew the reception of the believing Gentiles, to be the will of God. And when it was given, in the first instance, Peter did not hesitate, to acknowledge their covenant relation, by their baptism. " Can any man forbid water, that these should not be baptized, who have received the Holy Ghost as well as we? And he commanded them to be baptized." When called in question for what he had done, he said, " As I began to speak the Holy Ghost fell upon them. For as much then as God gave them the like gift as he did unto us, what was I, that I could withstand God?" To this evidence they all submitted. *When they heard these things they held their peace.* The Apostles also, baptized, not adults only, but the *households* of such; *them and theirs*, as appears by the instances of the *Jailer, Lydia,* and *Stephanus*.

IT

It may be said, "If the word of God is his covenant with us; and if his covenant is with such as have his word; and if such with whom his covenant is, have a right to the token of it; all this doth not reach the case of infants, that such should be considered as having the word of God, and in covenant; and as having a right to the token of God's covenant with them. For *they* know nothing of, nor are to be considered as having, the word of God, that his covenant should thereby be with them." This objection, if it would prove, that infants cannot be considered as having a right to the token of it, would prove, that the infant *Israelites*, could not be in covenant, and have a right to the token of it; *contrary to known fact*. It therefore would prove too much.

Nor is it *fact*, that Infants are not to be considered, as having, and believing the word of God, when their parents have it, and educate their children in the belief of its being the word of God; and instruct them in the truths of it. Children are, in the sacred scriptures, regarded, as having, with their parents, and with them believing, the revelation, in the belief and truths of which, they are educated, and instructed by them. In this manner our Saviour considers them, when he saith, *one of these little ones, which believe in me.*

The word of God is to us, and to our children in our generations. Thus God himself speaks of his covenant in my text. This word, the promises, and precepts of it, respect, not any one generation only, but the *present*, and *succeeding* generations; "My covenant between *me* and *thee*, and thy seed after thee in *their generations:*" and as the word of God respects the present, and succeeding generations, it is not for us to say, that his word is not to our *children*, nor his covenant with them; and that it *cannot be*, because of their infancy. The word of God in the text, was his covenant with Abraham, and with his seed in their generations.

erations. His feed the believing Gentiles are ; and with them (as the feed of Abraham in the fenfe of the covenant) is God's covenant, in *their generations*, as it was with the Ifraelites. And it is, in ordinary *fact*, that children, educated in the belief of revelation by their parents, and by them inftructed in the truths and precepts of it, do (when become capable of underftanding) believe and acknowledge the revelation, which they were educated in the belief of. And they are, in the outward adminiftration (or difpenfation) of the covenant, regarded as believing and having divine revelation, with their parents ; and as being together with them, in covenant. They were fo confidered under the former difpenfation, and Chrift fo confiders them, when he fpeaks of little children as *believing in him.*

DEISTS deny revelation as fabulous, and are not to be confidered as having divine revelation ; nor can, properly, be fo confidered. As the Jews, who deny revelation by Chrift, and the truth of the gofpel, cannot, properly, be confidered as having the gofpel, but in propriety of fpeech, have not the gofpel ; fo deifts or infidels, are not fuch as have the word of God, in the fenfe of this difcourfe ; nor are they, (according to this difcourfe) in covenant, as thofe who have the word of God. Nor are their children to be confidered as having the word of God, and therefore as in covenant ; but as denying the word of God with their parents, by whom they are educated in the denial and rejection of it. Neither are fuch parents, or their children, to be regarded as thofe that have the word of God, and are in covenant, any more than the heathen, previous to their belief or reception of the gofpel.—Neither can fuch parents as deny the gofpel, and divine revelation, in any felfconfiftency, either receive the token of the covenant themfelves, or defire it for their children, as a divine inftitution.

BUT

But having his word (the revelation which God hath made to men) we are in covenant: (His word being God's covenant with us) and denying and rejecting, the revelation which God hath made, we have not his word, and are not in covenant; and it is inconsistent with being in covenant. This we learn, by the Jews, broken off from the stock of Abraham, and their covenant relation to God, by their denial and rejection of the gospel; and by the Gentiles, being brought into the stock of Abraham, and covenant relation, by the belief or reception of the gospel; and by this also, viz. that the Jews, if they continue not in the unbelief, or rejection of the gospel, shall be graffed (or brought) *in again* into their former covenant relation, from which they were broken off, by their unbelief.

If the denial of the revelation God hath made, had consisted with being in covenant, the Jews should not have been broken off, by their unbelief and rejection of the gospel. On the other hand, if we are not in covenant, by the belief and acknowledgement of the revelation God hath made to us, the Jews will not be brought, or graffed in again, *if they abide not still in their unbelief:* But that they shall be, is the express assertion of the Apostle. As long as the Jews acknowledged the revelation God made to them, they continued in their covenant relation to God. (Branches of the stock of Abraham)—when they denied the revelation made to them by God, they were, by their unbelief broken off from the stock of Abraham, (from their former covenant relation) and the Gentiles, who believed the gospel, were graffed in; brought into the covenant relation, from which the Jews, by their infidelity, were broken off.

Then commenced the accomplishment of the prophecy abovementioned,—" Ye are not my people, and I will not be your God. Yet the number of the children of Israel shall be as the sand of the sea. Where it was said unto them, ye are not my people, there it

shall

shall be said unto them, ye are the sons of the living God." Further—while the Jews were God's visible covenant people, the token of his covenant belonged to them in their generations; and *from their infancy.* The same may be said of the believing Gentiles, succeeding them as God's visible people.

VII. The advantage of being God's covenant people, consists in that which *constitutes* their covenant relation to God. Viz. having the oracles of God—the light—the precepts—the ordinance of his word and worship. From these advantages, the infidel is excluded, by his infidelity; for he regards revelation as *fiction*, and its institutions as *mere human invention*—its precepts as without divine authority—and its truths as *fables*. It is the increase of infidelity, and of such as deny the covenant relation of the children of christian parents, that have a threatening aspect upon the visible church of God at present.

With respect to revelation, and covenant relation, infidels are no better than the heathen, ignorant of revelation; " Aliens from the commonwealth of Israel, strangers to the covenant of promise." But the believing Gentiles, are " Fellow heirs, and of the same body, and partakers of his promise in Christ, by the gospel. No *mere strangers* and *foreigners*, but fellow citizens with the saints, and of the houshold of God." The adult heathen are to be baptized upon their conversion to Christianity, or professed belief of the gospel. So are infidels or deists, who before denied the truth of the gospel. But such as acknowledged divine revelation, and are baptized, are in external covenant relation to God; and to them belong all the priviledges, and they are bound to all the duties, belonging to those of Christ's visible church, as they become capable of them; unless they cut themselves off from the visible church, by apostacy, (or infidelity) or are cut off by excommunication for some scandal and obstinacy, on account of which, as our Saviour teacheth us, they

are

are to be regarded no otherwise than the heathen. Of baptism, as the christian circumcision, and the token of the covenant, it may be said, "That it is *a seal of the righteousness of faith*, and cannot, therefore, belong to infants, incapable of faith.

But this makes not any thing against the administration of the token of the covenant to infants. For it is *a seal of the righteousness of faith*, as a seal or token of such a way of justification, viz. by faith; and the seal or token of this way of justification, belongs to infants, with the same propriety as to adults; such being the way of justification for those of every generation; for the *parents*, and *their children* after them. Such being the way of justification for both, the external token of it belongs, with equal propriety, to either, (or both.) That by faith, is the way of justification for those of every generation; and the external token or seal of this way of justification, (according to the covenant) belongs as properly to those in covenant, of a succeeding, as to those of a preceding generation.

Was not the token of the covenant, a seal of the righteousness of faith, (or of such a way of justification, viz. by faith) when it was received by Abraham? Was not the same the way of justification for his son *Isaac*, and for those of the *posterity of Isaac* in succeeding generations? And did not *Isaac*, and others in his succeeding generations, receive, the token of the covenant, and *seal of the righteousness of faith*, at eight days old? The seal of the righteousness of faith, (the way of justification for both) was to be received by parents, and their children, according to divine appointment. The token of the covenant, being *a seal of the righteousness of faith*, did not import, the faith and righteousness of the subjects, when it was received by them. This could not be, with respect to all the Israelites, at eight days old. It was rather a token, or seal, of the covenant, and of righteousness by faith according

cording to it; which God gave to Abraham for himself, and for his posterity in their generations. And baptism, considered as a seal of the righteousness of faith, is not therefore to be denied children, any more than circumcision was to be denied such, for the same reason. Nor is the covenant being a promise of eternal life, any reason wherefore the token of it should not belong to infants: For it is as much a promise of eternal life to our children, (and on the same terms) as to ourselves; and the token of such a promise, (as doth the promise itself) as properly belongs to their children, as to adult parents.

The advantage of being in covenant (agreeable to what has been observed already) is, in having the oracles of God; the light, precepts, promises, and all the motives of his word; together with the divine institutions of it. These are means of that spiritual and everlasting good, which God bestows upon those of his visible church, according to his good pleasure. Among these advantages and means of spiritual and everlasting good, is the administration of the external, and visible token of God's covenant with us; minding us of his covenant with us, and with our children, and a mean of our faith and hope in God, for ourselves and our children; and of exciting and encouraging us, to seek to God, for the blessings of his covenant, for ourselves and our's. By the token of it, *administered to our children*, we are minded of God's covenant with us, *and our children*: this (as a mean) is also adapted to excite the parents, to a care to keep God's covenant themselves, and to inculcate this on their children. By the token of God's covenant the remembrance of it is to be kept up, and perpetuated, for our benefit as above: for the token of the covenant administered by divine appointment to our children, imports that the grace and blessings of it, extend to us in our generations, and that, for ourselves, and ours, we may seek to and hope in God for them.

But,

But, whatever the advantages of external covenant relation may be, it is for us to remember, that having the word of **God**, and being in covenant, is *one thing;* and keeping God's covenant (whereby we are entitled to the future blessings of it) *is another.* Many Israelites, when in covenant, did not keep **God's** covenant with them; and many nominal Christians do not. These may say, *Lord, Lord, open to us. We have eaten, and drunk in thy presence, and thou hast taught in our streets.* But he will say, *I know you not: depart from me.* If we *Obey not the gospel of our Lord Jesus Christ, salvation* will be far from us. " He shall be revealed from heaven, with his mighty angels, in flaming fire, taking vengeance on them that obey not his gospel. And it shall be more tolerable for Sodom, in the day of judgment than for such."

It would have been agreeable to me, to have closed here, and not to have added another discourse; and I should have done it, had not the opinion of many worthy characters, been an objection to the preceding discourse, which it will be thought needful, and appears reasonable, for me to take notice of. This requires a second discourse; and that I close the first here.

SERMON XIX.

IT will be objected to the sentiments of the preceding discourse, " That when the scriptures speak of the *believing Gentiles* as the *seed* of Abraham, such as have saving faith are intended: such therefore are those who are in covenant, and their children with them. The parents then, who have a right to baptism for their children, are such only as have saving faith, and are themselves truly pious: and, consequently, must be such as are (in the judgment or opinion of the church) christians indeed." This, I apprehend, to be the great objection

objection to the preceding discourse. Some attention must, therefore, be given to it.

It is not denied, that the scriptures speak of being *children of God*, and *the seed of Abraham* in the *highest sense*; such as implies saving faith. But, this notwithstanding, they also speak of *faith*, of *being children of God*, and *the seed of Abraham*, with a respect to external *covenant relation*, and that belief of the gospel which is common to nominal christians; and that whence they are so denominated.

PARTICULAR texts may be true of, and applicable to *faith*. *The children of God*, and *seed of Abraham*, in either, or each of the above senses: neither is it very uncommon, to find passages of scripture *true*, in a twofold sense. But it is sufficient to my purpose, if the scriptures teach us, that external covenant relation *is* by such a belief and acknowledgment of the revelation God hath made, as is common to nominal christians: and this *is* the truth, as appears by the case of the Jews, as stated in the New Testament. They were broken off from their *olivetree*, that is, from the visible church of God, and their former external covenant relation, by denying the truth of the gospel, the revelation God hath made by his Son. Not only so, but, *If they abide not still in unbelief*, they shall be graffed in again; be again brought into their covenant relation, as before. We know the unbelief whereby the Jews were broken off, viz. denying the gospel—the word of God, and revelation by Christ. And, according to the Apostle, if they do not continue in the unbelief whereby they were broken off, shall be graffed in again—be again brought into their former covenant relation. This is sufficient to teach us these two things— first, that denying the revelation God hath made to men, is inconsistent with being in external covenant relation to God—and 2dly, that we are brought into it, by the acknowledgment, or belief of the revelation God hath made. For otherwise, the Jews would not have

have been broken off from their covenant relation, by denying the revelation God hath made in the gospel; nor will be again brought into it, when they shall no longer deny, but acknowledge such revelation made.

By such belief, therefore, or acknowledgment of divine revelation as is opposed to infidelity, and common to nominal Christians, we are in, and the Jews shall be again brought into, external, and visible covenant relation to God. The Jews, broken off from external covenant relation, by denying the revelation God hath made, and to be brought into it again, whenever they shall no longer continue their denial of it, puts it beyond any reasonable doubt what an unbelief it is, which is inconsistent with being in external covenant relation, viz. the denial of the revelation made to us; and what that belief is whereby we are externally in covenant, viz. that belief or acknowledgment of revelation, which is opposed to the denial and rejection of it, and is common to nominal Christians. And this further appears by the 8th of Acts, where it is said of the *Samaritans,* " When they believed Philip, preaching the things concerning the kingdom of God, and the name of Jesus Christ, they were baptized, both men and women. *Then Simon himself believed also? and when he was baptized, &c.*" The sacred historian, when he wrote this, knew (of Simon at least) that he had not any saving belief of the gospel. Notwithstanding, he affirms the same belief of Simon, as he doth of the rest; and that he was, thereupon, baptized, as were others who believed; and makes not the least distinction between the belief of Simon, and that of the rest, who were baptized; saying, that they believed, and that Simon himself also believed. This (if words can be) is affirming Simon's belief of the preaching of Philip, as well as that of the rest who were baptized by him; and it shews that the sacred historian is not to be understood, as speaking of a saving faith in those baptized; but of a belief common to them,

P p   Simon

Simon with the rest. Others of them, indeed, might have a saving faith, when Simon had not; but such is not the belief respected by the writer, in the account he gives; but a belief, common to Simon and others, who heard him preach, and were baptized by Philip. Therefore the belief respected by the sacred historian, can be no more than such as nominal christians have of the truth of the gospel revelation. But Simon's belief of his preaching, was regarded by Philip as receiving the gospel he preached, so as to be in covenant, and to have a right to the external token of it in baptism; which was administered to him.

It may be objected, " If Simon was in covenant by his belief of the doctrine of Philip, and had a right to have his covenant relation recognized by baptism; how could the Apostle say to him, *Thou hast neither part nor lot in this matter?*

This admits of several answers. 1. Philip, and the Apostles in their preaching, doubtless taught salvation by Christ in eternal life. And this may be what the Apostle respected, when he said to Simon " Thou hast neither part nor lot in this matter; for thy heart is not right in the sight of God. For I perceive that thou art in the gall of bitterness, and in the bond of iniquity." Accordingly the Apostle exhorted him to repentance, requisite to future salvation; as is the duty of the ministers of Christ, towards such of the visible church, as are of a character similar to that of Simon.

If we are not satisfied with this, and consider the Apostle as respecting the visible church, and a standing therein, when he said to Simon, " Thou hast neither part nor lot in this matter:" Then

2dly. Simon must be considered as one of those our Saviour speaks of, *who for a while believe, and afterwards fall away.* Though Simon, with others, believed the word preached by Philip, and had with them, been baptized, as one that believed, he might afterwards apostatize, or relapse into infidelity again, and
thereby

thereby be cut off from his external covenant relation, agreeable to what has been said of infidelity in the preceding discourse. And the Apostle, by his conduct, discovering the apostacy of Simon, by which he was cut off from the visible church, tells him, " Thou hast neither part nor lot in this matter;" that is, was no longer of, nor had any connection with Christians, or standing in the visible church. And this may be the right view of Simon's case. Whatever belief he had entertained of the doctrine of Philip, his relapse to infidelity, (inconsistent with his remaining in, and belonging any longer to the visible Christian church) appeared, by his conception of what was done by the Apostles, when the Holy Ghost was given through the laying on of their hands, as done by some magical art, which he did not understand, and hoped to obtain of them by money. This appearance of his apostacy (upon the principles of the preceding discourse) fully accounts for the words of the Apostle to Simon above cited, if we consider them as a denial of his belonging to the visible church. Whether this or the preceding answer, are either of them satisfactory, or not, yet

3dly. ONE thing is evident, and sufficient to obviate the objection, viz. whatever the Apostle intended by his words to Simon as above, he did not intend, that he (Simon) had not believed the preaching of Philip—had not been in covenant, and had his covenant relation recognized by his baptism ; or that (being baptized into Christ) he had not been received into the number of the visible church. For that he did believe the preaching of Philip, had been baptized, and, by his baptism, had been received into the visible church, were *certain facts ;* and the Apostle did not, by the words in question, mean to deny them. The evidence, therefore, of being in covenant, by that belief of the gospel which is common to nominal Christians, arising from the belief

lief and baptism of Simon, suffers no diminution by the words of the Apostle, upon which the objection, under consideration, is founded.

The word of God, according to the preceding discourse, is his covenant with us; and such as have his word (believed, or acknowledged, by them, to be the word of God) with them his covenant is made; and they are in covenant with God. This we have now found confirmed, by what the Apostle saith of the Jews, broken off by their denial of the gospel, viz. that they shall be *graffed in again* (or brought again into covenant relation) *if they abide not still in unbelief*, or in their denial and rejection of the gospel. We find the same confirmed also, by the baptism of Simon, upon his belief of the gospel, which could be no other than such as is common to nominal Christians.

It should also be considered—that our relation to God, by a saving faith, is spiritual, and invisible; and not that which belongs to the visible church of Christ, collectively: And these appellations, *Holy, Children of God, seed of Abraham, &c.* when given to those collectively, who are of the church of Christ, are not given, to denote their saving faith, and their hidden, spiritual, and invisible relation to Christ; but their common, external, and visible covenant relation.

Of the Israelites, and their external covenant relation, it is said, "The Lord abhorred them, because of the provoking of his Sons and his Daughters," (Deut. xxxii. 19.) And such among the Gentiles are so called as receive the gospel, and forsake idolatry. (2 Cor. vi. 17.) Wherefore come ye out from among them, and be ye seperate, saith the Lord; and I will receive you—and ye shall be my Sons and Daughters.

Their faith also, when affirmed of Christians collectively, (or of Churches) respects the faith common to nominal Christians, and to churches of such. " Ye are all the children of God, by faith in Christ Jesus,"

Jesus," saith the Apostle to the churches of Galatia. However true this might be of many individuals of them, and of saving faith, and filial relation to God in the highest sense, yet it is not reasonable to think, that the Apostle here intended it, or expected to be understood, of saving faith, and filial relation to God in the highest sense; for he affirms it of *all of them*, without exception. And it is improbable at least, that it was true of all of them, (understood of saving faith, and of filial relation to God in the highest sense) and we cannot reasonably so understand it, of all that belonged to the churches of Galatia. Hence there is reason to believe, the Apostle had not, in the words above, respect to saving faith, and filial relation in the highest sense; but to their external covenant relation. The epistle he wrote to them is a further evidence of this; for by it the Apostle doth not, seem to think of them all, as being children of God, by saving faith in Christ. " I marvel that ye are so soon removed from him that called you into the grace of Christ. Who hath bewitched you, that ye should not obey the truth? My little children of whom I travail in birth again, untill Christ be formed in you. I am afraid of you lest I have bestowed upon you labour in vain." These texts, have not the appearance of the Apostle's thinking them all children of God by a saving faith in Christ. He respects rather, the belief of the gospel, and that covenant relation, which were common to them, and to all nominal Christians, when he saith, *Ye are all the children of God by faith in Christ Jesus.*

And the manner in which the Apostle supports this assertion, is a further evidence of it; viz. by their baptism. " For as many of you (saith he) as have been baptized into Christ have put on Christ. There is neither *Jew* nor *Greek*—ye are all one *(church or body)* in Christ." The Apostle then, in his preceding assertion, had respect to their Christian baptism, and common covenant relation to God. If he did not, respect their

their baptism, and external covenant relation, in saying, *Ye are all the children* **of God by faith in Christ Jesus,** why doth he support, the assertion by their being baptized into Christ, and being all, of whatever nation, one church, or body, in Christ? The Apostle, when he saith "Ye are all the children of God by faith in Christ Jesus," respects their reception of the gospel, and external covenant relation; for in this respect only, were his words true of all of them.

There are passages of the scripture, argued in support of this opinion, viz. that none ought to be received into the Christian Church but such as are visibly pious persons, or Christians indeed. It will be thought incumbent on me to take some notice of these. Our Saviour's parable of the *good seed,* and *tares,* appears to be urged the most plausibly, in favour of this opinion. In it our Saviour expounds *the good seed,* of *the children of the kingdom,* and the *tares,* of *the children of the wicked one;* and represents the former, to be of *his sowing,* and the latter, to be of the *devil's.* But by this parable we cannot, with any certainty, determine the will of Christ, that such only be received into his church as are pious persons; and therefore, that such only, (as far as we can judge) are to be received as members of it.

The kingdom of heaven, in the Evangelists, is put for the dispensation of the gospel and the blessings of it, as well as for the visible church; and it is put for the gospel dispensation, or the blessings of it, in other parables in the chapter, which contains this of *the good seed, and tares :* and is, probably, so used in this parable. *The world is the field,* in which the good seed, and tares are sown; and (understanding *the kingdom of heaven* of the dispensation of the gospel) the parable teacheth us, the efficacy of the gospel with some, by the power and grace of Christ; and the wickedness of others, under the dispensation of it, by the instrumentality of Satan. And the *kingdom of heaven*

ven being put for the dispensation of the gospel, the pious, are properly *the children of the kingdom*, as those *begotten by the gospel*; or such with whom the gospel, in the dispensation of it, hath its proper and saving effect; and the children of the *wicked one*, are those disobedient to the gospel—living in sin under its dispensation, and *children of the devil*. Thus considered the parable teacheth us the saving efficacy of the gospel with some, and not with others: rather than such, as it is the will of Christ should belong to his visible church.

In the parable preceding this of *the good seed*, and *tares*, viz. that of the *sower* and the *seed sown, the kingdom of heaven* is the dispensation of the gospel; for, in his exposition of it, our Saviour calls the gospel *the word of the kingdom*. And in the parables which follow this of the *good seed* and *tares, the kingdom of heaven* is put for the gospel dispensation, or the blessings of it. And *the kingdom of heaven* being used for the dispensation of the gospel, or the blessings of it, in other parables of the chapter, increases the reason for so understanding it, in this parable of *the good seed and tares*. In one of the parable's that follow in this chapter, our Saviour likens *the kingdom of heaven, to a net cast into the sea, which gathered of every kind*; which, when full, was drawn to the shore, and a seperation made of the good and bad; in the application of which, our Saviour saith, "So shall it be at the end of the world; the Angels shall sever the wicked from among the just, and shall cast them into the furnace of fire." This parable respects *the gospel dispensation*, and the close of it at the end of the world, and in the same manner, our Saviour applies the parable of *the good seed and tares*; which is an evidence of the same intended by *the kingdom of heaven*, in each parable.

As I have said, *The kingdom of heaven*, is the dispensation of the gospel. *The world, the field*, in which

which the good feed, and tares are sown. *The good seed*, are those begotten by the gospel, or obedient to it, and, therefore, *children of the kingdom*. *The tares* are the wicked, who obey not the gospel, and are *children of the devil*. The parable admits, (at least) of this construction; and doth not, therefore, afford any certain conclusion (to say the least) that it is the will of Christ, his visible church should consist of such only, as are truly pious, and that none be received into it, but those, who are visibly such.

" But Christ speaks of the *good seed* as sown by himself, and the *tares* by the devil ; and this shews that the former are of his church, agreeably to his will ; and that others being in it, is *of the devil*." It shews that the pious of the earth, are so by his gospel, grace, and agency ; but not that it is his revealed will, that such only should constitute his visible church, and that none should be received into it but those, who are visibly such. (Christ may be said to sow good seed, as his gospel injoins piety, and, is adapted to it, as a mean thereof ; and as the pious in the world, (which is the field) are such by his efficacious power and grace. Nor does Christ, sowing the *good seed*, seem to be of different import, from what is said of his visible church of old, *I had planted thee a noble vine, wholly a right seed.* Again, *my beloved hath a vineyard : he sowed it—and planted it with the choicest vine.*

But none pretend, that, by the revealed will of God, the Jewish church was to consist of such only, as were pious persons ; and that such only were to belong to it, as were, visibly pious, why then should this be inferred, with respect to the Christian church, from (his being said to sow *good seed in his field*, which he tells us is the world) and the devil *tares*. It is common in the scriptures to ascribe what is good, to God, and wickedness, to the Devil, and to the lusts of men ; and Christ teacheth us, by this parable, to do likewise ;

also,

also, not to attempt to seperate the righteous and wicked here; but to leave this to be done by him, at the end of the world.

But, after that which came upon Ananias and his wife. "*Of the rest durst no man join himself to them; but the people magnified them; and believers were, the more added to the Lord.*" This teacheth us, that afterward, none of those, who did not believe the doctrine and testimony of the Apostles, durst join them, yet what was done, and known, proved a mean, of many believing the word preached by the Apostles; so that hence, the more believed their word, and joined the Apostles, and their followers. Whether the faith was such as is saving, is not said. With some of them it might be, and with others, nothing more than a belief, or persuasion, of the truth of the gospel, common to professed and nominal Christians.

" But Philip told the Eunuch, he might be baptized, if he believed with all his heart." This imported his right to baptism, if he was indeed convinced and persuaded, that Jesus, whom Philip preached to him, was Christ the Son of God. And the Eunuch answered, *I believe that Jesus Christ is the Son of God.* All Judah, and Benjamin, and strangers of Ephraim, and of other Tribes, when gathered at Jerusalem, *entered into a Covenant, to seek the God of Israel, with all their heart and soul. And all Judah rejoiced at the oath: For they had sworn with all their hearts:* (i. e. With a sincerity, which men may have in their promises, in distinction from any intentional deceit.)—It is not credible that all Judah were indeed pious men; and made this oath, with a pious, and gracious sincerity of heart.

" But the Apostle saith of the Lord's supper, *He that eateth and drinketh unworthily, eateth and drinketh damnation to himself, not discerning the Lord's body.* Therefore, to partake of this ordinance, not having saving faith, is to our own damnation." By eating and drinking

drinking unworthily, the Apostle intends doing it, not in a solemn and religious, but in a disorderly and riotous manner, (as did the Corinthians) to satisfy their hunger, and indulge their appetites to excess. *Not discerning the Lord's body*, is not understanding and regarding the elements, as the emblems of the body, and blood of Christ, broken and shed for us, and to be received as such, and in remembrance of him; and not distinguishing eating and drinking in the ordinance, from that which is to satisfy hunger, and gratify the appetite. Such disorderly, irreligious, riotous eating, and impious profanation of the ordinance as was among the Corinthians, the Apostle respects, when he speaks of eating and drinking unworthily, and to damnation; and not their eating without saving faith. To be satisfied of this, we need only to notice the direction the Apostle gave, how to avoid it; (i. e. eating and drinking to damnation.) "If any man hunger, let him *eat at home;* that ye come not together *unto damnation.*" (The same word as in V. 29th.)—We know there is no connection between a full stomach and saving faith, or piety of heart; or between the exercise of either at the table of the Lord, and *eating before we go from home;* and had the Apostle intended, by *eating and drinking unworthily, and damnation to himself,* doing it without saving faith, and piety of heart, he would not have given such a direction for avoiding it, as *eating at home,* before they came to the table of the Lord.

WITH respect to the marriage supper. The King coming to see the guests, and saying to one of them, "How comest thou in hither, not having on a wedding garment?" This close of the parable, respects the final judgment, and teacheth us, that though we are of his visible church, if void of real religion, Christ, at his second coming, will not own, but reject, and condemn us to the punishment of the wicked.

As

As far as my limits allow, I have noticed objections to the preceding difcourfe ; according to which, fuch as have divine revelation (believed by them to be his word) have the word of God, whereby his covenant is made with them ; and, being baptized, have the token of his covenant with them, and are in external covenant relation to God. The children alfo of fuch (educated by their parents in the belief of revelation, and by them inftructed in it) are confidered in the preceding difcourfe as having, and believing the word of God, or divine revelation with their parents, and in covenant together with them.

Such children (as they become capable of it) are bound by the word and will of God to all the duties, and have a right to all the privileges of God's covenant people ; are to obey the precepts, and to obferve the inftitutions of his word.

Heathen, ignorant of revelation ; Jews, who deny revelation by Jefus Chrift, and reject the gofpel ; and Deifts, who deny all revelation, are out of the queftion. But, as under the former, fo under the gofpel difpenfation, fuch as have the revelation God hath made (believed by them to be the word of God) with them is his covenant, and they are to obferve well divine commands and inftitutions. This is incumbent on all nominal Chriftians, come to years of fufficient underftanding, or capacity

It may be faid " If we baptize the children of all baptized parents, who educate their children as mentioned above, we may in fome, if not in many inftances, baptize children of parents who are offenders, and not free from fcandal." If parents are fcandalous offenders, in any refpect, they are to be dealt with agreeable to the gofpel, for their good, and in brotherly love ; but that their children (educated in the belief of it, and inftructed in divine revelation) are not to be confidered as believing revelation, and having the word of God, and in covenant ; and that they are not to receive

receive the token of God's covenant with them, because of some offence of their parents, is doubted.

Their parents are supposed to educate them in the belief of revelation, and to instruct them in it; and such children (for the reason that any are) are to be considered as having, and believing divine revelation, and in covenant. Infidelity, as hath been considered, cuts off parents, and their children with them, from covenant relation; and the excommunication, of such as cannot be reclaimed, may do the same. For such Christ teacheth us, are to be accounted by us, *as the Heathen*. But discipline, previous to excommunication, doth not destroy covenant and church relation. " If any man obey not our word, note that man, and have no company with him, that he may be ashamed. *Yet count him, not as an enemy, but admonish him as a brother*." A man then, may be under the censure and admonition of the church, and still continue in his covenant and church relation, and is to be regarded, and admonished, as a brother. And, if children are in covenant with their parents, how are they cut off from it by that in the parent, which doth not cut off the parent himself?

" But if children of parents above mentioned be admitted to baptism, discipline will be greatly weakened, if not destroyed." The weight of gospel discipline is in itself, or in what it is; and we are not to expect to give weight to it, by what doth not, but by that which doth, belong to it.

The discipline Christ hath enjoined, with respect to an offending brother, all nominal Christians are bound to observe towards such a one, when made acquainted with his offence; and if all such, would faithfully reprove, and admonish him of his crime, in the spirit of meekness and brotherly love, the offender, would have all his neighbours and brothers, acquainted with his errors, kindly, and affectionately, noticing him of, and cautioning him against it, and endeavouring, by their influence

influence, to reclaim him. *(Individually, and alone in the first instance.)* This would be a mean of convincing and reforming him, which, it would seem, could rarely fail of its effect. But if it should, and all those abovesaid, should again admonish him as before, two or three of them at the same time (trying their united influence with him) such their further repeated admonition, and joint influence, added to the former, must be of greater weight still with the offender, for his conviction and reformation. But if this also should fail, his offence is to be told to the church ; (or an assembly of Christians) and their joint influence, as a body, and the weight of their censure, and admonition, if need be, are to be tried with the offender. This discipline, duly observed, and the offender avoided, that he may be ashamed, few, very few, would be found proof against. But if any are, Christ teacheth us to regard them no otherwise than as heathen or infidels, no more in covenant or church relation. *Let him be unto thee as an heathen man and a publican.* But until this takes place, and as long as the offender is under discipline for his recovery, the words of the Apostle above cited, teach us, he is to be regarded as a brother. With respect to his children, (supposed to have a Christian education) they are, according to the preceding discourse, to be considered as those that have the word of God, and are in covenant. The reason which hath been given wherefore any children are in covenant, and have a right to the token of it, is, by the supposition, true of the children in question.

" But if the Christian Church, consists of all such as have the sacred scriptures, (acknowledged by them to be the word of God, or a divine revelation which God hath made to us) and are baptized into Christ, it will be impossible to support discipline in it." Say then, that Christ is *a hard master*, injoining that which cannot be done.

ALL nominal Christians are to observe the injunctions of Christ; let them do this (which they acknowledge to be their duty, and that they are bound to do it, by the will and authority of Christ, and in obedience to him) and Christian discipline will be among them. There is no greater difficulty in it, than that of observing Christ's laws; and this, all that have the gospel, believe it to be a divine revelation, and acknowledge the divine mission of Christ, must own themselves bound to, by the highest authority.

"BUT can we have any proper evidence that parents will educate their children in the belief of revelation, and instruct them in the truths and precepts of it, so long as the parents themselves do not publicly profess their belief of revelation, made to us in the scriptures of the Old, and New Testament; and do neglect any of the institutions of the gospel?"—I have no objection to their making a public profession of their belief of a divine revelation contained in the scriptures.

WITH respect to their neglecting any of the institutions of Christ, such scruples have been raised in the minds of many, by the opinion of some pious divines, respecting their right to a participation of the Lord's supper, that notwithstanding their neglect of it, there may be many instances in which it is reasonable to believe, of parents who neglect to attend upon and partake of the Lord's Supper, that they will give their children a Christian education; and, in particular cases, the churches and ministers of Christ must judge, respecting the education of the children, as the sentiments, and character of the parents give reason to believe; and baptize such children, as they have reason to expect will have a Christian education.

CONCLUSION.

WE were, in our forefathers, *Gentiles far off*; but

but are now *brought nigh, by the gospel—are children, not of the night, and of darkness, but of the light, and of the day—not of the bond women, but of the free.* The promise, made to Abraham, is unto us, and to our children, and to as many as the Lord our God shall call. And on the terms of the covenant the everlasting blessings of it shall be ours, and our children's. These things call for gratitude to him, who hath brought us out of darkness into marvelous light, and calleth us to his kingdom and glory—unto his eternal glory, by Jesus Christ. "In every nation, he that feareth God, and worketh righteousness, is accepted with him. The partition wall is broken down, and there is neither Jew, nor Greek, Barbarian, Scythian, bond or free." All are *one* in Christ, who came preaching peace to them that were *far off*, and to them that were nigh. "We are no more strangers and foreigners, but fellow citizens with the saints, and of the household of God." But let not any of us forget the *wide* difference there is, between being in external covenant relation to God, and being entitled to the great and everlasting blessings of his covenant. External covenant relation is by God's word to us, which is his covenant made with us; it is by the gospel of the grace of God. The gospel of our salvation sent unto us, believed or acknowledged by us to be the word of God. But an interest in the everlasting blessings of the covenant, is not without the belief of the word of God in which we keep his word. Therefore, *having the word of God*, let us believe it, and in the Saviour the Son of God, according to it; not with an inoperative dead faith, but that which is influential, and practical; productive of a spirit and practice, desires, and hopes, correspondent to the truths believed. And, *having the promises of God*, let us cleanse ourselves from all filthiness of flesh and spirit, perfecting holiness in the fear of God; and live, as the grace of God, which bringeth salvation, teacheth us; denying ungodliness, and worldly lusts, soberly, right-
coufly,

eoufly, and godly, in this prefent world. Otherwife, having the word and promifes of God, will, ultimately, profit us nothing. " For if we fin wilfully, after we have received the knowledge of the truth, (or live in wilful finning, under the light of the gofpel) there remaineth no more facrifice for fins ; but a fearful looking for of judgment, &c. The Lord Jefus fhall be revealed from heaven, with his mighty angels, in flaming fire, taking vengeance on them that know not God, and obey not the gofpel." Doctrinal knowledge, or profeffion, alone, will not avail to our final falvation. " The wrath of God is revealed from heaven againft all ungodlinefs, and unrighteoufnefs of men, who hold the truth in unrighteoufnefs."

THAT we may not receive the grace of God in vain, *the gofpel of the grace of God, and of our falvation,* fent to us, we muft receive the truth in the love of it ; believe his word, and keep it. " God giveth us all things, pertaining to life and godlinefs, through the knowledge of him that hath called us *to glory, and to virtue.*" Therefore, " Giving all diligence, add to faith virtue, knowledge, temperance, patience, godlinefs, brotherly kindnefs, and charity. So an entrance fhall be miniftered unto you abundantly, into the everlafting kingdom of our Lord and Saviour Jefus Chrift. As obedient children *follow Chrift ;* not fafhioning yourfelves according to the lufts of our former ignorance. " But, as he that hath called you is holy, fo be ye holy in all manner of converfation ; becaufe it is written, be ye holy, for I am holy." The everlafting bleffings of the covenant, are all our falvation ; let them be all our defire. Be not languid in your defire, nor negligent in your purfuit of them. " Reaching forth towards that which is before, prefs forward towards the mark, for the prize of the high calling of God in Chrift Jefus." " Of thefe things I will not be negligent, to put you in remembrance. Yea, I think it meet, as long as I am in this tabernacle, to ftir you up,

by

by putting you in remembrance; knowing, that shortly I must put off this tabernacle. Moreover, I will endeavour, that ye may be able, after my decease, to have these things in remembrance."

With respect to external covenant relation—For all advantages of it be thankful;—seek spiritual and everlasting benefit thereby; and neglect no divine institutions for that end. Baptism, the token of it, minds us of God's covenant with us, and our children, that our hope may be in God for ourselves and ours. *He keepeth covenant and mercy to a thousand generations; and remembereth his covenant forever: The word which he commanded to a thousand generations; his covenant with Abraham, and oath unto Isaac.* Adults, that live without baptism, and parents, neglecting that of their children, do (in their measure) contribute to God's covenant being forgotten, and not kept in remembrance by his appointed token of it. They rather live (by the neglect of its memorial) in the *denial* of God's covenant, than in the *acknowledgment* of it. Let not the ordinance of God, (instituted to be a token of his covenant, and to be observed in remembrance of it) be neglected, or his covenant forgotten. *His truth and faithfulness; his name and memorial, endure throughout all generations.*

Christ, who gathers the lambs in his arms, and carries them in his bosom, said, "suffer little children, and forbid them not to come unto me; for of such is the kingdom of heaven;" laid his hand on such, and blessed them. Fail not to bring your children to him in his ordinance, for his blessing, in thankful remembrance of his covenant with them, and with prayer to, and hope in God for them. The children of his ancient people, God calls *sons and daughters, which they had borne unto him;* the prophet saith of the church under the gospel, *They are the seed of the blessed of the Lord,* (or of Abraham) *and their offspring with them;* Christ saith, *Of such is the kingdom of heaven;* and his apostle,

tle, *The promise is unto you and your children.*" Denying our children the token of God's covenant, hath a different language, with respect to them, from the above in sacred writ. Its language is, a denial of God's covenant being with, and of his promises to them ; and is too much like saying to them, *Ye are not of the Lord's heritage : go serve other gods.* When God and his prophet, Christ and his apostle, held the above language respecting children, shall we not regard them as the lambs of Christ's flock, who said *Feed my lambs ?* When Christ is said to feed his flock like a shepherd, to gather the lambs in his arms, and to carry them in his bosom, shall we forget that God's word and promises are to our children, and his covenant with them, and deny them his token of it ?

THE word of God, in the truths, and grace it reveals ; in its precepts and promises ; and in the hope it brings, is as truly to our children, as to ourselves ; and is his covenant with them, as well as with us. God's covenant is with us in our generations, by his word ; as it was with the posterity of Abraham in the time of Isaac. None doubt that his covenant was with them in their generations ; or their right to the token of it from their infancy. And why doubt it with respect to us, to whom his word and and promises are, as they were to them in the former dispensations ? Certainly God's covenant was with Abraham, and his seed after him in their generations, for an everlasting covenant. His seed the believing Gentiles certainly are. Is it not then with them in their generations ? Yes with them in their generations also ; and to them in their generations, belongs the token of his covenant with them.

I WILL not hint at a limitation of the divine mercy, with respect to children that die without baptism, through the neglect of their parents.

WHEREIN the word of God is not explicit, we are not to venture upon assertion. But, where there is no claim, God, if he sees fit, may suspend his favour to our children, upon their parents observing his institution respecting them. And we find, that God said of the uncircumcised child, *That soul shall be cut off from among his people;* which imports some material evil to the child. Our Saviour also saith, *unless any one* (See the Greek) *be born of water, and of the spirit, he cannot see the kingdom of God;* which respects baptismal, as well as spiritual regeneration. These passages of sacred writ, deserve the serious attention of parents. They (at least) should learn to beware of neglecting any divine institution, with respect to their children.

The growth of infidelity, the encreasing neglect of infant baptism, and consequent disregard of the institution, are of threatening aspect upon the visible church of Christ among us; and are to be sincerely regretted.

Let us believe, and obey the gospel of Christ, and reform all neglects of his institutions. So shall, He that walketh in the midst of the golden candlesticks, and holds the stars in his right hand, be with and bless us.

SERMON XX.

UPON THE DISCIPLINE OF CHRIST'S CHURCH.

MATTHEW XVIII. 15, 16, 17, 18. *Moreover, if thy brother shall trespass against thee, go and tell him his fault between thee and him alone: if he shall hear thee, thou hast gained thy brother.*

But, if he will not hear thee, then take with thee one or two more, that in the mouth of two or three witnesses every word may be established.

And if he shall neglect to hear them, tell it unto the church: but if he neglect to hear the church, let him be unto thee as an heathen man and a publican.

Verily I say unto you, Whatsoever ye shall bind on earth shall be bound in heaven; and whatsoever ye shall loose on earth shall be loosed in heaven.

IN human society government and subordination are necessary for the preservation and well-being of it's members. Man as a rational being is accountable and the proper subject of law. His happiness and dignity are essentially promoted by subjection to authority and discipline.

For this cause, the Redeemer of the world, when he came down from heaven to set up a kingdom amongst men and to select to himself a family from the apostate race of Adam thought, it necessary to institute a system

of

of laws and ordinances for the government of his followers. By the obfervance of thofe laws and ordinances they will effectually confult their own beft interefts and fecure the favour of their divine King and Saviour.

CHRIST, as King exercifes a providential dominion over all the creatures of God; and a fpiritual dominion over his church upon earth, and the innumerable hofts of fanctified fpirits in heaven. Among his fpiritual fubjects he reigns by the power of truth. His kingdom is within them, a kingdom of light and perfuafion. His laws are obeyed, only, with the confent of the affections. A main defign of his adminiftration is to render his fubjects happy in the way of obedience and to prepare them for the unmixed enjoyments of his love, by making them "a peculiar people zealous of good works."

THE methods he has taken to eftablifh his authority in his vifible church ought to be diligently ftudied and well underftood by us, as we would wifh to prove ourfelves to be his legitimate offspring.

MY defign is to treat of the difcipline and government of Chrift's church upon earth. Previous to a confideration of the main fubject I fhall premife feveral truths which bear a relation to it. As

1ft. CHRIST JESUS is the fole Legiflator of the church.

HE is King in Zion. All things are put under Him. All judgment is committed to Him. And He is head over all things to the church. Having finifhed his teftimony of divine truth he denounced a heavy curfe upon all who fhould prefume to add any thing to his word or diminifh any thing from it. He has left no authority either with men or angels to prefcribe any laws or ordinances for the government of his members. The writers of our facred oracles while under the miraculous influences of the Spirit revealed to men the truths and inftitutions of Chrift: But without fupernatural affiftance from the fpirit of Jefus no man has authority to

impofe

impose doctrines or duties upon his disciples. The power of making laws being reserved by Christ in his own hands, no church, nor any officer of the church has a right to ordain rites and ceremonies of worship or rules of discipline for the gospel-kingdom.

2dly. THE rules for the government of the church are all published in the holy scriptures.

THOSE writings are the criterion and standard to which every ordinance of discipline is to be referred, and a system of discipline is to be approved, only, as it harmonizes with that unerring standard the scriptures, not the customs and practices of any church upon earth must determine what is right and proper in discipline. The scriptures must controul all steps and processes in the church. It is, therefore, a very presumptious error in those who subject the church of Christ in the conduct of their spiritual and religious interests, to the laws of civil communities or to the authority of ecclesiastical rulers. The holy oracles are the only measure of right and wrong in conducting the concerns of the church and it's members.

3dly. THE rules Christ has given in his word are ample and sufficient for all the purposes of christian discipline and holy living.

HE has taken a wise care to provide suitable and sufficient rules for the trial and issue of all causes in his earthly kingdom. These rules are not accommodated, merely, to the primitive, apostolic church, but to the family of Christ in all countries and ages to the end of time. His laws are all perfect ; they are promulged ; they are plain and intelligible to those who sincerely wish to understand them.

His officers are merely executive, confined to what they find written in the scriptures of truth. As far as they confine themselves to that unerring rule they have all power to bind and loose : when they depart from that rule they have no power at all. In the law and

and testimony we shall find ample directions for the government of Christ's church and kingdom upon earth.

A SUMMARY of christian discipline is comprised in our text and the salutary uses and effects of it are pointed out. I shall now endeavour to explain the principles of gospel administration in matters of discipline in a variety of particulars—And

I. I SHALL point out the purposes and ends to be answered by christian discipline.

THE obvious designs of discipline are, to secure the beauty, order and peace of the church—to manifest the dignity and glory of Christ as the Saviour of the church—and to bring the members into a strict conformity to their head. Discipline is to render Jesus and his laws precious to his children and respectable to those who are without—As the glory of Christ consisted in his moral rectitude, in being holy, harmless, undefiled and separate from sinners; so the honour of his members consists in their manifesting the same mind which was in him—in exercising that love of righteousness, that obedience to the law and that zeal for God which were the characteristics of their Redeemer.

ONE purpose of disciplining Christ's members is, to take off from the church all reproach as tolerating offences against their Master—as negligent of his glory—and inattentive to their mutual improvement and sanctification. It is to remove the reproach of the wicked who stigmatize the body for the faults of its members, and calumniate the whole for the delinquences of individuals.

GOSPEL discipline is to render the family of Christ respectable and terrible in the eyes of the world. The world continually scrutinizes the principles and practices of Christ's members; and the end of discipline is the preservation of pure doctrine and virtuous practice in the church. That the beauty of that holy society may silence the tongue of reproach and convince the conscience of enemies that they have no well
grounded

grounded objections to alledge against the followers of the lowly Jesus.

OTHER ends of this divine institution are, to confirm believers in duty—to quicken them in their spiritual progress—and to recover those who may have erred from the truth.

IN pursuing discipline christians should aim at the purity of the whole body—the admonition of all their members—the restoration of offenders, if possible, to a better life, and if not, to wipe away the reproach of their offences from the church by a due testimony against them. Thus by evangelical discipline christians will command the religion of Jesus to the veneration and love of all who behold their purity, benevolence and zeal.

PURITY is the first object of discipline; then peace, a peace grounded on purity—The good of the whole and especially of the person offending is an indispensable purpose to be answered in a course of discipline—Let this be always remembered, That the exercise of authority in the church is designed not for the destruction but for the edification of the body.

II. I WILL mention the temper of mind which ought ever to prevail in the exercise of christian discipline.

THE tender affections of cordial brethren should pervade the whole transaction according to that apostolic direction 1. Cor. xvi. 14. " Let all your things be done with charity." Love is the cement of christian society; mutual esteem and kind affection are the leading characteristics of christian professors. Hence our Lord told his followers " A new commandment give I unto you, That ye love one another." Nothing is undertaken and pursued among christians in a right and acceptable manner which is not dictated by a principle of unfeigned love. This heavenly affection should originate and conduct every process of discipline in the church of Christ. When this tender affection does
not

not manifest itself the process is irregular, unscriptural and injurious to that cause of Christ which it pretends to support.

A SPIRIT of retaliation, of revenge, of ostentation and pride is totally repugnant to the wholesome and successful discipline of Christ's house, and tends to mar it's beauty and order instead of advancing them. This then is a leading maxim in discipline, that the person who undertakes it must have a heart warmed with supreme love to Christ and an unfeigned love to his offending brother. Again

III. I SHALL designate the persons who are to undertake and pursue a course of discipline.

ALL Christ's members have a mutual care and oversight of each other; and are directed to exhort and admonish one another; and to watch over each other in the Lord. The relation they bear to one another is represented by the intimate union which subsists between the limbs and members of the same body. So that, " If one member suffer all the members suffer with it." It is, therefore incumbent on every individual of Christ's body the church, to feel themselves under obligation to regard the welfare of every other member, and to pursue the benefit of all their brethren in the way of discipline, if it be found necessary.

BUT it concerns Christians first to discipline themselves, by subduing their own hearts and lives to the laws of Christ. Before they enter upon the recovery of their brethren they must correct and amend their own offences. This is agreeable to that precept of our Saviour. " First cast out the beam which is in thine own eye and then shalt thou see clearly to cast out the mote which is in thy brother's eye." It is incongruous and irregular for one gross offender to attempt by discipline the correction and reformation of another. This would involve him in the absurdity of the one who is reprehended by the Apostle in Rom. ii. 21, 22. Thou, therefore, " Which teachest another, teachest thou not thyself?

thyself? Thou that preachest a man should not steal, dost thou steal? Thou that sayest a man should not commit adultery, dost thou commit adultery? Thou that abhorrest idols, dost thou commit sacrilege? One, who is himself an offender, cannot be thought so wise and faithful in managing discipline as a Christian of a fair character; nor can he act so much from true love and pious zeal as though he were himself governed by the laws of Christian love and purity. It is not proper that such an one should indulge himself, or be allowed by the church in commencing and pursuing a course of discipline with an offender, until he be recovered to a more inoffensive walk with God. A church process, conducted by a professor of a faulty and exceptionable character, dishonours Christ and wounds religion. Our Lord does not allow it in his gospel kingdom. But this he requires, that all Christians do so purify themselves as to be duly qualified for so benevolent and useful an employment.

WELL would it be for religion if members eminent for piety, for meekness, for wisdom, for self-government and for their affection to Christ and his members should manage cases of discipline: But when they omit it, even the frailest and weakest of his disciples must enter upon it as a testimony of their zeal for him and love to their brethren. When offences come none are excepted from earnest endeavours to remove them; but it is peculiarly incumbent upon the Officers and Fathers of the church to take the lead in the discharge of this important and solemn trust.

IV. I PROCEED to show who are the proper subjects of gospel discipline.

THESE are all the members of Christ's visible family who through the prevalence of temptations have fallen into gross doctrinal error or immoral practices. The scriptures view men as transgressors for corrupt sentiments in religion as well as for their immoral and

loose

loose practices. Both Heretics and disorderly walkers, when they prove incorrigible, are to be rejected.

NONE by their place and rank in the church, or by their civil dignities are exempt from the salutary restraints and corrections of Christ's laws.

HAVING once determined who belong to Christ's visible kingdom we have found who are liable for their offences to answer at the tribunal of his church. Without entering into the argument to prove the point I shall take it for a gospel truth, that all persons baptized into the name of Christ are sealed his members, are under reciprocal obligations to watch over each other, are bound to submit to the authority of the church, and are entitled to the privileges of Christian discipline in our Lord's visible family. So that those who neglect a care of baptized persons, children and youth, neglect their duty and deny to them one main benefit of their baptismal covenant.

THIS question of the right and privilege of baptized persons to the holy ordinance of discipline is not to be decided by the opinions and practices of negligent and slothful churches who omit the care of their souls: But it is to be decided by the authority of Christ speaking in the scriptures, who has told us, "That of these is the kingdom of heaven." All baptized persons, of age to receive the benefit of discipline, are entitled to the important and sacred privilege from the care of Christ's churches and from the individuals composing those churches. Again,

V. I AM to mark the offences which are proper matter of discipline.

HERE I observe, that all the faults and errors of Christians are proper matter for friendly rebuke and expostulation; but they are not all matters which require Christian discipline. For this would render processes in the church endless and impracticable. We are to bear one another's burdens and infirmities and not make

each

each other offenders for a word, for every incautious action or for every mistaken sentiment.

Those faults only are to be considered, as offences requiring discipline, which, when persisted in, endanger a man's salvation. Those faults demand discipline which betray a disregard and contempt of the Christian religion and draw into question the reality of grace in the heart. Trespasses inconsistent with the Christian profession and which, when persevered in, must exclude a man from the kingdom of heaven are the proper matters of formal discipline in the church. But those failings to which good men are incident even when their general reputation for religion is exemplary are to be corrected by the common exhortations and reproofs of a preached gospel and by the friendly offices of brotherly love and private counsel. But professors may not be called upon trial before the tribunal of the church for those incidental failings to which virtuous and pious men are liable every day of their lives.

When any conduct themselves in a manner palpably repugnant to their covenant vows and their sacred relation to Christ, and in a way reproachful to the Christian name and character, then are they to be called to repentance by a set course of Christian discipline and to be proceeded with, to their recovery or to an issue in which the honour of Christianity shall be vindicated from the reproach of countenancing such abuses.

This distinction of offences is both reasonable in itself and is supported by those declarations of holy writ which assure us, that the power of the church is to be exercised not for the destruction but for the edification of the body. Our text supposes, that the trespass must be of such a nature and aggravation as to be inconsistent with grace, and when the offender continues in it, will justify his brethren in considering and treating him, as a heathen man and a publican; i.e. " as a person who holds Christ and his laws in habitual contempt.

In those cases mentioned by the Apostle as proper matters of discipline such vices are specified as manifest a deeprooted depravity of heart viz. a contentious disorderly deportment in the church—fornication—covetousness—idolatry—railing—drunkenness—extortion and similar gross violations of the moral law.

In another place, we learn that heresy is a crime which claims the judicial cognizance of the church. By heresy we are to understand, not the lesser differences of opinion which take place among Christians: But those gross and fundamental errors which are palpably repugnant to gospel doctrine, and which deny the leading articles of our holy faith. For such heresies professors may incur the heaviest censures of the church and a final exclusion from it. But for those smaller variations of sentiment which may be reconciled to gospel faith and obedience, in the main points, the church may not proceed to cut them off from the outward ordinances and privileges of the kingdom.

If any of this description do so differ from us that they cannot walk with us to edification we must labour to enlighten and to retain them; but we may not proceed to treat them as heretics and contemners of the gospel.

Further: No offences of whatever nature are proper matter of a public process in the church which do not admit of scripture proof; that is, where the facts alledged cannot be substantiated by evidence equal to the testimony of two witnesses." For at the mouth of two or three witnesses every word is to be established in the church.

We may use frequent and urgent endeavours of a private nature to reclaim a secret offender, but we may not presume to bring secret offences into public process.

VI. I shall note the steps which are to be taken with offenders in the church of Christ.

It has been long controverted among Christians, whether the directions in our text apply to public offences as well as to those which are private and personal. The rule, evidently, applies to all trespasses of a private and personal nature. Some divines have alledged, that, by analogy or a parity of reasoning, the rule extends to those offences which are generally known and are directly against the whole church as the body of Christ. Without deciding, confidently, in this case, against the judgment of many great and pious interpreters of the scriptures, I observe, that the rule does not in it's letter extend only to those trespasses which are of the nature of personal injuries and to such as are known only to a few where religion has not been openly scandalized. It would seem that our Lord's views extended to such trespasses, as might be settled and satisfaction made for them, in a private way without coming to the cognizance of the church to determine upon the nature of the satisfaction to be rendered by the transgressor.

A good reason may be assigned why all offences should not come under the limitation of what are called, the first and second steps of discipline, and why private and personal offences should be treated in that way.

In private offences the guilt of the transgressor ought not to be made public; unless contumacy render it necessary for his recovery. In personal trespasses or injuries there is such a liability, in the injured person, to misapprehension and prejudice, that it is fitting, even in public offences, that he should take measures to heal the wound by a personal treaty upon the subject, and by the interposition of some friendly mediator. For such attempts often convince the offended person of his mistake; and he would certainly have a fairer opportunity by his placability to convince his offending brother of the wrong.

But

But when the offence is public, all seem to be equally interested in convincing and reclaiming the offender and of seeing the particular proofs that he is convinced and reclaimed. No plea can be made, that the process was dictated by prejudice or with an intention to expose to open shame since the offence is already known. In a private settlement the marks of penitence cannot be generally known and even a public acknowledgement in such cases must be void of the most satisfactory marks of a sincere contrition for sin.

I think it should have weight against extending the rule to all public offences, that the Apostle Paul, in giving his directions concerning the incestuous person, enjoins it upon the church, as a body, to proceed against him for his offence.

Nor in the case of an heretic, who is an open offender have we an intimation of any steps to be taken, but such as are of a public nature. Let each christian determine for himself and when he is convinced that private steps are, in all cases, to be taken, he is in conscience obliged to pursue them. Those steps will not mar the process. Nor do I imagine, that the omission of those steps ought ever to be plead in bar of a process against open and public offenders, unless in cases of personal injury.

In private and personal offences which, probably, include the greater number, the rule is plain and express, that the person offended shall go to the offender and in the spirit of Christian meekness and love tell him his fault in a secret manner. In stating his trespass he must labour to convince him by recounting the evidence of the fact and naming the witnesses; that the offender may be satisfied that the trespass has been committed and can be proved. He must labour to bring his brother to a better temper and conduct in future and with assurances of this tenor, apparently sincere he must rest satisfied and restore him in the spirit of meekness.

When

When this step fails of it's desired success, he is next, to choose some meet person of the church, (and reason dictates, that he should be one acceptable to the offender) or he may take two persons of this character and treat the matter over again, employing the labours of the attending brethren to convince and reclaim. If the offender be convinced—humble himself and engage future amendment and render due satisfaction, he is to be restored.

If he continue in his trespass he is to be reported to the officers and brethren of the church. His offence should be plainly and explicitly stated to the church, and the allegations being carefully and impartially examined judgement must be given according to evidence. Where the evidence amounts to the testimony of two credible witnesses, the accused must be convicted and gospel satisfaction required. Otherwise he must be acquitted.

When the process has not been conducted according to our Lord's directions it may not be sustained but the accuser after better information and faithful reproof be required to take the previous steps before he claim an hearing of the church.

Provided, the offender refuse to hear the church and return to his duty he should be admonished a first and, if necessary, a second time. When all this painful exertion of the church prove ineffectual he must be cut off from the church in a participation of gospel ordinances and privileges and be treated with severity as a traitor to the cause and religion of Christ. His brethren are bound to refuse him those common marks of respect which they may with propriety render to the men of the world, who know nothing of Christ nor yield any respect to his laws. Christians are prohibited so much society with excommunicated persons as to eat with them at a common table.

This severity, expressly, enjoined by our blessed Saviour, is the last and highest exercise of Christian tenderness

tenderness and fidelity; and when perseveringly exhibited will produce powerful effects; it will probably subdue the adamant heart of the offender. When he repents and manifests the sincerity of his repentance he is to be restored to forfeited privileges and to all the tender endearments of Christian love.

VII. I shall notice the effects which will usually follow a course of regular gospel discipline in the church of Christ.

No institution of our Saviour is more repugnant to the lusts and trying to the passions of men, than the discipline of his church.

The motives and designs of Christians in this matter are, often, misunderstood and grosly misrepresented. Indeed criminal motives, too frequently intermix themselves with the zeal of believers.

As nothing is more useful and necessary, and conducive to the honour of Christ and the reputation of his members; so there is nothing which the adversary of the church opposes with so much energy as a course of gospel discipline. He, continually, raises reproaches and contentions against the faithful advocates of Christian order and purity.

Formalists, hypocrites, false brethren, the world and the devil all unite and combine against this good and benevolent work. Hence some of the first effects of gospel discipline appear to be unhappy and disastrous. But charity and peace grounded upon purity being the end of this holy institution they will in the issue result from a course of wise and faithful discipline.

In this way the church will become respectable in the world and terrible to her enemies: She will be guarded against the intrusion of corrupt and wicked members: She will be healed of her formality, lukewarmness and hypocrisy. Hypocrites in Zion will be afraid. Believers will grow in grace and fast ripen for the pure employments and delights of heaven. Christ as the Saviour of the church shall be covered with glory. The church as his redeemed and sanctified bride, shall enjoy his enlivening presence and joyous approbation.

WHATEVER the church shall perform in a right manner and from pure motives shall be established; no efforts against her measures shall prevail; no daring offender shall elude the awful effects of her displeasure; no humble penitent soul shall find her consolations vain. For whatsoever she shall bind on earth shall be bound in heaven and whatsoever she shall loose on earth shall be loosed in heaven.

BUT alas when this holy discipline of the church is despised or neglected, then sinners in Zion are careless and secure in their error and wickedness. Men grow bold in their transgressions—dissolute unprincipled members are introduced into the visible family of Christ and the faithful servants of God are grieved and endangered by the multitudes of false and deceitful brethren who have crept in amongst them. The glory of the church is tarnished: The name of Jesus is blasphemed; irreligion and infidelity gain a temporary triumph; and great occasion is given to the enemy to scoff and blaspheme. The church degenerates and soon learns to symbolize with this evil world and the way is prepared for the display of God's wrath against his revolting heritage, until in the issue he will remove their candlestick out of it's place. Seeing then such manifold evils result from the abuse and neglect of Christian discipline, and such abundant and certain benefits follow the wise, constant and faithful administration of it let each professor of Jesus and every friend of his cause and kingdom apply himself watchfully and resolutely to this momentous duty. With our sincere endeavours we shall be sure of divine cooperations to render them in some eminent manner successful and useful to the glory of Christ and the prosperity of his church.

Relying

Relying upon this effectual aid, let us enter upon our master's service and commend ourselves unto him in well doing.

"Now to him that is of power to establish you according to our gospel and the preaching of Jesus Christ, (according to the revelation of the mystery which was kept secret since the world began, but now is made manifest, and by the scriptures of the prophets, according to the commandments of the everlasting God, made known unto all nations for the obedience of faith.) To God only wise, be glory through Jesus Christ for ever. *Amen.*

SERMON XXI.

DISSUASIVES FROM EXCESSIVE AND SINFUL DIVERSIONS.

ECCLESIASTES II. 1. *I said in mine heart, go to now, I will prove thee with mirth; therefore enjoy pleasure: and behold, this also is vanity!*

SOLOMON received from God, in early life as a special favor, distinguished wisdom. His first desires for it were laudable. Perceiving the necessary connexion between the happiness of his people, and the prudent administration of their public concerns, he earnestly sought wisdom, that he might be enabled to discharge the duties of his exalted station, with prudence and fidelity; that his own honor, and the national prosperity, and glory might be secured. But whatever were his first reflections and desires on the subject, he afterwards falsely supposed, that contentment and happiness might be obtained by an increase of knowledge in natural philosophy. Possessed of this delusive idea, he pursued his studies of the works of nature with unremitted exertions. He spake of trees, philosophically, from the hyssop to the cedar. And gave his heart to seek and search out by wisdom, concerning all things done under the sun. But, in the issue was disappointed of the satisfaction he expected.

REMAINING

Remaining uneasy, and being unwilling to conclude that happiness and contentment, were not attainable, in the things of the present world,—he resolved to pursue another course :—" I said in mine heart, go to now, I will prove thee with mirth ; therefore enjoy pleasure." Having formed this wild resolution, he immediately entered into all the extravagancies his riches could procure, his heart desire, or his lively imagination invent. When one object failed of gratifying his irresistible propensity for pleasure, he turned to another. For a season, he gave himself undue liberty in the use of wine—ran to the highest extravagance in buildings—to a vain mispence of wealth, in planting and ornamenting gardens of pleasure—in forming pools of water, and in surrounding himself with servants. He filled his palace with musicians of all kinds—his royal mansions with women of various nations ; and finally gave himself up to all the impunities of unhallowed love.

After having spent some time in the pursuit of pleasure ; and proving his heart with mirth, in full conviction of his folly, he said : " Behold this also is vanity." He found by experience that his unwise resolution had led him into a vexatious pursuit after that, which existed only in imagination.

Disappointment is the lot of all who seek for happiness in a round of diversions ; or in any of the alluring objects of this world. But few, if any, enjoy such advantages for the accomplishment of their desires, as were in the power of the king of Israel. His disappointment ought, therefore, to convince all of their folly, who give themselves up to this vain pursuit.

It is not supposed, however, that this remark, respecting the vanity of pleasure, refers to diversions of every kind, and degree : or, to the indulgence, on proper occasions, of a merry heart, which does good like a medicine. Some diversions are consistent with
piety ;

piety; are a great relief to the mind; and are highly improving and ornamental.

To distinguish between diversions innocent, or vicious in their nature, it is necessary only to remark, that the former are such as have a natural tendency, to preserve the health of the body—to improve the mind, and manners—to increase the innocent enjoyments of social life, and to *ameliorate* the heart:—The latter, have a contrary effect,—they tend to corrupt and depress the mind—to encourage, inflame and strengthen the evil propensities of the heart—to impair the health of the body—to render the manners brutal, and to minister to ungodliness.

To seek diversions in scenes of cruelty—in the fightings, and miseries of animals—in the dangerous exercise of racings—in the violent, and needless exertions of strength—in the idle exhibitions of uncommon courage, and extraordinary feats—in the mysterious tricks of common jugglers—in the merriment of inebriating cups—in the wantonness of impure love—in the indecencies of corrupt theatres, or in the impieties of a card-table, tends to all the evils and miseries above mentioned.

Such diversions as are innocent in their nature, become criminal, when carried to excess. They are excessive, when considered of importance, and are pursued with ardor,—When the mind and heart, by their influence are diverted from the duties of life, and the great concerns of eternity;—when they are unseasonable, and expensive;—and when no care is taken to render them serviceable. In all these cases they are direct evils. Behold they are altogether vanity!

I will now proceed to lay before those who pursue sinful and excessive diversions, such considerations as may have a tendency to dissuade them from their inconsiderate course.

The subject is such as requires plainness. I will not, through a false delicacy, bury my ideas in obscure language.

language. Such as are given to pleasure may expect a friendly openness.

I. This pursuit is injurious to your health.

The human system is not capable of sustaining excesses, any length of time. Irregularities weaken the animal powers, depress the spirits—irritate the nerves and nourish the seeds of dissolution. Where do you look for early debility, and a premature death? Is it in those who regularly follow their callings in life; carefully avoiding sinful diversions, and those sportive scenes which would expose them to various kinds of intemperance? Or, in such as involve themselves in pleasures—are daily found in the pursuit of sensual gratifications, and are regardless of the nature or degree of their sports? Whilst you perceive the former enjoying the pleasures of health, do you not often observe the latter suffering the pains of disease? And, indeed, every other distress—who hath wo—who hath sorrow—who hath contentions—who hath bablings—who hath wounds without cause—who hath redness of eyes? They, who, in the pursuit of mirth and pleasure, tarry long at the wine, and seek mixed wine for revelings! But in the end, these revelings bite like a serpent, and sting like an adder. They poison the body—waste the strength, and portray on the features the lineaments of death. This is a natural cause, why the wicked shall not live out half their days.

Be wise.—Consider the severe reflections you must endure, when suffering the pain of those diseases your excesses will produce. And learn to avoid those errors which have involved thousands in misery.

II. By pursuing sinful and excessive diversions you are in a course which tends to poverty.

The actual expenses of men of pleasure are great. A portion of time, in which they ought to be attending to their temporal concerns, is misspent. Their affairs become embarrassed. And they soon plunge themselves into the miseries of want. They beggar
their

their families, and press them down with sorrows derived from their own follies. "*He who loveth pleasure shall be a poor man.*" Yea, he shall be poor in estate—poor in name—poor in mental improvements—and poor in spiritual enjoyments. "He who followeth vain persons"—pursuers of mirth and pleasure—"Shall have poverty enough"—though "He considereth not that poverty will come upon him." He is like that slothful servant, on the deranged condition of whose field, Solomon remarked:—"Lo, it was all grown over with thorns, and nettles had covered the face thereof, and the stone wall thereof was broken down!—And concerning the owner he said, "So shall thy poverty come as one that travelleth, and thy want as an armed man."

III. When you have said to your heart—"I will prove thee with mirth; therefore enjoy pleasure"—have you obtained the pleasure you sought? Rather have not your pursuits been attended with perplexity, and followed with disappointment?

When you have spent a day in idle sports; or a night in reveling, lewdness, or gambling; having given yourselves up to the gratification of your wild desires—deprived yourselves of your necessary repose—disturbed the peace and order of your families, wounded the feelings of your connections and friends, and have retired from the scene of your confusion, and vice, have you then found pleasure in reflecting on what was past?

I will not enquire what satisfaction you received when engaged in your excesses, for whilst the time was passing you was devoid of reflection; as devoid of reflection as the ox that is led to the slaughter; or the fool to the correction of the stocks. But, when the scene is ended, reflection returns. You find that you have reveled—have gambled—have spent your time in wickedness, impairing your health—corrupting your minds—violating the laws of society—spending your wealth—

wealth—offending your God, and degrading human nature. When reflecting on these things, do you find the pleasure sufficient to counterbalance the pain?

Probably, you endeavour to exclude reflection, and strive to preserve the appearance of calmness and ease; and affect a total indifference as to any sensibility of your wickedness. Do you not, to your companions in folly, speak of your excesses with an apparent satisfaction? At the same time, is your heart free from the anguish of remorse? Does it not upbraid you of duplicity? And do you not find that, "the way of sinners is hard."

When Solomon spake of the pleasures of lewdness, he observed that, "The lips of a strange woman drop as the honey comb; and her mouth is smoother than oil:"—But, observe the sequel, "Her end is bitter as wormwood, sharp as a two edged sword. Her feet go down to death; her steps take hold on hell." Here is the pleasure. The honey drops are converted into wormwood. The smooth and insinuating language of seduction, by which the simple are led astray ends, as in the anguish of a double edged sword entering the heart. The much fair speech of the *impure*, with her deceitful kisses, together with her perfumed, and alluring bed terminate in the reproaches of conscience, which, as a dart, strike through the guilty soul. Such as pursue this pleasure, are as a bird which hasteth to the snare, not knowing that it is for his life. The lewd have cast down many wounded; yea, many strong men have been slain by her. Her house is the way to hell, going down to the chambers of death.

And, where is the pleasure? True is that declaration of Solomon, "Thou shalt mourn at the last."

From a contemplation of the miseries of lewdness, I would turn your attention to those of reveling, and gambling.

You have spent a night at the card table. What have you won? What have you lost? What time have you

you mifpent? What laws have you broken? What oaths and imprecations have you uttered?

SUPPOSE you have won: can you receive your winnings with an approving confcience? You muft be fenfible that you have no right to fport with property; or to leave it needlefsly to the decifion of a lot. To expofe it by gambling, is making the providence of God fubfervient to vile purpofes. When a lot is fanctified by the civil power to effect fome valuable, or benevolent object, it may be juftifiable to become interefted: But in this cafe, you expofe it wantonly, needlefsly, to gratify the vile paffion of avarice, or to obtain a momentary pleafure. What fatisfaction then can you take, in receiving, and ufing property acquired in this manner? Poffibly you may have become fo hardened, as to have loft all fenfe of the evil. If fo, it is to be feared, you are beyond the hope of recovery.

ON the other hand, what are your reflections when you have loft? If one gains, another neceffarily loofes. When you have left your property to the decifion of *chance*; and *chance* has been againft you; and in a few hours you are ftripped of the earnings of many days: Does this give you pleafure? I truft you will readily anfwer in the negative, when you reflect upon the paffions excited; and call to mind the horrid oaths—imprecations—curfes, and blafphemies uttered againft *chance*; or otherwife againft the *providence of God*, in confequence of this lofs.

WHERE then is the pleafure of gaming? It cannot reafonably confift in gaining or loofing. Does the charm lie in a reiteration of the fame round of thoughtlefs play? And is this a diverfion of fo much importance as to be worth purfuing? Will the pleafure it gives counterbalance all its attendant evils?

THE inexperienced, who have juft entered on this myftery of iniquity, have not a proper fenfe of the evils to which it tends. They begin by fpending an hour or two at the table, merely as a matter of diverfion.

fion. This habituates them to the game. Finding it but a dull round of thoughtlefs action, in order to ftimulate engagednefs, they begin to expofe property---a little at firft, only to excite attention ; this little foon loofes its effect, and larger fums are expofed. The wicked and inconfiderate diverfion is now ended, and the game becomes an object of property and avarice. The winner is willing to continue to increafe his gains ; and the lofer feels that he has a right to continue, to recover what he has loft. Temptations to fraud and injuftice, become violent. Heaven is impioufly invoked. Paffions rife, and foul language fucceeds. In this manner the night is fpent, and the way is now prepared for the continuance of the fame baneful practice. They repeat it, and foon loofe all fenfe of the evil. The iffue of the gambling table is commonly *intoxication*, which produces revelings, uproar, confufion, broken glaffes, violence, fwinifh conduct, beaftly ftupidity, and the horrid orgies are ended only by the burial of reafon in the rotten grave of inebriety.

IV. Excessive and finful diverfions, deprefs the mind, corrupt the heart, and deftroy the character.

You muft be fenfible that the pleafures you purfue are of an ignoble kind. Calculated to gratify the evil propenfities of the annimal nature. Of confequence they muft be debafing to the foul, by rendering it fubfervient to the beaftly appetites. A fenfe of moral obligation is hereby weakened. Every focial affection is deftroyed. You become unfeeling, as to the diftreffes of your fellow creatures ; and infenfible of the duties you owe to your God. Every mean of improvement in the knowledge of divine things is laid afide. And when not engaged in more wicked diverfions, your time is fpent in trifles.

But remember, that God has endowed you with rational fouls ; and has bound you to conduct virtuoufly by laws, by love, by mercy, by promifes of happinefs, and by threatnings of judgment. Turning your attention,

tion, therefore, to such satisfactions as arise from excessive and sinful diversions, evidences such a false estimate of true happiness; such a disregard to the divine goodness, and such a depravity and degradation of the intellectual powers as must, on reflection, fill you with shame. You are thwarting the kind purposes of heaven: And whilst boasting of reason, are acting a most unreasonable part.

Your character suffers. What right have you to expect the deference and good will of your fellow creatures, when you pay so little attention to your own character, to virtue, or to the salutary laws of society? Surely you fall under the detestation of the virtuous. By pursuing this course you will soon be ashamed to appear among men of principle and character, because you have neither. And you will feel that your presence is a disgrace to men of virtue and respectability.

How much better is it to consider and pursue those things which are lovely and of good report?

V. Excessive and sinful diversions are in violation of the law of God, ensure the divine displeasure, and render singularly awful the scenes of death and judgment.

Every rational creature is responsible for his conduct to his Creator. Reason and responsibility are inseperably connected. Accordingly God hath appointed a day, in which he will judge the world in righteousness. All must stand before the judgment seat of Christ, and receive the things done in their body, whether good or evil.

You are naturally inclined to remove from your minds all sense of your accountability; and to free yourselves from the restraints you are laid under, by the solemn truths of revelation. But these truths are unalterable. Till heaven and earth pass, one jot or one tittle shall in no wise pass from the law, till all be fulfilled. On that day, in which, God will judge the secrets of men you must answer for all your conduct.

Know

Know thou, that for all these things, God will bring thee into judgment. Know thou—indulge no doubt of the event. Flatter not yourselves with the deceitful and soothing notions, that in some mysterious and inconceivable way, you will escape. Let not the solemn ideas of death, and a future judgment pass your minds, as fugitive thoughts ; making no influential or abiding impressions thereon. When contriving sinful diversions, let the solemn idea of a righteous retribution, in the coming world, check your vain desires. And when in the practice of folly, remember, you are laying up in store things which must be manifested at the last day.

You are apt to employ all your thoughts upon your sports and pleasures. If things of a serious nature sometimes press on your minds you endeavour to stifle reflection, and to erase from your hearts every impression which may tend to imbitter your carnal joys.

Why do ye thus ? You are not insensible that hereby you aggravate your folly, incense your God, enhance the terrors of future judgment, and drown yourselves in perdition.

Instead of pursuing this course, you ought to be thankful that God has endowed you with reason, made you capable of reflection, given a revelation of his will, directed you to a virtuous line of conduct, encouraged your pursuit in it, threatened your deviations from it, opened to your view the consequences of virtue and vice, and as the benevolent parent of the universe solicits your attention to those objects in which are involved your real and eternal happiness.

If you are not thankful for these things ; but on the contrary violate the divine will, strive to throw off restraints, forget your accountability, put far away the evil day, pursue vanity, and run to excess, thoughtless of the displeasure of God, and fearless of the future judgment ; and thereby make a sacrifice of yourselves to the prince of disobedience ; surely, when brought

into

into judgment you will deprecate your folly, and feel that heaven is juſt in pouring upon you the vials of everlaſting wrath.

As judgment will not be delayed, how will you appear before God? What reflections will you have at death upon your preſent ſinful diverſions? How will the idle ſports and gay ſcenes of the preſent world appear to you, when preſented to the tribunal of Jehovah? There the books will be opened, and all your follies laid before you. Feeling the weight of that guilt in which you are involved, will you not then call to the rocks and mountains to hide you from the preſence of your offended Judge.

Do theſe things appear light and trifling, becauſe they are future?

Are you determined to walk in the ſight of your eyes, and in the ways of your heart,—to ſet reaſon, conſcience, and the fear of God aſide—to ſtrew your paths with pleaſure—to eat, drink and be merry—to fill your head and heart with vanity—to proceed in ſports and revelings—to follow the lewd to their beds of tapeſtry—to purſue unreſtrained, and to ſatiate your thirſt for the unhallowed pleaſures of ſenſe? and that, becauſe judgment is delayed? Alas!—Mortals conſider!—Oh! what bitterneſs you will find in the end!—Your dying beds will be filled with thorns, and your ſouls with the anguiſh of the never dying worm!

I shall cloſe with ſome general remarks.

The apoſtle, when ſpeaking of the perils of the laſt days, and the cauſes by which they ſhould be produced, mentions this as one, that, "men ſhall be lovers of pleaſures more than lovers of God." And it is evident from experience, that in proportion as pleaſures are purſued, religion decays—falls into diſrepute, and the troubles of the pious increaſe. As they oppoſe by their example and reproof, theſe vain and inconſiderate purſuits, they fall under the diſpleaſure, and meet with the reſentment of thoſe who are given to diſſipation.

By

By the decay of piety, and the general disregard to things of a serious nature, we must conclude, that the love of pleasure is predominant at the present day. Indeed we have other, and sufficient evidences of this melancholy truth. Things sacred, are called in question. Some unprincipled writers have ridiculed the Scriptures, and blasphemed the name of Jesus. The influence of virtue is almost overpowered. It has become unfashionable, and exposes to ridicule, to practise christian virtue in its purity.

The incarnation of the son of God; the doctrine of the atonement, and most of the sacred oracles, in some circles, are become the common topics for the display of licentious wit; and the religion of nature is highly and extravagantly commended, whilst none is practised.

But notwithstanding these lovers of pleasures more that lovers of God, are struggling to overthrow the Sacred Oracles, and to nullify the unalterable laws of Jehovah; yet, the Scriptures will prevail. Perhaps not, however, till thousands have inconsiderately involved themselves in perdition:—I say *inconsiderately*, for it is evident the reigning infidelity, does not arise from a candid examination of the evidences by which christianity is supported. Instead of examining the subject with that serious and persevering attention its nature demands, the Scriptures are thrown aside by many, without even a perusal.

This is a matter of lamentation to all the friends of the peace and happiness of mankind. It naturally tends to the ruin of the rising generation, to a dissolution of all the bands of society, to universal disorder, and to innumerable perils.

Let these lovers of pleasure remember, that although they may call in question the divine authority of the Scriptures; and thereby find their fear of God dissolved, and restraints against their excesses removed, and may rejoice therein, yet, that it is but a temporary ry delusion. The scene of their licentiousness will soon end, and eternity will open upon them.

THE unhappy influence this prevailing libertinism has on the rising generation is apparent. Hereby a sense of moral obligation is removed from their minds, fears of a just retribution are weakened, and desires for present enjoyment increased. Having pernicious examples before them, of some in high life, and of others advanced in age, they pursue their sinful diversions without reflection or remorse. Their appetites being keen for pleasure, and their judgments not being matured by experience, they rejoice in these destructive examples, as a self justifying argument.

THE present licentiousness of youth is not, however, to be attributed wholly to the reigning infidelity, nor to the pernicious examples of unprincipled men. Much is owing to parental negligence. Alas!—Parents reflect on yourselves:—Where is your family religion? Where are your lectures of virtue to your children? Where, your pious examples? Your sacred regard to things of infinite importance? and your united influence, and persevering endeavours to restrain the young?

I AM sensible that undistinguished censure would be unjust; for, however degenerate we may have become, yet there are a few who bear an exemplary testimony against the infidelity, and licentious pleasures of the age. Who, by prayer in their families, acknowledge the being of a God—train up their children in the principles of *christian* virtue, and set before them examples of piety.

IT is, however, obvious, that characters of this description are thinly sown. A great proportion of parents give up their children to the blind guidance of their uninstructed reason: And to pursue unrestrained, the paths into which they are led, by the impulse of their depraved hearts.

THE misery in which parents involve themselves by such indifference, is just. THE

The hearts of the virtuous bleed for the youth who have the misfortune to be placed under the care of such unnatural guides.

Youth, remember, however you may be wronged by those who gave you being, that the benevolent Parent of all has not left you without instruction. Wisdom is crying aloud; she uttereth her voice in the streets; she crieth in the chief place of concourse; in the openings of the gates, in the highest places of the city; and in the most tender, and persuasive language urges your compliance with her dictates. In her right hand she holds out for your encouragement, length of days and in her left, riches and honours. Her fruit is better than gold, yea, than fine gold; and her revenue than choice silver. Hear her call; attend to her instruction; keep her commandments, and live. Forsake her not, and she shall preserve thee: love her, and she shall keep thee. Exalt her, and she shall promote thee: she shall bring thee to honour, when thou dost embrace her. She shall give to thine head an ornament of grace: a crown of glory shall she deliver to thee.

Is it painful to see youth running to excess; regardless of the nature of their sports, and prostrating every virtuous principle at the shrine of forbidden pleasure? How much more so, to see those who are advanced in life, following their idle and vicious sports; when they have families grown to observe their irregularities: And who need the influence of a better example.

It is shameful for grey hairs to be found in the way of folly.

Let all be wise, and avoid such diversions as are inconsistent with the love and practice of piety; and strive to improve in things lovely.——Amen.

SERMON XXII.

HABITUAL GROWTH IN GRACE ESSENTIAL TO THE CHRISTIAN CHARACTER.

2 Peter iii. 18. *But grow in GRACE.*

THE Apostle **Peter** writes to all Christians. He informs them that there will be false teachers and scoffers in the latter, or gospel days. He cautions against hearkening to seducers, and being shaken in mind. Against being led away by the error of the wicked and falling from our own stedfastness. And as the mean to prevent this, and secure our own comfort, he directs us to grow in grace. I shall attempt to show

I. The import of the phrase *grow in Grace.*

II. The propriety of the direction, or give the reasons why Christians should labour to grow in grace.

III. That growth in grace is essential to the true Christian character.

I. Let us consider the import of the phrase grow in grace.

The word **Grace**, in scripture use, has various significations. Originally and strictly it signifies a gift. Hence the Apostle uses it to signify liberality or a free contribution. (2 Cor. viii. 19.) It frequently signifies the blessings and benefits which flow to us in and by

Jesus

Jesus Christ. We are saved by grace. It is needless to mention all the acceptations of the word. Suffice it to shew how it is to be taken in the text. And it signifies much the same as the word virtue, viz. a good disposition, good habits and good actions flowing from them. He is a virtuous man, whose mind is well disposed. And whose discourse and behaviour are correspondently good and excellent. Grace here signifies a disposition of mind truely and habitually pious, and a behaviour and conduct correspondent to it and proceeding from it, or, in other words, such a temper and conduct as is agreeable to the gospel. The seat of it is in the mind. The disposition or temper of mind is what God chiefly regards. "It is a good thing that the heart be established with grace." We should be well grounded in the truths of religion, and replenished with every pious disposition and habit. Our actions should flow from an heart replenished with grace. "We should teach and admonish one another, and sing praise, with grace in our heart: Our speech should be always with grace." Should flow from a pious disposition, and carry a tincture of it, that we may edify others. In the whole of our conversation, "we must have grace to serve God acceptably." All our actions must flow from a believing, loving, obedient disposition of soul, must be conformable to God's will and aimed at his glory.

These pious dispositions and habits of soul are termed gracious ones, and such a behaviour and conduct are termed gracious or godly, partly because they are freely given by God to his children, and by the influences of his spirit they are disposed and enabled to live unto God and have their fruit unto holiness; and partly because such dispositions, habits and conduct are pleasing to God. In this sense the word grace is frequently used, thus Noah and Moses found grace in God's sight, i. e. conducted so as to please God and obtain favour of him.

WE

We may hence learn the import of the expreſſion "grow in grace." It implies,

I. That Chriſtians are here in a ſtate of minority. It is children that grow. Chriſtians are here as children growing up to maturity, that they may enter upon the poſſeſſion which Chriſt has purchaſed and our heavenly Father has reſerved for us. We ſee and know but in part; but when we ſhall become men, we ſhall no longer ſee darkly through a glaſs, but know as we are known.

II. To grow in grace, ſuppoſes that Chriſtians are in a ſtate capable of growth and improvement. The hypocrite, who was never born of God, has not a principle of grace within him, and therefore is incapable of growth in grace. But the real Chriſtian, who is born of the ſpirit and made partaker of a divine nature, is capable of growth in grace. True grace will not be finally loſt. The divine ſeed remains in the good man. Thoſe, who drink of the water which Chriſt gives, have in them a well of water ſpringing up into everlaſting life. Love to God and divine things, and hatred of ſin will grow ſtronger and ſtronger. No man can ſay that he has arrived to ſuch a degree in grace that he is capable of no greater attainments. The Apoſtle Paul did not think himſelf perfect, "But forgetting the things which are behind, he reached forth unto thoſe which are before, and preſſed towards the mark for the prize of the high calling of God in Chriſt Jeſus."

III. To grow in grace ſuppoſes that there ought to be proper care and exertions on our part to that end. Chriſtians are not to be ſlothful in the buſineſs of religion, but fervent in ſpirit ſerving the Lord. To be followers of thoſe who, through faith and patience, inherit the promiſes. To give diligence to make their calling and election ſure, to add to their faith knowledge, virtue, temperance and all the graces of the Chriſtian temper. And though we are beholden to God for divine

vine influence to enable us to grow in grace, as well as for the original implantation of good difpofitions in us; yet ordinarily growth in grace is in proportion to our care and endeavours in improving the means of grace and influences of the divine fpirit offered us. The fcripture informs us that it is God who gives men power to get wealth, and alfo affures us that the hand of the diligent maketh rich. Thefe affertions are confiftent. It is owing to the rain and funfhine that the fruits of the earth grow and come to perfection; yet he, who cultivates his land beft, ordinarily has the greateft crop.— He, who improveth his talents beft, gains moft by the improvement. The more diligent we are in every duty, the more will every good difpofition be ftrengthened, the more pleafant will the path of duty be, the more conformed to God fhall we be, and the more meet to be partakers of the inheritance of the faints in light. I proceed

II. To fhow the propriety of the direction in the text, or to give fome reafons why Chriftians fhould labour for growth in grace.

On a candid confideration, we fhall find that fuch a direction is proper on feveral accounts.

I. Because Chriftians in general are too carelefs in this matter. They do not take proper care to make advances in the divine life. The world courts their affection and engroffes their attention. They need, therefore, to be frequently reminded of and ftirred up to their duty. To give diligence to add to their faith virtue, knowledge, temperance, patience, godlinefs, brotherly kindnefs and charity. And to make their calling and election fure. Minifters fhould not be negligent in putting Chriftians in mind of thefe things.

II. Because growth in grace evidences an intereft in Chrift. Grace in a weak ftate is hardly difcernible. It is common for Chriftians, when they examine themfelves by the marks given in God's word, to have

a mixture

a mixture of doubts and hopes. This arises in part from the weakness and imperfection of grace. But if the Christian finds that he grows in grace—that his love to God and hatred of sin increase—that pious dispositions grow stronger—that gracious habits are more confirmed, and the ways of duty more easy and delightsome: It is a satisfying evidence of Christian sincerity; and he, in these ways, makes his calling and election sure to himself.

III. Because growth in grace is much for our comfort. Many are in great uncertainty about their state, in bondage through fear of death, and enjoy but little consolation. The reason of this is, their not growing in grace. Hence they are void of those evidences of sincerity which arise from growth in grace, and, consequently, the comforts which those evidences afford. Death, judgment and eternity are of solemn consideration—scenes which we must all try. We all dread misery and wish to be happy. Therefore, to have solid evidences that we are interested in the saving benefits of the Redeemer's purchase, and a good hope that we shall be accepted of our Judge, and obtain eternal life affords great comfort. Moreover,

Growth in grace is comfortable in itself. It affords present satisfaction to the good man; as it causes the ways of religion to become more and more easy and agreeable to him. Some duties, at first seem hard to a Christian: But when he is exercised in the ways of godliness he finds by experience that "Wisdom's ways are ways of pleasantness, and all her paths are peace."

I add, that the Christian, who improves well the talents committed to him, will receive divine light and consolation. "To him that hath," that is, who improveth what is committed to him "shall be given." To those who improve divine influences and advantages aright, "God giveth more grace." "God will shed abroad his love in their hearts, and create joy greater than that of harvest, or of those who divide the spoil."

If

If Christians are negligent in duty, they deprive themselves of these consolations.

IV. The direction in the text is highly proper, as the way to prevent declining in religion is to labour to grow in grace. The only way to prevent going backward, is to be zealous to press forward in religion.—Not that, I suppose, grace in a true Christian will be lost. The Apostle, however, cautions to " beware lest we fall from our own stedfastness;" and, to prevent this, directs us to grow in grace. Christians by profession may apostatize. Real Christians may hearken to seducers, and be led into errors, and hearken to temptations, and fall into great and scandalous sins to the dishonour of God and the wounding of their own consciences. Therefore, if we would please God, prevent spiritual maladies, and preserve an healthful and vigorous frame of spirit, we must labour to grow in grace.

V. The direction is highly proper, because growth in grace will render our conversation beautiful and alluring to men. Our Lord directs us, to let our light so shine before men, that others, beholding our good works, may glorify our heavenly Father. The gospel directs us to be harmless and blameless in the midst of a crooked and perverse people before whom we are to shine as lights in the world. It is grace that makes the righteous man more excellent than his neighbour—that causes his conversation to shine with a peculiar lustre, and appear beautiful and attractive to all beholders.—And the greater his improvement in grace, the more beautiful and winning will his conversation be. The law of God will be in his heart, his mouth will speak of wisdom, and his tongue will talk of judgment.—Words fitly spoken, how beautiful are they? They are like apples of gold in pictures of silver. And not only the words, but the behaviour of an advanced Christian is beautiful and alluring. He is honest and upright in his dealings, prudent and peaceable in his behaviour,

serious

serious yet not morose, affable yet not frothy or vain, courteous, condescending and benevolent to all. Those must be lost to a sense of goodness, who would not love and wish to possess such amiable qualifications.

VI. This is a proper direction, as growth in grace is necessary to carry us safely and honourably through the duties, and, especially, the trials to which we may be called in our Christian course.

Some of the duties to which God calls us are hard to flesh and blood: Such as mortification and self-denial. An improved state of grace is necessary in order to our discharging them in such a manner as is honourable to God and to our Christian profession.

But, besides duties, there are various trials and sufferings to which God in his providence may call us. A considerable growth and improvement in grace is very necessary to enable a Christian to go through them in a becoming manner—to submit to the divine disposal with patience—to justify God under the evils and calamities he brings upon us—to trust God in times of great darkness and trouble, and wait on him for help and relief in his own time and way.

It needs some proficiency in the school of Christ to say as Job in affliction, "Though he slay me, yet will I trust in him." To cleave the closer to God—to hate sin more—to love God better—to walk more stedfastly and humbly with him—to comfort ourselves in him, and rejoice in him when outward comforts fail. To chuse suffering rather than sin—to endure torture rather than accept deliverance on sinful terms argues improved grace.

When preferment is offered, and death threatened, the unsound professor greedily catches at the bait. Improved grace only resists the temptation.

There is need of improved grace to get the benefit of afflictions and trials. There is such a thing as a Christian's getting real good by sore afflictions and heavy trials—a greater good than deliverance from them.
The

The Psalmist could say, "It is good for me that I have been afflicted." If the Christian sees more of the vanity of the creature—of his own imperfections, and need of pardoning grace and divine aid—if he longs for freedom from sin, nearness to, and full enjoyment of God, or, if he finds any lust or corruption mortified—overcomes any temptation—has his sincerity and interest in God's covenant cleared up, or the light of God's countenance lifted upon him; any of these is sufficient to make amends for the affliction. Improved grace is necessary to reap the blessed fruits of trials and afflictions.

VII. Lastly, every Christian should labour to grow in grace, that he may ripen for glory.

We are travelling towards the eternal world.— We hope for blessedness in that world. Surely then we should desire to be "Made meet to be partakers of the inheritance of the saints in light—to be conformed to the image of Christ—to grow up in all things into him who is the head and Saviour of his church," and should labour for it. Death is a great change. But not so great to an improved Christian as to others.— For he is in a good measure attempered to the heavenly world. The same disposition is wrought in his soul, which reigns in the breasts of the inhabitants above: viz. Love to God and to his fellow creatures. His hope and his treasure are there. And he has had some foretastes of the joys of that world. Therefore he can cheerfully obey the summons of death, while those who are not in an advanced state of grace die with fears and reluctance. The more grown in grace a Christian is, ordinarily, the stronger are his hopes, the less his fears, and the less his surprize when he arrives at the world of glory. All these are strong reasons why we should labour to grow in grace. I proceed

III. To show that growth in grace is essential to the Christian character: Or that true Christians do grow in grace.

To prevent mistakes, let it be remembered, that it is not asserted nor meant that this growth is in every instance immediately sensible or perceivable by the Christian himself, or by others. Agur was advanced in holiness when he said, "Surely I am more bruitish than any man, and have not the understanding of a man; I neither learned wisdom nor have the knowledge of the holy." Paul stiles himself "less than the least of all saints." Good men see so much corruption in themselves that they doubt, sometimes of the being of grace in themselves: At such seasons they cannot discern its growth.

Let it be further noted that it is not meant that grace in a good man grows every day—that it has no checks, intervals, or even decays. The contrary is evident. Grass and fruits may receive checks by unseasonable weather. Corn may wither, and yet be revived by friendly rain, grow and come to perfection. David seems for some time to be in a declining frame of spirit, after his sin in the case of Uriah. Until Nathan the Prophet came to him with an awakening parable. After that he was recovered and grew in grace.

Grass and fruits may grow, yet the growth not be immediately perceptible. In process of time by comparing them with what they were, we see that they have grown. So it is with grace.

Where grace is implanted in the soul by the regenerating influences of the divine spirit, it will grow and increase. "The water that Christ gives him, shall be in him a well of water springing up into everlasting life." "The meat which the son of man shall give unto you endureth unto everlasting life." He that believeth on me," saith Christ, "Out of his belly shall flow rivers of living water." What can more fully show that grace is a growing principle, and will increase in the regenerate soul? Such will have their fruit unto holiness, and in the end everlasting life." "He that hath begun a good work in Christians will carry it on

to

to the day of Chrift." In confequence of this, the good man fears God and efcheweth evil. His love to God and divine things, and his hatred of evil increafe and grow ftronger; and the ways of religion grow more familiar and delightfome. "He delights in the law of the Lord after the inner man. None of God's commands are grievous to him. With full intenfenefs of mind he ferves the law of God." And he does it with increafing pleafure. Thus, as Solomon obferves, "The path of the juft is as the fhining light, that fhineth more and more unto the perfect day." This is agreeable to Job's obfervation, "The righteous fhall hold on his way, and he that hath clean hands fhall be ftronger and ftronger." This is a divine promife: And it clearly holds out this truth, viz. that the true Chriftian, who has that faith which is genuine, fhall grow in grace, make progrefs in the divine life, and ripen for glory.

GRACE implanted in the heart is like a grain of muftard-feed; though it is fmall at firft; yet it grows to be a large plant refembling a tree. The feed of grace remains in a good man; nor is it an inactive feed, but a growing one, which, under proper cultivation, will bear much fruit. Accordingly Chrift tells his difciples, "I have chofen you, and ordained you that ye fhould bring forth fruit;" and he directs them to abide in him, that they may bear fruit.

THAT profeffor, therefore, who does not grow in grace, and bring forth the fruits of holinefs, has reafon to fear that he never had a principle of grace implanted in his foul. If there was a work of grace wro't in his foul, his foul is furely in an unhealthful and difordered frame, a frame in which he cannot enjoy the comforts of religion. And when a perfon is in this cafe, and yet not fenfible that any thing is wanting or amifs in him, he is in a very dangerous condition.— Lukewarm, Laodicean profeffors, who are ignorant of
their

their true state, and think it better than it is, are in danger of being rejected by Christ.

The true Christian's love to God increases. The divine character appears more amiable every time he contemplates it. Every time he views the divine law, it appears a more fit and excellent rule of conduct for the children of men. He delights more in it, and more earnestly longs for a conformity to it. He sees more of his own defects, and grows more humble. He is more sensible of his dependance on God for pardon of sin and for strength to resist temptation and to persevere in the ways of godliness. His heart is enlarged with gratitude to God for providing a Saviour, and opening a way through which to obtain remission of sin and grace and strength sufficient for our needs. He applies to God more frequently and more fervently for pardoning mercy, and quickening and strengthening grace. He is also careful to wait on God in all the ways of divine appointment, that he may receive spiritual nourishment and growth in grace. And though Christians may be ready to faint, when they see the difficulties they have to encounter, because they find they have no light in themselves; yet when they thus "Wait on the Lord, they shall renew their strength: They shall mount up with wings as eagles, they shall run and not be weary, they shall walk and not faint. They shall go from strength to strength, 'til they appear before God in Zion."

IMPROVEMENT.

I. It is worthy inquiry, whether the real cause why so many are in a sad uncertainty respecting their state is not their own carelessness and negligence? They do not duly press forward towards the mark for the prize of the high calling of God in Christ Jesus.— They do not give all diligence to make their calling and election sure.

Some look back on what they have experienced, perhaps a number of years ago. They imagine it was conversion;

conversion; but they are not certain, they perplex themselves with that. Our business is rather to go forward. If we grow in grace it is thence certain that we have grace. If we are negligent about growth in grace, we cannot expect the comforts of religion, the evidence of grace and the good hope founded upon it.

Some indeed expect assurances of an interest in Christ from the immediate witness of the spirit: But they are mistaken. "The spirit of God does indeed bear witness with our spirits that we are the children of God. This witness, however, is not an immediate, but a mediate one. "The spirit witnesseth with our spirits," therefore we must take pains with our spirits. The spirit works in the souls of Christians those graces which are the condition of the promises. And he irradiates the soul to see the work which he has wrought. Satan would persuade the soul that no such work is wrought. The divine spirit excites to self examination, and in that way assists them to discern the fruits of the spirit. Good men obtain a good hope through grace.

II. Hence let us be persuaded to examine ourselves, whether we grow in grace. Let us, however, beware of trying ourselves by false marks and of concluding in our own favour upon false promises.

Do not conclude that you grow in grace because you increase in knowledge. Knowledge is desirable, and our religion must be founded on it. But men may attain great degrees of knowledge and yet have no true grace.

Do not conclude that you grow in grace because you are zealous in religion. There is a bad zeal as well as one that is commendable. A selfish or party zeal may increase and arrive to as high a pitch as Jehu's when the zealot is destitute of grace.

Do not conclude that you grow in grace because you are greatly affected with things of a religious nature. You may be greatly affected with the death of
Christ.

Chrift. You may be as much affected, perhaps, with any other tragical ftory.

Do not conclude that you grow in grace becaufe you are more frequently in your clofets. Defire of reputation, or the force of confcience or felf love, or hypocrify may prompt to that.

Do not conclude your growth in grace from the good opinion others entertain of you. There are fome who have a name that they live, when they are dead: i. e. Are reputed to be Chriftians, when they really are hypocrites. Hymeneus and Philetus doubtlefs were renowned for piety, elfe their fall would not have fhaken the faith of fome of the faints. Again,

Conclude not that you grow in grace from this, that you love Chriftians better than you did. You may love fome better than you did becaufe, on acquaintance with them, you find them of a fweeter temper, or becaufe they agree with you in fentiment or practice, are of the fame party—or from fome other felfifh confiderations.

Would you know whether you grow in grace, try yourfelves by marks more certain than thefe.

Do you find that your love to God increafes—that it is really ftronger than it was in time paft? Are you more fenfible that you are always in his prefence? and is that fenfe more pleafant to you? When your fpirits are low, and you enjoy no fenfible divine communications, is it a confolation that God knows your ftate; and do you long for nearnefs to him. Do you open your mind freely to him? Do you find in yourfelves a ftedfaft defire to pleafe God, and to avoid whatever is difpleafing to him? Do you find that you efteem and prize God's laws more highly? Do you fee it's excellency more clearly, and long more ardently for a perfect conformity to it? Are you habitually reconciled both to his commanding and difpofing will, and find that your will is more readily difpofed, in every circumftance, to fubmit to whatever God would have

done,

done, borne or forborn? Can you in times of trouble cast all your cares on God, and possess your soul in patience? If so, these are good evidences of growth in grace. Further,

How is it with regard to your fellow men, do social affections strengthen, and unfriendly passions languish? Do you love your enemies, pray for, and seek the good of those who seek your hurt? Do you labour to overcome evil with good? This is truly a Christian temper.

Again, do you grow more humble, and find your mind more emptied of pride and haughty imaginations than it was? Humility is a silent, but most excellent grace. God resists the proud, but dwells with the humble.

Do you see more and more the uncertainty and vanity of all creature enjoyments, and set your affections on things above? Do you long and labour for a growing conformity to God, and a meetness to enjoy him, call on him for mercy more frequently and fervently, and have your hopes and expectations from him only.

If these things are in you, you grow in grace.

III. Labour to grow in grace. In this way you will honour God and religion, and promote your own comfort.

You may ask, in what way must I labour for growth in grace? I answer; by a diligent attendance on the means of grace—on all ordinances of divine appointment. You cannot expect to attain the end, if you neglect the means. Read and meditate on God's word day and night. Attend on a preached gospel—wait on God at his table—keep the sabbath holy—reverence God's sanctuary—keep your heart with all diligence, and take heed to your ways. Walk uprightly before God and man. Often look forward to the future and solemn scenes which await you, and often reflect and examine yourselves, and consider what preparation

ration you have made for them. Repent of your sins and miscarriages; and beg pardoning mercy of God: Beseech him to keep you from falling, to present you faultless before the throne of his glory, and to accept you in his beloved Son Jesus Christ our Lord and only Saviour. *AMEN.*

SERMON XXIII.

ON WHAT CONSTITUTES A CRIMINAL CONFORMITY TO THE WORLD.

ROMANS x. 2. "*And be ye not conformed to this world.*"

PEOPLE, who enjoy the sacred Scriptures, most generally acknowledge, that they are under obligation to regard the will of God which he has revealed to them; and to seek a treasure in heaven, and not upon earth. But unhappily the depravity of our heart has too strongly attached us to the things of sense. Many, in their conduct, appear to labor more for a portion in this world than for an inheritance in heaven. Surely it may be said, "A deceived heart hath turned them aside."

"No man," our Savior teaches us, "can serve two masters." "Ye cannot serve God and mammon." The apostle, therefore, when he beseeches Christians by the mercies of God, that they present their bodies a living sacrifice, holy, acceptable to God, which is their reasonable service," subjoins the command, "And be ye not conformed to this world." Another apostle supposes christians "to know, that the friendship of the world is enmity with God : whosoever therefore will be a friend of the world is the enemy of God."

Two things call for our attention.

I. When people are criminally conformed to this world: And

II. The importance of not being conformed to it.

Several things will be observed in answer to the question,

I. When are people criminally conformed to this world?

1. People are criminally conformed to this world, when they have more ardent desires to possess its enjoyments, than to promote the honor of God, and prepare to dwell with him in his kingdom.

God, to whom we owe allegiance, is the only self existent and infinite being. Every other existence depends on him. He is the author of all good. His love sent Christ to die for men. His infinite greatness and excellency, and what in his love to mankind he has done for our salvation, unite to lay us under obligation to him. His first commandment requires, that " we love the Lord our God with all our heart, and with all our soul and with all our mind." And in harmony with this he expressly forbids to " have any other gods before him."

There is no urgency of temptation that will justify a departing from his holy way. To be christians you must follow Christ," though to do it you " forsake father and mother, wife, children, brethren and sisters, and even your own life."

Mankind were created for the service and glory of God. The present life is their time of trial and preparation for his future kingdom. It is now that you are to lay the foundation to glorify and enjoy God, through eternity. To this your most ardent desires and all your exertions should be directed. " Whether therefore ye eat or drink, or whatsoever ye do, do all to the glory of God." " Seek ye first his kingdom and righteousness."

Now, what is the first object of our concern? What end is first in our view in all our labours? Are our warmest desires toward God, and the things of his kingdom? And do we seek these more than the riches or any of the gratifications of the present world? Are those of us who are poor in earthly substance, satisfied with our lot, esteeming ourselves happy in having precious advantages to obtain an inheritance in heaven, of unspeakable felicity and eternal duration? And do they, who are rich in this world, use their goods in obedience to Christ, to make to themselves friends of the mammon of unrighteousness: which, when they fail, will receive them into everlasting habitations?

Christ, in one of his parables, has set before us a striking example of conformity to the world. A rich man, whose ground brought forth plentifully, thought within himself what to do, to provide room for all his fruits and goods, and confident of accomplishing his plans, meditated on the completion of them to say to his soul, "Soul, thou hast much goods laid up for many years; take thine ease, eat, drink, and be merry." All his concern was for this life. You hear no acknowledgement of God, or providence; no thanksgiving for the abundance which he enjoyed; no confession of sin, or thought of mortality; no concern to honor the Lord with his substance, or to provide for the enjoyment of God in his eternal kingdom.

2. People are criminally conformed to this world, when most of their time and thoughts are with delight devoted to it.

To employ our time and thoughts, with pleasure, upon things which possess our affections, is natural. Our minds entertain them without being wearied. But objects, which are viewed with indifference, or cold aversion, are soon dismissed and forgotten. The pious believer, whose heart is filled with divine love, thinks often of God, contemplates his perfections and providence,

dence, with pleasure admires his grace, and rejoices in the hope of seeing him as he is in heaven.

WHILE employed in the concerns of the present life, God is often in his mind. His desires ascend to the realms of glory, and raise his thoughts in humble supplications and praise to the sovereign Lord of all worlds.

EVEN the pleasure which he takes in earthly enjoyments, while it calls forth his thankfgivings to his divine benefactor, reminds him of the more precious felicity of enjoying God. And,

is this what we experience? Men of the world look for other pleasures, and give other employment to their thoughts. In their earthly pursuits, they do not care to have God with them; are unmindful of his presence, and forgetful of their own eternal concerns. Their body employs more of their attention than their immortal souls, and the things of this world, more than those which relate to eternity. If the word of God, or any alarming providence excite a momentary attention, their heart not pleased, quickly dismisses serious thoughts, and invites into it more agreeable imaginations. In pretending to wait on God, even on his holy day, and in his house of prayer, he often is forgotten, and the thoughts which should be devoted to him are occupied upon the world.

3. PEOPLE are criminally conformed to this world, when they rejoice more in having a prospect of earthly enjoyments, than in an equally encouraging prospect of securing spiritual and everlasting blessings.

IN proportion as men set their heart on any supposed good, they are made glad by a favourable prospect of obtaining it. The world flatters them with the view of earthly things; the word of God invites by the hope of eternal life. Which of these gives us the greatest joy?

THE bible, which you may read daily in your houses, the gospel which you may hear preached every sabbath, and the holy ordinances which you see administered, afford precious advantages to know the things of God, and seek his salvation. The outpouring of the Spirit, in exciting an awakened attention to everlasting concerns, and making many willing to hear in the day of Christ's power, adds to the hopefulness of the prospect of securing eternal life. And,

How are these priviledges viewed? How is the Spirit of God treated? Does the hope of salvation by believing in Jesus Christ give you more real pleasure, than any prospect of worldly prosperity? "Is gladness put into your heart more than in the time that your corn and your wine increase?" It is a criminal conformity to the world that makes men rejoice in earthly good more than in the blessedness of the kingdom of God.

4. People are criminally conformed to this world when in seeking its enjoyments they are not conscientiously obedient to the will of God.

God gives to his people as much of the world as he sees to be for their good; and does not allow them to take any forbiden steps to acquire its riches or gratifications. All injustice, and neglect of the distinction of right from wrong, are offensive to him. He saith, "All things whatsoever ye would that men should do to you, do ye even so to them." And in all your indulgences he directs you to have an ultimate regard to his glory. These, and other like precepts, and principles of action, should regulate your intercourse with your fellow men, and all your indulgences of pleasure. That you be temperate in eating and drinking; that you "Abstain from fleshly lusts which war against the soul;" that you be honest in your conversation, free from deceit in buying and selling; that you do not overreach the ignorant, nor "Grind the faces of the poor;" that you be faithful to keep covenants, and to fulfil engagements with your fellow men. They, who disregard these duties in using or seeking the world, are criminally conformed to it.

5. People

5. People are criminally conformed to this world when they follow the fashion of it disregarding the directions of God's word.

Many things, which are countenanced or at least excused by the world, and some in which it glories, are condemned by the laws of Christianity. Instead of the ostentation and haughtiness of pride and revenge, it teaches humility, peaceableness and forgiveness of injuries. The divine Jesus himself is a pattern of meekness, lowliness of heart, patience under abuses, and benevolence even to enemies. His religion is in like-manner distinguished, by the love which actuates his true disciples, toward all men. But

The benevolence of the gospel does not teach compliance with men in things which are sinful, nor indifference toward any command of Christ, notwithstanding the world may judge it to be unessential. We are strictly forbidden to call any man father upon earth, by obeying his opinion in things of religion rather than the word of God. In our condescension to men all the strictness of Christianity is to be preserved.

That conformity to the world is evidently criminal, which excuses the neglect of any divine institution, carelessness in sanctifying any part of holy time, irregularity of conduct in regard to the seasons of family worship, and the rest of sleep in the night, or indifference as to the truth of gospel doctrines, because of the variety of opinions which is found among Christians.

Christ teaches to be charitable toward men of different sentiments, and not to exclude them from our fellowship for not thinking with us in things not essential to the life or practice of gospel religion : But it is the world that teaches men not to have an opinion of our own respecting the doctrines of Christ nor to be conscientious and careful in all things to believe the truth.

It is the world also that looks on the outward conduct ; while God views the heart as of the first importance in obedience and religion. Out of the heart the
mouth

mouth speaketh; and the good man from his good treasure bringeth forth good things.

6. PEOPLE are criminally conformed to this world when of choice they neglect any of the institutions of gospel religion, or attend them in a careless formality.

THE good man is not ashamed in having respect to all God's commands. And he delights to draw near to God. The language which his heart speaks, is, "O God, thou art my God; early will I seek thee."— How amiable are thy tabernacles! The world uses other language. It has no delight in God, in his holy day as devoted to spiritual rest, and religious worship, or in sacred ordinances as institutions for approaching the divine presence. It is conformity to the world to omit secret and family prayer, or not to be constant in daily attending them, to be satisfied with observing only a part of the ordinances of Christ, to be willing to have frequently an excuse to neglect public worship, or in a pretended waiting on God to give liberty to the heart to wander from him, and with the fool's eyes to be at the ends of the earth, or occupied by whatever vanities afford it amusement.

THE preparation of men to assemble for religious services ordinarily corresponds with their manner of paying homage to God. The pious man is solicitous by selfexamination and prayer, to stir up a penitent, humble, believing and devout frame of heart, to honour God and receive religious improvement in attending his worship. They, who are conformed to this world, have other concerns on their mind. Their outward dress, and ornaments, which are to be seen of men, employ their attention. To these their thoughts are principally devoted. "What, know ye not that to whom ye yield yourselves servants to obey; his servants ye are to whom ye obey?"

7. PEOPLE are conformed to this world, when they are unfriendly to the requirements of Christ, which direct them to give liberally of their substance to the necessary support

support of his worship, and the charitable relief of the poor.

CHRISTIANITY considers men as God's stewards of the goods of his providence, and while it allows to take to themselves for their own necessities and convenience, as their circumstances will allow; it directs them both to do justice to all men, and to make him a pious acknowledgement of his right, in bestowing a due proportion of his goods to the support of his religion, and the relief and maintenance of his poor. "The laborer," saith Christ in a charge given to his ministers, "Is worthy of his hire:" "Is worthy," as an Apostle expresses it, "Of his reward." And a representation which Christ gives of the future judgment notices only actions of charity as entitling men to an entrance into heaven, and the neglect of them as occasioning the sentence, depart ye cursed into everlasting fire: "For I was an hungred, and ye gave me no meat: I was thirsty and ye gave me no drink. I was a stranger, and ye took me not in: Naked and ye clothed me not: Sick, and in prison, and ye visited me not." It is to no purpose that any in reply ask, when saw we thee in any of these needy circumstances and neglected the duties of charity? He will answer, "Verily I say unto you, in as much as ye did it not to one of the least of these" my brethren, "ye did it not to me. And these shall go away into everlasting punishment."

IN doing acts of justice, in which are included a reasonable recompence to Christ's ministers for their services performed by his appointment, with the support of Christian ordinances in obedience to his word, men are to be governed by the universal laws of equity. In acts of charity they are to be guided by their own judgment exercised under the influence of the general principles of christianity. God leaves us thus to the decisions of our own minds, that we may manifest what we are. But he tells us that we always have the poor with us, and when we will may do them good;

and

and that if any man have this world's good and seeth his brother have need, and all men are his brethren, and shutteth up his bowels of compassion from him, the love of God cannot dwell in him.

The world often makes a parade of doing justice and giving alms. God approves of upright and benevolent views in the heart. " If there be first a willing mind," in regard to deeds of charity, " It is accepted, according to what a man hath," and the ability which God hath given him to be liberal of his substance.

But when men possess the ability, and are called of providence to do alms, it is not of Christ but in conformity to the world that they are reluctant to give left haply as they say in their heart they themselves may want in old age, or their children may want after they are dead. " Cast thy bread upon the waters," saith the wise man; " For thou shalt find it after many days." And saith Christ, " Take no thought for the morrow: For the morrow shall take thought for the things of itself." In seeking first the kingdom and the righteousness of God, they, who trust in him, have his promise of enough of all earthly good; and not to believe him, in a practical dependence on his truth, is to be conformed to the world.

What further claims our attention in regard to this subject, is,

II. The importance of not being conformed to this world.

God, who possesses all possible excellency, and who gave being to all creatures, is the rightful sovereign of the whole creation.

But notwithstanding his infinite goodness and almighty power, a rebellion has taken place against him. The devil began it in heaven, and being cast out of those abodes of holiness, he tempted the parents of our race to sin; and by his success in seducing them into apostacy he became, as an Apostle calls him, the God of this world. As the prince of the world he reigns in the hearts of the children of disobedience, and holds all the wicked in allegiance to him, as subjects of his kingdom.

To destroy his hateful dominion, the church of Christ is set up among men; requiring them to return to God, and serve him in faith and holiness. The gospel proclaims pardon and life to those who come out of the devil's kingdom, and believe in Jesus Christ as their Lord and Saviour. Their day of probation is given to them that they may choose to whom they will belong, and show themselves by their works. At the same time all the authority of God, all the love of Jesus, and all their hope of eternal life by Christ command and urge them to renounce the devil, forsake their conformity to the world, and give themselves wholly to God, to be saved by Jesus Christ.

To comply with this appointment and demand of heaven, in opposition to the powers of hell, is the end for which you enjoy your day of probation, and all the privileges of grace. Your everlasting salvation depends on your doing it. The day of judgment will gloriously exalt Christ, and complete his triumph over all his enemies. Then they, who shall have presented their body a living sacrifice to God, shall be rewarded with eternal life; they, who are conformed to this world, will be doomed to eternal death.

The doom will be just; for conformity to the world violates the first obligation that you are under to God your creator and preserver, and to Christ your redeemer. "The friendship of the world is enmity with God," rejects his Son, and righteously exposes to his everlasting wrath.

And what can this world give to those who are conformed to it, that should allure you to risk the loss of all future happiness? How momentary is the longest earthly life? How uncertain you are of tomorrow? Conformity to this world can no more prolong the present life than it can give the future. It cannot even secure a succession of pleasure while you are here.

Sinful gratifications are deceitful, and like poisoned liquors produce moral, and often bodily disease and pain. Thus the first sin of the parents of our race, by which they thought to become as Gods, depraved the whole human nature, as well as turned man out of paradise, entailed death on his children, and brought the world under a curse.

Who, that is sober, does not see that drunkenness and gluttony are a deceitful road to pleasure; that they debilitate the moral and rational powers, destroy health, waste property, turn man to a beast, and bring on him shame, want, and an untimely and awful death? Other sins are like enemies of happiness. They debase the moral faculties, disorder the passions, subject the reason to prejudices, make man an enemy to himself; occasioning either senseless stupidity, or painful remorse and fearful forebodings of future misery.

Would you see an example of what the world can do toward making man happy, read in the book of Esther, the history of Haman, and hear him in the height of his riches and earthly grandeur, unbosom himself to his wife and select friends," yet all this availeth me nothing, so long as I see Mordecai the Jew sitting at the kings gate." So small a circumstance, which would not produce any emotion in a mind under the government of religion, was sufficient to deprive him of the relish of all his greatness.

To this unhappiness does conformity to this world reduce man, who, in his original, was made in the image of God. Such are the destructive effects of sin in vitiating our capacity to enjoy the good things of divine bounty. And do you, to whom the invitation is given to accept restoration to the likeness of your creator, choose to remain in your apostacy, slaves to the lusts of your father the devil? Shall sin reign in your mortal body, and hold you in bondage to the world? Think

of

of what your redeemer has done and suffered to purchase you spiritual freedom. Do you bear his name, and feel no gratitude for his death, nor any effectual desire to be conformed to his life? And has the love of God, of which Christ is the messenger to our world, no power over your heart, to raise your affections to things divine and heavenly? To what end are you favoured with the word of God, and the ordinances of gospel worship? Why are life and immortality brought to light, and salvation offered you freely on terms of grace? And what is the benefit of your being told that in God you live and move and have your being? If knowing all these, and with heaven and hell before your eyes, you disbelieve the truth of deity and follow the allurements of the deceiver? In vain are you informed of the resurrection of the dead, and of the glory of the saints, in coming from their graves in the likeness of the glorified body of Christ, if still your minds continue enslaved to the world. Yet do ye call yourselves Christians, brethren of him who in eminence is the Son of God? Are ye begotten to a lively hope by his resurrection from the dead? My friends, " Whosoever is born of God overcometh the world." And they who are truly disciples of Christ and worthy to bear his name, " Are not of the world," as he, when on earth, was " Not of the world." Be persuaded that your ruling affections and your manner of living decide your character. " If any man love the world the love of the Father is not in him."

In the view of God's majesty, holiness, and authority requiring you to be like him; of his love to men, and the death of Christ for their redemption; of the shortness of your continuance in the present world, the unsatisfying nature of earthly enjoyment, and the importance of this season of trial and preparation for eternity; and of the solemn importance of death, the resurrection, the final judgment, and eternal life or eternal death, be persuaded instantly and renewedly to

present

present your bodies a living sacrifice, holy, acceptable to God which, certainly, " Is your reasonable service; and be ye not conformed to this world; but be ye transformed by the renewing of your mind, that ye may prove what is that good and acceptable and perfect will of God."

SERMON

SERMON XXIV.

RELIGION FREQUENTLY CORRUPTED BY HUMAN SPECULATIONS.

COLOSSIANS II. 8. *Beware left any man spoil you through Philosophy.*

COLOSSE was a confiderable city in Phrygia, not far from Laodicea and Hierapolis. It is now in ruins; and the memory of it preferved chiefly in this epiftle, which the Apoftle Paul wrote while he was a prifoner at Rome, having learned their circumftances from Epaphroditus.

Though Paul had not feen them; yet he had a very earneft concern for their good. Therefore he wrote this epiftle to them, to caution and warn them againft deceivers, and eftablifh them in the Chriftian faith. He cautions them againft thofe who would "beguile them with enticing words." Errorifts and falfe teachers generally appear with a flow of zeal and earneftnefs in religion; they make great pretences; and "By good words and fair fpeeches they deceive the hearts of the fimple," who are not aware of their defigns. Againft fuch we muft be on our guard. There are fome who fpeak fair, yet we are not to believe them, becaufe there are feven abominations in their hearts.

hearts. Would we avoid their snares, we must be rooted in Christ, built up in him, and established in the faith, as we have been taught in the oracles of divine revelation.

In the text the Apostle gives a general caution, and warns us whence the danger is most likely to arise. "Beware lest any man," let him make what pretences to religion or knowledge he will, "spoil you," make a prey of you, or rob you of your Christianity. And this will most probably be attempted through a pretence to philosophy and superior knowledge; which is really in this view, but "Vain deceit." These men are deceived through the pride and vanity of their own hearts. They fancy they know more than others, and are "Vainly puffed up in their fleshly mind." They neglect divine revelation, and lean on their own understanding. They speculate on matters of religion.— They pretend to be refiners in religion, and to strike out more rational plans of worship; but they deviate from the path of truth, and, instead of improving, corrupt religion.

In this way religion has been generally corrupted; and there is great danger of its being still corrupted, and men despoiled of it, by those of this turn of mind.

That we may see this more clearly, I would observe,

That religion is a conformity to the will of God, in heart and life, in faith and practice.

That the will of God, respecting matters of religion, is made known to men by revelation. How much of God and divine things man would have known by the meer use of his rational powers, had he continued in his primitive state, we cannot determine. A revelation from God to teach men some important points in religion, for ought we know, might have been then necessary. Be that as it may; a revelation is needed in our present lapsed state, to shew us whether God will pardon sinners, and restore them to his favour, and on what terms. Such a revelation God has gracioufly afforded to the children of men. We have it in the fcriptures of the Old and New Teftament. This revelation was made at fundry times, as the circumftances of the world required. It is now complete. It contains all that is neceffary for us to know, believe and practife, in order to pleafe God and obtain falvation. Infidels have put in various cavils, and endeavoured by all their art and fubtilty to fhake and undermine the foundation of the fcriptures as a divine revelation.— But all their cavils and pleas have been folidly anfwered and refuted. The evidence that the fcriptures are a divine revelation is clear and irrefragable. Our religion therefore muft be conformable to the fcriptures and grounded upon them. Whoever, therefore, would lead us off from thofe to feek religion elfe where, or wreft the fcriptures from their genuine meaning, to fupport doctrines or tenets of man's invention, and would lead us to embrace fuch doctrines or tenets, would rob and fpoil us of our richeft privileges.

The Apoftle Paul was a man of great learning as well as piety. He was well acquainted with human nature, and with the hiftory of mankind. He knew how religion had been corrupted in various parts of the world, by whom, and under what pretexts. He knew that human nature was the fame, and that the fame temptations would be likely to prevail in future time, as had prevailed in times paft.

Religion had been corrupted by human fpeculations. God revealed to Adam his purpofe of fending a Saviour into the world, and appointed a way of worfhip for man. The true religion was taught by the Patriarchs to their children. When men increafed they had ftated inftructors. Noah was a preacher of righteoufnefs. His fons taught the true religion and way of worfhip to their pofterity. In procefs of time religion was corrupted and idolatry fet up inftead of the worfhip of the true God.

. This

This was done by men who boasted of learning and abilities superior to others. They did not like to retain the true God, and true way of worship, in their knowledge. They professed to point out and teach a more rational way of worship and scheme of religion. But "They became vain in their imaginations," or reasonings, "And their foolish heart was darkened; professing themselves to be wise, they became fools, and changed the glory of the uncorruptible God into an image made like to corruptible man, and" (what seems more strange) "To birds, and four footed beasts, and creeping things: They changed the truth of God into a lye." i. e. into an idol, which was imagined to be what it is not.

The common people, in former ages, were very ignorant, they had no books, no advantages to obtain knowledge. The learned were puffed up with pride. They delighted in disputing and making a shew of their knowledge. They assumed the title of Sophoi, wise men. The Apostle reproves them for their arrogance. "Professing themselves to be wise." Sophoi, wise men; "They became fools." The vulgar however were led by them. In process of time that title seemed too arrogant. They therefore took to themselves the more modest title of philosophers, which signifies lovers of wisdom. But though the title was more modest, yet the persons who took it were not. They made great pretences to knowledge and wisdom. But they shewed their folly in this, that they should think there was divine perfection, in a piece of carved wood, in a beast, or a serpent. Yet they led people to worship these under a pretence of it's being an advancement in religious knowledge—a more rational worship—a refinement in religion.

There ever have been persons of this cast; who fancied themselves wiser and deeper sighted in matters of religion than others, speculated in them, and, under pretence of refining and amending, corrupted it.

PHILOSOPHY was first studied, and religion first corrupted in Chaldea. Egypt was next the seat of learning; and religion was corrupted there, much in the same manner as in Chaldea, by philosophical refining.

ATHENS was the seat of learning next; and though they were superstitiously religious in the Apostle's day, and worshiped a multiplicity of Gods, yet the true God was to them the unknown God. Their philosophers seem to be the teachers of religion, at least of the moral part of it. Mysteries of religion, as they called them, that is, particular forms of worship, performed to this or that particular God or Goddess, were known only to the priests, not taught publicly—taught only to those who were training up to officiate in them, or to some noble person desirous to learn them. Their principal instructors were the philosophers. These were divided into various sects. Paul was encountered by the epicureans and stoicks. It is needless, and would be tedious to give an account of the different sects of philosophers and their different tenets. Whoever is acquainted with the writings of those philosophers, who lived in or near the apostle's day, knows that their philosophy consisted principally of logick, metaphysicks, and ethicks. Seneca's morals are among their best performances. That philosopher was undoubtedly acquainted with Paul at Rome, and got some of the best things he wrote from Paul. But how confused is he in many points? Had he believed and studied divine revelation, he would have given us a much better performance.

WHENEVER men have set up their own reason as the standard, and rejected divine revelation, they have given us very defective and maimed, and, in most instances, very absurd systems of religion. We need not go back to heathen writers for the proof of this. The writers among the most learned modern deists confirm it.

BUT

But it is not by the speculations of these only that religion has been corrupted. Christianity was early corrupted by the Gnosticks; men who made great pretensions to superior knowledge; likewise by Cerinthus, Ebion, the Nicolaitans, and other hereticks.

No man of any considerable note who has broached a new scheme in religion, how heretical or fanatical soever, but has had a number of followers, and some admirers. These admirers generally go into the extremes of those whom they follow, where they differ most from the opinions commonly taught and embraced, and frequently push them further than the original author designed, under pretence of superior knowledge or zeal; and many times not only pervert the truth, but the design of the original author. Thus religion is corrupted by degrees, and the sectaries become more corrupt than the first founder of the sect.

Metaphysical reasonings have been sometimes very prejudicial to religion. When men have taken wrong data, i. e. things for granted and as a foundation, which were not true, their reasonings from them, however specious, were not solid, and consequently not justly conclusive: The specious appearance of reasoning, however, has led others into mistakes and errors.

Notwithstanding the Apostle's caution in the text, christianity has been greatly corrupted, almost in every age, by men who pretended much knowledge, zeal, and piety. Many of the ancient fathers of the christian church, by endeavouring to reconcile Christianity to the doctrines of Plato and Aristotle, greatly injured it.

Popes, and even councils have dishonoured Christianity, and perverted the Christian system, by their speculations. Under pretence of rendering religion a more rational service, and the worship of God more devotional to us, and more acceptable to him, they have

have introduced a worship nearly similar to that of the heathen of old.

WHEREIN consists the difference between the ancient image worship and that of modern date? Between that they paid to their departed heroes, and that which is paid to the saints of the papal calendar? Were not the designs and ends professedly the same, viz. that they might obtain their influence with the supreme God for the benefit of the worshippers?

Have not the errors of popery been introduced and continued much in the same manner as the errors in the Jewish church in our Saviour's day? The scribes and Pharisees, men, who professed the greatest knowledge and zeal, collected or compiled many things in religious worship and practice, which they called traditions of the elders, and made them of equal or superior authority to the written law of God: and popes and councils have done the same: And both the one and the other have made void the express law of God by their traditions.

A too fond attachment to the philosophy of Plato and Aristotle in some, and an over fond attachment to the speculations of popes and councils in others, greatly impeded the reformation.

MEN of literature are, many times, too fond of the philosophical notions which they imbibed in the course of their education. Men of reading have their favourite authors. If any errors are contained in these, they are greedily and imperceptibly embraced and riveted in the mind. An eloquent preacher or an elegant writer is apt to be admired, and while the beauty of his style, or the sweetness of his oratory, captivates, his errors are not seen. Oratory was a branch of learning which the Apostle might well couch under the more general term philosophy, and might properly caution us against being led by it into error.

MEN of distinguished parts and learning, many times, relying on their own understanding and not on God,

embrace

embrace great and dangerous errors. When this is the case, they generally do much injury to religion. Most of the heretics, who have made any confiderable figure in the world, have been men of this fort. They prided themfelves in their parts and learning—were not content with the doctrines of religion commonly taught and received—fpeculated on them, and, under a view of correcting and amending, corrupted them. They were defirous, like Diotrephes, of having the preeminence, broached their peculiar tenets in fuch a manner as they thought moft likely to take with others, perhaps at firft with caution, and when they had got admirers and followers, more openly, carried a great fhow of zeal for purity of religion and the good of men with them, and fupported their tenets by a fhow of argument and with great confidence. By thefe means many have been fpoiled of fome of the beft parts of religion, and led into grofs and dangerous errors. And if the life of the herefiarch was blamelefs, and he reputed a man of piety, the danger has been the greater, and the herefy become the more extenfive.

The ignorant and unlearned, in which number is included the bulk of mankind, in moft ages and countries, generally follow popular leaders, both in religion and politicks. If a leader is famed as a wife politician and a good man, he has great afcendency on both of thefe accounts. This was the cafe with Mahomet. He was a fubtil politician; and pretended to be taught of God, by the miniftry of the angel Gabriel. By the help of a monk, he compofed his Alcoran, in which he ufed his utmoft fagacity and art to form a fyftem of religion wherein Jews, Chriftians and heathen could unite: But he corrupted judaifm and chriftianity to do it. His reputation was fpread abroad, his followers increafed, he foon had an army, propagated his religion by fire and fword, and laid the foundation of a great empire.

The fubtilty and craft of Mahomet, and the ignorance

norance of the people in that day and that part of the world were great. He was indefatigable, and had some remarkable advantages to carry his points. The bishop of Rome became pope, or the man of sin, much about the same time that Mahomet set up. Though the mystery of iniquity had been longer working in the bishops of that see, yet the popes arrived at the height of their power more gradually. A succession of bishops, each puffed up with pride at their elevation to the see of Rome, then the seat of empire, took every measure their cunning could devise to aggrandise themselves and the see. They gradually prevailed over the clergy, and by their means over the populace, their exorbitant power and titles were afterwards acknowledged by kings and princes who wanted their assistance.

Mahomet pretended that both Jews and Christians had corrupted their religion, and that he was sent as an extraordinary prophet, by God to reform what was amiss, and teach and propagate the true religion. In these pretences he was not singular, though he was unusually bold and assuming. For though the popes have added many ceremonies to divine worship under a pretence of making it more devotional and acceptable; yet most hereticks of note have pretended that religion was corrupted, either in doctrine or practice, and that their tenets were conformable to the original standard, the scriptures, to the doctrines and precepts of Christ and his apostles. Whoever will read the history of them, will find that this has generally been the case. How extravagant and wild soever were the notions they embraced or doctrines they taught, they pretended they were contained in the scriptures. But they commonly wrest the scriptures to make them comport with their speculations. The scriptures must be taken literally, or allegorically just as suits their scheme or notions.

Such teachers, how corrupt soever the doctrines are which they embrace and teach, generally make a
shew

shew of great zeal to reform errors and propagate truth. They usually pretend that something is amiss either in the doctrines or practice commonly taught and received, in those places where they go to preach, which needs to be reformed; and some of them insinuate that they are specially called of God to promote such a reformation—that they have had their eyes opened by the divine spirit to see the truth—they give out hints that the churches in those parts or their teachers are corrupt—that it is a dead time in religion, and that even good men are asleep—that it is time to rouse up—that if they would attend to their preaching, and open their eyes, they would see the truth. Thus " By good words and fair speeches they deceive the hearts of the simple." They cause them to think they are really what they pretend to be; and though " They privily bring in damnable heresies," yet " Many follow their pernicious ways, by reason of whom the way of truth is evil spoken of, and, through covetousness, they, with feigned words, make merchandise of them."

Reformation in religion has been necessary at various times; it was so when popery had overspread great part of the Christian world. The churches had embraced doctrines which the scriptures did not teach, and gone into practices which the scriptures did not allow. Should any of the churches thus deviate from the plain and essential rules of the scripture, a reformation would be necessary.

But when we see a man zealous to promote a reformation in the church, and introduce a new doctrine or practice, we should consider whether a reformation in those points is necessary in reality, or only in pretence—whether religion would gain or loose by it—whether the pretended reformer may not have some sinister views and base designs; and, what the consequences would be. Could we have a fair view of the aims of many of these speculating reformers in religion, we should find that either pride and ambition, a desire of popularity

popularity and applause, or some other selfish motive was at the bottom. Men may zealously affect you and yet not well.

If therefore we see a man zealously engaged to promote innovations in the churches, either in doctrine, worship or conduct, whatever pretences he may make to superior knowledge or sanctity, we have reason to suspect and watch that man. Should he endeavour to introduce his reforming plans into those churches, and among people who are found in the faith, and under pretence of love to the souls of men, and desire to promote purity in religion, censure those ministers of churches, whom God has owned and blessed, because they differ from him in some sentiments or practices; beware of that man. He has not the spot of God's children. He has not yet learned of Christ to be meek and lowly of heart—to esteem others better than himself—to speak evil of no man—to put on charity. Especially if you find that he is shy of the ministers of the gospel—if he shuns wise and good men—if he tries to work on the minds of the lowest class and most ignorant people—if he enters into their houses, and "Leads captive silly women," he has the marks of a seducer, who, "By good words and fair speeches deceives the simple." Let him first cast the beam out of his own eye, before he attempts to pull the mote out of another's. Let him reform himself, before he attempts to reform others. For generally such reformers are the persons who have the greatest need of being reformed.

The caution in the text is needed by us as well as by the Colossians. Mankind are much the same in all ages and countries. Some are disposed to lead, and others are disposed to follow them; and in every age there have been false teachers and men have been misled by them. We are told by the apostle Peter (Ep. 2. Chap. ii. v. 1.) That this will be the case.— There is a spirit of error as well as of truth. We have

many

many cautions against listening to seducers and being led astray. "The spirit speaketh expressly, that in the latter times some shall depart from the faith, giving heed to seducing spirits, and doctrines of devils." Some false teachers are so corrupt, and so engaged to propagate their errors, that they make no hesitation at " Speaking lies in hypocrisy." What base and sordid views have such!

Others are of an enthusiastic turn of mind.—They speculate on matters of religion, and very frequently run into the marvellous or mystical. They may have parts and learning: But their disposition to search out the mystical meaning of scripture, and explain it to others, and their confidence in their own judgment, accompanied with great zeal, has had an unhappy influence on others. They have been led thereby to enthusiasm and fanaticism. This has been greatly injurious to religion. For while numbers have been led away by such persons, others on the contrary have been induced to think religion altogether mysterious, to think the bible unintelligible or inconsistent. Men of parts and learning, by the tenets and conduct of these visionaries, have been influenced to discard the bible, and seek for religion from the light of nature. For men are apt to be on extremes.

Such apologies have been given for the bible, and divine revelation and the truth and excellency of the Christian religion have been so clearly demonstrated by pious and learned men, that the strong holds of deism have been overthrown. Nevertheless men of learning and genius, speculating on religion, on philosophical or metaphysical principles, have laboured to support deistical principles by wresting the scriptures. The endless punishment of the wicked is not consistent with their notions of divine benevolence. On this account the deists rejected divine revelation, because this doctrine was plainly held forth therein: But these latter speculators pretend to have found a salvo for that, in the scriptures, which the Deity overlooked, viz. That all men will be saved by Christ. But "Great men are not always wise." They have frequently corrupted religion by their speculations, and not less by these than others.

Whosoever diligently searches the scriptures with an honest desire to know the truth, will find, that, by the obedience and sacrifice of Christ, a way is opened whereby God can pardon sinners and receive them into his favour on a plan in which all the perfections of Deity harmonize. The terms on which we may be pardoned and saved are plainly revealed. Those, who comply with those terms, will be saved. Those, who reject them and continue obstinate and impenitent in sin, will be punished: And it is not in the power of language to express the perpetuity of punishment in clearer or stronger terms than the scripture does.

"To the law and to the testimony, whosoever speaketh not according to this word, it is because there is no light in him." "Though any man, or an angel from heaven, preach any other doctrine, than that contained in the sacred oracles, let him be accursed." "If there come any unto you, and bring not this doctrine, receive him not into your house, neither bid him God speed: For he that biddeth him God speed is partaker of his evil deeds." "These things have I written unto you concerning them that seduce you;" that, by these solemn warnings and cautions, you might beware of them, and, according to the direction of Christ, "Take heed that no man deceive you." "They shall deceive many: And, if possible, shall deceive the very elect." Therefore, "Let no man deceive you with vain words," or specious pretences of love, zeal, or purity.

The contents of religion are the most solemn and weighty. God has made us rational creatures, moral agents, capable of loving, fearing and obeying him, capable of endless happiness or misery. He has, in the sacred

sacred oracles, set life and death before us, and assured us "That he will render to every one according to his works. To them who by patient continuance in well doing seek for glory, honour and immortality; eternal life: But unto them that are contentious, and do not obey the truth, but obey unrighteousness, indignation and wrath; tribulation and anguish upon every soul of man that doth evil." That such will be punished with everlasting destruction.

We are to use the faculties and advantages which God has given us in examining whether the bible has the genuine marks and tokens of a revelation from God, and is to be received as such; or, in other words, whether the Christian religion is the only true religion. When we have examined the arguments for that, and found them conclusive; we are to take the scriptures for our rule in all matters of religion. Our next care should be to understand what that religion is which they contain—what we are to believe, what we should do, and what we should forbear. In the next place we must comply with our duty, both in heart and life.

We are not to turn aside from the path of duty to the right hand or to the left.

You profess the religion of Jesus. "As ye have therefore received Christ Jesus the Lord, so walk ye in him; rooted and built up in him, and established in the faith, as ye have been taught; that ye be henceforth no more children tossed to and fro, and carried about with every wind of doctrine, by the sleight of men, and cunning craftiness whereby they lie in wait to deceive."

We should take heed that we indulge no bias or prejudice in our minds. If we have any favourite set of notions, or any particular doctrine or practice, which we are fond of and wish to be true, or wish to support by the scriptures; in such case we are in great danger of embracing error. For men will strongly argue themselves

themselves into a belief of what they wish to be true, and fancy they find support for it from the scriptures.

We ought to look to the Father of lights, by fervent prayer, in the name of Christ, for the teachings of his spirit with his word, to lead us into all truth and duty—to preserve us from the errors and snares to which we may be exposed, and guide our feet in the way of peace. We lack wisdom, let us ask it of God; he gives liberally and upbraideth not. God resisteth the proud, but gives grace to the lowly. The meek will he guide in judgment, and teach his way.

Let us therefore learn meekness of Christ, trust in the Lord, and not lean to our own understanding: Then will he guide us by his counsel, and keep us by his power, direct our hearts, and establish our ways, deliver us from every evil work, and preserve us unto his heavenly kingdom.

Now unto him that is able to keep you from falling, and to present you faultless before the presence of his glory with exceeding joy ; to the only wise God our Saviour, be glory and majesty, dominion and power, both now and ever. *AMEN.*

SERMON

SERMON XXV.

REASONS FOR FREQUENT MEDITATION ON DEATH AND JUDGMENT.

Psalm xxxix. 4. *Lord make me to know mine end, and the measure of my days, what it is; that I may know how frail I am.*

IT is conceived, that this psalm was written by David, when his mind was disquieted with a consideration of the prosperity of the wicked, and the adversity of the godly. Though, while the psalmist was musing upon the unequal dispensations of providence, the fire of passion burned within him; yet he prevented his passion breaking forth into reproachful reflections against God. "I said, I will take heed to my ways, that I sin not with my tongue. I will keep my mouth as with a bridle while the wicked is before me." Either in my presence, or in my mind. "I held my peace even from good, and my sorrow was stirred." When the psalmist opened his mouth, and spake with his tongue, he made the prayer of the text. "Lord make me to know mine end, and the measure of my days, what it is; that I may know how frail I am." While David contemplated his end, the shortness and uncertainty of his own life, and the life of other men, and that after death comes the judgment, when every man shall

shall receive according to his works. It served to calm his mind with respect to the dispensations of providence in the prosperity of sinners and the adversity of the righteous: He resolves to rise above the frowns and flatteries of this world, and to make God his hope, his only portion.

In attending to the text, I shall attempt to shew, the import of David's prayer—the importance and advantage of keeping the shortness of life, and the certainty of death and the judgment in sight.

I. We will shew the import of David's prayer in the text.

"Lord make me to know mine end." It is not to be conceived, that in this petition, David expresseth a desire, that he might be informed of the exact time, the year, and day when his life should end. It was not the usual method of divine procedure, thus to ascertain men of the time of their exit. God hath kept the day of death a secret from men, (no doubt) for this wise reason, that they might not defer a preparation for it, but be always ready. Agreeably we have this counsel from Christ, "Therefore be ye also ready: For in such an hour as ye think not, the son of man cometh." Mat. xxiv. 44.

This petition might express the desire of David, that he might be fully established in the belief of his dissolution; that he might keep death in sight; daily feel himself a dying man, constantly exposed to have the thread of life broken, and the grave opened to receive him.

"And the measure of my days, what it is."—We might here observe again, that the psalmist doth not ask to be informed of the exact measure of his life; how many years, months and days he should continue in this world: But that he might know the measure of his days to be very short: That he might constantly bear it upon his mind that life was uncertain and momentary. He desires to feel the truth of that declaration

tion of the apostle James. (James iv. 14.) "For what is your life? It is even a vapor that appeareth for a little while, and then vanisheth away." Agreeably to this feeling, the psalmist observes in the verse following the text, "Behold thou hast made my days as an hand breadth, and mine age is as nothing before thee, verily every man at his best state is altogether vanity."

"That I may know how frail I am." The last clause of the text is a clew to the proceeding, and furnisheth us with the reason, why the psalmist desired to know his end, and the measure of his days: He was desirous to keep death in sight, and the shortness and uncertainty of life, that he might be sensible what a frail dying man he was, and in this apprehension of the matter that he might be in constant readiness to meet death, and appear before his Judge. We pass

2dly. To shew the reasons for frequent meditation upon the shortness of life, upon death and the judgment that follows, and the advantage that may arise from it.

1. This may serve to cure men of envy and impatience.

It is probable that the psalmist felt something of the rottenness of envy in his bones when he penned the context; the fire burned while he beheld the wicked in prosperity, and the righteous plagued all the day long: But when he turned his attention to his end, when he beheld death in full prospect, the measure of his days short and the judgment following upon life being closed; he appears to lose this envious spirit, and embraceth a calm state of mind. And, why should not a view of the shortness of life operate in this way? Why should men be envious and impatient, when they are to tarry here but for a moment, when they are constantly in danger of death? What ground is there for envy and impatience, when the life of all men is upon the same precarious foundation as our own, and man at his best state is altogether vanity? The time of life is

too

too short and uncertain to render it worth our while to make a great ado, about our own worldly circumstances, or the situation of others. Were men to continue in this world for ever, it might alter the matter, and put a different face upon prosperity and adversity: But as this is not their continuing city, it is foolish and sinful to make a great noise and bustle about their circumstances in life, and by envy and impatience render our breast like the troubled sea, which cannot rest, but casteth up mire and dirt.

If men are under the rod of God by a connection being broken; by being divided in twain, or a limb taken off, why should they be impatient? Though the wound bleeds freely, and is very painful to endure: Yet it is to be endured but for a day. Death is near us even at the door, and the next blow which he gives may fall upon our guilty head, and his hand is already raised, armed with the deadly weapon. Is it not because we think of living long in this world, that the death of our friends is so excessively painful to us, that the sword is so keen that we not only sigh, cry, and groan, but are prone to murmur and complain when we feel it! Were we to follow our friends the next week or day, this, methinks, would help to silence us, and check our impatient spirit. No man can say how soon his life may be finished: And if he felt himself a dying man in a dying world, it must to a degree break the edge of his sorrow, remove his impatience, and calm his restless soul. Especially this view of life would have this tendency, when we considered death introducing us to judgment, when we must give account of ourselves to God, and receive according to our works. Envy and impatience under the afflicting hand of Providence are exercises of mind exceeding criminal, and offensive to heaven, and we may well dread to have them produced at the bar of God, for we could not justify this temper before our Judge, though the affliction had been ever so pungent under which we exercised it.

To

2. To contemplate life in its shortness and finished by death, may serve to teach men the evil nature and the destructive consequences of sin.

When death is contemplated, and we see men dying round us, and feel ourselves following, do not our thoughts repair to the procuring cause of this mortality? Do we not consider sin, as commissioning death against us, and breaking the ground to receive us! Do we not recollect that passage of holy scripture, Rom. vi. 11. "Wherefore as by one man sin entered into the world, and death by sin, and so death hath passed upon all men, for that all have sinned." Death is the wages of sin. The dissolution of the body was one thing intended in the death which was threatened to our first parents should they eat of the forbidden tree. When they were called before the bar of God this was one part of the sentence passed upon them. Gen. iii. 19. "For dust thou art, and unto dust shalt thou return." We cannot well avoid including temporal death in the sentence, for it is particularly mentioned, "Unto dust shalt thou return." From this sentence we are more easily taught the death of the body than the death of the soul, though spiritual and eternal death are included in it. When the death of the body is considered as the fruit of sin, the evil nature and destructive consequences of it are represented in a striking manner. What waste doth death make in our world! What multitudes hath it swept from the stage of action! Innumerable have gone to the grave, and death is daily gaining trophies in our world. Death spares neither age nor sex. It is not contented with withered limbs, and a conquest over those who are stooping for years. Death attacks the gay and sprightly; those, whose breasts are full of milk, and whose bones are moistened with marrow; it cuts down those who are in the prime of life and heighth of usefulness; it breaks the strongest connections, and tears those asunder who are one flesh, who feel more like one than twain.

C c c

twain. Nor doth the infant escape the avenging sword of death; frequently he is introduced to life, draws a few breaths, and breathing out his soul in dying groans, quits the stage of action before he can discern between good and evil.

YEA death triumphed over the Lord of glory.—The son of God was found in fashion as a man, and humbled himself, and became obedient unto death, even the death of the cross. Such was the evil of sin, that, to atone for it, Christ must make his soul an offering; as without shedding of blood there was no remission; Christ our passover was sacrificed for us; he bore our sins in his own body on the tree.

WHEN we thus take a view of this world, as a dying one, and consider sin as the procuring cause of this waste and devastation of the race of Adam, must it not represent sin as exceedingly sinful and destructive?

A CONSIDERATION of the shortness of life may serve to heighten our sense of the evil of sin. The antediluvians lived to a much greater age than generations of men at the present day. The men of the old world rose to such a heighth in wickedness, and the earth was so filled with violence that God determined to sweep off the inhabitants by a flood of waters. To prevent the increase of wickedness, the age of man is curtailed, and by degrees reduced to threescore years and ten. Such was the evil nature of sin, and so prone were men to practise it, that their age was made a hand breadth, an inch or two of time that they might not have opportunity to rise in sin, and become giants in iniquity, as did the antediluvian world.

WHILE death is making such devastation in our world, wasting one generation after another, taking our friends from our side, and rending them from our bosom, let us learn the evil nature of sin, and the destructive consequences of it; and may we be excited herefrom to cleanse ourselves from all filthiness of flesh and spirit, perfecting holiness in the fear of God.—

The

The death of the body is but a small part of the wages of sin. Sin is the death of the soul. The second death awaits the sinner, and unless we repent we shall all likewise perish. By timely repentance and faith in the redeemer let us seek an escape from eternal ruin. Being united to Christ by faith, though we must undergo a dissolution of the body, yet we shall escape the second death, and the body will be raised at the great day fashioned like to Christ's glorious body, and we shall be forever happy with the Lord.

3. A FREQUENT meditation on the shortness of life, of death and judgment, may serve to check men in their immoderate desires after the world and their excessive pursuit of it.

THE world hath charms, which, it is not a little difficult for a corrupt heart to resist. 1 Tim. vi. 10. "The love of money is the root of all evil; which, while some have coveted after, they have erred from the faith and pierced themselves through with many sorrows."

2 TIM. iv. 10. "For Demas hath forsaken me, having loved this present world; and is departed unto Thessalonica."

THE devil, knowing the charms of the world, improved it in his endeavours to tempt our Saviour into sin. Mat. iv. 8, 9. "Again, the devil taketh him up into an exceeding high mountain, and sheweth him all the kingdoms of the world and the glory of them: And saith unto him, all these things will I give thee, if thou wilt fall down and worship me." Charming and bewitching as the world may be to a corrupt heart; yet to keep death and the measure of our days in sight, may serve to check our immoderate desires, and eager pursuit of it. It had this effect upon David. Agreeably he observes in the 6th and 7th verses of our context, "Surely every man walketh in a vain shew: Surely they are disquieted in vain: He heapeth up riches, and knoweth not who shall gather them: And,

now,

now, Lord, what wait I for? My hope is in thee." Why should men pursue the world with excessive warmth, when they cannot enjoy it but for a short season, perhaps, not for a day? yea, when their soul may be required of them this night, and they be called to judgment? Of what avail was the wealth of the rich man in the parable who lifted up his eyes in hell torments, and not a drop of water was afforded him, to cool his parched tongue? One reason why men pursue the world to excess must be this: They keep death and judgment out of sight, and promise themselves long life and prosperity in the world.

May not the man, who adores mammon as his God, be addressed, to feel the importance of keeping death, and the judgment in sight; Thou fool, who art chasing after the world till thou art out of breath; bring the judgment before thee, and place death at thy side: Take him with thee into thy fields, vineyards and garners: Let him attend thee in all thy worldly pursuits; let him look thee full in the face, when thy fever for the world runs high and thy pulse is full; and will not this check thee in thy career? Contemplate the rich man who lost his soul for the world, and lifted up his eyes in torment, and will not this moderate thy fever for earthly things? Thou mayest soon be taken away: Then where are those things which thou hast provided? What comfort will they administer, when thou art secluded from heaven, and ingulphed in woe?

4. To keep the shortness of life in sight, death and the judgment in view, will serve to moderate the desires of men after the pleasures of the world.

The fool in the parable, Luke xii. 19. "Saith to his soul, soul, thou hast much goods laid up for many years; take thine ease, eat, drink, and be merry." From whence doth this inconsiderate declaration take rise, but from keeping death and judgment out of sight and presuming upon long life? "Soul, thou hast much goods laid up for many years," therefore for ma-

ny

ny years, " Eat, drink and be merry." Had this fool heard that declaration from God, Luke xii. 20.— " Thou fool, this night thy foul shall be required of thee," it would have marred his worldly joys, and poisoned every sensual cup.

May not the man of pleasure be addressed, to place death in the midst of his sensual enjoyments? Let the man, who looks upon the wine when it is red, place death before him: when he sets at the jovial table with his merry companions, passing the flowing bowl, and frequently replenishing it; while he deals out his cards to his friends in excess and riot, let him place the judgment before his face; let death haunt him as he retires late at night, heated with wine, and wearied with the game; let death attend him to his bed-chamber and there address him, *I shall soon be with you;* take this method, thou son of pleasure, and will it not marr your joys, excite you to forsake your cups, and burn your cards?

Let the wanton, impure person, who improves the black and dark night, to sleep in the lap of his Delilah, and gratify his lust with his lascivious mistress, contemplate death and judgment, and will it not add wings to his feet and cause him to fly the chamber of uncleanness and for his life escape her presence, whose way leads to death and whose steps take hold on hell?

Let the fool, to whom it is sport to do mischief, bring death and judgment to view, while he ranges the streets, orchards and melon-yards of his neighbour in the execution of his mischief and sport, and will not this check him in his mad career, and make him cease from his mischief and folly? Eccle. xi. 9. " Rejoice, O young man, in thy youth, and let thy heart cheer thee in the days of thy youth, and walk in the way of thine heart, and in the sight of thine eyes; but know thou, that for all these things God will bring thee into judgment."

5. Frequent

5. Frequent meditation on death and judgment, tends to put men upon a preparation to meet death, and appear before their Judge.

Death must be contemplated would we be prepared to meet it: The judgment must be attended to, would we be found of our Judge in peace. It is difficult to contemplate death and the judgment to come without fear, and trembling, and being put upon enquiry what shall we do to be saved? "When Paul reasoned of righteousness, temperance and judgment to come, Felix trembled." A contemplation of these important, interesting realities, may well make every man tremble, who feels unprepared to appear before his Judge. It is from a principle of fear that men are excited to escape the wrath which is to come. Paul persuaded men from this principle. 2 Cor. v. 11.— "Knowing therefore the terror of the Lord, we persuade men."

Though a contemplation of death and eternal judgment, may give us present pain, and marr our worldly joys, yet it is medicinal—it is necessary; it is infinitely better to endure this salting, than to be salted with eternal fire. As all are interested in death and the judgment of the great day, let all be entreated to think of these things, and so think as to be prepared for them. Death and the judgment will come whether we think of them or not; they will not tarry. Fly to the Saviour, and make the Judge your friend; then all things are yours: death is yours; then you may sing the song of triumph, 1 Cor. xv. 55, 57. "O death where is thy sting? O grave where is thy victory?" Thanks be to God who giveth us the victory, through our Lord Jesus Christ." Then being called before the bar of Christ, the Judge will pronounce, Mat. xxv. 21. "Well done thou good and faithful servant; thou hast been faithful, over a few things, I will make thee ruler over many things; enter thou into the joy of thy Lord." Deut. xxxii. 29. "O that they were wise,

that

that they underflood this, that they would confider their latter end"—to which prayer let all the people fay, amen.

SERMON XXVI.

THE FINAL AND TOTAL DISAPPOINTMENT OF THE WICKED.

PROVERBS XI. 7. *When a wicked man dieth, his expectation shall perish.*

OBSERVE 1st. THE subject of this affirmation. "A wicked man." It applies to all of this description.

Observe 2dly. THE object of this affirmation. "His expectation." It includes every expectation which he had formed relative to the enjoyment of good. This is as indefinite and unlimited as the other.

Observe 3dly. THE issue of his expectation. Shall *perish*." Shall utterly fail of accomplishment. What he looked for will be removed very far and forever from him.

Observe 4thly. THE certainty of this event. "*Shall* perish." It is not barely possible, nor merely probable but it is absolutely certain. It is vain to flatter the heart with a different issue.

Observe 5thly. THE time in which this disappointment will be most strikingly manifested and most fully and lamentably experienced. "When a wicked man *dieth*, his expectation shall perish." Agreeably to this view of the text we may

I. CONSIDER

I. Consider the character which is drawn.

II. The objects of expectation.

III. The disappointment of it as it ordinarily happens in this life.

IV. The time mentioned in which it will be total and final.

I. The character which is drawn—" When a wicked man dieth." This includes those who are wilfully ignorant of the truth, stupidly insensible of moral obligation, grosly vicious, openly regardless of their own spiritual interest, and indifferent to the consequences of their conduct. Not only those who appear deeply corrupt, but formalists; who, ignorant of the power, content themselves with the form of godliness; who give God bodily service but deny him the devotion and complacency of their heart. Those who have that friendship for the world which is enmity against God. Those, it includes, who do not embrace Jesus Christ as a suitable, a sufficient, an only and a divine Savior. Those who do not exercise evangelical repentance for violations of the law of God both in heart and life. It includes, in a large sense, all without distinction and exception who are unrenewed by the spirit of grace and are, of course, unregenerate: not allowing that pious descent, water baptism, christian education, profession, or a good visible deportment make any material and essential change. So much for the character drawn. I pass

II. To illustrate the objects of expectation. "His expectation."

1. Wicked men have groundless and absurd expectations from the world. They eagerly desire it: they highly estimate it: they hope for very much from it: they labor most assiduously for it: they greedily seize it: they tenaciously hold it: they wish long, even always, to enjoy it. No labors, difficulties or dangers usually check the ardor with which they pursue it. These often stimulate to more vigorous and unremitted exertions. They yield themselves wholly to the pursuit.

suit. They let the world command their time, engross their attention and reign uncontrolably in their hearts. They treat it as their portion, as the sovereign good. They worship it as a god. Some offer their hearty devotions at the shrine of wealth, some at that of honor, and others at that of sensual pleasures. As the apostle John comprizes all that is in the world under these three heads: "The lust of the flesh, the lust of the eyes, and the pride of life." 1 John ii. 16. Dazzled with that which is showy, judging according to present appearances, unused to investigate the nature of earthly things thoroughly, and unwilling to receive the truth, the wicked hastily conclude that the things of the world will furnish a good suited to their rational nature, sufficient for ample satisfaction, and abiding as their own existence. They deceive themselves with golden dreams of happiness. Seek continually for that which they do not find, which has not been found, and which never will be where they seek it. Disappointed in one instance and in one pursuit they renew the search, continue their work and hope against hope. Neither their own experience, nor that of others nor the testimony of heaven to the truth cures them of their error and folly. They drink in delusion as water.

2. Wicked men, when they attend superficially to the subject, expect to live here several years and enjoy frequent opportunities to prepare for the most solemn future events.

Some do live to be old. They conclude that they shall reach old age. It appears to them more probable that they shall than the contrary. Health they enjoy. It may be youth. At least they have not passed their manhood. With common prudence they expect to prolong life during pleasure. Should sickness excite their fears; yet the cause will soon be removed and their fears speedily allayed. To morrow, in all desirable respects, will be as this day, even much better. With the continuance of life they connect an equally long enjoyment

joyment of their religious advantages. Long shall they have the word of God with them: seasons both to hear and read the word. Sabbaths will be granted to them. Neither instruction nor reproof, warning nor persuasion will be withholden from them. They guard laboriously against what might awaken attention, produce solicitude, rectify their mistakes and effect a change of conduct and temper. They resemble their own situation to a beautiful piece of painting where light and shade are happily blended by the pencil of a masterly workman.

3. WICKED men conclude that future repentance will be easy, pleasing and certain.

WHEN sober and thoughtful they may say within themselves and to others, with one, who probably never did repent, when we have a convenient season we will call up the subject in thorough earnest. Tired at last of the hurries of business, the pursuits of ambition and the toils of pleasure; mortified with the empty dreams of fancy; weary of seeking rest in an unsettled and fluctuating state; and convinced of the infatuation of wasting life upon this world; they flatter themselves that they shall both acknowledge the importance and necessity of evangelical repentance, and readily repent. Their understanding will guide and govern their will. They shall discern what is best and approve what they thus discern; undo the past, resolve right for the future and choose the practice of piety. They suppose that all from without and all from within will combine to facilitate repentance. It will then be much more expeditiously effected than at any former and a very early period. They count upon small or no opposition to it from their own heart, enured to disobedience and folly, nor from the world nor the great adversary. They think not of the encreasing strength of corrupt habits. What is aimed at is to omit the present performance of acknowledged duty, blunt the force of consideration and strengthen presumption. In

their

their opinion, to which they pertinaciously adhere, they are wiser than seven upright persons who can render a reason. They mean to judge for themselves when it is most expedient to repent; and, though blinded and warped by prejudice, they feel confident of judging right.

4. The wicked flatter themselves that the view which they entertain of their practice in general will not be soon nor easily changed.

Though they may have devised many mischievous devices, left the paths of uprightness, walked in the ways of darkness, and rejoiced to do evil, they strangely smooth the rough brow of wickedness and palliate in various ways the worst actions. To that mass of conduct which has not a good report of the truth they endeavor to reconcile themselves. None, they say, are perfect: in all things the best fail: faults and vices are common among mankind; many are equally blameable; blame divided becomes a cypher; temptations are frequent, sometimes strong; it is difficult to resist them: their nature is morally disordered; their bent to do evil or neglect duty is not at once restrained; they have performed many useful services; the useful will ballance the useless; the outwardly good excuse the bad; a large number of improper actions they have willingly forgotten; besides a merciful God will not severely treat his erring and offending creatures. Thus they persuade themselves that the criminal part of their conduct is not very odious and faulty; and that they shall afterwards think as favorably of it, in the main, as they now do; at least that conscience will not deeply wound their repose and mar their enjoyments.

5. The wicked form an opinion of their hearts which they propose and hope long to retain: they do not, at present, contemplate the probability of a distant very material change.

They seldom, if ever, admit the scripture description of the unrenewed heart. " That the carnal mind is is enmity against God"—that, habituated to evil, it "is deceitful above all things, and desperately wicked:" that there is a deep fountain of iniquity within; that corrupt hearts may be aptly compared to bodies of putrefaction; to a vault which contains dead men's bones; to will that which is displeasing to God and oppose that which is always pleasing to him is usual for sinners:. The springs of their conduct, and the ends which they pursue, and the objects which they prefer, and the continual exercises of their hearts pass commonly with few and feeble censures: at least, they are inefficacious. They do not conceive that God hates and threatens their prevailing temper; that it is impossible for God to commend it; that they contract heavy guilt by the indulgence of it; that the *motives* of what they have done, which was proper, will plead more strongly for their condemnation, than the *matter* of their actions will for their salvation; that an essential change of temper must constitute their preparation for happiness. Many, not viewing the moral disorder as deep and alarming, consider the cure as easy and the change more in form than substance, in degree than in kind.

6. THE wicked imagine that their present notion about death and the consequences of it will vary little hereafter.

THEY think little about it; habitually treat it as a trifle; they make no provision for its arrival. It seems like a dream to them. Though persons die in every part of the world every year, they hear of it or read the account, loose their acquaintance and friends, attend other's funerals, and sometimes they are diseased and pained themselves, still they have very little to do with this subject: they do not think in earnest about their own death. Whether they shall die is scarcely settled in their minds; or whether it will be a very trying season; whether they shall endure much distress, or sustain any real inconvenience by it; whether it will be better or worse with them after for their indifferency is
undetermined.

undetermined. What they shall do in the end does not reform their lives, nor commonly alarm their fears nor share their attention.

7. The wicked expect that in some way they shall escape the wrath of God; which is threatened against sin.

Their opinions may be different; their notions undigested and unsettled. The effect of them is uniform; neglect to prepare for the great day. Some look for safety or impunity because the time of sinning has been short; conjecturing that present sufferings may be adequate to the full demerit of sin: others suppose that they have rendered too many services to mankind to experience lasting disadvantages beyond the grave: others have been the subjects of convictions, fears, sorrows and reformations; hence they flatter themselves with hopes of safety: many encourage themselves in carelessness or formality from the supposed character of God; all mercy: some fancy that he does not hate sin so much as has been asserted; or that his threatnings may be dispensed with; or that, perhaps, he never was in earnest; his threatnings are used merely as warnings; temporary expedients to answer the purposes of his general government; this notion they may the more readily imbibe as sinners will never desire and urge God to execute them upon themselves. They impose upon their hearts a belief that those anticipations of recompence which at times assail and distress them may be the offspring of a wrong education. They are willing that the Judge of all flesh should possess the weakness and caprice and unmeaning pity of fond parents or of rulers destitute of suitable qualifications for their dignified places. They suppose that God will be as partial as they can wish him to be: that at last he will be quick to hear them when they cry to him: though they have been slow to hear his voice and turn at his command. These may be the objects of the expectation of the wicked.

III. I pass

III. I pass to the disappointment of it; "Shall perish." We will here consider the ordinary fate of it in this life. To do it a particular review of the several articles already mentioned will be requisite.

1. THEIR expectation from the world will perish.

PROVIDENCE reads useful lectures to them on the nature of the world. Their own experience is adapted to prove that vanity and vexation of spirit constitute much of worldly men's portion: that man hath very little of all his labor and of the vexation of heart, wherein he hath labored under the sun. Ecclef. ii. 22. As to solid enjoyment it may be asserted, that all his days are sorrows, and his travail grief: yea, his heart taketh not rest in the night. This is also vanity. Ecclef. ii. 23. When all things are weighed in an even ballance, they have, as we say, their labor for their pains. They weary themselves for a thing of nought. For the happiness of the present time consisteth not in worldly abundance. It has ever been proved that he, who loveth silver, shall not be satisfied with silver; nor he that loveth abundance with increase. When goods increase, they are increased that eat, or need, them: the abundance of the rich will not suffer them to sleep. Their continuance is uncertain. Security cannot be obtained. They perish by evil travail. They take to themselves wings and fly away. The offers of the world are vain, the smiles are deceitful, the frowns are sometimes severe, its troubles are sinking and irremovable. Its riches are uncertain, its honors precarious, its pomp and glory fading, its pleasures fleeting and delusive. Those, whose hearts have been lifted up with these things, trusted in them and rioted upon them, have found that the owners were discontented and unsatisfied. That these have not profited them in the day of evil. "Men of low degree are vanity, and men of high degree are a lie: to be laid in the balance, they are altogether lighter than vanity. Pf. lxii. 9. "God accepteth not the persons of princes, nor regardeth the rich more than the

the poor." Job xxxiv. 19. Such persons "walk in a vain shew: they are disquieted in vain." Ps. xxxix. 6.

2. The expectation of long life and the enjoyment of future more eligible seasons for repentance will likely perish.

The mass of mankind die at an early period. Our life is represented as vanity. Our age is declared to be nothing. Our days are called an hand breadth. In innumerable ways is life exposed to be cut off. The instances in which this expectation has perished can't be told for multitude.

The enjoyment of future and more eligible seasons is also uncertain and improbable. Should life be prolonged the best seasons for repentance may slip away and not be repeated. Childhood and youth are short and return not. Persons may remove their place of abode to their disadvantage; they may loose their health or their understanding; they may contract an habit of presumption and neglect of appointed means. Opportunities for a regular attendance upon them may be interrupted or irrecoverably lost. God has not bound himself to continue despised blessings. Hence, grounded in part on this uncertainty, is the dispatch which we are required to make. "Whatever thy hand findeth to do, do it with all thy might." Ecclef. ix. "Remember thy Creator now in the days of thy youth." Ecclef. xii. "Seek ye the Lord while he may be found." Ecclef. lv. "Agree with thine adversary quickly." Matt. v. "A little while is the light with you." John xii. "But now commandeth all men every where to repent." Acts xvii. "That now it is high time to awake out of sleep." Rom. xiii. "Awake thou that sleepest, arise from the dead—redeem the time, because the time is short. Ecclef. v. These and similar passages serve as beacons to warn us of the danger of trusting to future seasons and to check a common and fascinating delusion. While sinners do not re-

pent

pent the decree may be sealed, the commandment may go forth and the day of grace close.

3. The expectation that future repentance will be easy, delightful and certain shall perish.

How groundless it is the following thoughts may show. Persons may die without the least premonition. They may be violently seized, followed with sharp pains or fainting sickness; wholly occupied with their bodily troubles, unable to attend to their secular concerns—much less to the weightier concerns of the soul; they may be deprived of the regular exercises of their reason; it may be altogether suspended. This has often been the case. Besides, use familiarizes both virtue and vice. When evil habits are once contracted the conquest is attended with much difficulty. Those, who have long been exercised to corrupt and cursed practices, will seldom quit them. Those, who have long disregarded instruction, slighted warning, disrelished rebuke, resisted restraint, grieved the Spirit and misimproved or neglected divine institutions, will probably pursue this course to the end. They will not, of themselves only, subdue corrupt tempers, refuse the evil, hate folly and choose the good. Their opposition to repentance will be proportioned to the time in which they have voluntarily lived in sin. Great then is the improbability of divine assistance being afforded. The condition of such is discouraging, difficult, alarming and almost remediless. At last sinners will find that the difficulties are mountainous: that the whole is the reverse of what they foolishly imagined.

4. The continuance of their favorable opinion of their own conduct is most likely a vain expectation.

Their misconstructions will cease. Their former palliations will appear but cobweb subterfuges. Their self justification will strike them as a futile attempt at self deception. What they once pretended to approve they will at last condemn. Those actions, which they seemed to suppose proceeded from a due respect for God and their fellow men, proceeded only from natural conscience, fear of wrath, hope of profit or the workings of animal nature. Those, which glittered before their own bewildered imaginations, will be discerned to be an abomination with God. The approbation, which some sinners look for, will be turned into detestation. Could they feel as easy with their conduct as they once did they would gladly purchase the ease at a dear rate. But the truth will undeceive them.

5. The partial and false opinion which the wicked form of their own hearts will sooner or later perish.

They are deceived. They deceive themselves. They labor to do it. They do it in defiance of the representation which the bible makes of the human heart. They hold fast deceits. But finally, except they die as with a lie in their right hand, the truth will be perceived by them; though it may be reluctantly avowed by them; though it may be hated by them. They will be convinced that their heart is very impure—full of odious tempers, contains the seeds of all evil—that they have been ensnared, enslaved and ruled by it. That they themselves are viler than the beasts that perish; deserving of loathing and rejection forever. The hope derived from the small depravity or fancied goodness of their hearts will utterly fail them when conscience faithfully discharges its duty.

6. The expectation of the wicked respecting death will perish.

They removed far from themselves this evil day; as they view it. They flattered their hearts that, perhaps, it would not come; or not till they were willing for it; or that it would not be so forbidding as they had supposed. But it approaches. At the time appointed it delays not. Its aspect is grim. Its advances, if gradual, are steady and irresistible. They must become a prey to this mighty conqueror and destroyer of mankind. It appears to them a most formidable enemy. With inexpressible reluctance they yield to its
power.

power. But they muſt yield. "There is no man that hath power over the Spirit to retain the Spirit; neither hath he power in the day of death: and there is no diſcharge in that war: neither ſhall wickedneſs deliver thoſe that are given to it." Eccleſ. viii. 8. By dying they leave the body in which they have lived a conſiderable time, on which they may have doted, which they may have delicately fed, which they may have abuſed and idolized. They leave a ſtate of probation and preparation. They go into an untried, unknown, unchangeable ſtate; for which they are unprepared. A preparation for death may then appear very important and eſſential. More ſo than all other things under the ſun. A ſudden change will exiſt in their views. Former errors will fly like chaff before the whirlwind. The difference may ſeem almoſt incredible to themſelves. Doubtleſs they would fain think and feel as they did in proſperity and eaſe. But the dream will now vaniſh and the bubble burſt.

7. The expectation which the wicked feed of eſcaping the wrath of God will finally periſh.

Sinners are apt to miſconſtrue divine patience into a ſilent connivance at their folly. Becauſe his hand does not ſpeedily take hold on judgment they are ready to imagine that he is really or altogether like themſelves. But the time cometh in which God will reprove them and ſet their ſins in order before them. Pſ. l. They will yet know that he is not a God that hath pleaſure in wickedneſs: neither ſhall evil dwell with him; the fooliſh ſhall not ſtand in his ſight: he hateth all the workers of iniquity. Pſ. v. The word is gone out of his mouth in righteouſneſs; it ſhall not return empty: they ſhall eat of the fruit of their own ways, and be filled with their own devices. Prov. i. Deſtruction ſhall be to the workers of iniquity. Prov. x. The wicked are reſerved to the day of deſtruction. Job xxi. 30. The unprofitable ſervant ſhall be caſt into outer darkneſs. Matt. xxv. Tribulation and anguiſh, indignation

and

and wrath will be the lot of all that do evil and turn not from it. Rom. ii. Except ye repent ye shall all likewise perish. Luke xiii. He that believeth not shall be damned. Mark xvi. It will at last go ill with impenitent sinners: they shall lie down in sorrow. Isa. iii. and l. God is not unable nor unwilling nor undetermined whether to execute his threatnings on those who will not work righteousness and follow holiness. These in their execution, appear from the word of God, to be commensurate with their own existence. The same expressions being applied to the divine existence, to the happiness of saints and to the misery of the wicked. Human language does not furnish expressions of more awful import, larger extent and superior energy. Such a punishment equals the demerit of sin. The satisfaction demanded for the forgiveness of offenders; and the one which was accepted, was made by him who thought it no robbery to be equal with God; and who is expresly called the true God and eternal life. Philip. ix. 1 John v. There is an essential difference of temper between the righteous and the wicked; this difference may be more clearly seen at death and still more strongly marked in the day of judgment: this difference will be perpetual. Plainness is used and care is taken by the inspired writers to guard the readers of their writings from a dangerous error. These and similar observations will, finally, if conscience is well instructed and awake, strike conviction into the souls of sinners. The basis of their former opinions will appear radically defective. The falsehood, which has been their confidence, and the lyes which have been their refuge, will disappear before the light of revealed truth. The hail will sweep away the refuge of lyes and the waters of God's wrath will overflow the hiding places: their covenant with death will be disannulled, and their agreement with hell broken. Isa. xxviii. Their devices are unprofitable: they will prove a bed shorter than that a man can stretch himself upon it, and the covering much

too

too narrow to wrap himself in it. They have foolishly dreamed of peace while destruction was hastening. No provision is made for those who reject Christ. There being salvation in no other: neither is there any other name under heaven given among men whereby they can be saved. Acts v. Thus the objects of this expectation, with the expectation itself, shall perish.

IV. I PROCEED to notice the time in which it will most strikingly appear to be final and total, "When he *dieth*, his expectation shall perish." Sinners meet with adversity. In different parts of their life many unpleasant events fall out. But they reluctantly submit to them. They fortify their minds against them. They devise various ways to remove them. None to derive spiritual benefit from them. They labor to confront the truth, to quiet conscience, to silence fears and live at ease and pursue their favorite courses. Thus we read. "Though while he lived, he blessed his soul: and men will praise thee when thou doest well to thyself. He shall go to the generation of his fathers; they shall never see light. Like sheep they are laid in the grave; death shall feed on them; their beauty shall consume in the grave. Be not thou afraid when one is made rich, when the glory of his house is increased: For when he dieth, he shall carry nothing away; his glory shall not descend after him." Ps. xlix. "For the dead know not any thing, neither have they any more a reward here: for the memory of them is forgotten; neither have they any more a portion forever in any thing which is done under the sun. For there is no work, nor device, nor knowledge, nor wisdom, in the grave whither thou goest." Eccles. ix. Death closes the scenes, takes down the stage, removes the actors and finishes the whole drama of life. All go to the judgment seat of Christ to receive according to their doings. Nothing at death but religion can, on spiritual grounds, allay fear, inspire with hope, administer relief, and give the victory over death and the grave. All other objects of expectation

expectation will quit the distressed and distracted, the guilty and polluted soul. They will be utterly destroyed root and branch. They will appear empty as chaff, unsubstantial as the wind and delusive as a dream. It will appear that madness was in the heart. Man that is in honor, and understandeth not, is like the beasts that perish. Eccles. ix. Ps. xlix.

Let me now call upon sinners to *consider the nature of the disappointment, the time and circumstances of it.* Unless your ears are dull of hearing: unless you have shut them and become like the deaf adder. Consider before the evil which shall come, unless you repent, comes upon you: lay up sound wisdom and live. This disappointment involves *all your expectations.* If any object was untouched it would afford consolation. If only the smallest or small objects were affected you might support yourselves under it. But it sweeps away all on which you relied; from which you expected profit.

Consider that the *principal subject of suffering is your soul.* How keen its sensations! How bitter its reproaches! How vast the injury which it must sustain!

Consider that this disappointment will come on you *when you need more abundant support.* In the last extremity, to have every thing fail you: When dying, to be pained with blasted hopes, vain delusions, unsatisfactory enjoyments, fearful anticipations, despairing apprehensions and stinging reflections beggars language to describe. How trying, how terrible, how overwhelming the condition of such persons!

This disappointment *will be final and compleat*—Will you consider of it? Could you hope for a favorable change, that you should recover what you had lost and enjoy even that and much more and what is much better the present and such a temporary loss might be easily borne; yea cheerfully and gratefully: if that loss prepared for and insured richer enjoyments. But it is not so. As the tree falls, it lies; as death leaves you,

you, judgment finds you. It is appointed unto all men once to die, and then comes what? another state of probation? No, but the judgment. Heb. ix. When you will receive according to the things done in the body whether they be good, or whether they be evil. Ecclef. xii.

CONSIDER that this *difappointment will be aggravated by this thought that means were employed to prevent this evil.* You have not dwelt in darkness, nor sat in the region and shadow of death. You have lived in Immanuel's land: Light has shined around you. The oracles of God have been with you. What is needful has been plainly revealed to you. It has been the work of Chrift's minifters to fet the truth before you: to declare the whole counfel of God to you; to prefs the belief of the truth and enforce the difcharge of chriftian duties upon you. How then muft you load yourfelves with reproaches becaufe you would not improve the light; you would not walk in the light of divine truth? but you hated the truth and quarreled with your duty; you neglected holinefs and thus flighted your own happinefs. No relief will voluntary ignorance, will wilful difobedience afford you. You will be beaten with many ftripes. When you recolieft, at laft, how frequently, how affectionately, how folemnly, how faithfully you have been inftructed, perfuaded, warned and rebuked and you were not profited, the reflection muft bite like a ferpent and fting like an adder.

CONSIDER alfo *that this difappointment may be much unexpected to yourfelves; that this will heighten the evil.*

UNEXPECTED and fudden evils fall with double weight. You, finners, are dreaming of light and peace, of fafety and falvation. When lo! darknefs and trouble, death and deftruction come upon you. Let me then, from compaffion and love to your beft intereft, call upon you to leave the hurries of bufinefs, the dreams of fancy and the fcenes of diffipation, and go into your clofets, retire into yourfelves and look carefully into your

your moral state. Know what a change you must experience: realize what must be the end of your favorite course. Be persuaded to adopt such measures. Adopt them soon. Necessity lies upon you. Too soon you cannot attend to a reformation and to conversion. You will not, in future, enter upon this important work with prospects equally bright, and hopes equally strong as at the present time. Life is uncertain—health precarious—reason may be disturbed—means denied—the day of divine patience may come to an end—the Spirit's influences be withheld. Attend then speedily to this interesting subject. Be as prudent and assiduous and vigilant as you and others usually are in the management of your secular concerns. The reasons for such conduct are solemn as death, weighty as salvation, forcible as eternity. You must keep your own souls diligently. It is your duty to guard seasonably and effectually against this disappointment. You must look well to it that when this world leaves you and you leave this world a portion in heaven may be secured to you.

To give additional efficacy to these considerations reflect upon the difference both living and dying between the condition of the wicked and the righteous.

"The fear of the wicked," which he sometimes has, "shall come upon him; but the desire of the righteous shall be granted." The hope of the righteous shall be gladness, but the expectation of the wicked shall perish." "The wicked is driven away in his wickedness: but the righteous hath hope in his death." As the whirlwind passeth, so is the wicked no more; but the righteous is an everlasting foundation." Prov. x. and xiv. "The man that wandereth out of the way of understanding remaineth in the congregation of the dead." Prov. xxi. "But understanding is a well spring of life to him that hath it." Prov. xvi. "The way of the wicked is darkness; but the path of the just is as the shining light that shineth more and more unto the perfect day." Prov. iv. "Many sorrows shall be to
the

the wicked : but he that trusteth in the Lord mercy shall compass him about." Pf. xxxii. " Light is sown for the righteous, and gladness for the upright in heart." Pf. xcvii. " Though the wicked spring as the grass and the workers of iniquity do flourish : they shall be destroyed forever." Pf. xcii. " But the Lord is the refuge of his people : he is their place of defence and salvation." Pf. xci. " These shall go away into everlasting punishment, but the righteous into life eternal." Matt. xxv. Lay these things to heart, consider your ways and fly from the wrath to come.

SERMON XXVII.

THE HAPPY AND GLORIOUS STATE OF THE RIGHTEOUS.

Proverbs xi. 8. *But to him that soweth righteousness shall be a sure reward.*

BY sowing righteousness means working righteousness. The more common acceptation of the term righteousness in the old testament denotes sincerity in our treatment of God, integrity and justice in our intercourse with the world; the steady and cheerful discharge of duty in general. The works of such, performed in the strength and presented in the name of Christ, will be accepted. They will be rewarded not according to any intrinsic merit which they possess but agreeably to the promise of the covenant of grace.

The point for illustration may be exprest nearly in the words of the text. That to the righteous there is a sure reward.

I. Describe the character—" Him that soweth righteousness."

II. Notice the reward.

III. The time and place in which this reward shall be more fully conferred.

IV. Show the certainty of the bestowment— Then the improvement.

I. Describe

I. DESCRIBE the character. "Him that soweth righteousness."

SOWING righteousness is of the same large signification with many other scripture expressions; which describe true religion. As the following. "The kingdom of God is not meat and drink, but righteousness and peace, and joy in the Holy Ghost." Rom. xiv. 17. This kingdom of God denotes a spiritual one erected in the soul; consisting in holy dispositions and virtuous actions. "And that ye put on the new man, which after God is created in righteousness and true holiness." Ephes. iv. 24. Righteousness here may more immediately point to the duties which respect our neighbor; and holiness to those which respect God: or righteousness may import a divine or new nature implanted in the heart by the Spirit, fitting for and inclining to pious exercises: holiness may denote, an exclusion of all corrupt mixtures in our religion. "Awake to righteousness and sin not." 1 Cor. xv. 34. This includes an holy life, spiritual rectitude, inward and real conformity to the rule of right. "That we might serve him without fear, in holiness and righteousness all the days of our life." Luke i. 74, 5. That we might undismayed and continually obey God in all things; that we might be universally religious. Righteousness and holiness being often connected, may include a discharge of obligations to God and man. It is the same as sowing to the Spirit, who shall of the Spirit reap everlasting life.' Gal. vi. 8. as walking in the Spirit—living in the Spirit. That is guiding and governing ourselves according to the motions, influences and instructions of the Spirit: or according to the doctrines and requirements of the word of truth, which was written under the guidance of the Spirit of holiness. It is the same as to do justly, love mercy, and walk humbly with God. It falls within the limits of righteousness to render to all their dues. To God the services which belong to him: To men all that justice and respect and love which
they

they may claim from us: To ourselves that benevolence and beneficence which belong to rational and accountable and immortal creatures. To estimate and advance every interest proportionably to its intrinsic or relative worth. He, that chooses and pursues such a course, founded in reason, described and required in the oracles of God, making of it an established rule from which he would not willingly deviate, to keep a conscience void of offence both towards God and his neighbor and himself, sows in righteousness.

II. We will notice the reward annexed to sowing in righteousness.

1. Those who do it shall have inward peace. "A good man," we are taught, "shall be satisfied from within himself." Prov. xiv. 15. A consciousness of upright intentions and carrespondent pious actions is a deep source of satisfaction. It is a rich feast to the real possessor. He can fearlessly though modestly survey his fellow men. He is bold as a lion. Not that he is perfect; for in every thing he fails of what is demanded. Yet he aims and labors to fulfil the royal law of love and of equity; doing to others as he would in similar circumstances desire them to do to him. He looks inward without dismay and horror; sharing the testimony of a good conscience. He looks upward without servile fear, and mercenary hope. He humbly appeals to God how soberly and unblameably and honestly and godlily he behaves. He accustoms himself to impartial and profitable views of his heart and life. He calls himself to a strict account. Studies his heart: desires to know what manner of spirit he is of. He traces his conduct to a secret but true source, and rejoices when he finds that his works are wrought in God. "The work of righteousness," affirms the inspired prophet, "is peace, and the effect of righteousness, quietness and assurance forever." Isaiah xxxii. 17. The genuine friend of God possesses a peace to which all others are strangers. Which is independent of the applause and censure

sure of the children of disobedience. When evils threaten—when changes come—when revolutions happen in the world he stayeth his mind on God and enjoys sweet peace. He doubts not, while he trusts in the Lord, of a good issue. He knows who can, and who will make the wrath of man to praise him ; and who is able and is determined to restrain the remainder. Pf. lxxvi. And who has promised that all things shall work together for good unto them that love God and are called according to his gracious purpose. Rom. viii. His soul is brought into subjection to the will of God. Reason, enlightened by the word and sanctified by the Spirit of God, sways its sceptre over the appetites, affections and all the motions of the heart. A due proportion exists among the powers, order prevails, and harmony reigns.

2. He that soweth righteousness will probably obtain the favor of all, and will certainly share the esteem of the excellent of the earth.

A christian spirit and deportment will usually screen persons from abuses and secure to them many kind offices. Those, that do good, and appear to delight in goodness, will receive good from others. Those, who are diligent and sober, ingenuous and discreet, meek and humble, patient and forgiving, honest and liberal, will, for the most part, be respected, spoken well of, improved and assisted as there may be need. Persons must overpower moral principles, overlook the distinction between a man and a brute and glory in their shame before they can coolly insult or despise unaffected and noble virtue. The righteous is more excellent than his neighbor. Prov. xii. 26. Not only in the view of God, but of the generation of God's people. They, approving the things which are excellent, discerning what is fit, abounding in knowledge and judgment, delighting in the law of God, and exemplifying of it in their conduct, esteem, love and associate with those who sow or work righteousness. They esteem such highly,

speak

speak most respectfully of them, mark, with gratitude to heaven, their spiritual growth and rejoice exceedingly in their divine confolations, and anticipate with rapture an everlasting refidence with them in the kingdom of their Father and Savior.

3. He that foweth righteoufnefs enjoys the blessing of God continually.

There is a bleffing upon the perfon and upon the family—upon the profperity and adverfity—upon the defigns and labors—upon the meditations and charities—upon the civil and religious privileges of the upright—Upon the word of truth; both read and preached; upon the Lord's day—upon the inftitutions of religion—upon the means of fanctification. He is bleffed with righteoufnefs. Conformably to this view of his fituation we read. "The Lord blefleth the habitation of the juft." Prov. iii. 33. "Bleffings are upon the head of the juft." Prov. x. 6. "The memory of the juft is bleffed." Prov. x. 7. "He fhall receive the bleffing from the Lord, even righteoufnefs from the God of his falvation." Pf. xxiv. 5. "Bleffed is the man that delighteth in the law of the Lord; and in his law doth he meditate day and night. He fhall be like a tree planted by the rivers of water, that bringeth forth his fruit in his feafon: his leaf alfo fhall not wither; and whatfoever he doeth fhall profper." Pf. i. 1, 2, 3.

4. He that foweth righteoufnefs enjoys the fpecial prefence and covenant favor of God.

God fills heaven and earth with his effential prefence. In this view he never can, for a moment, be far from any of his rational creatures. But in his omniprefence and omnifcience multitudes do not felicitate themfelves. The thought that God beholds them every inftant, obferves all their actions, infpects their heart, perfectly underftands their moral character and retains forever his knowledge and will judge them according to the gofpel of Chrift excites their fear, produces difguft and breeds hatred. It mars their peace. It infufes a fting,

when

when realized, into every temporal enjoyment. But it is not so with the sincere friends of religion. The special presence of God is with them to guide them, protect them, to encourage them, to sanctify them, and comfort them. He makes his face to shine upon them: lifts up the light of his countenance upon them. He makes with them an everlasting covenant, even the sure mercies of David. Numb. vi. 25, 26. Isa. lv. 3. He comforts them with the forgiveness of their sins—They have the witness of the Spirit that they are the children of God; and hence heirs of God, and joint heirs with Christ. Rom. viii. 16, 17. He puts joy and gladness into their hearts and fills their mouth with praise. If in the light of the king's countenance is life; and his favor is as a cloud of the latter rain. Prov. xvi. 15. and as the dew upon the grass. Prov. xix. 12. If many entreat the favor of the prince. Rev. xix. 6. How much more is the special presence and favor of the infinite God to be carefully and constantly sought, to be highly valued and gratefully acknowledged; and how exceedingly must those be priviledged who enjoy them? His favor is life, and his loving kindness is better than life. Pf. lxiii. With him is the fountain of life. Pf. xxxvi. The upright shall always dwell in his presence. Pf. cxiii. 13. God will make such most blessed forevermore. Pf. xxi. Thus the righteous have a reward in possession as well as one in reversion: one in hand and one in prospect. Godliness has the promise of the life that now is and of that which is to come. 1 Tim. 4.

III. I pass to consider the time and place in which this reward will be more fully conferred.

The present is a militant state, the future a triumphant one: this is one of trial, that of recompence: this of discipline, that of reward. Both graces and enjoyments are now imperfect. Both under divine cultivation, saints being God's husbandry, are growing and ripening for heaven. Troubles await the just. If need be they are in heaviness through manifold temptations.

tions. 1 Peter i. 6. Snares spread their way; difficulties attend their progress in religion: enemies disturb and harrass them. Their own follies produce heavy complaints. Their intercourse with the things of the world indispose them too much and too often for a close walk with God. Their almost unavoidable connexion with those who know not God, who do not love our Lord Jesus Christ, nor set their affections on heavenly objects, deadens, at times, their keen relish for spiritual exercises, veils their evidences of grace and swells their sorrows. Owing to their indiscretion and negligence, their cowardice and coldness, their pride and discontent, their avarice and worldliness God sometimes hides his face from them, they walk in darkness, experience fear and maintain sharp conflicts with their enemies and meet with mortification and disgrace. The powers of darkness triumph in their advantages. This life is a wearisome pilgrimage. They loath it, they would not live here always. Job vii. 16. A portion only or in the things of this life would be insupportable to them. Saints cannot admit the thought of everlasting imperfection, dulness and darkness and coldness. Such barrenness and emptiness; such doubts and fears as they experience here if continued ever would make existence an indescribable burden to them. Though God never forsakes nor forgets them. For though the righteous falleth seven times he shall rise: God is able to hold him up; and he shall be kept by the mighty power of God through faith unto salvation. Prov. xxiv. 16. 1 Peter i. 5. In the way to their Father's kingdom above he allows his children to drink of the wine of consolation and to draw water out of the wells of salvation. He gives them an hope of seeing the glory of God: that hope which purifieth the soul, even as he is pure: good hope through grace which is an anchor to the soul. Rom. v. 2. 1 John iii. 4. Heb. vi. 19. Hope of grace: and Christ is in them the hope of glory. God will not let them be moved away

from

from the hope of the gofpel; and the Spirit will ftrengthen them to give diligence unto the full affurance of hope unto the end. Col. i. 23. 27. Heb. vi. 11. An hope both of prefent and future fpiritual good which animates them in duty, fupports them in temptation, brightens the night of affliction, leffens the pains of dying and removes the dread of being dead. They have a well grounded perfuafion that annihilation is not their portion. They are affured that God will not leave their bodies forever under the dominion of the grave. Death, the laft enemy, fhall be conquered. " They are begotten again unto a lively hope by the refurrection of Jefus Chrift from the dead." 1 Peter i. 3. " So alfo is the refurrection of the dead: it is fown in corruption, it is raifed in incorruption: It is fown in difhonor, it is raifed in glory: it is fown in weaknefs, it is raifed in power: It is fown a natural body, it is raifed a fpiritual body. This corruptible muft put on incorruption, this mortal muft put on immortality." 1 Cor. xv. 42. 3, 4. 53. " For our converfation is in heaven; from whence alfo we look for the Savior, the Lord Jefus Chrift; who fhall change our vile body, that it may be fafhioned like unto his glorious body, according to the working whereby he is able even to fubdue all things unto himfelf." Philip. iii. 20, 21. When they walk through the valley of the fhadow of death they believe that God will be with them; that the rod of his power, and the ftaff of his promife will comfort them. Pf. xxiii. They believe that God will redeem their fouls from the power of the grave; guide them by his counfel, and afterwards receive them to glory. Pf. xlix. 15. lxxiii. 24. After a few more revolutions of funs and moons they expect to go the way whence they fhall not return. To go into an invifible ftate. Being made meet for it, they hope to partake of the inheritance of the faints in light. God himfelf having wrought them to this felf fame thing, and given them the earneft of the Spirit in their hearts. Col. i. 12.

G g g

2 Cor.

2 Cor. v. 5. Having set their affections on things above, and their life being hid with Christ in God, they expect, that when Christ, who is the life of christians, shall appear, they shall appear with him in glory: that then they shall be like him, and see him as he is; behold his face in righteousness; and when they awake be satisfied with his likeness. Pf. xix. 1 John iii. Col. iii. Their understanding will be enlightened by beams darted directly into them from the sun of righteousness. Their affections will be forever warmed by divine love: burning with the vehement ardors of the purest devotion. Their holiness will be perfect. Their happiness will be compleat and still growing. Their employments will be the noblest, most delightful, and improving which can be conceived of. Their joys will be exquisite, abundant, overflowing and eternally flowing into their souls. There will be a variety, a suitableness, a fulness, a constant increase and a perpetual enjoyment of good which altogether transcends the liveliest imagination. There will also be granted a clear discernment of its excellency and the keenest relish for it: that relish will be always unabated—that discernment always clear—the sources of happiness inexhaustible—The light of heaven will be an eternal day. There is no temple in heaven: for the Lord God Almighty and the Lamb are the temple of it. And the city has no need of the sun, neither of the moon, to shine in it; for the glory of God doth lighten it, and the Lamb is the light thereof. And the nations of them that are saved shall walk in the light of it. Rev. xxi. 22, 3, 4. Having washed their robes, and made them white in the blood of the Lamb, they are before the throne of God, and serve him day and night in his temple: and he that sitteth on the throne shall dwell among them. They shall hunger no more, neither thirst any more; neither shall the sun light on them, nor any heat. For the Lamb, that is in the midst of the throne, shall feed them, and shall lead them unto living fountains of waters: and God shall

shall wipe away all tears from their eyes. Rev. vii. 15, 16, 17. They shall eat of the tree of life which is in the midst of the paradise of God. Christ will give unto them a crown of life. They shall be made pillars in the temple of God, and shall go no more out. They shall be made kings and priests unto God. They shall sit with Christ on his throne. Rev. i. ii. iii. It is the pleasure of Christ that those, whom the Father hath given him in the covenant of redemption, should be with him where he is; that they may behold his glory which the Father hath given him; and the love which he bears him. John xvii. 24. They are to be perfect in the perfection, glorious in the glory, happy in the happiness, and compleat through the fulness which is in Christ, who is the head of all principality and power: In whom it pleased the Father that all fulness should dwell: In whom dwells the fulness of the Godhead. Col. ii. Thus the reward to him that soweth righteousness will be ample, superabundant, unutterable, and inconceivable. It will be fully expressive of the love of God, of the grace of the Lord Jesus Christ and the benevolence of the Spirit. It will reflect infinite honor upon the adorable Trinity and afford the highest possible satisfaction to the upright in heart.

IV. I proceed to show the certainty of this bestowment. It is called "a sure reward." From reason we could not have safely inferred such a reward beyond this life. What saints now receive from God may equal their service. In point of merit they have not any claim upon God. Had they obeyed the whole law they would have been unprofitable servants: they would have done no more than was their duty to do. What God gives in the present life might prove a full compensation for perfect obedience. But far more evident is the exclusion of the least merit when in every thing the best come short and in many wholly offend; when there is a body of sin and death in them. But God has informed us in his word what he will bestow

upon

upon his obedient children beyond the grave. The imperfection of reason is supplied by the fulness of scripture. We are favored with clear and sufficient information on this important subject. Our faith stands not in the wisdom nor veracity of man but in the truth of that word of God which liveth and abideth forever. 1 Pet. i. 23.

1. Its certainty may be argued from various particular and general declarations of scripture.

What is addressed to Abraham applies to all who have like precious faith. " I am thy exceeding great reward." Gen. xv. " In keeping of thy commandments there is a great reward." Pf. xix. " Surely there is a reward, and thy expectation shall not be cut off." Prov. xxiii. " Say ye to the righteous that it shall be well with him : for he shall eat the fruit of his doings." Isa. iii. " Great is your reward in heaven." Matt. v. " Every man shall receive his own reward." 1 Cor. iii. 8. " God is not unrighteous to forget your labor of love, work of faith and patience of hope in the Lord Jesus Christ." 1 Thess. i. 3. " Cast not away therefore your confidence," A well grounded hope, " which hath great recompence of reward." Heb. x. 35. " No eye hath seen, nor ear heard, nor mind conceived the things which God hath laid up for them that love him." 1 Cor. ii. 9. Thus, to omit many other places, various and explicit are the declarations of inspired truth. Now God is not a man that he should lie ; nor the Son of man that he should repent : Hath he said it, and will he not do it ? hath he spoken, and will he not make it good ? Numb. xxiii. 19. " Faithful is he that calleth you, who also will do it." 1 Thess. v. 24. God is able to fulfil his word, in which his children hope. He is of one mind : and who or what can turn him ? In the inviolable truth, in the almighty power and unchangeable mercy of God they have assurance of a reward. Hence God's people have exercised patience ; knowing that after they have done the

will

will of God they shall receive the promises. In a believing expectation of future glory they have not been disappointed: Hence we read: "That ye be not slothful, but followers of them, who, through faith and patience, inherit the promises." Heb. vi. 12.

2. It is easily and strongly argued from the design and work of Christ.

"He gave himself for us; that he might redeem us from all iniquity, and purify unto himself a peculiar people, zealous of good works," Titus ii. 14. "Christ loved the church, and gave himself for it; that he might sanctify and cleanse it with the washing of water by the word; that he might present it to himself a glorious church, not having spot, or wrinkle, or any such thing." Ephes. v. 25, 26, 27. He offered himself without spot unto God having obtained eternal redemption for us. Heb. ix. He became the author of eternal salvation unto all them that obey him. Heb. v. There are many mansions in his Father's house: he is gone to prepare a place for them. John xiv. And he will bring many sons to glory. Heb. ii. Grace is provided and glory is purchased by his blood for all that receive him. His design will be effected. He will see of the travail of his soul and be satisfied. Isa. liii.

3. It may be clearly argued from the work and earnest of the Spirit.

It is his work to create us in Christ Jesus unto good works: To fulfill in us the whole good pleasure of his goodness, and the work of faith with power. Ephes. ii. 2 Thess. i. To unite the soul indissolubly to Christ. Grace is a divine and immortal principle, secured by a promise. Christ hath obtained a more excellent ministry than the priests under the law, being a mediator of a better covenant; established on better promises. Heb. viii. Grace or the Holy Spirit dwelling in believers is in them a well of water springing up into everlasting life. John iv. It is the work of the Spirit to build them up in the most holy faith, keep them

them in the love of God, looking for the mercy of the Lord Jesus Christ unto eternal life. Jude 20, 21. Having begun a good work in them he will perform it unto the day of Christ. Phil. i. He will not forsake the work of his own hands; his mercy endures forever: he will perfect that which concerns them. Pf. cxxxviii. "Now, he that hath wrought us to this self same thing is God, who hath also given unto us the earnest of the Spirit." 2 Cor. v. This self same thing is an hope and belief of the everlasting enjoyment of God. The Spirit is a friend of truth. Never favors a work of error. Nor can a lye ever be from the Spirit of holiness. Believers are said to be sealed with that Holy Spirit of promise unto the day of redemption. Ephef. i. The renewing and sanctifying influences of the Spirit are the seal which God sets upon his people by which he knows them; by which they are distinguished from all others; and hence they will be delivered from every evil work, and established unblameably in holiness at the coming of Christ. They have peace of conscience, joy in the Holy Ghost, good hope through grace and everlasting consolation. The present consolations of the Spirit are the earnest of the approaching harvest in heaven. Like the first fruits under the law—like the grapes of Eshcol which assured them of a rich vintage when put in possession of the promised land.

PERHAPS some will say that a work of righteousness does not secure a future reward; because persons may not continue to sow in righteousness and so may fail of the grace of God unto eternal life. To which I reply that perseverance in holiness is both a *duty* and a *privilege* or covenanted mercy. It is a *duty*. Because christians are required to continue in Christ's word—to abide in him—grounded and rooted in the truth—to forget that which is behind and press forward to that which is before—to hold fast that which they have received—to let their path shine brighter and brighter—

their

their righteousness they must never let go—nor let their heart reproach them while they live—They must keep their heart with all diligence—They must ponder the path of their feet, and let all their ways be established. They may not turn to the right hand or to the left from following God—They must cleave to him as a garment to the loins of a man—They must not ever be weary in well doing. Thus perseverance is their duty—It is also the *privilege* and covenanted mercy of christians. Unto them "are given exceeding great and precious promises; that by these they might be partakers of the divine nature; it is secured by these promises that they, giving all diligence, should add to their faith, virtue, knowledge, temperance, patience, godliness, brotherly kindness and charity; that they should be filled with all the fruits of righteousness, and thus giving all diligence to make their calling and election sure, not unto God; for known unto him are all his works from the beginning; but unto themselves: for, by doing these things, they shall never fall: For so an entrance shall be ministred unto them abundantly into the everlasting kingdom of our Lord and Savior Jesus Christ. 2 Pet. i. Acts xv. Philip. i. They are encouraged, and assisted as well as required to be stedfast and immoveable, always abounding in the work of the Lord, forasmuch as they know that their labor shall not be in vain in the Lord. 1 Cor. xv. 58. The following instructions and cautions—as "Take heed lest any of you should seem to come short of that rest." Heb. iv. "Beware lest ye also, being led away with the error of the wicked, fall from your own stedfastness." 2 Pet. iii. "Look to yourselves, that we loose not those things which we have wrought, but that we receive a full reward." 2 John 8.—do not militate against the certainty of the reward. They were either given to nominal or real christians. If to the former, they teach us that their profession would be vain unless they held out unto the end; and if they apostatized from the faith their in-

sincerity

sincerity would be made manifest. If to the latter, to real christians, they are given to animate them to the utmost diligence and vigilance and fortitude lest a contrary course should betray them into indiscretions and snares. They are given to impress christians with the important place which means hold in the whole scheme of grace. That it is an everlasting truth, that they must work out their own salvation with fear and trembling, though God works in them both to will and to do of his good pleasure. Phil. ii. 13.

Though also we read of those who in time of temptation fall away, Luke viii. 13. it is evident they had no root in them, and believed only for a while. This event does not disprove a continuance in grace and final salvation. Though we read in Heb. vi. 6. That it is impossible to renew such again to repentance, it does not overthrow our reasoning upon the security of the reward of grace. For it is most likely that the apostle in this chapter gives us a description of the miraculous gifts of the Spirit which some then possessed, and of all other attainments which natural men possess, and declares that if any should fall from such an height into infidelity and an open and contemptuous rejection of the gospel of Christ their spiritual state would then be hopeless. The same character, I apprehend, is drawn in Heb. x. 29.

Neither doth what the *prophet asserts in the name of the Lord. Ezek. xviii.* 24. weaken our arguing upon the certain connexion between working righteousness and the reward. The passage is this. " But when the righteous turneth away from his righteousness, and committeth, and doeth according to all the abominations that the wicked man doeth, shall he live ? All his righteousness that he hath done shall not be mentioned : in his trespass that he hath trespassed, and in his sin that he hath sinned, in them shall he die." It is well known that God was the visible king of Israel—that they were his visible people—that he gave them many statutes

both

both moral, ceremonial and political—that a visible observance of them was required—that he connected with that observance temporal blessings and religious privileges. With this view of the subject the prophetic description of that righteousness, which was the condition of present favors, answers. Attend candidly to it. "But if a man be just, and do that which is lawful and right, and hath not eaten upon the mountains, neither lifted up his eyes to the idols of the house of Israel, neither hath defiled his neighbor's wife, and hath not oppressed any, but hath restored to the debtor his pledge, hath spoiled none by violence, hath given his bread to the hungry, and hath covered the naked with a garment; he that hath not given forth upon usury, neither hath taken any increase, that hath withdrawn his hand from iniquity, hath executed true judgment between man and man; hath walked in my statutes, and hath kept my judgments, to deal truly; he is just, he shall surely live, saith the Lord God." Ezek. xviii. 5, 6, 7, 8, 9. The slightest survey of this righteousness, which secured outward blessings, must afford decisive conviction that it does not amount to that inward renovation, that spiritual quickening—that divine transformation of soul—that inward indwelling of the Spirit with which eternal life is always joined: hence cannot disprove the sacred assertion that to him who soweth righteousness shall be a sure, a vast and an infinite reward.

If any should urge that they fear lest *some unfavorable event——some unforeseen accident——or some mighty enemy should rob them of this reward;* I have only to observe, that if you have passed from death unto life, you may be persuaded, that neither death, nor life, nor angels, nor principalities, nor powers, nor things present, nor things to come, Nor height, nor depth, nor any other creature, shall be able to separate you from the love of God, which is in Christ Jesus your Lord. Rom. viii. That Christ's sheep hear his voice, and he knows them, and they follow him: And he gives

gives unto them eternal life; and they shall never perish, neither shall any pluck them out of his hand. John x. 27, 28. Thus the reward is sure to them that work righteousness.

IMPROVEMENT.

I. REMARK the wisdom of the true friends of righteousness and holiness.

Wisdom, it is well known, consists in pitching upon the best end, in employing the fittest means, and in choosing the most suitable season to effect it. The best end is the attainment of the greatest good, the everlasting enjoyment of God: The best means to attain this end is the habitual and sincere discharge of universal duty: The best season for securing of it is the morning of life; and the only season is during the present life. If these observations are too evident to be soberly contradicted, it follows that the upright man is the wise man: in a religious view the only wise man. Religion introduces to a pleasing and beneficial acquaintance with the best beings. With *God the Father*; his perfections and character. With *Jesus Christ*, the only mediator between God and man. With *the Holy Spirit*, the quickner and comforter. With *the holy angels*; that excel in strength, and that are ministring spirits unto the heirs of salvation. With *the saints*, who are the excellent of the earth. Our work lies mainly with God through his Son and our Savior. He is our Creator and Benefactor. He is the Father of Mercies, the God of grace; our Lawgiver and Redeemer and Judge. We are always dependent on him. We every moment receive much good from him. We are unspeakably, yea infinitely indebted to him. We are accountable to him. We are saved not by works of righteousness of our own, but according to his mercy, by the washing of regeneration, and the renewing of the Holy Ghost, which he sheds on christians abundantly through Jesus Christ our Saviour; That being justified by his grace, we should be made heirs according to the hope of eternal life. Titus iii. 4, 6. 9.

Hence

Hence we should please him, seek our happiness in him, and yield our whole selves unto the Lord. A spiritual and an intimate acquaintance with God is preferable to a thorough knowledge of human arts and sciences, the policies of states, the civil laws of our own country, and the situation, climate and productions, manufactures, trade and commerce of the whole world. The upright man has attained that wisdom which is the principal thing. He has got that sound understanding which is a well spring of life to the soul. He knows his duty. He studies the word of God. The gospel reveals to him the author, the nature and the way of eternal life. How he can secure the favor and blessing of that being who can do for him very abundantly; who can overrule all events to his profit; and who can be his portion forever. This knowledge is with him. The favor of God is his special privilege—A conformity to God is his glory. The service of God is his employment. The hope of a reward in heaven is a cordial to him under all the trials of life. He is then exceedingly wise. His wisdom bears proportion to the prevalence of vital and practical holiness. Disregard them, you pious ones, the ridicule of a blind and the scorn of an atheistical world. Be not ashamed of the practice of righteousness. Pursue your work. Encrease in grace; abound in hope; live above the world; and long for the blessedness of heaven. Rather be ashamed of your leanness; of the languor of your devotions; of the weakness of your spiritual desires. The wisdom of sowing in righteousness appears from the nature, the greatness of the reward: from the condition and certainty of bestowment; the long enjoyment of it; the unalienable possession of it. Bless God for it. " For the Lord giveth this wisdom." Prov. ii. 6.

II. SEE how weakly and absurdly objections are urged and prejudices harbored against the practice of righteousness.

IN different ways the quarrel against religion is managed. But many urge, to reconcile themselves to
their

their habitual neglect of it, that the inducements are weak: that the reward is not adequate nor sure. They must serve God without present, without sufficient compensation. God is treated as an hard master; compared to an austere man. But this is to reject scripture declarations: to contradict the uniform tendency of moral causes; to attack the constitution of heaven; to confront the experience of the godly in all ages; it is to make God a lyar. This undertaking is arduous and impious. Nothing is more amply supported than that there is a sure reward to him that soweth righteousness. God loves the upright. They dwell in his presence. The secret of the Lord is with them that fear him. All the paths of the Lord are mercy and truth unto such as keep his testimonies. He makes with them an everlasting covenant, in all things well ordered and sure. They dwell in the secret of the Most High, and abide under the shadow of the Almighty. To them that are faithful unto the death he will give a crown of life. The experience of God's people in all ages has evinced his love to be marvellously and immensely great. Religion will not effectually shield us from every kind and degree of natural evil. But it prepares us for adversity: it lightens the stroke: it supports under it: it sanctifies what we endure: it assures, to patience and submission, a favorable conclusion. While under the discipline of their heavenly Father saints have peace of conscience and joy in the Holy Ghost. Many are the afflictions of the righteous but the Lord delivereth them, finally, out of them all. Pf. xxxiv. "Weeping may endure for a night, but joy cometh in the morning." Pf. xxx. 5. When true religion, like the bible, which contains and reveals it, is profitable for all things, such an objection can soon be answered; such a prejudice easily shown to be groundless. Except righteousness will bear severe but impartial examination, whence such declarations from the mouth of him who must know, who must utter, and must delight in the truth? "Happy is the man that findeth wisdom, and the man that getteth understanding.

understanding. For the merchandise of it is better than the merchandise of silver, and the gain than that of fine gold. She is more precious than rubies and all that we can desire. She is a tree of life to them that lay hold upon her, and happy is every one that findeth her." Prov. iii. Whence, unless it is so, do we hear him, who was full of grace and truth, declare?" Riches and honor are with me, yea durable riches and righteousness. My fruit is better than gold; and my revenue than choice silver." Prov. viii. Why, unless it is true, are we told that the fruit of the Spirit is goodness? Gal. v. 21. Why do we hear the righteous confess from one side of the earth to the other, Thy commandments, O Lord, are the rejoicing of our heart—they are our songs in this the house of our pilgrimage—we have esteemed the words of thy mouth more than our necessary food? How shall we account for such conduct? Shall we say that the whole generation of the upright have been fools and fanatics? But is it not an unfounded and an incredible assertion? How distinguished have very many of them been for discernment, judgment, steadiness and usefulness? We must then conclude that the prejudices which are so generally fostered against the practice of godliness are unreasonable and inexcusable. They argue the criminal depravity of the heart. When any do not obey God and present themselves to him living sacrifices holy and acceptable it proves that they hate heart and life holiness: that they will not renounce the flesh, the world, and the devil to sow in righteousness and receive a most glorious and sure reward.

III. Most grateful effusions of soul should accompany the information that God hath annexed a sure reward to holiness and righteousness.

Children do not merit of their parents because they hearken to excellent counsel, and obey reasonable commands and afford joint assistance for their mutual benefit. The citizens of a state do not because they conform to the wise provisions of government; and uniformly

formly do that which is requisite for their common welfare. Sufficient compensation might be found in the good effects naturally resulting from such conduct. Neither do saints merit of God. In every thing they fail. It is of the Lord's mercies that they are not consumed. What God bestows upon them is for the sake of Christ. Through him he has communion with them. He brings them very near to him. He makes an everlasting covenant with them. He offers them beyond the largest wish—beyond every created imagination. He gives them durable riches. He bestows upon them crowns of righteousness. He provides for them rivers of pleasure in heaven. He gives as though he could not give enough. He rewards their faithful services an hundred, yea a thousand fold beyond their intrinsic value. His grace in Christ is exceeding abundant towards them. **The motives to christian duties are vast as infinity, lasting as eternity.** Your tongue then, christians, should celebrate the praises of God. Your hearts should overflow with gratitude. You should bless the name of the Lord while you have any being. You should acquaint yourselves thoroughly with a work; and delight exceedingly in it; and pursue it steadily which is to employ you forever above.

IV. We remark the incomparable excellency of the sacred scriptures.

They are a light to us. They are adapted to guide us into the truth—to make the simple wise—to direct us in the way of peace—to give us solid hope—to afford us strong consolation—to assure us of the reward of righteousness; both in this world and in the next—to confirm our faith in the important points of an everlasting state; of the reservation of an inheritance incorruptible, undefiled, and that fadeth not away, for all those that serve God. For this knowledge we are indebted to a special revelation. What some of the heathen conjectured: about which many doubted; more disbelieved; and the most were ignorant of; we, through the tender mercies of God, know; the day

spring

spring from on high having visited us to give light respecting salvation by Christ. While we compassionate those that grope in darkness; and while we pray for infidels, and tremble for the fate of scorners and despisers, let us hold the word of God in the highest estimation and view it as infinitely better than thousands of gold and silver.

V. The subject furnishes solid ground for patience under the trials of life.

We are born to trouble. Many are the afflictions of the righteous. " Whom the Lord loveth, he chasteneth; and scourgeth every son whom he receiveth." Heb. xii. Exclusive of the necessity and present benefit of such discipline, which proves like a refiner's fire, and like fuller's soap, the future reward of patience and hope, of faith and submission overballances present sufferings; sweetens the rod and inflames with love to a wise and merciful providence. " For our light affliction, which is but for a moment, acceptably borne, worketh out for us a far more exceeding and an eternal weight of glory." 2 Cor. iv. 17. Who would not blush to complain or faint when corrected that believed the truth?

VI. We conclude that if there is a sure reward to the godly there is also a just but different recompence of reward to the impenitent and unbelieving. One is as certain as the other. Is as deducible from the righteousness as the other is from the mercy of God. Is as clearly, as frequently, and as strongly declared in the volume of inspiration. If those that work righteousness, that love mercy, walk humbly, grow in grace and perfect holiness in the fear of God are rewarded with peace of conscience, the special presence and favor of God, and the final and everlasting possession of all desirable good in heaven: then those of an opposite character; i. e. temper and practice; who do not love God supremely, nor their neighbor disinterestedly; who do not seek the kingdom of God, nor hunger and thirst after righteousness, nor prize heaven above this world,

and

and love holiness more than they do sin, must be filled with their own devices: such, under the incalculable advantages of the gospel, cannot escape an aggravated doom; even the damnation of hell. Are the upright by the washing of regeneration and the cultivation of the fruits of the Spirit qualified for future happiness; and are they, by the covenant and oath of God, secured of everlasting life? Impenitent sinners are by their temper fitted for destruction: and God has bound himself to execute a righteous sentence of condemnation upon all those that love not our Lord Jesus Christ in sincerity. If light is sown for the righteous and gladness for the upright in heart; then darkness and trouble; sorrow and destruction are the portion of sinners.

VII. Let all be persuaded to sow in righteousness.

1st. Because there is no other way in which the reward can be obtained.

2dly. Because the reward will infinitely compensate your service.

3dly. Because neglect to do it argues unprovoked and criminal abuse of the mercy and grace of God in providing and offering and promising such a free and an immense reward to godliness.

4thly. Because if you loose the reward by your folly, you perish forever.

5thly. Because the attainment of it will bring everlasting glory to God.

Let these plain and solemn considerations sink down into your hearts and live in them.

VIII. Let those, who hope and wait for this full reward in heaven, be animated to much diligence, to holy fervor of spirit, to abundant service for God, to continual encrease in holiness. See to walk worthy of God, who hath called you unto his kingdom and glory by Jesus Christ, to whom be glory forever, AMEN.

TABLE OF ERRATA.

OWING to the diversity of hands among the writers of the Sermons and a want of thorough knowledge of them, several errors have happened; the principal of which are here corrected: a few of less consequence are omitted.

Page 9, 11 line from top, for *is* read *are*.—P. 11, 2 f. bott. for *are* read *is*.—P. 31, 12 f. bott. for *shalt* read *shall*.—P. 32, 22 f. top, for *have* read *hath*.—P. 32, 23 f. top, for *agreeable* read *agreeably*.—P. 51, 12 f. top, for *habitation* read *conversation*.—P. 52, 15 f. top, for *faults* read *fruits*.—P. 66, 10 f. top, for *though* read *those*.—P. 72, 3 f. bott. for *create* read *great*.—P. 78, 15 f. top, for *they* read *there*.—P. 116, 10 f. bott. after *Godhead* read *of the Spirit*.—P. 153, 16 f. bott. for *oppose* read *oppose*.—P. 209, 4 f. bott. for *pleasure* read *pleasures*.—P. 253, 14 f. bott. for *grave* read *grace*.—P. 277, 4 f. top, for *articles* read *article*.—P. 304, 12 f. top, for *faith* read *both*.—P. 328, 13 f. top, for *command* read *commende*.—P. 341, 18 f. top, for *impunities* read *impurities*.—P. 395, 14 f. bott. for *promises* read *premises*.—P. 399, 9 f. top, for *proceeding* read *preceding*.—P. 416, 10 f. bott. for *Ecclef.* read *Isaiah*.—P. 419, 14 f. bott. for *really* read *nearly*.—P. 428, 15 f. top, dele *within*.—P. 430, at the bott. for *strings* read *stings*.—P. 436, 14 f. bott. for *laid up* read *prepared*.—P. 443, 17 f. bott. for *them* read *then*.—P. 448, 3 f. bott. for *See to walk* read *Walk thou*.

www.ingramcontent.com/pod-product-compliance
Lightning Source LLC
Chambersburg PA
CBHW022138300426
44115CB00006B/249